The Architecture of the United States

An Illustrated Guide to Notable Buildings
A.D. 1115 to the Present
Open to the Public

MERRY CHRISTMAS

TO

JOHN

FROM

1985

The Architecture of the United States

Volume 3
THE PLAINS STATES
AND FAR WEST

G. E. Kidder Smith
Fellow, The American Institute of Architects

in association with

The Museum of Modern Art, New York

Introduction by David Gebhard

Anchor Books
Anchor Press/Doubleday   Garden City, New York
1981

The Architecture of the United States is published simultaneously in hardcover and paperback editions.
Anchor Books edition: 1981
Anchor Press edition: 1981

This book is the third of a three-volume series—*The Architecture of the United States*. The others are: *New England and the Mid-Atlantic States,* and *The South and Midwest.*

PHOTO CREDITS

Jorgé Figueroa of *Modernage* made—beautifully—most of the prints in the book, with the rest made by the author. For "outside" photographs in this volume, the author is deeply indebted to the following:

Page 17 Courtesy of Museum of the American Indian, Heya Foundation
Page 67 Courtesy of U. S. Army Corps of Engineers
Page 197 ESTO photo courtesy of the architect
Page 437 Courtesy of Powell Symphony Hall
Page 545 Courtesy of KTHI
Page 608 Courtesy of Skidmore, Owings & Merrill, architects
Page 719 Courtesy of Patrick King
Page 757 Courtesy of Lawrence Halprin
Page 779 Courtesy of the National Park Service

Library of Congress Cataloging in Publication Data

Smith, George Everard Kidder, 1913–
    The architecture of the United States.

    Includes glossaries and indexes.
    CONTENTS: v. 1.   New England and the Mid-Atlantic states.—v. 2.   The South and Midwest.—v. 3.   The Plains states and Far West.
    1. Architecture—United States—Guidebooks.
I.   New York (City). Museum of Modern Art.   II.   Title.
NA705.S578   917.3'04926
Hardcover edition ISBN: 0-385-14676-0
Paperback edition ISBN: 0-385-14677-9
Library of Congress Catalog Card Number 79–8035

To DFKS

who enriched every page
—and every hour

Foreword

This guidebook was initiated (1967) and first sponsored by the Graham Foundation for Advanced Studies in the Fine Arts under its then-director (now emeritus) John Entenza. In 1978 the Foundation, under the directorship of Carter H. Manny, Jr., FAIA, gave me a supplemental stipend to complete and update my research. The National Endowment for the Arts, first under Roger L. Stevens and then under the ever-helpful Nancy Hanks, assisted by Bill N. Lacy, gave me two substantial fellowships, while the Ford Foundation contributed two grants at critical moments, and the Museum of Modern Art a grant-in-aid. To the two Foundations, the Endowment, and the Museum, my lasting gratitude: this demanding project would not have been possible without their financial and moral support.

Objective of Book   The purpose of this guidebook is to help establish architecture more fully in the cultural life of the United States. For "architecture" is largely unknown to the public, all but ignored in general art courses at our universities, and—with the pioneering exception of New York's Museum of Modern Art—rarely shown in our museums. By pinpointing excellence and introducing the reader and traveler to distinguished building, it is hoped that the book will encourage interest in the heritage of this country's architecture. For unless we develop more discernment regarding urban and architectural quality, we will continue to commission and produce the mediocrity which characterizes most of our cities and buildings today.

This guide does not pretend to be a history of architecture in the U.S.A.—its author is an architect and critic, not a historian. The book is intended to serve as a commentary on a cross section of each state's architectural resources from earliest times to the present. It is by no means an inventory of memorable works—at only twenty buildings per state one arrives at a thousand entries—but it will critically examine structures considered representative of major periods of development. (There are, of course, many more than a thousand notable buildings in this country, but today's book economics severely limits the number which can be included.) Some states, particularly the older and the more populous, obviously have a greater range of distinguished work than the more recent or more sparsely settled.

Selection of Buildings   A compilation such as this must reflect the selective process of one individual. However, every building described has been personally examined and, with my wife's perceptive aid, an on-the-spot, preliminary report written. The final choice represents a winnowing of over three thousand structures to half that number. With few exceptions each is at times open to the public.

The lengthy research connected with the preliminary selection of the historic buildings was greatly facilitated by the books and articles of architectural historians and other specialists in the field, to whom I am deeply indebted. Though there is no up-to-date overall history of architecture in this country at present (1980), several promising ones are now in production. There are, however, a number of useful volumes on various periods, regions, and architects, and these are mentioned in the text when quoted. For selecting contemporary examples I relied on my extensive architectural file, which contains speedily retrievable articles on almost all buildings of merit published in the last forty years. Conversations with architects and historians kept matters topical. Because of limits of space, only those engineers, landscape architects, and related specialists who played a major design role are listed.

As regards choice of buildings, some readers may, of course, harbor favorites which have been irritatingly omitted, while other structures may be puzzlingly included. However, to bring *de gustibus* up to date, the late Mies van der Rohe and the late Walter Gropius—architects and educators of great significance in this country—each thought little of Le Corbusier's chapel at Ronchamp in eastern France, a building most hold to be one of the century's most important. Frank Lloyd Wright's disagreement with most of the architectural profession is well documented.

Omission of Some Building Types No private houses have been included in this guide, though several harmonious streets of such houses are listed. However, a few private buildings are so stimulating on the exterior that they are mentioned with the cautionary note of sidewalk viewing only. Some contemporary suburban corporate headquarters and similar works of distinction were omitted at the request of their managements. All correctional institutions were bypassed and only a few mental institutions written up. The most sincerely regretted absence is that of a number of fine new buildings which had not been finished when we were last on the scene. More than twelve years were spent on this project and though three updating grants were made, inevitably in a country as large as this we missed some outstanding new work, plus some historic museum-houses which only recently have been opened. Sadly, some buildings discussed here undoubtedly will **disappear** in the next few years.

State and City Guidebooks Although this book of necessity omits many important buildings, old and new, this lacuna is partly eased by the realization that an encouraging number of comprehensive local architectural guidebooks is becoming available. Hopefully, every state and major city will eventually have a critical guide to its outstanding buildings. The local offices of the American Institute of Architects— listed in most telephone books—can often be of help, as can state tourist boards. Many cities and towns have an annual house tour, usually in the spring, when homes otherwise not open to the public can be visited.

For all architectural exploration, state and city maps are essential for time-saving travel.

As this book is primarily a field guide and reference source, the photographs are necessarily small. For a "visual data bank" of architecture in the United States see my two-volume *Pictorial History of Architecture in America* (American Heritage/W. W. Norton, 1976).

Caveats The structures described herein generally are open on the dates, days, and hours indicated, but it would be wise to check on these. Admission might range from 25 cents to a number of dollars, and, like hours, is subject to change. If no admission charge is indicated, the entrance is probably free although this, too, can vary.

There are times—a dreary winter day for instance—when even the Parthenon fails, when Pentelic marble cannot inspire. So it will happen that buildings extolled here can disappoint: moreover some might show their years before their due or have undergone serious alterations since last visited. In addition, this book is admittedly a cheerful report, probably at times too cheerful, but I am, for better or worse, an optimist in the first place and, secondly, if a structure was not considered outstanding it would not be included.

Prior to publication, the description of each building was sent to its architect or the appropriate historical body for correction of possible error. The responses were of the utmost help in corroborating and correcting data, and I am deeply grateful to those national and state agencies, dedicated historical societies and curators, fellow architects, and individuals who so generously and constructively helped check the text. I only wish that there were space to list them all individually.

It is well to keep in mind that in some cases even specialists will disagree, often in dating, occasionally even in the attribution of the architect of a historic building. The dates of the buildings begin with the generally accepted date for commencement of construction and the finish thereof. Major alterations, when known, are also listed. It is thought that the facts given here represent the most recent research; in most cases data came from information at the source. The National Register of Historic Places (1976), U. S. Department of the Interior, was also of great help. If there are errors, however, the fault is, of course, mine.

In Summary The United States with its geographic range, size of population, ethnic richness, and financial means produces more architectural probing, offers more excitement, and achieves a greater volume of outstanding new work than any other single country. But lest this encomium seem comforting, it must be immediately added that for the most part, our town planning lags far behind that in Scandinavia, our land usage both in city and suburb is lamentable, and our low-cost housing generally inexcusable. Moreover I am uneasy about much work now being turned out. A few architects, properly publicized, seemingly are more concerned with conjuring novelty for novelty's sake, or with producing seductive exhibition drawings, than they are willing to be vexed by the tough, three-dimensional realities of a client's program, his money, or the annoying details of site and climate. Professional responsibility—let alone societal responsibility—appears to be of little moment. We are increasingly witnessing what Siegfried Giedion called "Playboy Architecture." Many of these idiosyncratic excursions will look trivial twenty-five years from now when, one hopes, the house or building will be paid for. Architecture should be concerned with creating significant space, not scene painting. Nonetheless, we in the United States still have a workshop with a vitality unmatched elsewhere, and if we take a greater interest in what is being built (and torn down), we can create a finer tomorrow. This is what this book is about. The author would appreciate corrections and suggestions.

G. E. Kidder Smith, FAIA
September 1980

163 East 81st Street
New York, NY 10028

ACKNOWLEDGMENTS

This book would not have been published had it not been for the constant help and encouragement of Martin Rapp, the Museum of Modern Art's spirited and talented Director of Publications. Stewart Richardson, former Associate Publisher at Doubleday—and a friend of long standing—was his stalwart cohort. Both have given me wonderful support. Editors Elizabeth Frost Knappman and Eve F. Roshevsky, and Harold Grabau, Adrienne Welles, and Patricia Connolly, copy editors, went over the manuscript with many suggestions for its betterment, and Loretta Barrett shepherded a staggering mass of material through production. Thanks also to Marilyn Schulman, our designer.

I am particularly grateful to the four eminent architectural historians whose introductions give such illuminating perspective on the background and forces which helped' shape the buildings in the three regional volumes. Dr. Albert Bush-Brown, chancellor of Long Island University and co-author with the late John Burchard of the encyclopedic *The Architecture of America,* contributed a superb introduction to the architecture of the Northeast—Volume 1—and also commented pertinently on the text for individual buildings. Professor Frederick D. Nichols of the School of Architecture of the University of Virginia and an author long known for his brilliant studies of Jefferson and the architecture of the South wrote the first introduction for Volume 2. Professor Frederick Koeper, a specialist on the buildings of the Midwest—his *Illinois Architecture* is one of the finest state guides—sets the stage for the second part of Volume 2. The indefatigable David Gebhard, whose guidebooks to the architecture in California and Minnesota are classics, gives great insight to the work of that vast sweep of states west of the Mississippi in Volume 3. To all four I am deeply indebted for their sterling contributions.

But the two individuals who dealt with every word of every sentence—always to their betterment—were my wife and Patricia Edwards Clyne. My wife advised on the field selections of buildings, wrote almost all of our on-the-spot reactions, navigated when not driving (we covered some 135,000 miles/217,000 kilometers), and shared twelve years of work, most of it under pressure conditions. (She also shared the delights of finding many extraordinary buildings in this extraordinary country.) The material simply could not have been gathered nor the book written without her constant help, judicious taste, and glorious companionship. When travel was over—once forty-seven different motels in fifty-six nights—and I had typed the text with semilegibility, Pat Clyne, the distinguished author and speleologist, took over. She tackled the oft-confused (and sometimes windy) language of 2,800 pages of manuscript, rationalized constructions, minimized malaprops, inserted the forgotten, removed the superfluous, all in a superb editing job. She then typed each page so beautifully that it could be framed. With these two lovely and talented daughters of Minerva the task became not only possible but pleasurable.

VOLUME 3 ACKNOWLEDGMENTS

In addition to those who gave invaluable assistance in checking data on individual buildings, the following were of outstanding help:

Alaska Susan F. Edelstein, Superintendent, Sitka National Historical Park; R. L. Shalkop, Director, Historical and Fine Arts Museum, Anchorage.

Arizona William C. Bolton, Tuzigoot National Monument; T. Dwayne Collier, Montezuma Castle National Monument; Gary M. Hasty, Chief of Interpretation, Canyon de Chelly National Monument; Rev. Kieran McCarty, OFM, Mission San Xavier del Bac.

Arkansas The Arkansas Territorial Restoration; Lucy Robinson and Barbara Brigance, Arkansas Commemorative Commission.

California G. A. Fialho and staff, Department of Parks & Recreation, San Simeon Area; Stephen Garrett, Director, The J. Paul Getty Museum; Rev. Reginald McDonough, OFM, Old Mission, San Miguel; The Municipal Arts Department, City of Los Angeles; Sandy Snider, L. A. County Arboretum; John C. Worsley, FAIA, State Capitol Restoration.

Colorado Convention & Visitors Bureau, Denver; Denver Art Museum staff; the Superintendent, Rocky Mountain National Park; Gilbert R. Wenger, Acting Superintendent, Mesa Verde National Park; David Wicks of the Denver Landmark Preservation Commission.

Hawaii Henry J. Bartels, Curator, Iolani Palace; Sara Holmes Boutelle, the Julia Morgan Association; James W. Foster, Jr., Director, Honolulu Academy of Arts; James C. Luckey, Lahaina Restoration Foundation; Barnes Riznik, Director, Waioli Mission House Museum.

Idaho Jim Davis, Idaho State Historical Society; Dorine Goertzen, Idaho State Division of Tourism.

Iowa Amana Society, Don Shoup, manager; Iowa State Historical Department; Margaret Keyes, Director, The Old Capitol, Iowa City; Max A. Smith, President, Poweshiek County National Bank.

Kansas Julie A. Wortman and Larry A. Jochims, Kansas State Historical Society.

Minnesota The Minnesota Historical Society and its numerous staff members; Dick Ferrell of the Pillsbury Company.

Missouri The American Institute of Architects and Betty Lou Custer; The Landmarks Commission, Kansas City; George McCue; W. Joan Marshall, National Park Service, Jefferson National Expansion Memorial; Kevin Lee Sarring, Old Post Office, St. Louis.

Montana John Hayt, Montana Historical Society.

Nebraska Nebraska State Historical Society; Bill Fink, Homestead National Monument.

Nevada Betty Hood, Curator, the Bowers Mansion; W. E. Wieprecht, Nevada Division of Historic Preservation and Archeology; V. B. Wilkinson, Bureau of Reclamation, Lower Colorado Region.

New Mexico Walter P. Herriman and Jim Trott, Chaco Canyon National Monument; Thomas W. Merlan, State Historic Preservation Officer, with Dr. Bainbridge Bunting and Dr. Myra Ellen Jenkins; William L. Schart, Park Ranger, Aztec Ruins National Monument; Michael F. Weber, Museum of New Mexico; Arthur H. Wolf, Director, Millicent Rogers Museum.

North Dakota C. L. Dill, Nick G. Franke, and Kurt P. Schweigert of the State Historical Society of North Dakota.

Oklahoma John R. Hill, Curator, Oklahoma Territorial Museum; Mrs. George Metzel, History and Archives, Boston Avenue United Methodist Church.

Oregon Richard H. Engeman, Jacksonville Museum; Arthur Spencer, Oregon Historical Society.

South Dakota Bruce Schumacher, Siouxland Heritage Museum.

Texas Wayne Daniel, Fort Concho; Martha Doty Freeman, San José Mission; Galveston Historical Foundation; David McDonald, Superintendent, José Antonio Navarro State Historic Site; Louise E. Nixon, Gillespie County Historical Society; Mitchell A. Wilder, Director, Amon Carter Museum.

Utah Paul L. Anderson, Manager, Historic Buildings and Sites Section, The Church of Jesus Christ of Latter-day Saints.

Washington Earl D. Layman, City Historic Preservation Officer, Seattle.

Wyoming William H. Barton and Philip J. Roberts, Wyoming State Archives and Historical Department; Kelly Marting, Yellowstone National Park.

Contents

Introduction

David Gebhard

The Early Years, 1820–60: Geographically, the region from the Mississippi to the Pacific Coast represents one of America's most varied series of landscapes. It also represents a play between specific environments which still remain somewhat untouched, and landscapes which have gone through a major transformation at the hands of man. The eastern segment of this region, from the Mississippi River to the eastern slopes of the Rocky Mountains, was and still is a world of contrasts, where the eastern woodlands slowly, and in some cases rapidly, give way to the open grasslands of the Great Prairie, which in turn thins to the far west where the prairies become increasingly arid. The partly hilly country of the Mississippi Valley merges into the undulating prairie lands which only change when the Rocky Mountains are reached. Rainfall and ranges of temperature introduce different zones which crisscross in diverse ways from north to south, and east to west.

Similar divergences exist within what often is referred to as the intermountain region. Changes here are often extremely abrupt, ranging from high-altitude snow-covered mountains, to well-watered valleys, to almost desert-like conditions in the interior of the Great Basin. Finally the narrow zone west of the Coast Ranges produces a complicated series of microclimates as complex as one can find anywhere in the world.

The imprint of man's manipulation on these environments has been appreciable, producing both negative and positive results. The deciduous and coniferous forests of the Mississippi Valley have generally disappeared, giving way to rich, cultivated fields and pastoral lands. To the west, in the open plains, the long- and short-grassed prairie lands have in most cases been turned into cultivated acres. Logging and mining have transformed whole sections, ranging from northern Minnesota to the Pacific Northwest, and extensive federal water projects have created a series of new Edens, such as the interior San Joaquin and Imperial valleys and much of coastal Southern California.

Each of these Western regions has provided just enough in the way of appreciable difficulties so that it encouraged either a submission to it or a manipulation of the landscape on a scale generally unknown elsewhere in the United States. If one wishes to discover (or creatively invent) a single feature characteristic of this entire region it is the play between each of these native environments and the cultural and material baggage brought by one or another of the groups who have come into the area. In pre-European times the area in and around the Mississippi and its major tributaries, such as the Missouri River, accommodated groups of river valley agriculturalists who built permanent villages along the waterways. The siting of these prehistoric villages, the specifics of their layouts, the dwelling type and their ceremonial structures were generally influenced by examples from the East and the South; they were then a Western extension of an Eastern Woodland culture on the agriculturally marginal plains. These native Americans managed to accommodate themselves to this different environment, but these accommodations were kept to a minimum. Great ceremonial centers like the Caddoan site of Spiro (in Oklahoma), or the proliferation of effigy earthworks in Wisconsin, Iowa, and Minnesota, illustrate how forms and approaches to an environment derive from outside of the area.

The characteristic dwellings of these Native Americans, the semisubterranean pit house, the bark-, grass-, or reed-covered wigwams, and the skin-sheathed tipi, so closely associated with the Plains native people, were house forms which originated elsewhere. The Northern and Central Great Prairies, the Plateaus, and the Great Basin were from the earliest time areas which were impinged on from outside. From the archeological evidence currently available it would appear that each of these native peoples brought with them that which was familiar. They were of course forced to adapt to the new environment or they could pursue the alternative of moving on and leaving it. But insofar as possible, they, like the later European settlers, would seem to have attempted to keep as many of their older, familiar values as possible. Like other Native Americans they sought to control their environment through the highly abstract device of beliefs about their world and their relation to it. While their ability to manipulate their environment physically was limited, they nonetheless did imprint their presence on the land in the way of ceremonial circles, configurations of stones, vision-quest shelters, and through drawings and paintings placed on rock surfaces. Visually all of these Native American manipulations of their environment remained subservient to the natural quality of the place, but still they openly set aside a segment of the environment as something which especially reflected man's presence.

A similar minimal impact on the land resulted from the first centuries of European contact with the region. It was not until the mid-eighteenth century that the French laid out the City of St. Louis (1764), later replanned by the Spanish (1796). In California in the last half of the eighteenth century the Spaniards from Mexico laid out their chain of missions, and their equally important towns and military presidios. While there were theoretical differences expressed in the settings and configurations of these early French and Spanish towns in the west, their basic underlying ingredient was the Classical gridiron plan. The French, in their plan for St. Louis, elongated the grid parallel to the Mississippi River and then encompassed it with walled fortifications which hinted at the European medieval as well as Renaissance city. The Spanish composed their cities with a more complex set of ingredients: the mission church and its secondary buildings, the military presidio, and finally the central plaza, which was to form the eventual core of the new city. The plaza, however, as a central organizing feature, did not always end up as a successful unifying element for most of the Hispanic settlements in California. The single-floor adobe houses of the early 1800s were built in what seemed to be a loose, almost randomlike pattern, either around the presidio or outside of the confines of the plaza. Before the hefty impact of the Anglos began to be felt in California, the general impression conveyed by these Spanish communities was that of small rural villages. They became visually unified man-made artifacts, not through planning, but as in early eighteenth-century Santa Barbara, through the unity of forms, of white wall surfaces, and of red tile roofs.

The Anglo surveyor's grid, which dominated American planning through the nineteenth century, was not then that much different from the early patterns imposed on the land by the French and Spanish. The Anglos' scheme tended to be neutral, and tended to be non-ending so that it could accommodate untold growth. Its three basic ingredients were a public square of usually one block, often reserved for a county or city building; a main street, which might or might not bear any relationship to the public square; and the transportation linkage with the outside world. The location of the dock, pier, or livery, if it was a pre-1850 Midwestern community, or the railroad station and perhaps yards in the latter part of the nineteenth century, was also conceived of as separate from Main Street and the public plaza. This looseness of the Anglo village or city plan was just another device to encourage flexibility of land use within the community.

The earliest settlements of the first half of the nineteenth century in the middle and upper Midwest closely mirrored the patterns of settlements which had been established to the east. With only a handful of exceptions, all of these town sites were situated on waterways which offered the possibility of both transportation and power. But while the nineteenth century could and did respond romantically to the scenic qualities of a meandering stream or broad river, the community's relation to the waterway was almost always exclusively a utilitarian one. Because of the limited impact of man on the early-nineteenth-century Midwestern environment, the people of the time could have their cake and eat it too. The beauty and natural quality of the river was still close at hand, even if mills, docks, warehouses, etc. lined the waterfront of the village or newly developing city.

The rural environment equally reflected the initial low-keyed impact of the settler, coupled with the traditional European response to a pastoral landscape. In Iowa, Minnesota, eastern Missouri, and Oklahoma the rectangular cultivated fields and open pastures eventually melt into what appears to be native coppice or forests. The suggestion of a series of small scale (the usual 160-acre/65-hectare homestead plot) conveyed by the fenced fields and narrow dirt roads was repeated in the small scale of the buildings which comprised the farm complex. The chaste, simple white clapboard farmhouse hinted at, but did not dramatically insist on, its Greek Revival heritage. This hinted-at quality was usually restricted to the basic gabled proportions of the structure and the general symmetrical disposition of windows and doors. Outright Greek (or even Federal) detailing seldom occurs either within or on the exterior of these puritanical farmhouses. If Classic detailing was introduced it was often limited to the principal entrance, which might boast a simple Classical entablature or pediment, and a recessed composition of side lights and doorways. The real entrance to the farmhouse was in the one-story kitchen wing. Here one finds the first general use of porches—a feature which was to assume great importance in the late-nineteenth-century rural and suburban dwellings.

Before 1860, the small to larger urban environments tended to reflect the latest architectural fashions of the principal cities of the East closely. Civic buildings, such as state capitols and county courthouses, started out by employing the Greek Revival imagery—a columned, pedimented structure surmounted by a drum and dome. Later the verticality of the Italianate began to modify the older Classical language. Generally commercial architectural—ranging from retail stores, offices, and banks—expressed the forms and details of the Italianate Renaissance as it was interpreted at the mid-century. Most of the commercial buildings were conceived of at the time as purely utilitarian structures, devoid of any architectural intent. Yet the architectural predilections of the period always came through, with the result that warehouses, small factory buildings and mills were often stronger as designs than other buildings in the community. Church structures posed one of the occasional exceptions to the predominance of the Greek and Italianate modes. While many of the pre-1860 Midwest and on to California congregations built in the Greek Revival Style, an equal number showed a strong preference for the Gothic.

Before the Civil War the imagery of the urban or suburban dwelling found in the Midwest or in California tended to be a decade or so behind its Eastern counterpart. Throughout the area the same sequence occurred: first the Greek Revival and then the introduction of Italianate features, and finally the emergence of full-blown Italianate dwellings. In plan almost all of these dwellings (whether large or small) employed the traditional side or central hall plan, with the kitchen generally arranged as a separate, single-story wing to the rear or side. By the early 1860s a few of the more posh and "advanced" dwellings had central heating instead of fireplaces and stoves, gas lighting, and some interior plumbing.

From the first, the Western dwelling modified and then abandoned the older medieval heavy timbered framing method. By the 1840s the light stick balloon frame was close to universal in use for wood frame and sheathed buildings. While brick and stone load-bearing walled structures still enjoyed traditional prestige, the wood balloon frame was thought of as being highly advantageous, not only because of low cost, but also because it could be erected rapidly. The Midwest on to the West Coast actively participated in the inventive use of architectural imagery that we today loosely label "Victorian." The ease of working in redwood and the mildness of climate led to a florescence of High Victorian architecture on the West Coast. The often illustrated Carson House in Eureka, California (1884–85), by the prolific firm of Samuel and Joseph Cather Newsom, is rightly considered as *the* example of the American Queen Anne. In the years immediately after the Civil War the Italianate mode was the most popular, not only for residential architecture, but equally for commercial and institutional buildings. The fondness for the Italianate continued on for a much longer period (until the 1890s) in San Francisco and in other cities of California. In Kansas City, St. Louis, and Minneapolis/St. Paul, the Italianate was often intermixed with elements of the Second Empire Style (Mansard roofs, tower pavilions), and with sawed and turned work which we associate with the Eastlake Style. All of this was followed in the late 1870s and on through the 1890s by the Queen Anne, the Richardson Romanesque, and versions of the Classical Renaissance tradition. In the early 1890s the Romanesque mode, the Classical, and the Beaux Arts became standard fare. In Mid and Far Western residential architecture the Colonial Revival rapidly began to modify and eventually to replace the earlier Queen Anne and Richardson Romanesque.

By 1890 the major urban centers from the Mississippi Valley to the Pacific were closely in line with the changes in fashion which were taking place in the East. Architects from outside the area, like H. H. Richardson and Burnham and Root, were occasionally designing buildings in the West, and their Eastern work, which was well published in professional journals, was clearly followed by Western practitioners. The rapid development of America's architectural profession in the 1880s, coupled with the economic prosperity of the West, drew many competent architects to the major Western urban centers.

The Years 1895–1941: The sense of the Midwest as the heartland of America—the place where the real and essential values of America were preserved and practiced—lent an added element of optimism which was reflected in urban planning, in cultural activities, and in a concern for political and social reform. The nationwide City Beautiful Movement, personified by Chicago architect Daniel H. Burnham, left its stamp on numerous Midwestern and Western cities. Denver's extensive state and local Civic Center (1904–17) represents one of America's most successful realizations of the ideals of Classical order, while the individual buildings which comprise San Francisco's Civic Center (1912–36) constitute America's most impressive monument of the Movement. The civic centers of smaller cities, ranging from Duluth, Minnesota (1908–30), to Stockton, California (1924), indicate how even modest-sized communities could effectively share this ordered world.

The imagery of the City Beautiful Movement, that of the Classical Beaux Arts, was realized in several major monuments: Cass Gilbert's opulent Minnesota State Capitol in St. Paul (1893–1904), or the picturesquely situated Washington State Capitol at Olympia (1911–28, Wilder and White). In the 1920s the Beaux Arts passed into its next phase combining the Classical and Moderne, and once again the Mid and Far West were in the forefront with such buildings as the Liberty Memorial in Kansas City (1921–26, H. Van Buren Magonigle) and the Oregon State Capitol at Salem (1935–38, Trowbridge, Livingston & Keally).

Urban and suburban park systems, often coupled with interurban rail systems, transformed the utilitarian image of the city into something which was more livable and urbane (at least for the middle and upper middle classes). Though Minneapolis' famous park system, or San Francisco's Golden Gate Park both antedate 1890, they saw their full realization in the thirty-year period from 1890 through 1920. The spread of suburbia itself continued ever more rapidly, and by the early 1900s, builders/developers were beginning to lay out large-scale subdivisions of single-family middle-class housing. The English ideal of the country house experienced its American version from 1890 through 1930. Extensive estates for the upper middle class and the very wealthy were established in the countryside near the principal urban centers. Minneapolis had its Lake Minnetonka and San Francisco had its array of extensive estates "down the Peninsula." This was the time too when even further retreats from the urban world came to the fore—symbolized in California by Carmel as an artist's (Bohemian) retreat, and Santa Barbara (and adjacent Montecito) as a Voltairian haven where the wealthy could symbolically cultivate their gardens far removed from the cares of the everyday world.

After World War I, suburbia and the urban core of the cities quickly began to orient themselves to the automobile and its needs. Streets, parkways, and highways were increasingly the prime concern of those who, in the earlier decades, had been involved in the City Beautiful Movement. In the more "advanced" West Coast cities and especially in and around Los Angeles, the auto and the way that it was used began to destroy the preeminence of the urban core. In Los Angeles itself the auto-oriented *de facto* planning arrested the growth of the city center as the heart of the community and replaced it with a series of linear urban corridors and secondary urban cores. Drive-in facilities and the later freeways were fully presaged during these years.

In the Midwest and on the Prairie, the rural landscape was changed in several ways. In the smaller towns the earlier preeminence of a church, or the drum and dome of a county courthouse, was dramatically replaced by the tall cylindrical grain storage elevators. By 1930 the ribbons of concrete highways with their gentle curves and undulating response to the terrain had come to challenge the thin linear ribbons of steel rails of the railroad. But while the economics of the Mid and Far West were still closely tied to the great railroad systems, the private car and the new highways were increasingly becoming the familiar way that one traveled not only to the nearby town, but also to the city.

During the 1920s the Midwestern and Western farm units were becoming larger and larger, and such features as silos of concrete, hollow tile, or brick strongly injected a machine image that matched the increased use of machinery in the production of crops. From a distance it was now the tall cylindrical silos that established the presence of the farm center. In some cases the precise geometric form of the silo was reflected in the octagonal or cylindrical form of the barn—a form which had come into its own during the previous two decades, 1900–20.

At the turn of the century much of the Western prairies and the intermountain region were still very much the frontier. On the open grasslands it was the thin, barbwire fences continuing over the horizon, coupled with an occasional railroad line or road, that openly indicated this was no longer the unconquered West. Here the grouping of ranch or farm buildings was low and small of scale. The wooden branding corral asserted its visual importance over that of the single-story ranch house and other buildings. The presence of the ranch complex was often reinforced by stands of cottonwood trees planted for shade, not as in the Midwest by trees planted as a series of windbreaks, which enclosed a whole farmhouse, or by an occasional elm which shaded a green lawn.

On the West Coast the agriculturally rich valleys of the Pacific Northwest, such as Oregon's Willamette, hinted at their Midwestern as well as their Northeastern sources. The great irrigated valleys of California and especially that of the interior San Joaquin conveyed a different quality from that of the rest of the Mid and Far West. In California the farm complex of buildings was almost always dominated by a high, wood-sheathed truncated support for a square water tank. With its mild climate and available water, the California farmhouse surrounded itself with a virtual jungle of trees, shrubs, flowers, and lawns. Nearby the imposed rectilinear pattern of the irrigated fields was reinforced by extensive rows of blue gum eucalyptus, which effectively acted as windbreaks.

Since the small and large cities of the Midwest and West were still very much new, it should not be surprising that the numerous technological developments of these years were quickly put to use. In industrial and commercial architecture the great innovations emanating from Chicago—the steel frame, the cladding of buildings in terra-cotta, the extensive use of glass—occurred in Midwestern buildings very shortly after their initial introduction. The elevator, steam, hot water, and forced-air heating (and even modes of cooling) were to be found in the principal commercial buildings of every large Midwestern and Western city. In the Far West the favored new structural material was reinforced concrete (which had been used as early as the 1880s in the San Francisco Bay region by Ernest Ransome). Reinforced-concrete buildings of appreciable size began to be constructed in the 1890s, and even the idea of leaving the tactile surface remaining from the board pattern of the forms came into being as early as 1889. While steel framing was the preferred structure for high-rise buildings, the West Coast experienced an impressive renaissance in the use of concrete, ranging from the tilt-wall structures of the San Diego architect Irving J. Gill, to a remarkable array of public and private low-rise buildings constructed during the 1920s.

In its own way the architectural images employed in the four decades after 1890 were as varied as in the previous "Victorian" period. Throughout the Midwest and the West late Victorian architecture continued to be built into the early 1900s. A case in point would be in San Francisco, where a good share of its remaining Victorian wood architecture dates from after 1900. But at the same time, one would find it difficult to distinguish examples of urban commercial and public institutional architecture of the Mid and Far West from those of the East. Beaux Arts Classical imagery was the preferred fashion for the skyscraper, whether in Kansas City or Seattle. Suggestions of the medieval and of eighteenth-century Georgian architecture, all used highly correctly, were employed for churches, schools, libraries, universities, YWCAs and YMCAs.

In the years from 1895 to 1941 a succession of waves of intense nationalism swept across the United States. In the East and to a lesser extent in the Mid and Far West this nationalism was expressed in a revival of America's own Colonial architecture. The late Queen Anne and what we call today the Shingle Style were early manifestations of this nationalist urge—an urge which was assertive and imperialistically aggressive, and at the same time retreated into nostalgia. California and especially Southern California "one-upped" the national scene by creating its own regional nationalism, first in the Mission Revival (1890–1915), and later during the 1920s in the Spanish Colonial Revival. By 1930 the urban and rural landscape of much of California was highly distinct from that of the rest of the country. This distinction was not just a question of architectural images, it was equally a result of the approach taken to landscape architecture and to planning. The (almost) universal presence of Hispanic imagery which came into being in Southern California by 1930 was due to a general consensus which existed at the time—a consensus which led to the creation of official as well as unofficial architectural controls which would ensure this unanimity of imagery.

Another oblique symbol of nationalism was the California bungalow. While many of the bungalow's specific sources (and its philosophy) came from the English Arts and Crafts Movement, its ideal of returning to the simple life suggested the not too distant past of the American frontier. And as was the case again and again in American architecture, the California bungalow adroitly managed to conjure up an antiurban aura of the frontier, while at the same time it created a near perfect machine for living. The way that it was crafted meant it could be a mass-produced builder's product, or a real live do-it-yourself enterprise.

Not only was much of suburbia—as we know it today—a product of the twenties, so too was the character of downtown—of Kansas City, St. Louis, Minneapolis/St. Paul, Denver, Seattle, Portland, San Francisco, Oakland, and Los Angeles. Many of the dominant commercial high-rise buildings of the downtowns of these cities date from these years, and the theme of the Classical civic temple surmounted by a skyscraper tower first came to the fore in the Oakland City Hall of 1914 (by Palmer, Hornbostel & Jones), and its culmination was reached in Bertram Goodhue's Nebraska State Capitol Building at Lincoln (1919–32). The skyscraper as a symbol of business or governmental bureaucracy rapidly changed its imagery during the 1920s. At the beginning of the decade the Beaux Arts held sway (with an occasional exercise in the Gothic); by the end of the period the Classical tradition had gently given way to the Zigzag Moderne (Art Deco). The Foshay Tower in Minneapolis of 1926–29 (by Magney and Tusler) was indeed an exotic obelisk, but its detailing was Moderne, and it functioned well as an advertising device. Government as just another business was effectively symbolized in the Zigzag Moderne skyscraper form of the City Hall and Ramsey County Courthouse in St. Paul (1931–32, Holabird & Root; Ellerbe Architects), and in the Moderne skyscraper on the prairie, the North Dakota State Capitol at Bismarck (1932–34, Holabird & Root). In Los Angeles, the Moderne Richfield Building, sheathed in black and gold terra-cotta (1928, Morgan, Walls and Clements), was a near-perfect business machine, with its two-level parking garage, its restaurants, lounges, barbershops, and its fully controlled environment of refrigerated air conditioning and warm-air heating.

Compared to the East, the Midwest and Far West were a hotbed of radical high-art architecture. The tendrils of the Midwest Prairie School extended from Minneapolis, especially in the work of Purcell and Elmslie. Their Woodbury County Court House at Sioux City, Iowa (1915–17), represents a culmination of the movement. In California, Irving J. Gill maneuvered the Mission Revival image so that his puritanical buildings have rightly been compared to the early Modern work of the Europeans. It was Southern California as well which became the one and only American outpost of Modern architecture of the twenties and thirties—first with R. M. Schindler and Richard J. Neutra, later through the works of Gregory Ain, Harwell H. Harris, and Raphael Soriano. In the Bay Area of San Francisco, a milder, highly livable version of Modern imagery occurred in the houses of William W. Wurster, Gardner A. Dailey, and others.

While the Great Depression of the 1930s substantially reduced private building activities, the decade still turned out to be a key one for American architecture. Through federal funding (generally the WPA) many changes took place in the urban environment—new parks, streets, public housing, and the construction of a wide variety of public buildings including schools, city halls, recreation buildings, and the like. The facilities at many of the state and federal parks were expanded, and highway improvements furthered the cause of the automobile. By 1941 Los Angeles had emerged as the preeminent automobile city of the mid-century. The first of Los Angeles' freeways, the Pasadena freeway, was begun in 1934 and completed in 1941; linear strip commercial development continued; and single-family housing of suburbia pressed out in all directions. The shopping center, which had its beginnings in both the Midwest and in California in the late 1920s (the Country Club Plaza in Kansas City, 1922–28, Edward B. Delk and E. W. Tanner; and Cathay Circle in Los Angeles, 1926–27, D. Gibbs), was well on its way to becoming the core of the new urban community. Drive-in architecture flourished; drive-in supermarkets were joined by drive-in movie theaters, restaurants, florists, shoe repair —almost anything. The large-scale motion picture palaces of the twenties were replaced by small suburban motion picture theaters which looked to their parking lot as much as to the street.

The imagery of the 1930s was also highly distinct from that of the 1920s. In commercial and governmental architecture, the Beaux Arts and the Zigzag Moderne gave way to the Streamline Moderne, with its white stucco curved surfaces and glass bricks. The Classical traditions were cleansed even further. As was true elsewhere in the country, the luxury of Rome and the sophistication of Athens were replaced by the primitive atmosphere of Sparta. In domestic architecture the wide variety of borrowed images of the twenties was abandoned for the new nationalism of the white clapboard, green-shuttered Colonial. In California the Hispanic episode of the Spanish Colonial Revival was modified, and the Monterey Revival and the California ranch house came to the fore producing an image which could be regional and national, Hispanic and Anglo.

The Years 1945 to the Present: The thirty-five years since the end of the Second World War have experienced several momentous planning battles, all of which are still present today (1980). The first and major clash was between the traditional view of the cities' downtown as the core of an urban landscape, and the close to universal tendency after 1945 for urban communities to grow horizontally. It was in the early 1930s that Frank Lloyd Wright (in his projected Broad Acre City, 1932) had argued for the primacy of suburbia, the linear commercial city, and the automobile. Well before this, at the beginning of the twenties, Los Angeles planners had been devoting their attention to seeing how the horizontal city could be realized. After 1945 (and even before) in every major Midwestern and Western city the urban core was either arrested in its growth or began to decay. Suburbia, the shopping center, and the freeway as a linkage came to constitute both the reality and the ideal.

As in the East, extensive areas of St. Louis, Kansas City, Minneapolis, Oakland, and San Francisco were bulldozed clear for projected urban renewal. In most cases, the wastelands of empty space resulting from urban renewal remained for decades; generally when they were built upon, the new ended up being tawdry and deplorable. At the end of the sixties there were some affirmative changes in the overall pattern of the gloom produced by urban renewal. Starting with its Nicollet Mall (1958–62, 1967, Lawrence Halprin and Associates) and the enclosed "Skyway" pedestrian bridges, Minneapolis has managed to bring about one of the few instances in the United States of a successful reassertion of the primacy of the traditional urban core, although it should be pointed out that Minneapolis' new core is also effectively serviced by an extensive new freeway system. Los Angeles and its surrounds simply went on their own way, horizontally connecting together a seemingly endless number of small and medium-sized urban centers.

The post-World War II rural landscape of the Midwest and West has not changed in any degree comparable to that of the urban/suburban landscape. The beautiful pattern of freeways with their double ribbons of concrete and curvilinear geometry of interchanges has been imposed on an older environment. The major changes which one might notice have to do with the current need for water and energy, especially in the Far West where the great dams of the 1920s and 1930s have been joined by both large and small concrete and earth-filled dams. The California Aqueduct (1959–72, Department of Public Works, State of California), which, like the pattern of a pathway in an eighteenth-century English garden, winds its way through the San Joaquin Valley, is as momentous in its implications as any freeway or horizontal expansion of a city. The high-voltage lines equally dominate sections of the rural landscape, with their high open metal towers which now crisscross the plains, mountains, and valleys of the West.

The close to universal acceptance of the bland Corporate International Style in the post-World War II years produced an array of commercial and governmental buildings that we still find difficult to appreciate, even with a hefty nostalgia for the 1950s. The Midwest and Far West, like the rest of the United States, are filled with examples of these thinly clad boxes. Perhaps in a way it was advantageous that urban renewal was not initially successful. For in the case of Minneapolis, San Francisco, or downtown Los Angeles, the dominant new buildings which we encounter today were built at the end of the sixties and later. On the whole these later examples will age more gracefully and very likely will become even lovable in the years to come.

The ideal for the suburban middle- or upper-middle-class dwellings after 1945 was the California ranch house. Like the earlier California bungalow, here was a democratic architectural image—an expensive architect- (or catalog-) designed example—differing only in size from its 1,200-square-foot/111-square-meter builder's version. In the Midwest the ranch house might partake a little more of the imagery of the Eastern Colonial, but its open plan and informal relation to the out-of-doors indicate its Far Western sources.

The Midwest experienced a sprinkling of high-art examples of Modern architecture during the pre-1965 period. Eero Saarinen's Jefferson Memorial Arch in St. Louis (1965), Minoru Yamasaki's Northwest National Life Insurance Building in Minneapolis (1963), and Pietro Belluschi's Equitable Building in Portland (1948) are all-too-rare occurrences of high-art architecture. Basically the commendable level of architectural design which we associate with the Midwest occurred after 1965. This is equally true of the Far West, with the major exception of domestic architecture. Just as Los Angeles represents a high point for the early Modern of the twenties and thirties, so too did it during the fifties and early sixties. The Case Study House program of John Entenza and his magazine *Arts and Architecture* created an image of the Modern which had a worldwide impact. In the Bay Area the "Woodsy" tradition provided the source for California's next national/international export, the vertical shed-roof box. The Sea Ranch condominium (1965) by Charles W. Moore and William Turnbull (along with Donlyn Lyndon and Richard R. Whittaker) became an instant international landmark.

Another California export of the late 1960s was the do-it-yourself wood butcher's house which blossomed forth in semi-dropout communities throughout California, especially in the north. Here a cultivated back-to-nature crudeness was coupled with open nostalgia for the past, using old stained-glass windows, doors, water closets of the 1920s, and craftsman framed oak furniture. Architects and builders were not oblivious to this nostalgia and by the seventies the shingle-clad craftsman image had become a norm for the new subdivision houses. Even commercial architects took up the theme with rough wood shake walls and roofs, board and batten walls, and leaded glass windows.

A potpourri of recent and more distant past imagery has now entered the scene, not only in the Far West but in the Midwest as well. We can now have lunch in a railroad car or a "Victorian" station, and dinner in a French château or half-timbered English pub. The amusement park, ranging from Disneyland in Anaheim (1955 and later) to Magic Mountain in Valencia (1970 and later), has strongly affected the symbolism of nostalgia. The culmination of the current fascination with historic imagery is unquestionably the J. Paul Getty Museum in Malibu (1972–73; Langdon & Wilson, Stephen Garrett; Norman Neuerberg; Emmet L. Wemple & Associates), a symbolic re-creation of a luxurious Roman villa. Only this Roman villa, like a contemporary shopping center, is oriented around the auto and its parking garage.

As is true for the rest of the country, historic preservation is one of the most potent new forces in planning and architecture. No small or large urban landscape in the Midwest has escaped or will escape the new scrutiny which preservation concerns are forcing upon them. Hand in hand with preservation are numerous environmental concerns, many of which will appreciably slow the transformation of both the urban and rural landscape. Even in Los Angeles, which is often mistakenly thought of as being non-historical, preservation and environmental concerns are having a deep impact, and in smaller communities like Ferndale and Eureka it now seems reasonable to hope that their "Victorian" character will remain. In Kansas City, St. Louis, Minneapolis/St. Paul, and Denver, one major monument after another is being recycled for new and often very different uses.

The architects' commitment to the Modern is still dominant, but the imagery employed to express this commitment is rapidly changing. Philip Johnson and John Burgee's IDS Tower in Minneapolis with its Crystal Court (1968–73) and Cesar Pelli's (Gruen and Associates) Pacific Design Center in Los Angeles (1975) provide a good indication of how Modern architecture has viewed itself at the end of the sixties and into the seventies. As the work of the late 1970s indicates, the Modern movement is anything but dead in the Mid and Far West, and historicism which was laid to rest in the 1940s is equally alive and vital. The interplay between the two may well keep each of these from repeating the architectural sterility of the 1950s.

ORGANIZATION OF BOOK

The three volumes of this guidebook describe the architecture of three geographic regions with (roughly) the same number of buildings in each: Volume 1—New England and the Mid-Atlantic States; Volume 2—The South and Midwest; and Volume 3—The Plains States and Far West. The states are arranged in alphabetical order, and each state begins with a map showing by numbered dots the relative geographic location of cities containing buildings described in that state. The cities are also listed alphabetically and if there is more than one building in a city they appear in approximate chronology. As is explained, the structures which are in boldface type in the state index are of general interest, whereas the others are more for architects, architectural historians, and other specialists. An index and glossary appear in each volume.

Alaska

Fairbanks 3–5

Anchorage 1–2

Kenai 8

Skagway 12

Juneau 6–7

Sitka 9–11

ALASKA

The buildings in boldface type are of general interest. The others are for the specialist.

Anchorage
1. **Historical and Fine Arts Museum** (1968/1974)—Schultz/Maynard; Kenneth D. Maynard
2. Anchorage Natural Gas Building (1969)—Crittenden, Cassetta, Wirum & Cannon

Fairbanks
3. **Native Village, Alaskaland**
4. **Commons, University of Alaska** (1969)—Crittenden, Cassetta, Wirum & Cannon
5. **Rasmuson Library and Fine Arts Center, University of Alaska** (1969)—Francis B. Mayer

Juneau
6. Old Witch Totem Pole (c. 1860)
7. St. Nicholas Orthodox Church (1893–94)

Kenai
8. Church of the Holy Assumption (1894–96)

Sitka
9. Sitka and the Russian Heritage in Alaska (early 19th century)
10. **Sitka National Historical Park and Its Totem Poles** (mid-19th and 20th centuries)
11. **Centennial Building** (1966–67)—Allen McDonald
    Visitor Center (1965)—John Morse & Associates

Skagway
12. **Broadway and Its Buildings** (pre-1900)

1 Historical and Fine Arts Museum (1968/1974)
7th Avenue at A Street
Anchorage, Alaska

**SCHULTZ/MAYNARD, ARCHITECTS (1968); KENNETH D.
MAYNARD, ARCHITECT (1974)**

A small, flexible, multisubject museum containing a variety of displays
concerned with Alaska's art, plus an illuminating insight into native
(i.e. Aleut, Indian, and Eskimo) cultural contributions. The rectangular building is faced with a deep ocher brick and topped by a continuous cornice. The frieze, by Alaskan artist Alex Duff Combs, consists of five standardized panels repeated in series. The windowless
exhibition rooms, particularly the high ones at either end, form quiet,
efficient settings for the displays. One might wish for an outdoor extension, plus more on habitats, but altogether the museum itself provides
a fine setting for its first-rate interpretations of the native contributions
of this extraordinary state. Kirk, Wallace & McKinley were consulting
architects.

*Open Tues.–Sat. 9–6, Sun. 1–5, except holidays; in summer, Mon.
9–6, Tues. and Thurs. 9–9*

2   Anchorage Natural Gas Building (1969)
Spenard Road at 31st Street
Anchorage, Alaska

CRITTENDEN, CASSETTA, WIRUM & CANNON, ARCHITECTS

Accented by a well-sculpted freestanding plaque, whose prominent placement beside the road "announces" the building to the speeding motorist, and neatly set back behind a low wall with proper planting, this small sales and office structure sets a commendable standard. Its inset ground floor and thorough detailing are carried through with finesse. Construction is of steel frame and dark anodized aluminum panels. The sculpted plaque—semiabstracting the state's natural features and wildlife—was designed (1970) by Alex Duff Combs, who used glazed ceramic relief on concrete. The gas, for which the company has the distribution franchise, comes from the Kenai Peninsula, the oldest developed fields in Alaska.

Showroom open during business hours

3   Native Village, Alaskaland
W on Airport Way, N at Peger Road
Fairbanks, Alaska

Alaskaland was built for the Centennial of the Territory-State in 1967, and among its better exhibits is this reconstruction of building types seen (or once seen) in the three different native cultures of Alaska: Eskimo, Aleut, and Indian. Though the three are ethnically related, especially the Eskimo and Aleut, they are generally considered different peoples: altogether the three number today around 60,000. The cheerful, generally peaceful Alaskan Eskimo—they rarely warred—are the most numerous. They live basically along the coast, their greatest concentration being near the mouth of the Kuskokwim River. Their cousins continue some 5,000 miles/8,000 kilometers along the Arctic Ocean and its innumerable islands, across to Greenland and down to Labrador. There are also Eskimo still in Siberia. The Alaskan Eskimo who live on St. Lawrence Island—roughly 50 miles/80 kilometers from the U.S.S.R.—speak a Siberian dialect and, reputedly, have occasional contact with the Asians. The sea for all of them is the source of their food, clothing, and "wealth." (A small minority of Eskimo do live slightly inland along rivers where they depend primarily on caribou or salmon for their sustenance; the name "Eskimo" means "eater of raw flesh.") Some experts think the Eskimo language is remotely related to the Ural-Altaic family (the Altai Mountains of central Asia are contiguous to the U.S.S.R., Mongolia, and China). The Alaska Indians were, and to a certain extent still are, found in the interior below the Yukon River (the Athapascans), and along the southeast coast (Tlingit and Haida). The Aleuts—who were among the first peoples in North America—live, as expected, in the fog-shrouded, volcanic-created Aleutian Islands and at the end of the Alaska Peninsula. These unfortunate people were almost exterminated by the Russian fur traders, diminishing from some 25,000 souls to less than one-tenth that number when the United States purchased "Russian America," retitling it Alaska. The present population of these understandably reclusive people is probably only a few thousand of native blood.

The Fairbanks "village" compound, albeit set in an artificial and occasionally commercial milieu, gives some understanding of the shelters erected by people with few tools, less material, and a climate which ranges from hostile to semireasonable. Obviously the Eskimo igloo is not represented, but it should nonetheless be kept in mind that the Alaskan ice igloo is not a permanent dwelling; it is a temporary shelter

especially useful when on hunting trips or traveling. A skilled builder can make an igloo in an hour or two utilizing only a knife. In the far more northerly Canadian islands and Greenland, where the temperature is colder and driftwood rare, the igloo was and is a more utilized form of winter shelter. Kaj Birket-Smith in his book *Eskimos* (Crown, 1971) mentions that "This obviously very primitive form is . . . also used by some of the Koryak," the Mongoloid people of northeastern Siberia. Peter Freuchen, the famous Eskimo explorer, describes the typical igloo (*iglu* or *igdlo* means a house of any material) as being 12 feet/3.6 meters in diameter and 9 feet/2.7 meters high at center. The "permanent" Alaskan Eskimo house is built of vertically placed driftwood—whale ribs when available—and sometimes with a bit of stone, the whole covered with sod and semiburied in the ground, the interior being lined with skins. They are typically 12–14 feet/3.6–4.2 meters long. Like the igloo, they have long insulating *tossut* or "tunnel" access, the tunnel also serving as storage area on one side and low kitchen on the other. With the coming of warmer weather in spring and summer, these sod houses leak from the top and fill with water at the bottom from melting permafrost, at which time the family moves into a conical tent generally of caribou skins or seal skins. The Diomede Island "skin house" at Alaskaland is a summer dwelling of drift log frame and split walrus hides as covering. In most villages now (like the distressing Barrow, the northernmost settlement in the U.S.A.) where sufficient lumber has been brought in by whites, the Eskimo prop ramshackle buildings on pilings, and live thus all year round.

Open daily 12–6, year round

---

4 Commons (1969)
University of Alaska
College Road (AK 3)
Fairbanks, Alaska

CRITTENDEN, CASSETTA, WIRUM & CANNON, ARCHITECTS

As a key unit at the entry of a burgeoning university, this commons must provide visual importance and also fit handily within the pedestrian circulation pattern, both of which it does well. In spite of awkward grade conditions which dropped the building almost a floor below the approach, the stepped-down entry has been capably handled. The dining room is enclosed by glass on three sides, with an elevated outrigging of vertical wood louvers. This gives the windows both sun and glare protection in addition to recalling the forest beyond. The interior of the dining room has a ceiling profile of slightly canted planes; this geometry plus subtle touches of color eliminate any feeling of boxlike rigidity. A lounge, whose stained wood sheathing picks up the wood of the louvers, occupies the top of the building's two floors, with a broad roof terrace around it.

Open during school year

---

5   Rasmuson Library and Fine Arts Center (1969)
University of Alaska
Fairbanks, Alaska

FRANCIS B. MAYER, ARCHITECT

Holding down a motley collection of older buildings, this complex provides a much-needed spatial anchor for the center of the campus. The

five-story library which forms one side of the "plaza" is the major unit. Others include a 1,072-seat recital hall for the music department, a 450-seat drama theater and a small laboratory theater, a Great Hall (which doubles effectively for less formal recitals), and a full art department with studios. Architecturally the functions are clearly expressed in plan and space and their divergent forms are well articulated. Structure throughout is of reinforced concrete with pebble aggregate concrete panel walls. Copper-tinted mirror-glass surrounds the main-floor reading rooms and those on the top floor, with two floors of stacks in between. A competent cluster of functions.

Open Mon.–Fri. 8–5, Sat. 1–6, Sun. 11–6, except holidays

6   Old Witch Totem Pole (c. 1860)
by Village Library
Juneau, Alaska

Freud and Lévi-Strauss, among others, have written on totemism and its phratry, but it remained for the clans of the Northwest Coast Indians to raise totems to their greatest heights, at least artistically. Their magnificent carved and painted heraldic rejoicings celebrated family history, mythologic beliefs, deaths, and even potlatch (i.e. "celebratory") one-upmanship in spectacular terms. (Some were 60 feet/18 meters and more high.) But, alas, nineteenth-century missionaries considered them idolatrous—which, of course, they were not, being primarily pedigrees—and if they did not pull them down themselves they urged their charges to do so. Totem pole carving thus became a moribund art and even those poles which were "spared" eventually rotted, though made of cedar. Moreover the Indians themselves, when discovering that their own family totem was decaying, found it easier to carve a new one than to preserve the old. Those that remain are now state treasures and there is a growing interest in reviving the art. The Old Witch Totem shown here—it "relates" a mother-in-law problem—was moved to Juneau from Sukkwan, a village near Hydaburg on Prince of Wales Island. Southernmost Alaska was the center for totem pole carving and the Haida, who carved this, one of the chief tribes practicing the art. (See also the description of the Sitka National Historical Park and Its Totem Poles.)

---

7   St. Nicholas Orthodox Church (1893–94)
326 5th Street
Juneau, Alaska

A minute and architecturally modest church of Russian parentage but some Victorian details. The octagonal body, with gabled entry on one side (note belfry), is topped by a bold octagonal roof with an onion-domed cupola atop and a cross above. The tiny interior, almost half sanctuary, is of interest chiefly for its collection of vestments and several outstanding old books. The church was built primarily for those native Indians who were converted to the Russian Orthodox religion, and is thought to be the oldest still standing in Alaska. It is listed in the National Register of Historic Places.

Frequently open

8 Church of the Holy Assumption (1894–96)
Kenai, Alaska

Founded by the Russians in 1791, Kenai was revived by Standard Oil
in 1963 when its wells gushed forth. In between these dates the somewhat primitive church-and-chapel was erected, itself originally established in 1846. Primitive in plan and scarce polished in detail, it is
nonetheless one of the best of that dwindling handful of structures
recalling Russian cultural influences which carried on (at least reli-

giously) long after Alaska was acquired by the United States. The church's scaled-down metal domes quaintly and faintly suggest the ancient Byzantine origin of its rites. Would that there were more such examples. The church is listed in the National Register of Historic Places.

If not open inquire at caretaker

---

9 Sitka and the Russian Heritage in Alaska (early 19th century) Sitka, Alaska

Alaska's discovery by the Russians occurred when Vitus J. Bering, a Dane in the service of Peter the Great, sighted the St. Elias Mountains on July 16, 1741. (Mount St. Elias is 18,008 feet/5,486 meters high.) Sitka, founded in 1799, was the first major settlement, and the town

served as the Russian capital from 1808 to 1867 when Secretary of State Seward purchased what was to become the forty-ninth state for $7,200,000. (This cost was approximately 2 cents an acre or $12.28 a square mile. Overkill of seals and otters, coupled with fashion's reduced demand—furs being the Russian financial backbone—helped prompt the sale.) At Sitka, also, the American flag was first raised over the new territory. The most prominent early figure in the development of Sitka was Aleksandr Baranov (1747–1819), a trader, and he so dominated the development of the Russian American Company that his imprint was paramount. In 1799 he made the town (now Old Sitka) his capital and when this was destroyed by the warlike Tlingit Indians three years later, he reestablished what is now the present city 6 miles/9.6 kilometers to the south. Baranov's venture was commercial and fur-dominated, similar to the privately financed expedition to Jamestown, Virginia, in 1607. He and the settlement prospered; the town remained the capital, officially New Archangel, even after Mr. Seward's purchase. (Alaska, incidentally, was almost totally neglected by the federal government for decades after its purchase.)

Unfortunately little of merit remains from the years of Russian occupation and culture. The **Russian Orthodox St. Michael's Cathedral** in the center of town—important but of naive design—was dedicated in 1848 but burned in 1966, and though it has been rebuilt (of fireproof material) it is not quite the same. Fortunately its icons were saved though a large number had been stolen in the late 1860s. The **Russian Bishop's House** (1842–43), on Crescent Harbor, was neglected for years following the sale of Alaska to the United States. In 1972 it was incorporated into the Sitka National Historical Park (q.v.) and is now undergoing complete restoration. A modest but sizable building—it measures 76.3 feet/23 meters long—it will add considerably to the city's architectural background. Target date for completion is 1984. The **Blockhouse** (restored) off Seward Street is a nostalgic reminder, but little else of distinction has survived. (See also the Church of the Holy Assumption, 1894–96, at Kenai.)

The **Sheldon Jackson Museum** (1895–96), Lincoln Street, was the first poured concrete building in the Territory and also the first museum (founded in 1887). It houses an excellent collection of Eskimo artifacts. The museum is listed in the National Register of Historic Places.

---

10   Sitka National Historical Park and Its Totem Poles (mid-19th and 20th centuries)
.5 mile/.8 kilometer E of town on Metlekatla Street
Sitka, Alaska

Sitka's 107-acre/43-hectare park was established in 1890, was made the Sitka National Monument in 1910, and became the Sitka National Historical Park in 1972. At this late date the Russian Bishop's House was added to its care. (See Sitka and the Russian Heritage.) The Park is located on the spot which marked a turning point in Alaskan history, for it was here in 1804 that the Russians and the Tlingit Indians fought the Battle of Sitka, which was the last significant armed resistance of natives to the white man. (In "the lower forty-eight" the last major Indian battle took place in 1880.)

More cheerfully, the Park possesses a sterling collection of eighteen Tlingit and Haida totem poles set in a grove of spruce and hemlock. Some of these poles represented Alaska at the St. Louis Exposition of 1904; others are WPA copies. The tallest is the Chief Sonnihat Pole (more correctly Saan'a'heit) at 59 feet/18 meters. It is probably

accurate to say that totem poles were the outstanding esthetic achievement of the North American Indians.

Religious symbolism, it is important to note, is generally absent from totem poles: they primarily represent family trees, pride of ancestral heroism, "merit badges," social one-upmanship, and mortuary uses. And although their origin is disputed, totem poles may have evolved from interior "house pillars," then were moved outdoors to be attached to the front of the dwellings, and finally erected as freestanding "monuments in cedar" as they have been called. Supposedly the first described by Westerners were those seen on Cook's third voyage in 1778, though other parts of Alaska had been discovered almost forty years earlier.

The Haida, who inhabit the southernmost Alaskan and northernmost Canadian islands, are generally credited as being both the pioneers of the art and the finest carvers. (They were also superb canoe makers; some of their crafts measured 70 feet/21 meters long.) The word "totem" is from the Odjibewa, or a kindred Algonkin dialect, and means "his emblem." Eventually totem poles enjoyed a coastal spread of some 500 miles/800 kilometers. The once-great forest of this area, often with red cedars, supplied easily worked wood, while the winter rains encouraged indoor activity, often in cedar-planked multiple-family clan houses as large as 40 x 50 feet (12 x 15 meters). These were upheld by the carved "house pillars" mentioned. Perhaps paradoxically the "great age" of the totem pole was in the early and mid-nineteenth century when the introduction of metalworking tools by ship captains enormously facilitated carving. The increased wealth of many chiefs through the fur trade was also a factor in their proliferation. Though an iconography of sorts exists—the raven, eagle, bear, and whale are favored—totem poles are almost impossible to "read" by one not indoctrinated into the culture, as their subject matter represents personal achievement. The Haida, incidentally, at least those who survived the white man's diseases, probably led the easiest lives of the North American Indians because they enjoyed a reasonable climate and rich resources. They developed surprisingly elaborate social hierarchies including substantial ownership of slaves. Their splendid vertical culture ranks among our finest inheritance. (See also the Old Witch Totem Pole in Juneau.)

Open daily 9–5, except major holidays and Sun., Nov.–Mar.

The handsome **Visitor Center** (1965) in the Park was designed by John Morse & Associates for the National Park Service. In it, contemporary Tlingit and Haida artists continue in their artistic traditions by demonstrating wood and silver carving and bead and button techniques. There is also a museum/exhibit hall and an audiovisual program.

Visitor Center open daily except major winter holidays and Sun., Nov.–Mar.

---

11   Centennial Building (1966–67)
Harbor Drive
Sitka, Alaska

ALLEN McDONALD, ARCHITECT

Invitingly presiding over the waterside (on built-up land), surveying Sitka's panorama of sea, islands, and distant snowcapped mountains, Centennial Building serves as community and convention center. A

small regional museum, under the direction of the Sitka Historical Society, occupies its front section. Built with local stone base and wood sides, and dominated by a roof of well-sculpted planes, it serves its functions efficiently and handsomely. One of the most interesting exhibits is a thoroughly researched model of the town as it appeared in 1867, the year Alaska was purchased by the U.S.A. A colorful Tlingit Indian ceremonial canoe in front provides an appropriate introduction.

Open June–Sept., daily 9–9, Oct.–May 9–5

---

12 Broadway and Its Buildings (pre-1900)
Skagway, Alaska

Skagway—the Home of the North Wind—was the once thriving entry port for the unbelievable Yukon gold rush, that 1897–98 stampede of perhaps 30,000 or more determined men struggling into nearby Canada's Klondike. The town reputedly reached at its zenith a population (mostly transient) of some 10,000–20,000, the largest in the Territory. However, it quickly declined to less than 1,000 when more and more accessible gold was discovered (1899) across Alaska at Nome on the Bering Sea. Skagway thus almost collapsed (the population was reportedly 492 in 1930—the adjacent village of Dyea did disappear), but it fortunately revived somewhat during World War II

as a supply base for constructing the Alaska Highway. (The Japanese had captured Attu, Agattu, and Kiska islands in the Aleutians in 1942–43, and the highway, more than half of which traverses Canada, was a vital logistic U.S. supply line.) In the mid-1960s mineral wealth in the Yukon began to be shipped out and Skagway became a prominent ore-concentrate shipping point, its White Pass and Yukon Railroad, daringly built during the gold rush, finally coming into its own. (It also today makes a spectacular tourist excursion.) Throughout these ups and downs the buildings of the late 1890s survived, though many are semiabandoned, and this legacy, though modest, is important in any review of the architecture of the state. There is no significant individual structure but Broadway as a street will reward the dedicated, plus the followers of Jack London and Robert W. Service. Note that Broadway's surface is still gravel and its sidewalks are of wood and largely under a projecting canopy. The most frenetic structure is the Arctic Brotherhood Building (1899) near the harbor end of the street, with a facade totally decorated with sticks of driftwood, looking like some giant match king's last fling. A half block up the street stands the Golden North Hotel (1898, now open May 1–Sept. 30), with "dome" added in 1903 when the hotel was turned at right angles. Within is displayed a hair-raising collection of photographs of endless lines of miners attacking the murderous snows of White Pass and Chilkoot trails which lead over the Canadian border and then to the gold fields of the Yukon, still some 500 miles/800 kilometers away. A number of rooms of the Golden North have been comfortably restored as originally furnished (but with modern plumbing). There are other buildings of the time along Broadway but more important is the general, relatively unspoiled total character of the street. The Trail of '98 Museum (open May–Sept., daily 8:30–10 A.M., 3–8 P.M.), ex-McCabe College (1899–1900) and just off Broadway, though no architectural sensation, has a kaleidoscope of memorabilia of the gold rush period.

Fortunately the Skagway Historic District has been entered in the National Register of Historic Places so that this unique town will be preserved.

Arizona

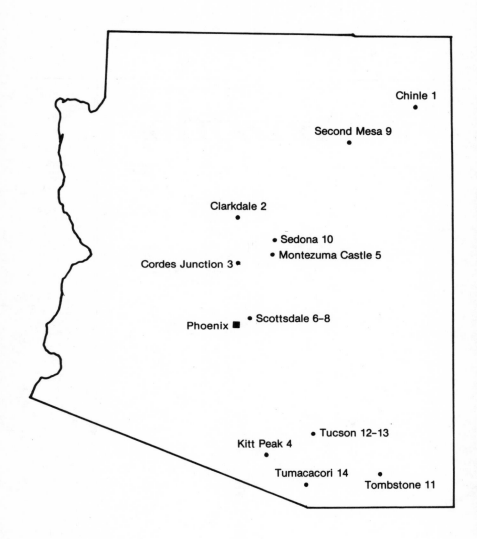

Chinle 1

Second Mesa 9

Clarkdale 2

Sedona 10

Montezuma Castle 5

Cordes Junction 3

Phoenix ■ Scottsdale 6–8

Tucson 12–13

Kitt Peak 4

Tumacacori 14

Tombstone 11

ARIZONA

The buildings in boldface type are of general interest. The others are for the specialist.

Chinle	1	**The White House** (1066–1275)
Clarkdale	2	Tuzigoot National Monument (1125–1400)
near Cordes Junction	3	Arcosanti (1970–)—Paolo Soleri
Kitt Peak	4	**Robert R. McMath Solar Telescope** (1966)—Skidmore, Owings & Merrill
Montezuma Castle	5	**Montezuma Castle National Monument** (c. 1100–1450)
Scottsdale	6	**Taliesin West** (1938–59)—Frank Lloyd Wright
	7	**Cosanti Foundation Workshop** (1962–)—Paolo Soleri
	8	**Civic Center** (1968–75)—Gonzales Associates
Second Mesa	9	**Hopi Cultural Center** (1970–71)—Gonzales Associates
		Old Pueblo of Oraibi (1300–)
Sedona	10	**Chapel of the Holy Cross** (1956)—Anshen & Allen
Tombstone	11	**Tombstone Courthouse State Historic Park** (1881–82)—Frank Walker
		Historic District (largely 1880s)
Tucson	12	**Mission San Xavier del Bac** (1776–97)
	13	Pima County Junior College (1970–)—Caudill Rowlett Scott; William Wilde & Associates; Friedman & Jobusch
Tumacacori	14	San José Mission (c. 1800–22)

1 The White House (1066–1275)
Canyon de Chelly National Monument, 6.5 miles/
10 kilometers E of
Chinle, Arizona

The White House at the base of this extraordinary canyon—a red sandstone Permian slash at times 1,000 feet/305 meters deep—is, like other cliff-dwelling examples throughout the Four Corners area, far more of nature than of man. But it represents, as do the others, such a logical, functional, and handsome fusion of home beseeching cliff that it offers rewards to all interested in our earliest surviving vernacular. Its precipitous location gave protection against flash floods, did not encroach upon the fertile river-watered land below, and offered reasonable defense. (These factors also prompted the development of Italian hill towns in the Middle Ages.) Nature, of course, furnished the

greatest share of the shelter, plus a beauty which will excite anyone frisky enough to hike down and back the 500-foot/152-meter drop to the canyon's broad base via a good but strenuous trail. (River-bottom Jeep trips—plus accommodations—are also available from Thunderbird Lodge.) The entire ruin consists of two sections: a lower against the base of the cliff and an upper from which the name is derived. ("White House" comes from the still-surviving white clay plastering of the central room.) The higher section (not accessible) is magnificently perched 40 feet/12 meters above the canyon floor—like the nest of a weird mechanical bird—its neatly squared buildings notched in the protecting cliffside. There are approximately eleven semiruined rooms in the upper part. Ladders gave access from the roofs of the lower buildings (visitable), which once rose three and four floors but which have been reduced by river and weather to ruined hulks today. (Unusually high water in 1930 did severe damage.) But even if one does not go to the canyon base, the rim automobile trip, especially with binoculars, will enlighten.

In 1931 the entire area, which covers 130 square miles/337 square kilometers and which also includes the Canyon del Muerto, was dedicated as the Canyon de Chelly National Monument. The region was occupied by the prehistoric Puebloan Anasazi culture beginning around A.D. 350, but the Pueblos left at the end of the thirteenth century because of the disastrous drought which seared the entire Four Corners area for a generation and more. (Also left are some three hundred known Anasazi sites in the Monument.) Around A.D. 1700 the Navajo—the largest of the Indian groups—migrated to the canyon and today it is their traditional home. Note their hogans scattered along the flat and fertile riverbed. These slightly domed, roughly circular, log and earth houses are virtually unique to Navajo culture. Hogans are related to the shelters of the Navajo's Athapascan cousins in northwest Canada, but their design changed from bark covering to hide to packed earth and sticks as the early migratory hunters and gatherers moved to and settled in the southwest U.S.A., arriving around A.D. 1000. The hogans' basically circular plan, however, remained though the older more conical form evolved into the low "dome" seen here. Religious symbolism was part of the mythology connected with these shelters and their basic orientation was eastward so that they would catch "the first blessing" of the sun. "Even Navajos with modern houses may have hogans for religious rites" (*The World of the American Indian,* National Geographic Society, 1974).

Overlook and trail always open; Visitor Center open Memorial Day–Labor Day, daily 8–7, rest of year 8–5, except Jan. 1, Dec. 25

2 Tuzigoot National Monument (1125–1400)
2.4 miles/3.9 kilometers SE of
Clarkdale, Arizona

Unlike cliff dwellings, the stone and adobe pueblo which overlooks the
valley at Tuzigoot is constructed, unembraced by nature, on top of a
120-foot/36-meter-high limestone knoll. Though it is in ruins today,
one can get a good impression of the building skill of the prehistoric
Pueblo Indians. The structure, which measures approximately
500 x 100 feet/152 x 30 meters, contains seventy-seven ground-floor
and fifteen second-floor rooms of generous size—12 x 18 feet/3.6 x 5.5
meters. Entry was gained by roof hatches: only three doorways were
discovered in the entire pueblo. The original population was swelled
to some four hundred around A.D. 1200, the fertile land and nearby

Verde River readily sustaining them. Yet the pueblo was abandoned after the 1400s. Disease, warfare, and internal strife are thought to have been the major causes. When the first Spanish explorers arrived in 1583 only Yavapai Indians in brush huts were living in the area. The ruin was excavated in 1933–34 by a team from the University of Arizona, and in 1939 the site was made a National Monument. An informative museum nearby houses the artifacts.

Open Memorial Day–Labor Day, daily 8–5: admission

---

3   Arcosanti (1970–   )
2.5 miles/4 kilometers NE of Cordes Junction exit of IS 17
   (c. 70 miles/113 kilometers N of Phoenix)
Cordes Junction, Arizona

PAOLO SOLERI, ARCHITECT

The philosophy behind the planning and buildings of Arcosanti, a community which will eventually accommodate 4,500–5,000 inhabitants, seeks an intimate, indeed revelatory, relationship between man and nature, a unity of those forces which shape—and which too often have misshaped—the world. Arcosanti's physical manifestation heralds arcology—architecture and ecology—and "is seen also as a societal framework that can give a higher quality to humankind's physical, psychological and aesthetic well-being." This "alternative urban environment" will preserve most of its site for agriculture and recreation, with only 13 acres/5.3 hectares of its 860-acre/348-hectare property being used for buildings. It will eliminate sprawl by sheltering all life functions—housing, work, education, recreation, shopping, religion, and culture—within one fantastic, twenty-five-story megastructure. Revering "The Theology of the Sun," it will depend upon it for most of its energy needs via a vast (5-acre/2-hectare) south-facing greenhouse and solar-heat-collecting unit stepped down the mesa in front. Waste and pollution will be almost non-existent, while the need for the automobile will wither.

Construction of the "first generation" units of Arcosanti began in 1970 and by the late seventies several substantial structures, all amateur-built, were out of the ground. The first which the visitor meets is the Crafts III Building (1977), an "exploded" box reception and restaurant center nearest the parking lot. This energetic design is charac-

terized by rectangular concrete panels, both poured and prefabricated, many of them pierced with large circular openings somewhat reminiscent of Louis I. Kahn's work in Bangladesh. Behind this rise two apses (both 1975), the nearer housing the foundry with the ceramics workshop where Soleri's famous bells are made. A short distance to the east spring twin in-line barrel vaults of prefabricated concrete sections forming a splendid open work space for the wood and metal shops (1972). Separated from each other by 6 feet/1.8 meters, they measure 63.3 feet/19.3 meters wide and 32.8 feet/10 meters deep. Work on the East Crescent, just east of the vaults, is expected to be completed in 1981. Residential but flexible in character, it will house sixty to seventy people. In time this can be used for studio and work space, functioning as a playground, meeting and performance place, and market. Other housing will progress when funding becomes available.

This exciting, almost Roman forum group of "supporting buildings" will—if financing materializes—be dwarfed and embraced by the megastructure mentioned, a gigantic, greenhouse-topped crescent rising directly behind, a building which will offer its inhabitants (as mentioned, up to five thousand) a new form of "urban" life in its Two Suns Arcology, the second sun being "the monumental miracle of evolution peaked by the mind and spirit of man." The 1977 model of this mind-boggling complex—which in cross section vaguely resembles an automotive engine block at a 45° angle (see drawing)—shows one of the most fantastic projects to come off any architect's drawing board. We and the world will not be richer if it does not materialize. Chimeric, cosmic, mystic, and almost beyond belief in imagination and complexity, this microcity in the desert may well develop new insights

for the metropolis of the future. Any major effort to harmonize man and nature and minimize the need for non-renewable sources of energy will bear some of the fruit which the world sore needs. This alternative to present-day urban chaos "will demonstrate that we can rearrange the structure of our cities and towns in a very different way."

Daily tours at 9, 11, 2, and 4, except Dec. 25: admission

4 Robert R. McMath Solar Telescope (1966)
Kitt Peak Observatory
**39 miles/63 kilometers W of Tucson on AZ 86, then 13 miles/21
    kilometers S on AZ 386**
Kitt Peak, Arizona

SKIDMORE, OWINGS & MERRILL, ARCHITECTS AND ENGINEERS

Most industrial and technical architecture takes a prosaic turn; here it has been lifted to imaginative heights using the simplest of shapes and the most mundane of materials. The McMath solar telescope—the

largest solar telescope in the world—is a "fixed" instrument 500
feet/152 meters long, 300 feet/91 meters of which are underground, and is angled at 32° into its mountain base. On its top (110
feet/33 meters high) an 80-inch/203-centimeter-in-diameter helio-
stat, driven with incredible precision, follows the arc of the sun. This
then reflects the solar image down the long optical tunnel (oriented
along a north polar axis) to a 60-inch/152-centimeter mirror at bottom which returns it to another mirror (48 inches/122 centimeters
in diameter) near the spot where the casing enters the earth. This
last shoots the sun's image into the observation room with its vac-
uum spectrographs for analysis. To prevent temperature and lateral
(from wind) fluctuations, which would upset extremely delicate calculations, the whole shaft is encased by a water-cooled wind shield whose
outer skin is the sun-reflective, white-painted copper sheathing which
we see. By placing the square solar tunnel and its square vertical support on diagonals relative to each other, a more functional shape
resulted—the relation minimizing wind pressure and facilitating rain
and snow removal. In addition, a geometric interaction which is extremely potent esthetically, both at a distance and close up, has been
created. A section of the telescope's interior at ground level is open to
the public. Here one can observe some of its workings and hear a
taped recording on its functioning. From the area's base height (6,760

feet/2,060 meters) one also enjoys far-stretching panoramas. The Kitt Peak facility, which is supported by a number of noted universities, was designed by the Chicago office of SOM, with Myron Goldsmith chief designer and William E. Dunlap partner-in-charge. It was named for the late Dr. Robert R. McMath, who with Dr. A. Keith Pierce proposed it.

Open daily 10–4, except Dec. 25

Note the mosque-like domes of the stellar telescopes which pepper the mountain (these are not open to the public). The Kitt Peak site was selected, after a long search, for sky clarity, lack of turbulence, freedom from lights, yet convenience to a city. It occupies land leased from the Papago Indians, on whose reservation it sits. Magnificent.

5   Montezuma Castle National Monument (c. 1100–1450)
2 miles/3.2 kilometers E of IS 17
Montezuma Castle, Arizona

Montezuma Castle, which lies some 27 miles/43 kilometers ESE of Tuzigoot and is of the same Sinagua culture, is the country's best-preserved cliff dwelling. Perched high in a limestone scarp (not accessible to the public), the Castle comprises the nineteen-room former home of forty-five to fifty Indians. They found here not only protection but water for irrigation (Beaver Creek) at their feet. The Castle reaches five stories, rising in stepped-back stages set on natural ledges in the cliff. An excellent National Park Service Historical Handbook (Series No. 27, 1958) details the complete history of the area and shows floor plans of the structure. The rooms have an average size of 100 square feet/9.3 square meters. The walls are constructed of limestone rocks held together by a mortarlike mixture of sand, clay, and water, and were then plastered inside and out with the same composition. Sycamore logs 10–12 feet/3–3.6 meters long form the ceiling supports, with layers of branches and mud on top. The few "windows" were tiny and placed near the floor. Access to upper levels was through the ceiling of lower rooms. Though nowhere as extensive as the great ruins at Mesa Verde, Colorado (q.v.), Montezuma Castle is better-preserved, being considered 90 per cent original. It was made a National Monument in 1906 with additional acreage added in 1937 and 1979. Like Aztec Ruins National Monument, New Mexico (q.v.), this too was misnamed, Montezuma (1466–1520), the Aztec emperor, never having ventured as far north as Arizona.

Park open Memorial Day–Labor Day, daily 7–7, rest of year 8–5: admission

---

6   **Taliesin West** (1938–59)
Maricopa Mesa
N on Scottsdale Road, E on Shea Boulevard 4.8 miles/7.7
    kilometers to gate
Scottsdale (Phoenix), Arizona

FRANK LLOYD WRIGHT, ARCHITECT

Frank Lloyd Wright always was concerned with what he called the "kinship" of architecture with its setting, admonishing students not, for instance, to build on top of a hill but beside it in partnership, not dominance. This philosophy finds ominous opposition in the Judeo-Christian Genetic injunction to "fill the earth and subdue it; and have do-

minion over . . . every living thing" (Genesis 1:28). Wright's father, incidentally, was for a time a Baptist minister.

Taliesin West is the Arizona setting for Wright's winter-spring headquarters. Of it he wrote, it "is a grand garden the like of which in sheer beauty of space and pattern does not exist, I think, in the world" (*On Architecture,* edited by Frederick Gutheim, Duell, Sloan & Pearce, 1941). To carry this out he purchased from the government 800 acres/324 hectares of land which he promptly set to work on. For the harsh, "savage" yet strangely haunting light and geography of this choice bit of Arizona, Wright designed a series of interacting, in-love-with-the-desert buildings which rank among his exalted works. (Reyner Banham, the perceptive but oft acerbic English architectural critic, calls it "a tribal encampment.") The Taliesin nucleus, prominent in its geometry of both plan and space, comprises the famous drafting room, with the private quarters linearly attached behind, and a theater to the left. Though the complex was begun in 1938 it was added to and refined for over twenty years, becoming in the process more permanent, more lived-in, more subtle. Originally used for only a few months in winter, occupancy gradually has increased. Since 1959 (the year of Wright's death) it has served, for extended periods, Taliesin Associates, the maestro's very busy successors, plus the Frank Lloyd Wright School of Architecture. Taliesin, incidentally, was a Welsh bard who lived around the sixth century A.D.: FLW was of Welsh descent.

The most striking units of Taliesin West are fortunately those nearest the entry: the drafting room mentioned above—note its masterfully assured roof angles—and the theater detached at left. The latter burned in 1964 but has been completely restored. When these were first built they were roofed with canvas, which transmitted a soft enveloping luminosity. However, as substantial upkeep was required in an often harsh climate, cloth has been replaced by translucent plastic panels, with steel-reinforced rafters supporting them. Note the base, in fine contrast to the lightness overhead, especially the outside, of native boulders and mortar. These slightly inclined, horizontally striated walls —reminiscent of the Mayan stonework which FLW admired so much —constitute the most sumptuous masonry of the twentieth century. Partake, also, of the artful changes in levels, the programmed angles of circulation, and the quality of space in and between buildings; and, of course, the "silence and beauty" of the desert mesa. One of the country's greatest complexes, or as the distinguished architect Pietro Belluschi put it, "The years have not diminished the elemental quality of Taliesin West. More than other works by the master, it shows how to grasp the mood of the land and transform it into a place of harmony and beauty" (AIA *Journal,* May 1973: Dean Belluschi was chairman of the AIA's 25-Year Award jury).

Tours daily 10–4, on the half hour, except major holidays: admission

---

7   **Cosanti Foundation Workshop** (1962–)
     **6433 Doubletree Road (1 mile/1.6 kilometers W of North
        Scottsdale Road)**
     Scottsdale, Arizona

PAOLO SOLERI, ARCHITECT

Paolo Soleri, the country's visionary conceptualist, and utopian molder of architecture and ecology into "arcology," is also one of the most

spectacular draftsmen of our time. Born in Turin in 1919, Soleri conjures incredible coᶜmic cities of the future. He transfers thousands of thoughts to a roll of tracing paper which might well unfurl for a hundred feet (30 meters). His sketches are accompanied by fascinatingly intricate models, largely of acrylic plastic, towering structures which are as much geometric sculpture as urban portents. Yet for a man who has so captured the imagination of architects, students, and public alike, his completed works—beyond his famous sketches and his book *Arcology* (MIT Press, 1969)—are distressingly few. This, fortunately, is being changed with the beginning of a fantastic new "city" in central Arizona called Arcosanti (q.v.), a complex which will take years to finish. His earlier buildings include an Outdoor Theater (1970) in Santa Fe, New Mexico (q.v.), and this workshop-dwelling maze northeast of Phoenix. This latter lies not far from Frank Lloyd Wright's Taliesin West— where Paolo himself once worked (1947–48), coming from Italy to be with Wright. Part troglodytic, and all hand-built—mostly by student-apprentices—this highly informal cluster recalls the fact that the very first settlers on this land, the Indian Basket Makers of the first to seventh centuries A.D., all saw fit to dig into the ground before building above it. (The Indians used willows, reeds, and branches to roof their shallow excavations.) Soleri and his dedicated disciples have fashioned their workshop, living quarters, and small museum mostly out of concrete, these elements often cast in desert silt with spontaneous improvisation—an intriguing lot they are. Do not expect to see evidence of T-square or triangle, but circles, arcs, and apses abound—as do the justly famous Soleri ceramic and bronze wind bells (the sale of which helps support the Cosanti Foundation).

Open daily 9–5, except Jan. 1, Dec. 25

---

8   Civic Center (1968–75)
George Avenue between 1st and 2nd Streets
Scottsdale, Arizona

GONZALES ASSOCIATES, ARCHITECTS

The philosophy behind the planning of these three buildings—city hall, library, and Center for the Performing Arts—is highly unusual and highly effective. An entire cross section of the population of Scottsdale (which abuts the east boundary of Phoenix) was consulted before

planning commenced. Community reactions and ideas were solicited to involve the people in the shelter of government as well as in the choosing of its officials. From numerous meetings with the architects, town officers, and some four hundred residents, the notion evolved that the city hall, being the spot where decisions concerning most citizens were made, required maximum accessibility by the public to its offices. As a result the city's Council Chamber is the core of the building, forming an open, slightly sunken cockpit about which are grouped —with no doors or partitions—the three major branches of activity used by the public: finance and city clerk, planning and engineering, and parks and recreation. An ambitiously branched skylight with colored panes (over the cockpit) gives accent to the capably handled lateral and vertical spaces. The library is somewhat similarly conceived, with the periodical "room" and lounge forming an inviting, sunken, and off-center focus, and the reading areas, including a separate one for children, fanning from this. The Center for the Performing Arts, the last unit built (1975)—the other two were completed in 1971—houses a 750-seat theater, a 200-seat cinema, plus additional city offices. The relationship of the three buildings to each other and to the beautifully landscaped park (by the architects) is excellent. The architecture leans pointedly to the heavy-walled, small-windowed adobe image, but with the local sun intensity this regionalism stems from an understanding of forces, not transient fashions.

Open during business hours

---

9 **Hopi Cultural Center** (1970–71)
(with motel and restaurant)
on AZ 264, 5.3 miles/8.5 kilometers W of intersection with
AZ 87
Second Mesa (Oraibi), Arizona

GONZALES ASSOCIATES, ARCHITECTS

Responding sensitively to the difficult exposure of an upland mesa (6,450 feet/1,966 meters altitude), and respecting gently and logically the plain, small-window traditions of the region, the architects have put together a compatible and inviting complex of buildings. Located in the heart of the vast Hopi Reservation (on one of the main roads to Canyon de Chelly, see The White House), it surveys sometimes desolate, often awesome, and occasionally exciting scenery. The Center—actually a small museum and sales shop—plus restaurant and thirty-three-room motel (Box 67, Second Mesa, Arizona 86043; telephone [602] 734-2401) should do much to explain the area's culture while providing first-rate creature comforts for those seeking to explore the reservation. The inviting Cultural Center and restaurant occupy the highway side, with the motel units placed away from the road, grouped in pueblo-fashion clusters about well-scaled courtyards. Stuccoed concrete block was used throughout.

Open daily

Unfortunately the historic and nearby **Old Pueblo of Oraibi** (1300–)—one of the oldest continuously inhabited spots on the continent and once the largest of Hopi settlements—is disintegrating. Because of administrative dissension and the lure of greater opportunities, many of its inhabitants are moving to the newer and lower town and trading post, taking, in some cases, their vigas and stones with them to erect a new dwelling. Their parallel rows of houses, basically north-south-oriented, are fast crumbling, as are their thirteen kivas.

---

10   Chapel of the Holy Cross (1956)
off AZ 179, 3.8 miles/6.2 kilometers S of intersection with
·US Alt 89
Sedona, Arizona

ANSHEN & ALLEN, ARCHITECTS

In an overall setting suggestive of the not-distant Grand Canyon, and with an immediate background of towering, vigorously sculptured red sandstone cliffs, the architects have gracefully introduced an evocative memorial chapel. From the approach road the building almost extrudes from its dramatic site. The prominent (90-foot/27-meter-high) cross,

which fits in and slightly projects beyond the end walls, commandingly
rises from the ground between two outcroppings with the chapel's sides
resting on top of them. A partially elevated road leads up the cliffside
to the parking area just below the chapel, unfolding a succession of
panoramas as it goes. One then takes a sinuous footpath which snakes
around the bluff permitting glimpses of the chapel, which, when one
arrives, one sees perched proudly and independently on its pinnacle instead of being a mere adjunct of the cliff behind. The path and, at top,
the carefully convoluted balustrades which double as outdoor benches
establish a contrast against the sharp geometry of the chapel. The
church's side walls are parallel in plan but angle sharply upward in
profile toward the sanctuary while inclining slightly inward toward the
roof. The 12-inch/30-centimeter-thick reinforced concrete walls were
poured in place in 8-foot/2.4-meter sections. The nave measures 62
feet/19 meters long by 26 feet/8 meters wide. Both ends are of
glass. The cross, which projects one third of its depth into the nave itself, is sufficient to act as a sunshield for the dark (against glare) glass
which fills the chancel end. The cross thus is also dominant inside the
church, where unfortunately its thickness (i.e. depth) makes it some-

what massive. A 13-foot/4-meter steel crucifix, gaunt but impressive, by Keith Monroe is attached to its inner face, while the altar is cantilevered directly from its lower part. The nave accommodates approximately fifty souls in permanent pews which line the two sides and part of the rear, with chairs available for the open center section if needed. Sacristy, office, and services fill the basement. The chapel was a gift of Marguerite Brunswig Staude to the Roman Catholic Church in memory of her parents. It forms a dramatic memorial, one that calls on none of the materials of the setting (however, the concrete is textured and integrally tinted), yet one which grows with majesty from it. The profusion of sculptural forms in the natural red rock site and the towering cliffs embracing the building defied human competition; hence the dynamic simplicity of the chapel itself. (Mass is generally held at 11 A.M. each Sunday.)

Open daily 9–5

---

11   Tombstone Courthouse State Historic Park (1881–82)
3rd and Toughnut Streets
Tombstone, Arizona

FRANK WALKER, ARCHITECT

Many of the legends of the West when it was wild sprang from this mine-rich area—among them Wyatt Earp and the O.K. Corral. It is appropriate therefore to see the architectural background where Cochise County and Tombstone justice were sometimes dealt. (Cochise was a well-known Apache chief who died in 1874; from 1882–1931 this building served as the Cochise County Courthouse.) Though not, perhaps, a gem, the Courthouse is a surprisingly capable brick structure whose plaster over brick quoins, columned entry, and venturesome cupola recall influences from much farther east. An addition at the rear was made in 1904. Be certain to visit the courtroom on the upper floor. In 1958 the building was rehabilitated—having survived an ill-fated attempt at hotel conversion—and made into a history museum operated by the Arizona State Parks.

Open daily 8–5:30, except Dec. 25: admission

The town itself, now protected and partly rehabilitated, though uneven

and overly commercial, is worth a stroll along its covered boardwalks (restored). Almost all buildings date from the 1880s. The **Historic District**—including the Courthouse—was listed in the National Register of Historic Places in 1972.

---

12 Mission San Xavier del Bac (1776–97)
1.3 miles/2 kilometers W of IS 19 at San Xavier exit, c. 9.5 miles/ 15 kilometers S of
Tucson, Arizona

Spain took the Baroque movement in architecture—which began in Rome in the mid-seventeenth century—and molded it to the most fantastic and at times overreaching heights ever seen. This Iberian melding of Gothic, Renaissance, and Baroque influence—spiced by a bit of

Moorish—found reanimation in our own day in the work of the late Antonio Gaudí (1852–1926). Gaudí was a Catalan whose never-finished Sagrada Familia Church in Barcelona (1883–1926) is this century's most passionate "Baroque" expression. When the Spanish conquistadores, accompanied by their extraordinarily dedicated priests, explored and conquered Mexico (1519–1821) and what is now the southwest U.S.A., they dotted these lonely regions with a series of missions and churches that today enormously enrich this country's cultural heritage. Their architectural expression varied both chronologically and geographically, particularly in those outposts farthest from Mexico, such as northern New Mexico, where limited materials (mostly adobe) and unskilled Indian labor produced more primitive—but also more indigenous—results. In almost all of the Spanish-out-of-Mexico churches, however, violent contrasts are apt to appear, with plain walls erupting into great faeade accents of exuberant carving, of dazzling light-colored exteriors versus dark, mysterious naves, of simple and elaborate, of piety and semi-idolatry.

Epitomizing these tendencies, and resting like some strange ship tethered to a desert mooring, rises the pinnacle of Spanish religious architecture in this country: San Xavier del Bac. It was founded in 1692 by the incredible explorer and Jesuit, the Tyrolean-born Eusebio Francisco Kino (or Chini). But Father Kino's original chapel slowly disintegrated after his death (1711), and the church we see today was built much later.

In 1776 under the direction of the Franciscans, who in 1768 replaced the "troublesome" Jesuits, (whose order was "suppressed" by monarchs in Iberia and France in the mid-eighteenth century), the startlingly ambitious mission we now see was begun under Father Velderrain and finished by Father Llorenz. Its actual architect is unknown.

The church with its adjoining mortuary chapel is constructed of burnt brick with foundations of local volcanic stone. Its facade derives from Mexican prototypes (cf. the Cathedral of Chihuahua and SS Prisca y Sebastián in Taxco, among others). It is divided into almost equal thirds, with two plain, blindingly white square towers, topped by belfries, rising as guardians beside the intricately carved, soft red brick central portal. This ornately scrolled, boisterous (at times primitive) centerpiece leaps with enthusiasm from its quiet white frame to establish a smashing introduction to the church. Note that the vertical scrolls which contain the portal's two sides (and are echoed at the top where the portal projects as a false front) are repeated as a horizontal stringcourse with their ends curling upward on themselves to tie the whole front together. Note, too, the strange "scroll" buttresses at each corner of the tops of the towers where they lend support to the octagonal belfries (one incomplete). The portal "announces" the reredos within, or as William H. Pierson, Jr., succinctly put it in Volume I of *American Buildings and Their Architects* (Doubleday, 1970), "One of the most Baroque aspects of the San Xavier portal is the direct relationship it bears with the reredos behind the altar . . . the two are similar in design, both in [their] general shapes and divisions of space."

The dark and cool, vaulted and domed interior (compare the flat-roofed Spanish churches in New Mexico) is dominated by the almost unbelievable carved brick and polychromed stucco *retablo,* or reredos, flanked by richly treated transepts. This cavalcade of carving and decoration includes a cloth-draped statue of San Xavier in the center, with the Virgin above, saints flanking the two, angels and *putti* hovering about, all within firm architectural organization. There is no church interior north of Mesoamerica which can touch it, a hair-raising, sensational mixture of architecture and sculpture. It stems, via saltwater transmutation, straight out of the Spanish work of José de Churriguera, his architect father, four architect brothers, three architect children—and pupils. (The family, not surprisingly, added the word "Churrigueresque" to our panoply of architectural terms. The movement reached its climax in Salamanca, then traveled to Mexico, thus to Arizona and, more modestly, to other churches in Spanish possessions in the Southwest.) The "European" plan of San Xavier with its prominent transepts is roofed by five low ovoid domes, including one over each transept, and one high circular one over the crossing, all capably raised under the conditions. There are four windows in the high dome and in the nave walls, but none in the transepts. The nave itself suffers from an unfortunately ponderous "cornice" that runs along the spring line of the vaults, but this heaviness evaporates before the power of the *retablo.*

The church bid farewell to its Spanish missionaries in 1828 when the Franciscans were expelled following Mexico's independence. Its history throughout the rest of the nineteenth century was one of intermittent use, minor repairs, and considerable neglect, conditions complicated by the fact that no one was in full charge. Though earthquakes and lightning created minor damage, and weather took its toll, it was not until cracks in the dome appeared that the Catholic Bishop of Arizona authorized (1906) overall repairs and a sprucing up and expansion of the ancillary buildings. In 1949 full restoration under the aegis of a professional architect, E. D. Herreras, was undertaken, including retouching of the paintings by Henry Milan. The only intact survivor of the seven missions founded in Arizona, San Xavier is fortunately now in pristine shape. Spain's architectural efforts in Mexico reveal more expertise and finesse, but this, by far, is their greatest Colonial effort in the United States.

Open daily 9–6, except major holidays

---

13   Pima County Junior College (1970–   )
Anklam Road, 2.3 miles/3.7 kilometers W of IS 10
Tucson, Arizona

CAUDILL ROWLETT SCOTT, ARCHITECTS; WILLIAM WILDE & ASSOCIATES, FRIEDMAN & JOBUSCH, ASSOCIATED ARCHITECTS

Given the demanding semidesert Arizona climate it is surprising that so few contemporary buildings reflect this sometimes cruel yet often excitingly beautiful environment. However, the architects of this junior

college west of town have understood and taken advantage of these difficulties, and have transformed them into rewards. Hugging a ridge and utilizing the hillside's changes in levels, this spread-out, concrete grouping of various educational functions respects the blinding horizontality of the desert, playing off against it a series of open-air ramps and passages which burst from dark semienclosure into bright, green, and wind-sheltered courtyards. The experience of moving in and through the chain of units becomes a constant discovery of spaces. However, an educational plant is not primarily an architectural progression; it is a facility for generating thoughts and training hands, here 2,800 initially, 6,000 maximum. The rationale of this college, which has a marked emphasis on trades, has been as thoroughly attended to as has its sympathy with nature and its three-dimensional solid-void dramatics. The classrooms are often interior spaces, windowless and air-conditioned, forming an inner flexible core in each of nine conjoined buildings. Caudill Rowlett Scott were also responsible for landscaping, interior design, and graphics. James M. Hughes, Joseph W. Griffin, and Jack DeBartolo, Jr.—all of CRS—were the principals-in-charge.

Open during school hours

---

14 **San José Mission** (c. 1800–22)
    off IS 19, 19 miles/31 kilometers N of Nogales, c. 49 miles/79
    kilometers S of Tucson
    Tumacacori, Arizona

Though not one of the greatest Spanish missions, which the Jesuits and, later, the Franciscans built in the Southwest, nostalgic affection nonetheless goes out to the Tumacacori National Monument, abetted, no doubt, by its semiruined condition. (Actually the bell tower and mortuary chapel were never completed.) Moreover the nearby museum (1937) gives excellent background material on the peoples and conditions of this region nearly two hundred years ago. Like Mission San Xavier del Bac (q.v.), the first chapel on this site was founded (c. 1691) by Father Kino, but vanished long ago. The present church was built of the usual adobe, here made extra heavy against the Apache. Its facade is extraordinary with a semicircular, false gable end (perhaps to mirror the arched door and dome over the sanctuary) and with an attached "pediment" resting atop precisely aligned, offset pilasters. The niches formed by the coupled pilasters formerly contained statues of

saints. Surprisingly—compare San Xavier—the nave roof is not
vaulted but flat. The unusual baptistry (with walls 9 feet/2.7 meters
thick) attaches at right with belfry on top, its bulky width challenging
that of the church itself. The now demolished *convento* once stood adjacent. The church's last missionary departed in 1828, the Indians
themselves leaving it some twenty years later, with ruin—including the
collapse of the roof—setting in. In 1908 what was left was made a National Monument and the National Park Service was able to make
sufficient repairs, including a new roof, to stabilize the remains. A
major stabilization project is now in progress, the need to keep mois-
ture from eroding the adobe walls being a paramount concern.

Open daily 8–6: admission

Arkansas

ARKANSAS

The buildings in boldface type are of general interest. The others are for the specialist.

Conway	1	**Bailey Library** (1967)—Philip Johnson
Little Rock	2	**Arkansas Territorial Restoration** (1820s–40s/1941)
	3	**Old State House** (1833–42)—Gideon Shryock
	4	Trapnall Hall (1843)
	5	Capital Hotel (1872/1980)
	6	Mental Health Center (1964–65)— Wittenberg, Delony & Davidson
Prairie Grove	7	**Vineyard Village** (1830s)
Russellville	8	**Arkansas River Project and Dardanelle Dam** (1957–73)—U. S. Army Corps of Engineers

1   Bailey Library (1967)
Hendrix College
Washington Avenue and Independence Street off US 64 and 65B,
    NW edge of
Conway, Arkansas

**PHILIP JOHNSON, ARCHITECT; WITTENBERG, DELONY &
DAVIDSON, ASSOCIATES**

The Bailey Library forms an inventive, well-landscaped solution to
campus demand for space, particularly "logistic" space such as required by a library. Not only is the building athwart scholastic cross-

roads, the architects and landscape architect have designed it so that the sunken plaza in front can double for outdoor functions as well as entry. The plaza is, indeed, the spontaneous open-air core of the college, while the roof-deck on top of the library acts as a slightly elevated quiet area, with a connecting half-level that spouts a fountain from a 90-foot/27-meter-long pool. All grading has been handled to keep the library bulk so low that it enhances rather than intrudes upon the spaces framed by the older buildings surrounding it. These level variations are among the outstanding assets of the design. Moreover the earth berms insulate the library while eliminating the need for external upkeep.

One enters via the plaza in front to the below-grade front door but without experiencing a subterranean atmosphere. (However, a light well from the roof terrace over the front desk would have invigorated the entry.) The interiors—straightforward but not inspired—provide study rooms, carrels, seminar, administration, and work rooms, plus two levels of stacks. The library houses collections totaling more than 125,000 volumes. Joe Lambert was the landscape architect. Level changes and earth sculpture at its best.

Open during school year and limited hours during summer

---

2 Arkansas Territorial Restoration (1820s–40s/1941)
Third and Scott Streets
Little Rock, Arkansas

Miraculously saved from destruction in a deteriorating neighborhood and from the dubious distinction of serving as the Green Goose Beer Garden, this downtown block has been restored to its original condition of the 1820s, '30s and '40s when it was the heart of pioneer Little Rock. Mrs. J. Fairfax Loughborough sparkplugged this Restoration of thirteen buildings and their landscaping, persuading the state legislature to finance the work, which was completed in 1941. The state, which owns the Restoration, made a significant investment, not only preserving the past but saving the future.

The **Hinderliter House** was constructed (1826–28) only of oak logs chinked (as can be seen in the room on the second floor), but it was subsequently (1834) clapboarded over with cypress siding for greater weather protection. A porch and stairway were also added at this time.

The furnishings are largely original but with some reproductions. The **Noland House** (1840s) is the most substantial of the several dwellings of the Restoration, its brickwork and garden both of a high level. Note the porch across the entire off-street side with the two flanking dependencies, one housing the kitchen, the other the office. The **Conway and Woodruff houses** give further insight into the residential character of the period. (Note, especially, the kitchen in the Conway House.) Landscaping has been most successful. Altogether an excellent vignette of the early architecture of what became our twenty-fifth state only a few years later (1836).

Open Mon.–Sat. 9–5, Sun. 1–5, except major holidays: admission

3   Old State House (1833–42)
300 West Markham Street at South Center
Little Rock, Arkansas

GIDEON SHRYOCK, ARCHITECT

Rightfully the pride of Arkansas, this ranks among the freshest Greek
Revival examples in the country. Firm in profile, inventive in detail
(note the unusual "paneling" in architrave and frieze), it carries great
personality. The building was erected to serve as the new territorial
capitol, replacing the outgrown one seen in the Third Street Restoration. It was designed by Gideon Shryock, who had completed the state
capitol of his native Kentucky at Frankfort (q.v.) just a few years

earlier. It should be added that Shryock never personally visited Arkansas, and his clerk of the works, George Weigart, took charge locally, reducing the size of the building (with the aid of the governor) to meet the budget, keeping however the fine basic proportions. Although occupied in 1836, it was not fully completed until 1842. The brick stuccoed central block was originally connected to its two wings by "wooden houses" (probably porches), but these were replaced in 1867 (west) and in 1885 (east) by office structures to provide more clerical space. The cast iron seen today dates from these additions. At the same time the rear of the central building was extended toward the river. When the increasing population of the state outgrew these facilities, the legislature commissioned the scandal-heavy capitol (1900–17) down the street. (George R. Mann was the original architect, Cass Gilbert his successor.)

The Old State House was threatened with destruction until given a temporary reprieve for use as a medical school. Then in 1947—quality being recognized—complete restoration to the 1800s period was begun, under the architectural direction of H. Ray Burks and Bruce R. Anderson; since 1951 it has served as an Arkansas History Museum. The triple-tiered cast-iron fountain in front came (in part) from the Philadelphia Centennial Exposition: the first tier is original, the top two are replacements (1947).

Open Mon.–Sat. 9–5, Sun. 1–5, except major holidays: guided tours

---

4   Trapnall Hall (1843)
423 East Capitol Avenue
Little Rock, Arkansas

Looking as though it is a recent product of Country Club Gardens, the Trapnall House is actually over 135 years old. Though some sources claim that the house was based on a design by Gideon Shryock, who, it will be remembered, was the architect of the Old State House a few blocks away, recent research indicates that this was not the case. (Trapnall, like Shryock, was also Kentucky-born.) The house for years served as a relaxed, comfortable residence. Then, as the city moved westward, neglect set in (a bad fire making matters worse) and the house—like those of the nearby Territorial Restoration—went quietly downhill. And also like the Restoration, it was saved by a woman,

Mrs. C. M. Taylor, who recognized its fine but dilapidated lines and purchased it (1929) and gave it to the local Junior League as a memorial to her husband. At first used as a welfare center, the Greek Revival building was completely restored (1963) as a major rehabilitation example for the whole historic district. In 1976 it was sold to the State of Arkansas and designated as the Governor's Official Reception Center. It is now open to the public, being rented out for various social and business meetings. The interior has been furnished to adapt to its semipublic use, but the dwelling is still of architectural importance. There is an ongoing program of furnishings acquisition that will provide appropriate period background.

Open Mon.–Fri. 9–1, except holidays: also by appointment

---

5 Capital Hotel (1872/1980)
West Markham at Louisiana Street
Little Rock, Arkansas

CROMWELL NEYLAND TRUEMPER LEVY & GATCHELL, ARCHITECTS OF RESTORATION

This sterling example of a cast-iron-fronted building encountered declining years after World War II until rescued by a group of developers headed by architect Edwin B. Cromwell. It is now being handsomely renovated as a small (128-room) luxury hotel. Conven-

ient to much of downtown Little Rock, it adds enormously to the city's fabric and architectural richness. Originally constructed as an office building, it was remodeled into a hotel in 1876 with a fourth floor added (somewhat insensitively) in 1890. The hotel went its merry way for several generations as the social focus of the city until its lack of air conditioning and up-to-date facilities caused it to slip. Now due to vision and expertise, the hotel is being totally rehabilitated, playing a major role in the city. It will be the hub of a multi-use redevelopment of the area, including convention center, 400-room hotel, office building, and parking structure, and, hopefully, a park along the nearby Arkansas River. The hotel's original architect is not known. The building is listed in the National Register of Historic Places.

---

6 Mental Health Center (1964–65)
State Hospital Grounds
West Markham Street at Hooper Drive
Little Rock, Arkansas

WITTENBERG, DELONY & DAVIDSON, ARCHITECTS

This guidebook has avoided including mental facilities except for a few in the countryside: they are not places for the casual tourist. However, the hospital specialist will want to visit the O. E. Faubus Intensive Treatment and Administrative Center in downtown Little Rock. Be-

ginning with the problems of that most difficult of all hospital patients, the mental case, and working with superintendent Dr. George W. Jackson's philosophy of shelter, the architects have created an unusually sympathetic environment. There are friendly, undemanding, unregimented (but carefully supervised) spaces everywhere as the architecture reaches out with welcoming arms: "every corridor ends with a window." There are nooks for the lonely and spontaneous gathering spots for the gregarious, both inside and out. Patients can forgather in the large central courtyard, or sit quietly in one of the small "conversation" courts near each living unit. The design of these cloistered patios interlaces protection with challenging openness for the charges.

The basic layout consists of: (1) an administration building attached off-center in front; (2) a substantial one-story square block, raised on a prominent podium (approximately 160 feet/49 meters on a side), containing admission, treatment, and group facilities; and (3) six separate living units "plugged in" on three sides of the central block. The administration building, square in plan and partly elevated on pilotis, is architecturally self-important, but not the buildings concerned with patients. The canopy-surrounded central block contains one major court and three smaller ones, all interconnected with covered passages. The open courts alternate with the six treatment facilities (one for each living unit). Canteen, admission, and an intensive-treatment unit line the front of the elevated base with the patients' quarters on the other three sides. The six two-story, identical living units are connected to the central block by a second-floor passage. They each contain seventy-two double bedrooms, along with isolation room, restricted activity and mixed social activity areas, and nurses' stations.

The Faubus Center (which forms a part of an enormous, bland state hospital) treats approximately 440 souls, most of whom are returned to productive lives, in no small measure, it is fair to say, by having been sheltered by the architectural setting. Forget the formalistic administration building in front, but do look at the low-keyed buildings that form the central grouping. Fred E. Arnold and Robert B. Church III were in charge of design.

Open to the specialist on application

---

7   **Vineyard Village** (1830s)
    Battlefield Park, off US 62, just NE of
    Prairie Grove, Arkansas

The Vineyard Village collection of log structures, typifying an Ozark settlement of a century and a half ago, gives good background material on early living and building conditions of this hilly northwestern part of the state. (Prairie Grove is about 10 miles/16 kilometers southwest of Fayetteville.) The oldest units in the Village are the restored F. F. Latta house (in photograph) and barn—both built in 1834 but not standing on their original sites—the latter now serving as a community center. The stone well-house behind should also be seen. The school and church (once a dwelling) are of the same extremely simple notched-log construction as the Latta buildings, but were moved here

from the Ozark region. It is hoped that other buildings of the period will be added. More cohesiveness in layout and additional historical information on the buildings would be helpful, but the vernacularist will find the collection valuable. Battlefield Park was named for an important Civil War conflict which took place here in 1862.

Open daily 9–5, except Dec. 25

8 **Arkansas River Project and Dardanelle Dam** (1957–73)
1.7 miles/2.7 kilometers W of ARK 7, c. 5 miles/
  8 kilometers SW of
Russellville, Arkansas

U. S. ARMY CORPS OF ENGINEERS, DESIGNERS

The Arkansas River Project—more correctly the McClellan-Kerr Arkansas River Navigation System—is rehabilitating much of this area just as the TVA transformed the states which border the Tennessee

River and its tributaries. There are seventeen dams and locks on the river (twelve in Arkansas, five in Oklahoma), the final dam of which was completed in 1970, with the last powerhouse finished in 1973. This enormous undertaking was designed and constructed by the U. S. Army Corps of Engineers—the largest civil project in their history—and they have produced a sound job. The architectural quality of the powerhouses, shelters, and details (such as lamp standards) are not up to the inspired TVA level, but the technical aspects and the very act of making the river navigable from its Mississippi outlet to Catoosa (Tulsa), Oklahoma, is stupendous. Overall length is 446 miles/718 kilometers, total lift 420 feet/128 meters, and the minimum channel depth for barge traffic 9 feet/2.7 meters. The largest dam in the series is this near Russellville and Dardanelle (across the river), being 2,683 feet/818 meters long: its 124,000-kilowatt powerhouse was built in 1957–66, its 54-foot/16-meter rise lock in 1967–69. The powerhouse was designed by the Hydro-Electric Section of the Southwest Division of the U. S. Army Corps of Engineers in Dallas, Texas, in consultation with Sverdrup & Parcel in San Francisco. The lock and dam were designed by the Little Rock District, U. S. Army Corps of Engineers. In addition to making possible river barge navigation for eastern

Oklahoma and Arkansas and thereby attracting industry, the series of dams plays highly important roles in flood control (frequent flooding had often wreaked havoc along the river). It is also important in bank and silt stabilizaton, and, of course, in providing recreation facilities, while the powerhouses produce considerable non-extractive energy. It has been termed the "renaissance of a river": even more importantly, it has switched on the renaissance of a vast region.

California

CALIFORNIA

The buildings in boldface type are of general interest. The others are for the specialist.

Arcadia
1 E. J. Baldwin Guest House (1885)— A. A. Bennett

Benicia
2 Old State Capitol (1853–54)— Houghton & Ryder

Berkeley
3 **First Church of Christ, Scientist** (1910–12)—Bernard R. Maybeck
4 **University Art Museum** (1968–70)— Mario J. Ciampi & Associates

Carmel
5 Mission San Carlos Borromeo (1793–97)

Carmel Valley
6 Carmel Valley Manor (1962–63)— Skidmore, Owings & Merrill

El Segundo
7 Xerox Building (1966)—Craig Ellwood Associates

Eureka
8 William Carson House (1884–86)— Samuel and Joseph C. Newsom

Fresno
9 The Fulton Street Mall (1964)— Gruen Associates

Garden Grove
10 **Community Church** (1959–61)— Richard J. Neutra & Associates
Crystal Cathedral (1978–80)— Johnson/Burgee

La Jolla
11 La Jolla Women's Club (1913–14)— Irving J. Gill
12 **The Salk Institute** (1964–66)— Louis I. Kahn

Lompoc
13 **La Purísima Mission** (1813–18)

Long Beach
14 **Los Cerritos Ranch House Museum** (1844)

Los Altos Hills
15 **Foothill College** (1959–61)—Ernest J. Kump and Masten & Hurd

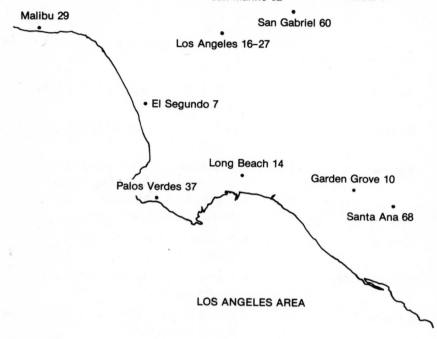

Pasadena 38–40
•

San Marino 62 •   • Arcadia 1
•
San Gabriel 60

Malibu 29
•

Los Angeles 16–27
•

• El Segundo 7

Long Beach 14
•

Garden Grove 10
•

Palos Verdes 37

Santa Ana 68
•

LOS ANGELES AREA

Los Angeles

See also: Arcadia, El Segundo, Garden Grove, Long Beach, Malibu, Palos Verdes, Pasadena, San Marino

16 **Bradbury Building** (1893)—George H. Wyman

17 **Hollyhock House** (1920–21)—Frank Lloyd Wright

Arts and Crafts Center (1920)— R. M. Schindler

18 St. Vincent de Paul (1924–25)— Albert C. Martin

19 Central Library Building (1925–26) —Bertram Grosvenor Goodhue

20 **Simon Rodia Towers/Watts Towers** (1921–54)—Simon Rodia

21 **Mann's** (formerly Grauman's) **Chinese Theater** (1926–27)—Meyer & Holler

22 Corona Elementary School (1935)—
Richard J. Neutra

23 The Village Green (formerly Baldwin
Hills Village) (1940–41)—Reginald
D. Johnson, Wilson, Merrill &
Alexander; Clarence S. Stein

24 University Research Library (Unit
1, 1964, Unit 2, 1971)—A. Quincy
Jones and Frederick E. Emmons

25 Pacific Design Center (1975)—
Gruen Associates

26 Federal Aviation Building (1974–75)
—Daniel, Mann, Johnson &
Mendenhall

27 **Bonaventure Hotel** (1975–77)—
John Portman & Associates

ARCO Tower and Bank of America
(1972)—Albert C. Martin &
Associates

Union Bank Building (1966)—
Harrison & Abramovitz and Albert C.
Martin & Associates

Security Pacific Bank (1974)—
Albert C. Martin & Associates

Los Gatos   28 **Civic Center** (1964–65)—Charles D.
Stickney and William R. Hull

Malibu   29 **The J. Paul Getty Museum** (1970–
74)—Langdon & Wilson

Monterey   30 **Old Custom House** (c. 1827–46)

31 **Larkin House** (1834–35)

Oakland   32 **Paramount Theatre** (1931)—Miller
& Pflueger

33 **Oakland-Alameda County Coliseum
and Stadium** (1966–68)—Skidmore,
Owings & Merrill

34 **Oakland Museum** (1967–69)—Kevin
Roche/John Dinkeloo & Associates

Oceanside   35 San Luis Rey de Francia (1811–15)

Palo Alto   36 Main Library (1957–58)—Edward
Durell Stone

Palos Verdes   37 **Wayfarers' Chapel** (1949–51)—Lloyd Wright

Pasadena   38 **David B. Gamble House** (1907–8)— Greene & Greene

39 The Stuart Company (1957–58)— Edward Durell Stone

40 **Art Center College of Design** (1974– 75)—Craig Ellwood Associates

Petaluma   41 **Petaluma Adobe State Historic Park** (1836–46)

Redding   42 Convention Center (1969–71)—Van Bourg & Nakamura, Smart & Clabaugh

Sacramento   43 State Capitol (1861–74/1976–82)— Miner F. Butler

44 Governor's Mansion (1877–78)— Nathaniel D. Goodell

San Bernardino   45 City Hall and Exhibit Hall/Convention Center (1972–73)—Gruen Associates

San Diego   See also La Jolla

46 Mission San Diego de Alcalá (1808– 13)

47 **Hotel del Coronado** (1887–88)—Reid & Reid

48 San Diego Stadium (1966–67)— Frank L. Hope & Associates

San Francisco   49 **Victorian Houses** (largely 1860–1910)

50 **Haas-Lilienthal House** (1886)—Peter R. Schmidt

51 **Palace of Fine Arts** (1913–15/rebuilt 1965–67)—Bernard R. Maybeck

52 **Hallidie Building** (1917–18)— Willis Polk

53 **Ghirardelli Square Redevelopment** (1864–1915/1964), **The Cannery Remodeling** (c. 1895/1969), **The Ice House Rehabilitation** (1914/1969)

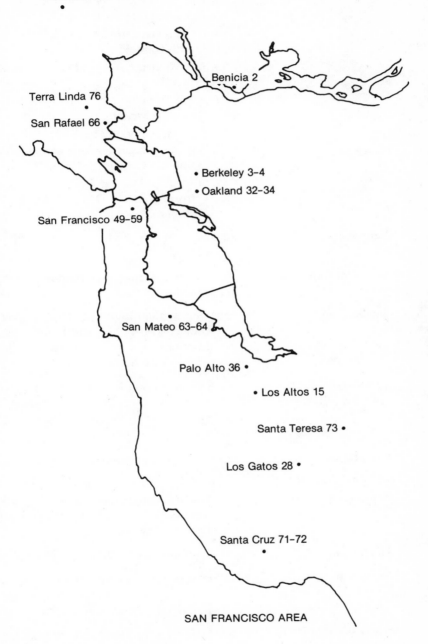

Petaluma 41

Benicia 2

Terra Linda 76

San Rafael 66

• Berkeley 3–4

• Oakland 32–34

San Francisco 49–59

San Mateo 63–64

Palo Alto 36 •

• Los Altos 15

Santa Teresa 73 •

Los Gatos 28 •

Santa Cruz 71–72

SAN FRANCISCO AREA

54 Four Fifty Sutter Building (1928–29)—Timothy L. Pflueger
55 **Golden Gate Bridge** (1933–37)—Joseph B. Strauss
56 **140 Maiden Lane** (1948–49)—Frank Lloyd Wright
57 Alcoa Building (1965–67)—Skidmore, Owings & Merrill
58 Bank of America (1968–71)—Wurster, Bernardi and Emmons with Skidmore, Owings & Merrill
59 Student Union, San Francisco State University (1974–75)—Paffard Keatinge Clay

San Gabriel
60 Mission San Gabriel Arcángel (1792–1805)

San Juan Capistrano
61 **San Juan Capistrano Mission** (1776–1806)

San Marino
62 **Huntington Library** (1919–20), **Art Gallery** (1909–11), **and Botanical Garden** (1904–   )—Myron Hunt and Elmer Grey; William Hertrich

San Mateo
63 College of San Mateo (1967–68)— · John Carl Warnecke & Associates
64 Hillsdale High School (1955–56)—John Lyon Reid & Partners

San Miguel
65 Mission San Miguel Arcángel (1816–18)

San Rafael
66 **Marin County Civic Center** (1959–62/1967–69)—Frank Lloyd Wright and Taliesin Associates

San Simeon
67 **San Simeon** (1919–47)—Julia Morgan

Santa Ana
68 **Orange County Court House** (1964–65)—Richard and Dion Neutra with Ramberg, Lowrey & Associates

Santa Barbara
69 Mission Santa Barbara (1812–20)
70 Santa Barbara County Court House

Santa Cruz

(1928–29)—William Mooser &
Company

71 **University of California at Santa Cruz**
(1963–   )—various architects

72 **Kresge College** (1972–74)—MLTW/
Turnbull Associates and Charles W.
Moore Associates

Santa Teresa
(San Jose)

73 IBM Santa Teresa Laboratory
(1975–77)—McCue Boone Tomsick

Sea Ranch

74 **The Sea Ranch** (1965–   )—Moore,
Lyndon, Turnbull & Whitaker

Squaw Valley

75 Cable-Car Terminal (1968)—Shepley,
Bulfinch, Richardson & Abbott

Terra Linda

76 Commerce Clearing House (1970–
71)—Marquis & Stoller

Thousand Oaks

77 Civic Center (1972–73)—Robert
Mason Houvener

1   E. J. Baldwin Guest House (1885)
Los Angeles County Arboretum
301 North Baldwin Avenue at 210 Freeway
Arcadia (E of Los Angeles), California

A. A. BENNETT, ARCHITECT

Among the non-bosky benefits of the Los Angeles County Arboretum are several buildings which illustrate the early architecture of this region—all that remains of a 13,000-acre/5,260-hectare ranch. The oldest—though reconstructed—is the house originally built in 1839 by Hugo Reid. Immediately adjacent stands a Gabrielino Indian wickiup. Across the small lake and built almost as a *folie,* is the Queen Anne Cottage, a guest house for the most famous owner of the property, E. J. "Lucky" Baldwin. Its Victorian stick-work has been carefully renovated by Maurice Block, including the original colors. Baldwin's matching coach barn (1897) stands nearby. A good group, fortunately acquired by the Los Angeles State and County Arboretum in 1954.

Open daily 9–4:30, except Dec. 25: admission

2   Old State Capitol (1853–54)
First Street at G
Benicia, California

HOUGHTON & RYDER, ARCHITECTS

Those interested in the spread of the Greek Revival from coast to shining sea—plus those concerned with mid-nineteenth-century California
history—will find this relic worth a visit. Its temple-like, in antis, pretensions, however, are only partially consummated. Built supposedly in
the incredibly short time of three months, the capitol was used for less
than two years before the legislators permanently transferred to Sacramento (1854). The Benicia building then served as courthouse,
church, lodge, and school until thoroughly put back into shape by the
State Park Commission (1956–57).

Open daily 9–5, except holidays

3 **First Church of Christ, Scientist** (1910–12)
2619 Dwight Way at Bowditch Street
Berkeley, California

BERNARD R. MAYBECK, ARCHITECT

On first entering this church one must pause and move slowly, for its subtle ambience unfolds with measured grace. The wide, horizontally couched nave, built in an era of vertical pseudo-Gothicism, envelops one in an atmosphere of inner architectural harmony. Yet this joyous, peaceful quality—one elusive in any period of religious building—cannot be pinpointed, nor does it lie in a study of details. The answer to

its excellence is found in the triumphant mantle of the overall interior
and in the transcendency of its unity, not the assemblage of its parts.
Maybeck synthesized completely the "oneness" mandate which the
church's building committee had given him. The auditorium is so art-
fully woven together, one forgets that whispers of the Byzantine, the
Gothic, Art Nouveau, and the Japanese—to name the most prominent
—are all apparent. More important, they are all working together to
produce an intricate whole without the least being a potpourri of
styles. Moreover, Maybeck called for utilitarian concrete, asbestos-
cement board, and factory sash in the construction; he was one of the
first to use such industrial materials for a prominent building. (Cf.
Frank Lloyd Wright's Unity Temple of 1908 near Chicago.) The huge,
unplaned timber double trusses rest on freestanding concrete columns,
their diagonal lines throwing a focus on the chancel and its centrally
placed podium. Their angled lower chords and the modest touches of
color in their gold-painted plaster inserts keep these massive roof supports from seeming oppressive. Other touches of color, plus accents of
richly modeled concrete capitals atop the concrete piers, and the indirect bowl lights of hammered steel fuse happily together. There is a
slight glare problem from the two side windows—the nave is far finer

with the lights on—but there is no problem with religiosity or architectural glory. The exterior builds up intriguingly at the entrance though the sides tend to an amalgam of influences which at times becomes disjointed and even labored (such as the extravagant pergolas atop the columns). But this is carping; the church is one of the greats —a seminal building in the development of California's architecture. The Sunday school wing was added in 1929 by Henry Gutterson.

Tours Sun. 12:15; otherwise by telephone appointment with church office: (415) 845-7199

---

4 University Art Museum (1968–70)
University of California
Bancroft Way between College Avenue and Bowditch Street
Berkeley, California

MARIO J. CIAMPI & ASSOCIATES, ARCHITECTS

No concessions or promises greet one standing before this gallery except for the superb Calder in front. Neither do its mysterious angled walls of stepped-back, blank concrete (almost suggestive of a harshly scaled stronghold) extend an invitation to enter. However, on the inside the museum erupts with a galaxy of tiered and tantalizing spaces. The building's concept is based on five double-decked "platforms," each an exhibition space, lapped like cards in a fan formation as they step down the grade in sequential half floors, but all pivoting on a central entry "court," which also serves for displays. Its nine gallery areas (five over four), varying in length from 60 to 80 feet/18 to 24 meters, form slightly tapered cul-de-sacs, with entry at the open (and narrower) end on the court, and with a double-backing ramp to take one up or down a half flight to the adjacent space. Each exhibition room has a skylight across its far end but its three walls are windowless. The projections into the court of the four interconnecting gallery ramps and the longer access ramps create a stimulating, almost frenzied, series of spaces, all bathed in the potent illumination of the skylit central area with its deep trusses and angles. The main entrance is at level 2½ so that one immediately is thrust into a maelstrom of three-dimensional excitement. One looks down on the lower galleries, the lowest of which opens onto an outdoor sculpture garden, and up to the beckoning cantilevers. Each exhibit area, in proper contrast to the questionably

strong stimulation of the core, offers peaceful display space, undisturbed by through circulation as its basic entry-exit lies along the court side. (A hidden emergency stair is provided at the far end.) This solution forms a pointed contrast to Frank Lloyd Wright's somewhat similar use of an open "orientation" core at his Guggenheim Museum in New York (q.v.): Wright used spiral ramps both for galleries and for circulation, while Ciampi distinguished between these functions. One can visit all the exhibition areas, or skip any of them, utilizing the ramps at their open ends, without ever being out of touch with the central catalyzing core from which the whole generates. Outside of levels 2 and 3 there are small open-air sculpture terraces with ramps down to the sculpture garden, which can also be reached directly from within. A restaurant and lounge overlook this garden, while a two-hundred-seat theater-auditorium, plus the usual services, occupy the basement. The commission for the museum was won by Mario Ciampi in a national competition in partnership with Richard L. Jorasch and Ronald E. Wagner. Fractious and brutal—but stimulating.

Open Wed.–Sun. 11–6, except Jan. 1 and Dec. 25

---

5   Mission San Carlos Borromeo (1793–97)
Church Street between Camino El Estero and Figueroa Street
Carmel (Monterey), California

The church we see today so verdantly set in a gardened court was, a hundred years ago, a lonely wreck, its roof fallen in, its mission buildings destroyed. The second of the series of twenty-one missions founded by Father Junípero Serra—who lies buried near its altar—the church itself was stoutly constructed of stone, with an unusual vaulted roof whose three ribs of stone arches, properly buttressed on the outside, support within a half-barrel ceiling of lateral wood planks laid atop the arches. An inverted boat shape results, climaxed by a recent (1957) reredos. The exterior with its two unequally sized towers (the larger of Ibero-Moorish inspiration), a fine Baroque star-shaped window over the prominent door, plus the asymmetry of the approach and its garden setting develop a comely ambience. Secularized in 1834, the church shortly thereafter nearly collapsed: the roof did fall in 1851 and was incorrectly replaced in 1884. Finally in the 1930s it was given a complete restoration.

Open Mon.–Sat. 9:30–5, Sun. and holidays 10:30–5, closed Thanksgiving and Christmas

NOTE: *The California Missions,* by the Editorial Staff of Sunset Books, Lane Book Company, 1964, is highly recommended. Its nineteenth-century drawings and photographs are especially illuminating.

6   Carmel Valley Manor (1962–63)
Carmel Valley Road (c. 5 miles/8 kilometers E of CA 1—SE of Monterey)
Carmel Valley, California

SKIDMORE, OWINGS & MERRILL, ARCHITECTS

The intensifying problem of housing the elderly has rarely been as felicitously handled as this life-care, "purchase"—as opposed to rental—retirement community for 220 residents. With non-profit church affiliation (United Church of Christ), Valley Manor provides 171 living units, a dining room for those who elect to use it (most quarters have their own kitchen or light cooking facilities), meeting house, recreation and craft room, medical center, and chapel. The architecture, basically white stucco with trimly eaved redwood shingle roofs—its units grouped in clusters suggestive of a Mediterranean village—provides accommodations ranging from studio apartments to two-bedroom cottages. Scale, the variety of relationships between buildings, the sequential vistas, and the landscaping are excellent. Near Monterey but set back from the coastal fog belt, the Manor maintains its own transportation (though many residents have their own cars) to provide ready contact with town activities. It is so altogether comforting that there is a long waiting list. Sasaki, Walker & Associates were the landscape architects.

Meeting house and central area only open to public daily 9–5, except holidays

7   **Xerox Building** (1966)
    555 Aviation Boulevard at 135th Street, c. 2 miles/3.2 kilometers
    S of LA International Airport entrance
    El Segundo (SW of Los Angeles), California

CRAIG ELLWOOD ASSOCIATES, ARCHITECTS

Though the interior of the Xerox Building (formerly Scientific Data Systems) is only open to the public by appointment, the specialist wishing to see the outside of an ingeniously conceived, brilliantly detailed building would find it well worth inspecting. The expression of its structure and its penetration of the skin combine explicitness with pared elegance, the steel of its Greek-cross columns standing free of the building as they support the lightweight roof trusses (4 feet/1.2 meters deep) with mathematical aplomb. Just behind rise the concrete pebble-aggregate wall panels (16 x 17 feet/4.9 x 5.2 meters). These are steel-framed, poured flat on the site, and tilted into position, the framing channels remaining in place. Measuring 464 feet/141 meters x 560 feet/171 meters (in 48-foot/15-meter bays), the building—most of which is occupied with production facilities—was speedy and economical in erection. It is obviously the epitome of terseness in appearance. As Craig Ellwood has written, "The art and science of building is

the art and science of structure . . . My order is structure. My direction is refinement. My goal is perfection" (*Bauen + Wohnen,* November 1962).

Reception area only open during business hours

---

8 William Carson House (1884–86)
2nd and M Streets
Eureka, California

SAMUEL AND JOSEPH C. NEWSOM, ARCHITECTS

The eighteen-room Carson House is a private club—and not open to the public—but the exterior alone is such a spectacular example of gung-ho Queen Anne and Charles Eastlake (etc. etc.) that it more than merits a drive by. It is, indeed, probably the finest late Victorian exterior in the country, a culmination of profligate fancies haughtily— but gloriously—dispensed. Mary Mix Foley describes it "as a valedictory to every style which had gone before and a harbinger of others to come" (*The American Home,* Harper & Row, 1979). Completely restored in 1964, it is now proudly maintained.

Only visible from street

---

9   **The Fulton Street Mall** (1964)
    Fulton Street
    Fresno, California

GRUEN ASSOCIATES, PLANNERS; ECKBO, DEAN, AUSTIN & WILLIAMS, LANDSCAPE ARCHITECTS

The U.S. "downtown," almost universally made up of an uninspired collection of buildings, wretched urban spaces, and inadequate parking facilities, is not going to be "saved" unless people are attracted to use it by more than its variety of merchandise. Business, commerce, the professions of necessity will remain (largely) in the central business district, but the mobile housewife and family are in increasing numbers relaxing in suburban shopping centers. To bring the shopper back downtown, both the trip and the experience must be easy, indeed fun, and the goods plentiful. To this end Fresno (population about 190,000), as part of an overall planning survey, transformed one of its main streets—choked with automobiles and totally devoid of urban comity—into an imaginative and delightful pedestrian mall six blocks long with five three-block cross malls. Though automobiles are banished, ample parking facilities are close at hand with both open-air and garage options. Service vehicles use existing alleys and buses the newly created loop road nearby. The pedestrian mall itself offers playgrounds for the children, carnivals, bowers and shaded rest spots for the footsore. All are interwoven with bouncing fountains, flowing waters, a careful variety of regional trees (162 in number), gardens (some 19,000 plants), and sculpture, including an imaginative clock by Jan de Swart. The whole is unified by wall-to-wall sidewalks, the

spritely patterning of which emphasizes the trees, fountains, pools, and fixtures, and—cleverly via its design—encourages a cross flow of shoppers.

All high hopes have not materialized—due primarily to the opening of a huge shopping center (1970) 6 miles/10 kilometers from downtown. Yet the Mall, reinforced in 1978 by the Fresno County Health Department, is alive and sanguine. As a local bulletin put it: "Had we not taken the risk of building the Mall in 1964, most people are convinced our downtown would now be a disaster area." Some of the shops are still of minus visual value and many of the old signs are intrusive, but altogether the results are a success. The Mall sparked this activity but it is only the culmination of a careful (six-year) overall urban analysis for the 86-acre/35-hectare central area of the city. As Victor Gruen himself has said, "The Mall, per se, is not a solution," nor just an isolated prettying process: it is the key element in thorough urban rehabilitation. Edgardo Contini of the Gruen office was partner in charge of planning, greatly aided by civic officials, local businessmen and professionals, and indeed the entire community.

Always open

10 Community Church (1959–61)
12141 Lewis Street, immediately N of CA 22 and W of IS 5
Garden Grove (S of Los Angeles), California

RICHARD J. NEUTRA & ASSOCIATES, ARCHITECTS

The Community Church began as a worship-in-your-car church—useful for families with babies, the poor of dress, and the many handicapped and indisposed of this retirement area. It blossomed with Neutra's ingenious outdoor-indoor solution. The nave has pews for 1,700 while 1,400 persons in as many as 600 automobiles fan in a semicircle about the balcony so that they can see the minister and follow the service via their car radios. (Most of the east wall of the church is also openable.) Sixteen steel bents form the frame of the nave, with natural stone making a chancel wall. The church has been expanded several times with the fifteen-story Tower of Hope for classrooms and offices being added in 1968. Dion Neutra was the project architect.

Construction was begun in 1978 for an adjacent and—to judge from

drawings—fantastic **Crystal Cathedral** seating 4,000. The entire eight-sided building, including roof, is of glass. Designed by Johnson/Burgee of New York (see Index), it was dedicated in September 1980.

Often open in addition to Sun. services: apply at office

---

11   La Jolla Women's Club (1913–14)
Draper Avenue at Silverado Street
La Jolla (San Diego), California

IRVING J. GILL, ARCHITECT

The far too little-known Irving Gill (1870–1936) was one of the brilliant early advocates of the modern movement in the U.S.A. His work reflected the "morality" and "down with the past" thinking of Louis

Sullivan, for whom he worked (1890–93); his affection for Southern California and the arcaded geometry of its Spanish missions, though then largely in semiruins; plus an antiornament influence which he shared with his exact contemporary, the Austrian Adolf Loos (1870–1933). The two conceivably exerted a cross-fertilization influence on each other, but a mutual admiration for Sullivan's writings more likely accounts for some similarities in their work. Gill's work thus possesses a potent simplicity and in many cases, such as here in La Jolla, a rhythmic movement of multiple arches. His architecture might be described as shaved Spanish, flat-roofed and without moldings, but shaved at a time when most Iberian-inspired buildings were on the shaggy side. As Esther McCoy points out in her valuable *Five California Architects* (Praeger, 1975), Gill's professional popularity suffered markedly after the heavily decorated Churrigueresque Style became fashionable following the 1915 Panama-Pacific Exposition in San Francisco and San Diego's Panama-California International Exposition of 1915–16. (Mrs. McCoy also illustrates the very advanced tilt-slab concrete construction of the Women's Club.) Although Gill's greatest building, the Walter L. Dodge House (1914–16) in Los Angeles, was wantonly destroyed in 1970, this clubhouse in downtown La Jolla shows how advanced he was for his day. Though only open to the public on Saturday mornings, one can get a good grasp of his buildings' simple elegance at any time from the sidewalk. The interiors are of less interest. The building is listed in the National Register of Historic Places.

Open Sat. 9–12, except holidays

---

12   The Salk Institute (1964–66)
off Genessee exit of IS 5, W on Genessee Street
10010 North Torrey Pines Road
La Jolla (San Diego), California

LOUIS I. KAHN, ARCHITECT

This vast, haunting agora, flanked by angled walls focused on the infinity of the Pacific, provides a brilliantly formal setting on a gloriously informal site. The east-west-oriented court is lined with study towers—the private offices for thirty-six Fellows—arranged in two-story banks of nine per side and angled to face the sea. These re-

treats are separated from the two enormous blocks of laboratories, which frame the far sides, by an elaborate semiopen, semienclosed circulation cloister. The offices for the Fellows plug directly into the laboratories (a half flight down), each of which forms a structurally open rectangle 65 x 245 feet/20 x 75 meters in size and subdivisible at will. All three floors of the laboratories are topped by full-height (9 feet/2.7 meters) service floors which carry the trusses, freeing the labs beneath of the need of columns. In addition these floors provide total flexibility for the elaborate pipe- and duct-work which feed the experiments below. Projecting behind each laboratory block are five service towers containing toilet facilities and fire stairs. Every major element is precisely stated.

The rigidly symmetrical agora is fleetingly suggestive of Jefferson's University of Virginia. (Most of Kahn's buildings are symmetrical.) Thus to some observers this core seems a bit ill at ease in the free landscape of rolling hills, live oaks, and eucalyptus, with the blue sea beyond. Kahn himself worried about this and asked Luis Barragán, the noted Mexican architect and landscape architect, for suggestions. Barragán said, "I would not put a tree or blade of grass in this space. This should be a plaza of stone, not a garden" (*L'Architecture d'Aujourd'hui,* 142, II/III, 1969). The resulting effect, when one debouches from a coppice and enters the gates, is that one is immediately mesmerized by the space and by that pencil-thin channel of water bisecting the courtyard and aimed for mother ocean. Even the travertine paving is scored to emphasize the adventure to infinity, an impression abetted by the insistent perspective of the blank, angled walls of the studies. These studies, incidentally, alternate vertically with open porches in their four-story towers, the offices themselves immediately identifiable by their paneled teak facing. Walking through the articulated circulation between the study wings and the lab blocks—to Kahn "architecture is a thoughtful making of spaces" (*P/A,* April 1961)—one encounters passages of sunshine and shadow, freedom and enclosure. This experience is even more exciting than the simple Italian cloisters which Dr. Salk—who was an eager, knowledgeable client—initially had in mind. The laboratories themselves, with their divisible-at-will loft structural framing, stand in pointed contrast to Lou Kahn's famous Richards Medical Laboratory in Philadelphia (q.v.), whose genesis was the intimate in-touch-with-neighbor approach.

Onto the west (ocean) end of the Salk blocks are tacked—without the clarity which distinguishes the major elements—four floors of offices, plus lounge and restaurant on the ground floor, all overlooking the Pacific. At the opposite, or east (i.e. entry), end are the mechanical wings with open service floors so that future changes can be made without interrupting any research facility. Faculty housing is planned. Dr. August E. Komendant was structural consultant. The Versailles of the virus.

NOTE: The below-ground Cancer Research Animal Facility was added under the south terrace in 1977 by Naramore, Bain, Brady & Johanson in association with Deems/Lewis & Partners.

Informal tours, Mon.–Fri. 11, 12, 1, and 2, except holidays

---

13   La Purísima Mission (1813–18)
off CA 1 and 246, 3 miles/4.8 kilometers NE of town on
Lompoc-Casmalia Road
Lompoc, California

Almost all of the buildings seen here today stem from the rebuilding of 1934–49—secularization (1834), earthquakes, and vandalism having largely destroyed the original mission. Yet the overall impression is of well-researched authenticity. Moreover at La Purísima, as opposed to some of the more pretentious California missions, the visitor can clearly grasp from the unusual in-line (as opposed to quadrangular) architectural layout the full cycle of mission life. This involved housing and educating Indians; shops and quarters; facilities for accommodating travelers; and, of course, the chapel. Occupying an unspoiled little valley, La Purísima was first established (1787–88) some 4 miles/6.4 kilometers southwest of its present location but was destroyed by an earthquake in 1812. In 1813 it was moved to the present site on the famous El Camino Real. It became the eleventh of twenty-one Franciscan missions stretching from San Diego to Sonoma 650 miles/1,046 kilometers—each a day's good march from the other —which the more than energetic Father Junípero Serra (1713–84) planned for Alta California. (He lived to see nine established.) Mexico's freedom from Spain (1821) sparked the mission's troubled and disillusioned Chumash Indians to revolt (1824), and from then on the entire establishment went downhill, particularly after secularization. What was left was sold by then Mexican Governor Pio Pico in 1845. Used as a sheep ranch and sharecrop farm in the last century, and

sadly weakened by weather, the ruins and 507 acres/205 hectares were acquired by the state in 1935, and under experts and the Civilian Conservation Corps of the Depression work was commenced on its reconstruction. (The Union Oil Company donated part of the land including that on which the buildings stand.) The foundations and crumbled walls of the old mission enabled all buildings to be precisely located, while early sketches were useful in restoring their appearance. All materials used in the rebuilding, from adobe bricks (250,000) to hand-adzed beams, were authentically produced. Though not as sophisticated architecturally as several of the other missions, La Purísima gives fuller understanding of mission life. It is, incidentally, one of the most ambitious reconstructions in the West. Much recommended.

Open daily 9–5, except major holidays: admission

14   Los Cerritos Ranch House Museum (1844)
4600 Virginia Road, NNW off Long Beach Road
Long Beach, California

Heavily restored and in parts added to or altered, this U-shaped house nevertheless delivers a good impression of a *rancho* when the state still belonged to Mexico. Interestingly it was built by Don Juan Temple (né Jonathan Temple from New England), the cattle rancher who the next year purchased the secularized La Purísima Mission (q.v.) and grounds almost 140 miles/225 kilometers to the northwest. Built of adobe with redwood beams, Los Cerritos shows the influence of the so-called Monterey Style which later became so popular in California. Thoroughly renovated in 1930, it was purchased by the City Council in 1955 and is now run by the town's public library. The grounds and planting are excellent.

Open Wed.–Sun. 1–5, except holidays

15   Foothill College (1959–61)
12345 El Monte Avenue, immediately W of IS 280
Los Altos Hills, California

ERNEST J. KUMP AND MASTEN & HURD, ARCHITECTS

The thirty-nine buildings of Foothill College epitomize the classic California pavilion layout. As such it has deservedly exerted enormous influence on instructional building ever since. Its architecture at times approaches the overly picturesque (as in the roof "priority" with projecting beams—which double as gutters—and with extra-heavy shakes). Yet the basic plan, the astute rationalizing of construction on modular lines, and the total ambience are exemplary. Moreover, it is knit together and fortified by possibly the finest campus landscaping that one will see. Foothill was designed to give two years of instruction to 5,000 day students and an equal number at night. In 1980 this figure was approximately 7,000, both day and night. In addition, its cultural facilities, particularly the 971-seat theater and the gymnasium (both near parking lots) are also used by the community. The brilliance of planning of the 122-acre/49-hectare site can be seen initially in the fact that the campus proper is built on two plateaus, and although there are 3,000–4,000 automobiles parked about the low periphery of the "mesas" on which the college rests, no vehicles, except for service, are allowed on the campus: they are not even visible from it. The slight undulations and configurations of the hill topography have been employed for optimum utilization with relatively little earth moving necessary.

The buildings are grouped in clusters according to function, with teaching units at west, library near center, then administration, theater, and campus "center." The physical education plant is on a hill by itself, reached by a short bridge. Though in design they are relaxed just short of folksiness, they are based on a very hardheaded, economical yet flexible module of reinforced concrete frame and redwood walls: almost all buildings use a 60 x 68-foot/18 x 21-meter "space module" which can be subdivided at any 4-foot/1.2-meter point. A variety of sizes—from library to teaching units—are accommodated by this structural system, simplifying and speeding erection while simultaneously developing esthetic homogeneity but not monotony. In general appearance Foothill looks like a well-knit, one-story, educational village with friendly residential scale of vaguely Japanese ancestry. The wide overhangs of all buildings serve as outdoor corridors (there are

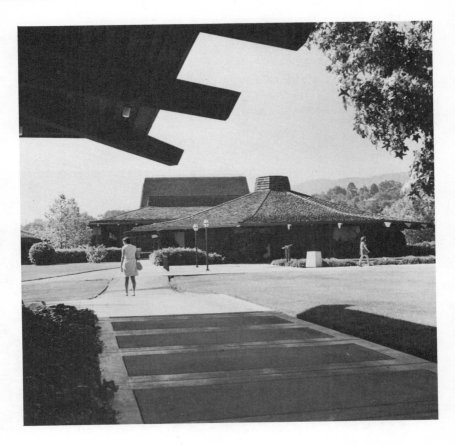

no inner ones) creating a continuity (plus some exposure during the brief rainy season). The outdoor spaces vary from the intimate courtyards adjacent to most class units to rolling vistas across the campus. The landscaping—by Sasaki, Walker & Associates—is not only superb visually (with some lacunae in upkeep), it is also functional in defining circulation by its artificial berms and "hills."

Pedagogical criticism might object that there are no home bases or rooms for the students who perforce must lug their books and possessions from class to class, while philosophically not feeling any identification, attachment, or peer security. Architecturally, Foothill—perhaps greater as a whole than as parts—presents a wonderfully attractive campus.

Grounds open daily

16 Bradbury Building (1893)
304 South Broadway
Los Angeles, California

GEORGE H. WYMAN, ARCHITECT

Spritely in spite of its years, and surviving the inconveniences of fire, earthquake, and semineglect in a once deteriorating section of downtown, this five-story building is one of the few commercial treasures of any period. Its top-lit central court, though somewhat cramped on the entry floor, radiates light and space above, while its lavish use of wrought iron (some think made in France) is wonderfully inventive, especially the "open" elevator cages. Once one of an endangered species of central-court, skylit "skyscrapers" (cf. the Brown Palace Hotel in Denver, Colorado), the Bradbury through a variety of happy circumstances (including use for charity balls) has come down to us basically intact, and in 1969 was handsomely restored and mechanically updated by the Bradbury Square Corporation. To underscore affirmation and approval the Southern California Chapter of the American Institute of Architects moved in when air conditioning had been installed, the second elevator put back in shape, and all returned to pristine glory, including the 50 x 120-foot/15 x 36-meter skylight. The exterior, of brick and sandstone (also restored), will not stop traffic, but step inside to see what a young draftsman—bolstered reputedly by a Ouija board—did with space, light, and loving attention to detail. It is listed in the National Register of Historic Places.

Open Mon.–Sat. 10–4, except holidays

---

17   Hollyhock House (1920–21)
Barnsdall Park
4800 Hollywood Boulevard just W of Vermont Avenue
Los Angeles (Hollywood), California

FRANK LLOYD WRIGHT, ARCHITECT

Wright's famous Barnsdall or Hollyhock House is the first of seven residences he designed in the Los Angeles area. It clearly shows his early interest in Mesoamerican architecture with its plain canted walls (here of wood "plastered with concrete and trimmed with cast stone") set off by a band of rich decoration. Hollyhock House (note the flower in the frieze) dominates a hill—which forms Barnsdall Park—on the eastern edge of Hollywood. Its cross-axial plan is of almost Roman monumentality, but its appearance, especially around its garden court and the circular pool, is domestic in scale. (The court was used for outdoor

theatrical performances.) With its projecting wings semienclosing space, the plan recalls that of the Imperial Hotel, on which Wright was working at the same time. On the interior note the dropped living room, the cathedral ceiling, and the indirect lighting. Observe, too, the channel of water from an upper outdoor pool to a lower one with detour around the fireplace. It is an interior more of units rather than of the spatial flow seen in Wright's Robie House in Chicago (q.v.). But what "units"!

Barnsdall Park occupies a site which Aline Barnsdall once planned for a center for the performing arts, but this never materialized, and in 1927 she gave house, studio, and the grounds of the former estate to the city "for recreation and cultural purposes." For some years indecision ruled, but as the plaque in front states, "In 1947 this building was reconstructed, furnished and equipped . . . by the Olive Hill Foundation, which was founded and endowed by Dorothy Clune Murray, in memory of her son." In 1971–75 further restoration was undertaken—termites having done great damage—and the house is now open for escorted tours. One of the greats.

The **Arts and Crafts Center** (1920) at·the entry was designed by R. M. Schindler, who also supervised the construction of the main house (Wright himself being mostly in Japan at the time). The Center was originally a studio-residence, one of a group that Ms. Barnsdall proposed.

Tours Tues., Thurs., first Sat. in month at 10, 11, 12, and 1, except holidays: admission

---

18 St. Vincent de Paul (1924–25)
Figueroa Street at Adams
Los Angeles, California

ALBERT C. MARTIN, ARCHITECT

In sketching even briefly a cross section of architectural developments in Southern California, it is requisite to include an example of the Spanish Colonial Revival which helped generate much of the region's appearance. The Spaniards left a residual and sturdy heritage in this, their onetime land, beginning of course with their famous missions. And when Bertram Goodhue was charged with designing San Diego's

Panama-California Exposition of 1915–16, he kept in mind the great Mexican cathedrals—as did Mr. Martin with this church. Goodhue not only "sought to embody the dream of a romantic past," he "fused all these sources—local, historical, and imaginary—in a new way" (*Architectural Record,* September 1978). Among the prominent offspring of that exposition is Los Angeles' St. Vincent de Paul, whose sides are properly simple while its tower and facade burst with rich sculpture, the latter—surprisingly—virtually a copy of the portal of Goodhue's California Building at the fair. Note the tower's pivotal role as a street fulcrum while the church's 45° placement at the intersection commands adjoining lots. The richness of the entry and the 151-foot/46-meter-high tower is repeated with enthusiasm on the interior. The nave ceiling is brightly painted while the Stations of the Cross sparkle with gold mosaics. The highlight, however, is the reredos which forms the climax of the 250-foot/76-meter-long nave. To quote the church folder, this background for the altar is in "carved, gilded and

polychromed wood after the sumptuous Churrigueresque fashion."
Though the iconography is complex the opulence is clear. Capacity of
the nave is 1,200. The church is constructed of reinforced concrete for
earthquake resistance: trim and sculpture are of limestone.

Open daily 7–7

---

19 Central Library Building (1925–26)
630 West 5th Street between Flower and Grand
Los Angeles, California

**BERTRAM GROSVENOR GOODHUE, ARCHITECT; CARLETON
MONROE WINSLOW, ASSOCIATE ARCHITECT**

One of Goodhue's last works (he died in 1924), Central Library not only represents a bold step but hints strongly of protomodern architecture. The smooth concrete walls are almost totally bereft of the historical motifs that typified the eclecticism of its day, while the window sash is the type used in industrial building. The architects have put the elements together with great skill, topping all with a colorful mosaic pyramid on the central tower. Lee Lawrie did the sculptured figures by the entry. Though the interiors—even the rotunda and reading rooms on the second floor—exhibit only modest spatial grandeur, their walls are richly covered with murals. Those in the rotunda-catalog room were painted on canvas (1927–32) by Dean Cornwell, and represent scenes from the "four great eras" in the history of Los Angeles. (The eras depict *Discovery, Mission Building, Americanization,* and *Founding of Los Angeles.*) In the dome are geometric decorations by Julian E. Garnsey. The History Room has a fine series of pictorial canvases by Albert Herter (1871–1950), while the other reading rooms have elaborately painted ceilings which current fluorescent lamps do everything they can to wash out. A full restoration of the library, it is hoped, will be undertaken.

Open Mon.–Thurs. 10–8, Fri.–Sat. 10–5:30, except holidays

---

20   Simon Rodia Towers/Watts Towers (1921–54)
1765 East 107th Street; E off Harbor Freeway (CA 11) on Century Boulevard, S on Central Avenue, E on 108th Street: follow signs
Los Angeles, California

SIMON RODIA, DESIGNER AND CONSTRUCTOR

Vladimir Tatlin, the Russian painter-sculptor (1885–1953), is generally credited with Constructivism. His work in making "void" as much an element as "solid" was carried to impressive heights in his 1920 project for a monument in Moscow, a design in which the spatial interpenetrations of the Eiffel Tower might well have been influential. (He had visited Paris in 1913.) Whereas Simon Rodia—born in an Italian village in 1879 and coming to the United States some twelve years later—had undoubtedly heard of the Eiffel Tower, it is more than doubtful that he knew of Mr. Tatlin. Yet Rodia, untutored and long unrecognized (he was indeed early mocked), was creating his own

constructivism at almost the same time as Tatlin but along the railroad tracks of south Los Angeles. Mr. Rodia, a tile-setter by trade, sought to give something to his adopted country in kindly recognition of what it had given to him—a sentiment invigorated no doubt by a not unworthy desire to be remembered. (We understand that he pored over the biographies of the great in his beloved Encyclopaedia Britannica.) Working always alone, with incredible dedication, Rodia erected with castoff steel reinforcing rods, wire mesh, and concrete—and without drawings or scaffolding—two major towers (104 and 100 feet/32 and 30 meters high) and several lesser ones. All were encrusted with what the art world would now call "found objects." Bottle bottoms and pieces of glass from junkyards, shells (some seventy thousand) from nearby beaches, colored tile fragments from construction sites, barrel hoops, broken plates—the ingredients are almost endless—all found their way into this patiently created work to which Rodia gave thirty-three years of his spare time. When he finished it in 1954, he left Watts, never to return. However, this is no rubbish collection, no casual assemblage, but a carefully stated esthetic achievement of fantastic imagination, fashioned lovingly through the years. If it seems more "folk" art than museum work, as of course it is, who cares? This is a museum in itself. But do not remain content with viewing the Rodia Towers from the sidewalk. Experience their spatial dynamism—this "participation in infinity" (Reyner Banham)—by walking in and about and through this dazzling web of three-dimensional virtuosity. Ingenious from the tensile engineering standpoint, the towers are absorbing as sculpture. Rodia made much from little, and the country is far richer for his labors. Whether we term it architecture or sculpture is secondary—as it is with Saarinen's breathtaking arch in St. Louis, Missouri (q.v.). The end product is molded space for the delectation of humanity. As the local guidebook (recommended) mentions, "The trivial . . . has lost its triviality." Simon Rodia, may he rest in peace, has given us the finest example of large-scale folk art in the Americas: an "extreme conception of an architecture without skin" (Ulrich Conrads and Hans G. Sperlich, *The Architecture of Fantasy*, Praeger, 1962).

Neglected and partly vandalized after Rodia's departure, the towers were purchased by two concerned admirers, William Cartwright and Nicholas King. They then organized The Committee for Simon Rodia's Towers in Watts, a volunteer effort to save them when the City Building Department condemned the towers (1959) as unsafe and "not conforming to building regulations." The outcry of architects, engineers, art lovers, and museum directors stayed their execution until tests by experts were made. When all the county's horses couldn't budge the towers—one shell fell off—reprieve was granted. The Committee was in charge of the towers until 1975, when they were given to the City of Los Angeles. In 1978 title was transferred to the State of California, but administered by the city's Cultural Affairs Department (formerly the Municipal Arts Department).

Open daily 9–dusk: admission

21 **Mann's** (formerly Grauman's) **Chinese Theater** (1926–27)
6925 Hollywood Boulevard at Orange Drive
Los Angeles (Hollywood), California

MEYER & HOLLER, ARCHITECTS

Of all the cinematic dream palaces of that age when the movies were king, Mann's/Grauman's—"the most famous motion picture theatre in the world"—now stands with few peers. (See also the Paramount Theatre in Oakland.) The exterior, as expected, displays dreamworld escapism, but the well-planned interior is remarkably restrained except for an ebulliently "Oriental" ceiling. A valuable cultural index of its day—and don't forget the hand prints of the stars in the pavement of the adroitly planned forecourt that entices one in before one knows it. Sid Grauman actually visited China in 1924, hence his inspiration.

Open daily for performances

22 Corona Elementary School (1935)
3825 Bell Avenue at Bear Avenue
Los Angeles (Bell), California

RICHARD J. NEUTRA, ARCHITECT

This famous school, really school annex, tiny though it be (five classrooms and kindergarten), pioneered such innovative concepts in educational architecture, at least at the elementary level, that it affected
school design in much of the United States. Richard Neutra
(1892–1970)—like several of his architectural cohorts—wanted to
make the classrooms airy and bright, and to open them out onto a
teaching terrace and play area by simply sliding one glazed half wall

behind the other. (In the Los Angeles area living and teaching outdoors can take place almost three quarters of the year.) He also sought
to eliminate the rigid, fixed-seat atmosphere which could be psycho-
logically hostile to young students—a notion which he may have gotten from his friendship with Sigmund Freud, once his fellow Viennese,
plus the antiauthoritarian teachings of John Dewey. To achieve these
ends Neutra had to use a one-story design, then an unusual proposition
but one in which his argument was "helped" by the 1933 earthquake.
When this height limit was accepted, he ran an inexpensive open-air
access corridor along one side of the north-south-oriented wing, putting a line of windows above to form a clerestory for bilateral light and
through ventilation. Ceiling height is 12 feet/3.6 meters. The west and
largely glazed side is protected from direct sun by a wide overhang and
an outrigging of louvers (originally awnings). The kindergarten faces
south. Today all is not as pristine as it was two generations ago—
asphalt has replaced grass and the hedges which divided the open-air
class areas are gone—but Corona still remains a building of great importance in the development of elementary school architecture in the
U.S.A. Dion Neutra made an addition in 1967.

Open during school hours

---

23   The Village Green (formerly Baldwin Hills Village) (1940–41)
**5300 Rodeo Road between Sycamore Avenue and Hauser
    Boulevard; S off IS 10 on La Brea Avenue**
Los Angeles, California

**REGINALD D. JOHNSON, WILSON, MERRILL & ALEXANDER,
ARCHITECTS; CLARENCE S. STEIN, CONSULTANT AND SITE
PLANNER**

The Village Green, until recently Baldwin Hills Village, is an outstanding example of urban land usage for domestic building—like the
other communities with which Clarence Stein was associated. Forty
years ago it triumphantly proclaimed lessons that we today—and will
tomorrow—incredibly ignore. Built (with FHA financing) and initially
owned by one man and now owned by the residents in common, it
shows what an enlightened developer with top-bracket designers can
do with 80 acres/32 hectares of then open farmland. Its principles are
so simple that one marvels that it has not spawned reasonable facsim-

iles across the nation, especially when those principles have been so financially rewarding that there has scarce been a day out of the 15,000 or so of its life when one of its 627 apartments has been empty.

The success of the development, like that of the earlier and influential Radburn in New Jersey (q.v.), stems mainly from the elementary fact that people and automobiles should each have their separate place, and that the former and their children and pets should not be menaced by the latter. Thus the overall plan was laid out as a superblock with seventeen garage courts (generally at right angles to the street) projecting inward about the periphery, and with low-density row housing zigzagged around these service areas. The main rooms of the houses—and their front doors—face onto the open parks that meander through the length of the development. Greenery and flowers are everywhere. Its "town houses" comprise both duplexes and one-story-over-ones—plus some one-story bungalows—which are entered from opposite sides. There are 275 one-bedroom units, 312 two-bedroom, and 40 three-bedroom houses, all of which have a private patio in back. (Brick serpentine-walled patios were added to those units without patios after World War II.) Though not architecturally inspired, they are competent and direct, their several muted colors giving quiet accents. A bit formalistic in overall plan and now lacking sufficient community facilities and shopping—many of the original shops were converted to living units—the Village Green/Baldwin Hills has yet many lessons for us today. In 1972 the project received the rarely given 25-Year Award for Excellence from the American Institute of Architects. Fred Barlow and Fred Edmonson were the landscape architects.

Since its conversion to condominium status (1978), its popularity has continued. However—and perhaps ironically—its initial family orientation has vanished. The Village Green is now an all-adult community with no children and no pets.

Inquire at office to visit

---

24   University Research Library (Unit 1, 1964, Unit 2, 1971)
University of California, Los Angeles
405 Hilgard Avenue, near Sunset Boulevard (Westwood)
Los Angeles, California

A. QUINCY JONES AND FREDERICK E. EMMONS, ARCHITECTS

The late Quincy Jones (1913–79) was one of the great humanists in the development of Southern Californian architecture. His influence was felt not only in his buildings but in his teaching, first as professor, then dean, of the School of Architecture and Fine Arts at the University of Southern California and as visiting critic at many other schools. He inspired young practitioners with a vital concern for creating a better environment and a better, more human shelter for all. Moreover he was able to upgrade significantly the prosaic "tract" housing, demanding natural land usage instead of the bulldozed sites which creep over the California landscape. Actually much of his extensive practice was domestically oriented, primarily because he liked people. Among his largest commissions is this two-stage Research Library. (A third building is scheduled.) On a campus of oft Byzantine obliquity, this library stands out with clarity. To minimize height, the first level is below grade but surrounded by a wide "moat" with a peripheral terrace and flowered embankment. The entry is via an inviting, covered but open "pavilion" which leads to the main (second) floor with loan desk, catalog files, general reading room, and offices. The third floor contains several large reading and study areas within the stacks along with carrels and a thoughtful outdoor reading deck. The three upper floors are

filled with stacks holding more than a million books, with a band of individual study carrels surrounding them. Construction throughout is of reinforced concrete to produce a loft-type structure where stacks can be placed anywhere—or the building eventually used for other than library purposes. The exterior is clad with precast pebble-concrete panels, with heat- and glare-resistant glass in the windows.

Open daily during school year

25 Pacific Design Center (1975)
Melrose Avenue at San Vicente Boulevard
Los Angeles, California

GRUEN ASSOCIATES, ARCHITECTS

A gigantic showroom and exhibit mart 530 feet/161 meters long, brightly wrapped in blue glass, that is almost guaranteed to slow the traffic between Beverly Hills and Hollywood—whence come most of the Center's customers. It was designed by Cesar Pelli of the Gruen office. Its 750,000 square feet/69,677 square meters of floor space accommodate display and office space for many of Southern California's firms which deal with contract and home furnishings, and it is laid out to provide optimum exhibition facilities. The cantilevered fifth and sixth floors open in the center onto an airily skylit galleria 85 feet/26 meters high, the feature which gives the PDC its distinctive profile. Mechanical services abut this to the north. Some semblance to London's famous Crystal Palace (1851) will come to mind—notably the roof— and in the Center's moduled glass envelope there is obvious similarity with the same designer's San Bernardino (California) City Hall (q.v.). The glass is transparent at eye level on each floor but backed with cement asbestos panels (to prevent heat buildup) elsewhere. The ground floor contains the International Design Center, a 400-seat auditorium, restaurants, banks, and public meeting rooms, with the second to sixth occupied by individual showrooms. A spacious hall at the entry cuts an angle through the building from the Melrose Avenue (public) side to the 1,150-car parking lot on the other. The scale of this arcade is good. The half cylinder on the facade contains one of the two banks of escalators. A 30-foot/9-meter grid was the basic steel-frame module. Edgardo Contini and Allen Rubenstein were partners-in-charge.

First floor open Mon.–Fri. 9–5, except holidays

26 **Federal Aviation Building** (1974–75)
Aviation Boulevard at Compton Boulevard
Los Angeles (Hawthorne), California

DANIEL, MANN, JOHNSON & MENDENHALL, ARCHITECTS

A smart edition of membrane building, here in glass, where a successful attempt was made to wrap corners and eaves with half rounds at the junctures of right-angle planes to express a continuous surface enclosure. The architects sought "a lightweight sculptural surface, where the building goes over the top . . . under the bottom, and also goes around the corner" (*P/A* 7:76 in quoting the designer). A shipshape encapsulation results which is as much philosophical architectural probing as it is efficient skin. Silver mirror glass—seemingly blue in reflecting the sky—and bright aluminum are the materials. The berm to the right of the entry adds highway interest to the Compton Boulevard side while creating a noise-relieved, open-air extension of the projecting cafeteria. Library, printing plant, and services fill the remainder of the ground floor with five floors above occupied in part by General Services Administration and, primarily, by the Federal Aviation Administration. (The Los Angeles airport lies 3 miles/4.8 kilometers to the north.) Anthony J. Lumsden was principal for design: Armstrong & Sharfman were the landscape architects.

Lobby open during office hours

27 Bonaventure Hotel (1975–77)
5th at Figueroa
Los Angeles, California

JOHN PORTMAN & ASSOCIATES, ARCHITECTS

Whatever else it may be or do, the Bonaventure adds a twenty-first-century note to Los Angeles' downtown, perking it enormously. The seemingly capricious (but well-composed) collection of five glass cylinders, the tallest thirty-five stories, evolved from the market need to provide approximately 1,500 rooms with a height restriction imposed by the redevelopment plan. The five cylinders provided the soundest solution. And the hotel has greatly enhanced its once uninspired Bunker Hill neighborhood. (The complex's mass and basic design obviously recall Detroit's Renaissance Center—q.v.—by the same architects.) On the interior, as with all of John Portman's hotels, the main floor revels in volumetric games with placid and almost ubiquitous waters establishing horizontal planes while six-story spatial tentacles probe mysteriously upward. Around each pier a new solid-void relationship unfolds. This tempting ambience—this calculated background for pleasure—was arrived at by imaginative handling of three dimensions,

not by tacked-on kitsch. In addition to hotel facilities, including a rooftop restaurant, there are five levels of shops. This resplendent caravanserai provides 1,474 rooms. Recommended.

Always open

Goodhue's Central Library Building (q.v.) stands just down 5th Street. New neighbors of the Bonaventure include: (1) The twin fifty-one-story skyscrapers **ARCO Tower** and **Bank of America** (1972) on Flower Street—Albert C. Martin & Associates, architects. Handsomely restrained, they are separated by a good plaza with sculpture (1973) by Herbert Bayer. A two-level mall runs beneath. (2) **Union Bank Building** (1966) at 5th and Figueroa, by Harrison & Abramovitz with Albert C. Martin & Associates. Note the sensitively camouflaged garage with a landscape plaza on the roof-deck. (3) **Security Pacific Bank** (1974), Flower at 3rd, by Albert C. Martin & Associates. This is a detached fifty-five-story granite-faced building overlooking a good urban park by Sasaki, Walker, landscape architects.

---

28 Civic Center (1964–65)
110 East Main Street at Fiesta Way
Los Gatos, California

CHARLES D. STICKNEY AND WILLIAM R. HULL, ARCHITECTS

A civil, anti-self-important civic center which shows that a small city (c. 25,000) can have commendable public architecture if it seeks it, in this case via a limited competition and a courageous administrator. The winning design placed the functions used by the public—administration, police, and library—on three corners of a square plaza elevated almost a half floor above grade, with the council chamber under the plaza but entered directly from the outside (as well as from within). The main staff-related functions of the three corner offices also occupy this lower level, and are interconnected around the council chamber. The landscaped terraces that lead up to the four sides of the plaza are cordially welcoming, while the views of the background trees and park between the offices which wrap the corners extend the vistas and tie the low-scaled building sympathetically to its wooded site. Windows are at times sparse, but the administration wing and the library both have a large skylight. The interior of the library, with its

separate children's wing, is low-keyed and inviting. Expansion of any one or all units was anticipated in the original design. Construction is of concrete with red brick walls, and these materials are repeated in the design of the plaza itself. Sasaki, Walker, Lackey Associates were the landscape architects.

Open during office hours

---

29 The J. Paul Getty Museum (1970–74)
17985 Pacific Coast Highway
Malibu, California

LANGDON & WILSON, ARCHITECTS

It would be easy to dismiss the Roman villa housing of the Getty Museum as an eccentric whim of an enormously wealthy man (who died in England and never saw it). This attitude of belittlement has indeed

received currency in the critical press. However, the Getty is far more than a seigneurial statement of aspiration or even idiosyncrasy. It offers, particularly on its main floor, an extraordinary collection of Greco-Roman art most of which is exhibited in an exemplary setting. (Mr. Getty became interested in this cultural and historic period when he first visited Pompeii and Herculaneum in 1912.) The building itself, including its garden and pool, is based directly on the plan of the second (or early first) century B.C. Villa dei Papiri in Herculaneum. This was excavated in the eighteenth century and carefully measured by Karl Weber, a Swiss engineer, in 1750–65. Standing on the coast outside the town, the villa was buried in mud in the A.D. 79 eruption of Vesuvius. (The villa reputedly belonged to Julius Caesar's father-in-law: its name comes from the still partly decipherable papyrus rolls—the most extensive ever excavated—found in the ruins.) Whereas a museum embracing a wide-ranging series of artistic periods (here up to the twentieth century) loses its architectural validity when housed in a reproduction of a two-thousand-year-old villa, for its main focus—the classical world—the Getty is unparalleled. And in addition to providing an authentic background for its antique collection, the building gives an immensely valuable depiction of the architecture of a scantily known era. Though obviously hypothetical above foundation level, this re-creation—not reconstruction—is as authentic as modern scholarship can conjure. Dr. Norman Neuerburg, the noted specialist on Roman domestic architecture, worked on the research for over three years. Country house depictions on wall paintings from demi-ruins in Pompeii, near Herculaneum, were of considerable help in decision-making.

The Getty's site, which had been purchased in the late 1940s and includes Mr. Getty's house, crowns a steep and narrow valley which offers from the top a view of the Pacific framed by eucalyptus and sycamore. First-rate technical facilities and a 124-car garage extend under the building with some open-air parking nearby. (The automobile accommodations, being limited by the difficult site, suggest the advisability of reservations mentioned below.) Because of the grade falloff the entry is not prepossessing. However, note the Roman-style paving stones of the driveway and the tufa, imported from Italy, of the wall. An elevator goes to the main level, where one is introduced to the museum by a 340-foot/104-meter-long peristyled garden. This is framed by Doric columns (curiously but authentically attenuated in the Hellenistic-Roman fashion) and highlighted by planting and a substantial reflecting pool. Excavations of the original pool at Herculaneum revealed a complete system of hydraulic controls. The planting faithfully utilizes the plant life of the first century A.D. when the garden of the Villa dei Papiri was destroyed. Emmet Wemple & Associates, the landscape architects, pored over Latin authors, documents, vases, and related works of art to create authentic landscaping—including bronze reproductions of sculpture and outdoor furniture and pergolas found in the ancient villa. The planting includes fruit trees, shrubs, flowers, camomile ground cover, etc., known to the Romans of the day. The colonnade is highlighted by first-century B.C. *trompe l'oeil* wall paintings in the Pompeian Second Style. Note the coffered bays framed by painted "columns" opposite actual ones; moreover no two bays are precisely alike in their decorative treatment. The detailing is extraordinary.

The two-story museum building stretches beyond the sides of the peristyle with a quiet scale that is emphasized by its south-facing porch and, above, its terrace. The entry vestibule is of unbelievable opulence —"a veritable feast of colored marbles" as the official booklet puts it, adding that "This type of decoration came into vogue in the late first century B.C. and was especially popular at Herculaneum." Note, too, the painted ceiling inspired by one in Pompeii. Every facet of the architecture (and planting) of the museum has historical antecedents: though sources for details vary, they are all authentic. The vestibule leads to an inner peristyle which reduces the scale outside to domestic proportions and also provides useful focus for the galleries—here classically oriented—which, with offices, surround it. The "filling in" of the lower flutings of the Ionic columns of the peristyle was a Roman device to keep the arrises (edges) of column flutings from being chipped in a high-traffic area. The bronze maidens about to draw water from the pool and the marble birdbaths are replicas of originals found in the villa.

The chief exhibits of the second floor are concentrated in several sumptuous period rooms—French decorative arts, primarily eighteenth century, were another of Mr. Getty's special interests. Other collections, particularly the contemporary, are less satisfactory. There are thirty-eight galleries altogether, twenty-two on the upper floor, all in excellent scale. As acquisitions increase—and the Getty's endowment is greater than that of any other museum in the United States and perhaps the world—a new structure may be built and the present museum devoted exclusively, and some think wisely, to the classical.

In exploring the museum be certain to see the West Garden with its Tea Room (open for lunch 10:30–2:30, refreshments until 4:30), and the East Garden with its Mosaic Fountain. Startling though the fountain's brightly polychromed mosaics and pebbles be, it is a precise copy of one still standing in the Casa della Fontana Grande in Pompeii. Stephen Garrett, RIBA, the museum's Director, was design consultant to the Trustees; Robert E. Langdon, Jr., was project director, with Edward W. Genter project architect; Emmet L. Wemple & Associates were the landscape architects, with Dennis L. Kurutz project director.

Open June–Sept., Mon.–Fri. 10–5, Oct.–May, Tues.–Sat. 10–5, except holidays: reservations suggested—telephone: (213) 454-6541

30   Old Custom House (c. 1827–46)
115 Alvarado Street, on Plaza at Fisherman's Wharf
Monterey, California

The King of Spain made Monterey the capital of California in 1775, but no structures of this era remain. When the newly created Republic of Mexico acquired the city and "state" in 1822 the first stage of this Custom House (the north end) was built—it is now California's oldest official (as opposed to clerical) building. The Americans briefly captured much of the state in 1846 (raising the flag on this Custom House), but it was not until two years later that California actually became part of the Union and shortly thereafter (1850) was made our thirty-first state. The Old Custom House, expanded from 1841–46, continued to serve its original functions until abandoned by the government in 1867. Subsequent commercial uses did not help the building's condition, but beginning in 1901 some restoration was made of its adobe and stone walls, and finally, in 1938, it came under the

state's purlieu and was fully restored. Though more of historic than architectural importance, the building is a good index of its time and place. It is listed in the National Register of Historic Places.

Open daily 9–5, except major holidays

---

31   Larkin House (1834–35)
Calle Principal at Jefferson Street
Monterey, California

This simple, hip-roofed adobe house with its encircling two-story veranda—the first in the state—is generally regarded as the pioneer example of the Monterey domestic vernacular which so influenced the subsequent architectural development of California. (It supposedly was also the first to have glass windows and an indoor fireplace.) Built as a combined store, office, and home, it later became a residence with the financial success of the owner, T. O. Larkin, who served here as consul to Mexico from 1844 to 1848. Though its walls are of thick

adobe in the Mexican-Spanish fashion long familiar throughout the Southwest, its framing is of redwood, here revolutionary. Note that the Larkin House, because of its second-floor wood balcony (primarily for access to the bedrooms) and its balustrade, carries a light even delicate impression, very different from one-story, solid-masonry structures. Harold Kirker writes in his beautifully researched *California's Architectural Frontier* (Peregrine Smith, Inc., 1973) that even "San Francisco was without a frame structure until 1836." As Kirker also mentions, Mr. Larkin, though he hailed from Massachusetts, spent ten years in North Carolina before he journeyed west. Thus it seems almost inevitable that the traditional tidewater dwellings of the Carolinas (Edenton, Beaufort, and Wilmington, let alone Charleston) with their "routine" double verandas influenced Larkin more than his native New England. As the Carolina double porches evolved, many feel, from Caribbean prototypes, the background of the Monterey Style becomes more and more fascinating. In any case the combination of the sturdiness and insulation of Mexican adobe with the tensile airiness of wood gave logical rise to the Monterey "style" which the Larkin House initiated. The house, along with many of its original furnishings, was given to the state (1957) by Mr. Larkin's granddaughter, Alice Larkin Toulmin.

Guided tours daily 9–4, except Tues. and major holidays: admission

---

32 Paramount Theatre (1931)
2025 Broadway
Oakland, California

MILLER & PFLUEGER, ARCHITECTS

The Oakland Paramount is an almost delirious example of Art Deco. Its exterior with its 110-foot/34-meter-high tile mosaic of enormous figures bifurcated by the projecting Paramount sign—which can be seen up and down the street—gives a hint of the prodigious, but it is the interior that rises to unequaled heights. A 58-foot/18-meter-high lobby forms a regal introduction with its side walls made of alternating vertical bands of warm artificial light panels and golden piers, while both ends and the ceiling are decorated with an almost luminescent grillwork. The grille, 12 inches/30 centimeters in depth, is made of

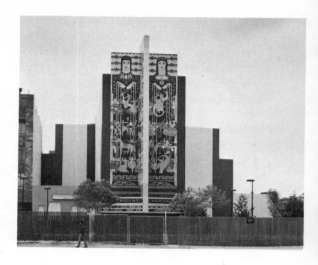

carefully composed metal "leaves," behind which indirect light shines with a greenish cast. As one moves laterally about the lobby the depth of the patterning "evokes the play of sunlight through a canopy of dense foliage." But whereas the foyer relies on stately luxuriance, the auditorium is unmatched in the United States or elsewhere for its refulgent splendor. Its gilded galaxies of whorls, patterns, and stylized figures are unbelievable. Furthermore this largesse extends over the stepped ceiling, while a solid-color curtain with silver and green appliquéd design calls attention to the stage. Outside and in, it radiates the dreamworld escapism with which the movies sought to beguile their customers. There will never be another like it.

After years of desultory life the theater was thoroughly reconditioned and restored (1973) to serve as the home of the Oakland Symphony and Oakland Ballet—then seeking proper quarters—as well as being open for other musical and related events. New seats were installed (reduced from 3,476 to 3,000 more comfortable ones), new rugs woven, and the whole brightly furbished. The building is now in the National Register of Historic Places. Timothy Pflueger was chief of design of the original building; Michael Dixon was the interior designer. Skidmore, Owings & Merrill were consultants for the renovation, with Milton Pflueger & Associates assisting.

Open for performances and public tours; telephone for hours: (415) 893-2300

33   Oakland-Alameda County Coliseum and Stadium (1966–68)
       **c. 5 miles/8 kilometers S of downtown Oakland off CA 17 (Nimitz
          Freeway) at 66th Avenue**
       Oakland, California

SKIDMORE, OWINGS & MERRILL, ARCHITECTS AND ENGINEERS

A keenly designed and engineered coliseum. It consists of a circular
drum framed by thirty-two gigantic (57 feet/17 meters high) x
members of reinforced concrete (poured in place), topped by an eave-
level compression ring. From this ring, 420 feet/128 meters in diameter, ninety-six cables are slung to a tension ring at the center (45
feet/14 meters in diameter), and on this net of cables the roof is laid.
Structurally impeccable, analyzed with the inventiveness for which
SOM is noted—here the San Francisco office—the Oakland Coliseum
presents a forceful image both by day and by night (when it is most
used). Enclosing yet independent of the structure stands a 70-

foot/21-meter-high wall of gray glass. Within rise banks of seats in two tiers, the upper of which fattens near the center. A circulation corridor separates the two near midpoint. From 11,000 to 15,000 spectators can be accommodated—depending on the character of the event —in seats which are brightly color-coded, as are the entry doors. It has facilities that range from basketball to ice hockey, with sufficient flexibility to take care of circuses. Ammann & Whitney acted as consulting engineers for the Coliseum roof.

Directly facing the Coliseum, and connected to it by an underground passage which can be used for exhibitions, rises the stadium for football, baseball, and soccer, seating 50,000 to 53,000. Its circular cup shape, 720 feet/219 meters in diameter, mirrors the cylinder opposite but purposefully does not compete with it, a scale diminution being achieved by "sinking" the playing field and lowest seats below grade and surrounding the stadium with an earth berm. Thus the spectators have only a half flight maximum up or down to their seats.

Open during events

---

34   Oakland Museum (1967–69)
1000 Oak Street between 10th and 12th
Oakland, California

KEVIN ROCHE/JOHN DINKELOO & ASSOCIATES, ARCHITECTS; DAN KILEY, LANDSCAPE ARCHITECT

The Oakland *Tribune* in the early part of this century predicted that Oakland would be "the Athens of the West" (an approbation later assumed by Berkeley), far outstripping its neighbor across the bay, otherwise known as San Francisco. Although this rosy notion did not quite materialize, Oakland in the past few years has matured with determination and foresight, and today offers much to both visitor and citizen. Among its most outstanding new buildings, and one of the most imaginative in the country, is the Oakland Museum—rather Museums, for there are three interconnected. Occupying four square city blocks, the building comprises a series of landscaped and terraced museum wings, lawns, and gardens, stepped down the grade with a flair that would appeal to Nebuchadnezzar. The architects had to provide exhibition spaces for California art, history, and natural science, and the chief problem facing them was to sort out these various functions, provide identity and circulation for each, yet tie them together in a

manageable whole which the public could readily grasp. The designers spent much time analyzing the cultural background and cultural needs of not only the city but the region, producing thus "a total museum related to the California scene." "Otherwise you are building shells for a function that may not exist," said Roche, "and you are building a monument, not a living thing" (Paul Heyer, *Architects on Architecture,* Walker and Company, 1966).

This "impossible" program has been solved with exterior brilliance on the court side with its series of dazzling planted terraces, and with reasonable success on the interior though complexity arises. The entry (at the upper level on Oak Street) provides a part-open, part-roofed introduction which gives onto the main art gallery with the permanent collection at the left, the gallery for circulating exhibitions to the right, with a panorama of spaces and view out in front. (The need for greater security has compromised some indoor-outdoor interaction.) The entrance to the main gallery is not prominent, and one (at least if right-handed) tends to turn to the door of the circulating exhibit space at the right, a two-story room entered by a balcony at the upper level which gives a fine overview of both room and contents. Tentacles of circulation lead from this gallery to the other exhibition spaces and occasionally to outdoor terraces as they step down the grade. California history (along with some parking) shares the same level as the temporary exhibition room. On the lowest level, and slid partly beneath the history wing, rests the natural sciences museum, plus more parking (for an overall total of two hundred cars). Both of these museums are identical in size and rectangular in shape. The natural sciences wing opens onto a large landscaped court, approximately 200 feet/61 meters on a side. It is framed by wings on two sides (the museum and a three-hundred-seat theater-auditorium placed at right angles), and by per-golas and property line wall on the other two. This courtyard doubles for exhibits and concerts.

As indicated, fully landscaped terraces—some with works of art—top all major and most minor changes of level, so that all outdoor promenades are marked by luxuriant planting, plus spatial and level changes that make exploration dramatic. Within, one can feel at times enmeshed by the labyrinthine circulation and by the lack of a domi-nant other than the temporary exhibits gallerv but the tension and release of spaces, interior and exterior, and the delights of the land-scaped terraces make this an extraordinary building.

Open Tues.–Sat. 10–5, Sun. 12–7

---

35   San Luis Rey de Francia (1811–15)
3.8 miles/6.1 kilometers E of IS 5 on CA 76 (Mission Road)
Oceanside, California

San Luis sits at ease on a comely ridge, surveying its valley and the to-kens of what had once been the largest and often the most agricul-turally productive of the twenty-one California missions. Suffering most of the ills attending the missions upon secularization (1834), the church itself at San Luis at least escaped collapse though stripped of every item of value. Undoubtedly its 6.5-foot/2-meter-thick brick-faced adobe walls were responsible for its preservation, as the mission lay deserted between 1865 and 1892. The length is 163 feet/49.7 me-ters and the breadth, 27 feet/8.2 meters. The church is unusual in having a transept and a dome (finished in 1829) over the crossing. Five bays marked by prominent pilasters, multidecorated on restoration to the point of artificiality, divide the nave, with a Renaissance-inspired altar and reredos filling the sanctuary wall. A well-scaled mor-tuary chapel, called the Madonna Chapel, opens on the right side of the nave. An interesting series of rooms with historic displays leads from the gift shop behind the arcade to the church proper. The patio at left, measuring some 500 feet/152 meters in size, once served as

the mission garden; however, the buildings which originally framed it were of one story, not two as at present. San Luis was rededicated in 1893 and work on its total reconstruction commenced as it was to function as a seminary. The mission still serves for religious instruction as well as housing a parish church. The single-towered exterior—some feel that two towers were originally planned—is now almost overly pristine. Be certain to take a look at the sunken garden and *lavandería* at the front left.

Open Mon.–Sat. 10–4, Sun. 12–4, except Thanksgiving and Dec. 25: admission

---

36 Main Library (1957–58)
1213 Newell Road at Parkinson
Palo Alto, California

EDWARD DURELL STONE ASSOCIATES, ARCHITECTS

A small, intimately scaled library, distinguished by its high-ceilinged reading room (with fireplace) and—most of all—by the relaxed, walled gardens at each end which serve as outdoor reading courts. Its

neighborhood character and the use of planting throughout are most appropriate. Eckbo, Royston & Williams were the landscape architects.

Open Mon.–Fri. 9–9, Sat. 9–6, Sun. 2–5, except holidays

---

37 **Wayfarers' Chapel** (1949–51)
Palos Verdes Drive South (c. 1 mile/1.6 kilometers E of Marineland)
Palos Verdes (Los Angeles), California

LLOYD WRIGHT, ARCHITECT

The architectural expression of the relationship between God and man and nature has been achieved with eloquence in this small (one hundred seats) chapel on picturesque hills which tumble down to the

Pacific. Designed by the famous (and eldest: 1890–1978) son of an
even more famous father, structure was kept to a discreet minimum
and the congregation is scarce aware that it is enveloped on the sides
and most of the roof by panes of clear glass set in a simple,
triangulated redwood frame resting on a local stone base. The chapel's
laminated wood arches, four per side, open to a Y-shape at spring-
point to make a roof of triangular (i.e. Trinity) planes. This religious
greenhouse is in turn wrapped and shielded by a wide variety of trees
and plants, samples of which—plus a tiny waterfall—are also found
within. Inasmuch as the chapel is basically transparent, solid roof

panels being at a minimum, there is no problem with glare (though sun heat was troublesome in the early years before the anticipated planting had matured). The 60-foot/18-meter-high campanile dates from 1954, and the cloister and library from 1957, their interconnection based on 30° triangles. The chapel belongs to the Church of the New Jerusalem, a sect based on the tenets of Emanuel Swedenborg (born Svedberg, 1688–1772), a remarkably learned Swedish scientist and theologian, who was much impressed by the Book of Revelation. He believed that there is a spiritual basis in all nature—a philosophy which Lloyd Wright beautifully interpreted. (Mr. Wright was also trained as a landscape architect by Frederick L. Olmsted.) One of the few genuinely sensitive houses of worship.

Open daily 11–4

---

38   David B. Gamble House (1907–8)
**4 Westmoreland Place, off North Orange Grove Boulevard, a half
    block N of Walnut Street**
Pasadena (Los Angeles), California

GREENE & GREENE, ARCHITECTS

Charles Sumner Greene (1868–1957) and Henry Mather Greene (1870–1954)—both trained at MIT—designed for David and Mary Gamble one of the great houses of the early twentieth century. Charles had a deep interest in Far Eastern art and Buddhist philosophy, and both had been impressed by the "medieval" Japanese Pavilion at the Fair of 1893 plus the aborning Shingle Style. At a time when upper-bracket domestic preference unhesitatingly regarded dusted-off "styles" of European vintage or U.S. neo-Colonial as absolutes, the brothers Greene erected a shingle house—"neo-stick," writes Scully—let it grow from the ground, projected outriggings of porches to catch the view and enjoy the breeze, and topped all by climactic sun-shielding roofs. The subtle progression from restrained to exuberant, particularly at the east end, is stunning: the lucid expression of structure, from rafter resting on beam down to minute junctures, is meticulous. The architects not only solved the problems of site, sight, and room layout, they did so with style, homogeneity, and integrity, while never forgetting function. Equally outstanding with freshness of design is craftsmanship. Each joint, each beam end, and, on the interior, every detail

including furniture and kitchen cabinets (at that time disdained by architects) are unsurpassed for workmanship. Note, particularly, the metal straps and wedges for binding beams together. An infatuation with intricacy of detail may at times take over, but take over with consummate elegance and regard for material. Incidentally, paint was never used, only stain. The shingled walls even are green-stained. The house, although of two full stories, was one of the prime examples in popularizing the California bungalow style—though here both large and expensive—bearing as it does resemblance to the wide-roofed, veranda-wrapped Bengali *bangla* of India (from which, of course, the name "bungalow"). The Greene brothers themselves designed over 150 bungalows in their long and busy practice. Fortunately in 1966 the Gamble House—one of their finest—was given by the Gambles' heirs, Cecil and Louise Gamble, to the City of Pasadena in joint agreement with the University of Southern California, a gift for which all can be thankful. In addition to being open to the public, the house is used for seminars and contains the Greene and Greene Library and the office of the Pasadena Foothill Chapter of the American Institute of Architects. It was designated a National Historic Landmark in 1978.

Open Tues. and Thurs. 10–3, also first Sun. of each month 12–3, except holidays: admission

39   The Stuart Company (1957–58)
    **3300 block, East Foothill Boulevard at Halstead Street (one
        block N of US 66)**
    Pasadena, California

EDWARD DURELL STONE ASSOCIATES, ARCHITECTS

A pharmaceutical palazzo which was highly influential in elevating
urban organizational headquarters from their routine mold, and making of them architectural showpieces (here combined with production
facilities). Stuart demonstrates that good architecture and landscaping
are stimulating for business and rewarding for staff morale. Mr. Stone

had shortly before completed the U. S. Embassy in New Delhi, and Stuart was designed the same year as the Palo Alto Library (q.v.). Many of the elements which can be seen in all three—grilles, reflecting pools, fountains, saucers of hanging plants—have been aped to ennui by now, but the Stuart Building was eye-opening to the business world when built. Its top (entry) floor—reached over a moat—is given to reception with a two-story atrium, and to offices, laboratories, and storage. Manufacturing facilities, taking advantage of the drop in grade, are located on the lower floor, along with the employees' dining room at the base of the atrium and opening onto the garden. Thomas D. Church & Associates were landscape architects; Maurice Sands, interior designer.

Reception area open during business hours

---

40   Art Center College of Design (1974–75)
1700 Lida Street (W off Linda Vista Avenue, c. 1 mile/1.6
**   kilometers W on Lida)**
Pasadena, California

CRAIG ELLWOOD ASSOCIATES, ARCHITECTS

Craig Ellwood, who has been called "a poet in steel," is one of the most ardent disciples of the late Mies van der Rohe, and for the energetic College of Design he has produced his most spectacular—and most Miesian—building. On the almost wild slopes of the San Rafael Hills a bit northwest of and overlooking the famous Rose Bowl, he has bridged a small canyon with an impeccable building 672 feet/205 meters long by 144 feet/44 meters wide. With its ends anchored on the ridges, the central part of the building, trussed by multiple king posts, leaps across the chasm with a free span of 192 feet/58 meters. The access road dashes underneath so that both on approaching and leaving the college there is an almost breathtaking levitation of mass and flow of tethered spaces. The freestanding triangulation of the "bridge" trusses is fully expressed and gives visual relief to what otherwise would be a tedious length. The end sections are both two stories high with the lower floor set two thirds in the grade (cf. Mies' Crown Hall in Chicago). The central area is occupied by administrative offices and library, with reception, offices, and exhibition space in the south wing.

Corridors line the outer periphery of most of the building, thus classrooms—debatably—are inset with light coming only from high transoms. The decision to place classrooms inside was determined by the school board and the architect in early studies (1970). This has had a plus value with the energy crisis because of the sun-shading which the outside corridors give the east and west sides while they themselves are not important thermally. The interiors are structurally expressive with ceiling and structure painted black and the walls white, with widely displayed student work providing color accents. The College of Design—one of the most noted in the U.S.A.—has architectural antecedents in Mies' never-built House in the Alps of 1934 and in Craig Ellwood's small Weekend House (1968) in San Luis Obispo (California). Some rigidity is evident in this one-building "campus" for a thousand students, and its remote residential location raises questions, but the result is a potent affirmation of two of the century's most characteristic materials—steel and plate glass.

Conducted tours Mon. and Wed. at 2 P.M., *Fri. at 10:30* A.M.; *telephone: (213) 577-1700*

41   Petaluma Adobe State Historic Park (1836–46)
  NE on Washington Road, SE at 3325 Adobe Road, c. 3 miles/4.8
     kilometers NE of
  Petaluma, California

This first-rate restoration, although only half the size of the original, gives an excellent idea of the private *ranchos* which characterized this former part of Mexico from 1822 to 1846. With the American victory over Mexico, hence the acquisition of California (1848), the Petaluma ranch, which covered 75,000 acres/30,350 hectares, began slowly to decline and was sold by its owner in 1857. In 1910 a patriotic California group bought and preserved what remained, but it was not until 1951 that the state's Department of Parks and Recreation acquired the ranch and began full-scale restoration of the half which was left. The

restorers were able to use almost 85 per cent of the adobe walls, many
of which were 4 feet/1.2 meters thick, and 20 per cent of the original
woodwork, some of it in the roof trusses being bound by rawhide. The
building might be said to combine the Monterey domestic vernacular
(see the Larkin House, Monterey), which was then developing, with
the long-prominent Spanish-Mexican patio layout (the original building formed a full square). It is completely surrounded by wide
overhanging eaves and peripheral balconies both on the out-facing
walls, which are windowless, and on the court side, the overhang and
balcony together serving the functions of sun and rain protection and
providing circulation. Much of the lower floor was used for storage.
Rancho Petaluma has been furnished with carefully selected or reproduced pieces of the period. It is a valuable example of the ranch
"house" of almost a century and a half ago.

Open daily 10–5, except major holidays: admission

---

42   Convention Center (1969–71)
Auditorium Drive off CA 299
Redding, California

VAN BOURG & NAKAMURA, SMART & CLABAUGH, ARCHITECTS

An almost totally flexible auditorium and convention center, capably handled in reinforced concrete. Everything from concerts to roller derbies to circuses can be efficiently housed, in addition to conventions and trade shows. Moreover the building is capable of simultaneously housing separate events. The exterior is forceful without exuding muscle, while the interior, though not resplendent, accommodates its multifunctions well.

Open during events

---

43   State Capitol (1861–74/1976–82)
Capitol Mall at 10th Street
Sacramento, California

MINER F. BUTLER, CHIEF ARCHITECT

There are numerous state capitols of greater architectural distinction, but none can match the arboreal majesty which envelops this substantial pile. Set in the 40-acre/16-hectare Capitol Park in the center of the city, this governmental enclave, now faced by a phalanx of state office buildings, luxuriates in the protection of an assortment of semitropical trees and flowering bushes. Moreover all buildings surrounding the park are limited to 75 feet/23 meters in height. Following a limited competition for the Capitol's design, work began on the excavations in 1860 but the cornerstone was not laid until the following year. The first occupants moved in during 1869 with final completion in 1874; later additions and changes took place, a six-story rear wing being added in 1954. In addition to Mr. Butler, who won the competition for the building, the following all played a role: Reuben Clark, Supervising Architect (1860–64); Gordon P. Cummings, Supervising Architect (1864–71); Krenitzer & Bennett (1871–72); and Gordon Cummings (1872–74).

In 1972 it was found by the State Architect that the Capitol would be unsafe even "in the event of a moderate earthquake." As a result, an almost complete reconstruction of the entire building was initiated (1976–82). Exterior walls have been heavily strengthened, all interior walls and floors have been removed and replaced, the roof structure has been retrussed, and the dome completely overhauled. The outside walls were stripped and wet-process shotcreted. Concrete flooring has been used instead of the original unreinforced brick arches,

wrought-iron beams, and wooden sleepers. Steel trusses and a new roof ensure stability. The copper covering of the dome has been replaced and will be left a natural verdigris instead of being painted (as it had been since 1893). The monumental cast-iron columns (40 feet/12 meters high, 4 feet/1.2 meters in diameter) and the ornament have been (or will be) restored. The decorative plaster, the painted designs, and the carved woodwork will be brought back to the 1900 period of the restoration—before the 1906–8 remodeling and "the overlays of modernization." A new museum will add to the substantial interest of the building itself. The project team for this enormous undertaking consists of John C. Worsley, architect and the owner's representative; Welton Becket Associates, architects; URS/John A. Blume & Associates, structural engineers; and on the Becket team Raymond Girvigian, historical consultant; Robert Mathews, project architect; Louis Naidorf, project designer; and Randall Myers, interior designer.

Guided tours from east entrance, Mon.–Fri. 10:30–1:30, except holidays

---

44 **Governor's Mansion** (1877–78)
16th and H Streets
Sacramento, California

NATHANIEL D. GOODELL, ARCHITECT

California abounds in a rich array of wooden Victorian houses—the state having come of age at that period—and although fires and earthquakes have taken their toll, many providentially remain. Among

the richest of the once maligned gingerbread school is this Italianate-Second-Empire-influenced former residence of the governor (but originally built for a local merchant). Almost all the clichés of its time can be found in its mélange of turrets, brackets, carvings, fish-scale shingles, and newel posts of passing magnificence. The interior commands a profusion of chandeliers and elaborate fireplaces but, having been the focus of attention of a series of governors' wives from 1903 to 1967, it lacks the consistent Victorian raffishness of the outside. The house now serves as a museum under the direction of the State Department of Parks and Recreation.

Open daily 10–5, except major holidays

---

45   City Hall and Exhibit Hall/Convention Center (1972–73)
Civic Plaza, 300 D Street
San Bernardino, California

GRUEN ASSOCIATES, ARCHITECTS

The selection of dark brown glass to envelop totally the municipal functions of a sunburned city is open to question; the results, however, are virile. The approach to the City Hall welcomes the visitor, with fountains along the way and with a spacious entry porch on pilotis. The overall form of the building is angled in profile and chamfered on the corners and edges to emphasize its tightly wrapped skin. And it is interesting to note that the module of the enclosing glass panels, three for windows and one for floor slab, is carried under the open entry as a soffit. Cesar Pelli, who was in charge of the design of the project, has long been known for imaginative use of glass, and its mercurial image properties are brought into full play in this "technological manifesto." The Convention Center is tucked under the City Hall, accounting for the latter's elevated position. The Council Chamber is at the rear of the main floor and can be entered directly. An open-air but covered garage is attached at the left with a convenient passageway to a department store. Dan M. Branigan was partner-in-charge.

Open during office hours

---

46 Mission San Diego de Alcalá (1808–13)
10818 San Diego Mission Road (E from city on IS 8 to IS 15, N on Mission Gorge Road, follow signs)
San Diego, California

The first of the California missions, thus California's earliest church, the mission seen today is, however, the fourth of its name and the third on this hillock. The redoubtable Father Junípero Serra founded San Diego de Alcalá in 1769 but it was relocated five years later to a site 6 miles/9.6 kilometers away for better farming conditions. This was burned by Indians the following year, and in 1776 construction of a larger church was commenced, only to have it almost destroyed by an earthquake in 1803. Another quake wreaked havoc so that when the present structure was completed in 1813 its "architects" had incorporated a series of heavy masonry buttresses for stability. In the 1840s San Diego de Alcalá, like the other missions in what was then Mexico, was secularized, and in mid-century was used for twelve years as a U.S. fort. Though returned to the Church in 1862, it was for decades in sad repair and in danger of totally disappearing—only half of the front remaining. After World War I its rebuilding was begun and the mission we see today was completely restored by 1931. It measures

150 feet/46 meters in length and 35 feet/11 meters in width. The church recently has been sparklingly renovated. The complex of church, patio, garden, mission school, and quarters gives a good impression of dedicated souls laboring in an agitated era.

Open daily 9–5, except Dec. 25: admission

47　**Hotel del Coronado** (1887–88)
1500 Orange Avenue
San Diego (Coronado), California

REID & REID, ARCHITECTS

This *grande dame* of resort hotels, one of the few remaining of its Queen Anne genus, still holds sway with almost regal assertiveness. Turrets and balconies embellish this behemoth of wood, along with a reputed 2 million shingles (nailed down by x hundred Chinese carpenters), while its interiors, especially the monumental 1,000-seat dining

room and the bars, are of a quality that any seaside resort today could envy. The hotel was planned, largely by James W. Reid, about a large court (150 x 250 feet/46 x 76 meters) filled with a "garden of tropical trees, shrubs and flowers," with its public rooms overlooking the ocean and bay. Its 399 guest rooms, now all with bath, originally had a fireplace each plus a wall safe. (Steam heat was installed in 1897.) Moreover they were—as was the rest of the hotel—illuminated by both electricity (the first hotel so supplied in the country: installed by Edison himself) and gas, this latter never needed. Although several of the public rooms have been changed through the years (notably— rather not notably—the Grand Ballroom), the oak-lined lobby with its wonderful elevators, the sugar pine dining room, and the bars remain substantially as built, and all beautifully maintained. Some 30,000 sprinkler heads were put in in 1916. The hotel's centennial is not too far off: may it hold sway over the Pacific well into its second century. Coronado/San Diego needs a structure of quality such as this, as a look up and down the strand at present-day buildings will confirm. Shingle-Queen Anne-Eastlake: architectural divertissement of a high order.

48   San Diego Stadium (1966–67)
Mission Valley, intersection IS 15 with IS 8 (US 80)
San Diego, California

FRANK L. HOPE & ASSOCIATES, ARCHITECTS AND ENGINEERS

The architects of the San Diego Stadium have taken its three facilities
for vertical circulation and made of them sculptural elements embracing
the modified horseshoe shape of the stadium itself. These comprise the
four cylinders of elevators for top-level seats (and for use by the handicapped), eight double-decked, high-speed escalators (reversible for up
and/or down use), and six spiral ramps (which can double for cart
servicing of the concession stands. Circulation and seating, service and
the served, are clearly stated entities. Moreover they are structurally
independent, hence could be built separately. The "illumination ring"
was then elevated above the arena by an extension of the main structure, making night-lighting a closely coordinated element of the design,
not a tacked-on afterthought. The resulting play of stadium horizontals

versus its verticals—both engineered with commendable refinement—
is dynamic, while the open space between stadium top and the elevated
lighting band gives an added three-dimensional fillip. Designed for
both football and baseball, the stadium seats 50,000 with armchair
comfort and excellent sight lines, with 5,000 seats, on groups of
rubber-tired dollies, movable for optimum visibility according to the
sport. The five banks of seats, the upper ones cantilevered and
columnless, are color-coded. Construction is of concrete, much of it
precast and prestressed on the site. Parking lots for 15,000 automobiles and 250 buses surround the field on all sides. There is even landscaping within the compound. Imaginative in concept, pared to bon-
iness (except in the ramps), economic in construction, and properly
served by its periphery of parking, this might well be the finest stadium
in the country. Frank L. Hope, Jr., was principal-in-charge of architecture, Charles B. Hope of engineering, R. Gary Allen project designer, and Ernest R. Lord project architect.

Open during events

---

49   Victorian Houses (largely 1860–1910)
San Francisco, California

No city this side of Bucharest has a more engaging collection of late-
nineteenth-/early-twentieth-century wooden houses than San Francisco.
Almost every residential district has its rewards but there is a rich
concentration in the hilly section vaguely delimited by Alta Plaza,
Lafayette Park, Jefferson Square, and Alamo Square, with Scott,
Steiner, Laguna, and California among the richer streets. The rise of
San Francisco as a city began with the gold rush of 1849, although at
first the prospect of wealth-for-the-panning almost emptied the streets,
stores, and ships of every able-bodied man. Gold, however, did bring
almost endless vessels through the Golden Gate, and thus laid the beginning of the city's continued position as shipping and banking capital
of the West Coast. The Victorian-Queen Anne-Eastlake period in domestic architecture was coming into its greatest popularity contemporaneous with this population growth, plus often sudden and vast
wealth. The heavily monied families built—with notable ostentation—
on Nob and other assorted hills, but almost all of these mansions are
unfortunately gone, many in the earthquake and fire of 1906. But even
the cheek-by-cheek modest houses, which were out of range of the fire,

express a frothy exuberance along the streets which prance over the city's hills and unfold breathtaking views. And it is as streets, not individual houses, that they most impress. Many of these dwellings are in sound structural shape (often they were built of durable—and then cheaply available—redwood), and though their plumbing and wiring may be questionable, the fashion for buying and rehabilitating them today woos an increasing number of smart house-hunters. There are reputedly over thirteen thousand surviving Victorian houses of merit: one firm alone has made over five hundred restorations. Their palette of carpenter Gothic covers a jaunty spectrum, and if the overall falters, most will indulge in rampant details. The bay window may not have been invented in this city—it has been around since sequestered ladies looked up and down the Euphrates—but the San Francisco Bay-bay vernacular represents its golden days. (Reputedly, nine out of ten houses of this period have them.) Those seeking more details will find a highly useful guide to the city's architectural heritage entitled *Here Today* published by Chronicle Books, 1968, under the aegis of the Junior League of San Francisco. It also carries an excellent inventory. The San Francisco Convention and Visitors Bureau, 1390 Market Street, issues a useful "Victorian House Tour" map.

Visible from street only

NOTE: See the following description of the Haas-Lilienthal House.

---

50   **Haas-Lilienthal House** (1886)
2007 Franklin Street
San Francisco, California

PETER R. SCHMIDT, ARCHITECT

An outstanding example of the Queen Anne Style, a house which escaped the 1906 earthquake and fire virtually intact. Perhaps even more remarkable, its all-redwood construction has withstood man-created depredations for the seventy-five years since nature revolted. Its wondrously gabled, turreted, and bracketed exterior—a veritable catalog Queen Anne—sports mandatory stylistic asymmetry and projected window bays, the bay on the corner topped by a round shingled tower whose conical roof vanishes in a series of diminishing nubbles. The interior, its ground-floor rooms sensibly connected by sliding doors in

the fashion of the day, was modified at the turn of the century and though more subdued than the outside still merits a look. The house was generously donated by the Haas-Lilienthal heirs to The Foundation for San Francisco's Architectural Heritage: it may well be the finest example of its style in the United States which is open to the public.

Open Wed. 12–4, Sun. 11–4:30: admission

---

51   Palace of Fine Arts (1913–15/rebuilt 1965–67)
Bay at Lyon Street
San Francisco, California

BERNARD R. MAYBECK, ARCHITECT

Maybeck (1862–1957) was at heart a romantic eclectic, and though his Beaux-Arts training in Paris had given him a Classic-inspired base, he generally essayed a more organic idiom, as in his houses and his

Christian Science Church at Berkeley (q.v.). For the Roman pomp of the Panama-Pacific International Exposition of 1915, however, nothing would do but back to the forum—with Piranesi standing in the wings. For this he created an intoxicatingly rich octagonal temple and colonnade with an arc-shaped gallery—for the art of the nations of the world—directly behind. The sketch for this thrilled the fair's commissioners, as the building did all. The Palace of Fine Arts indeed became so popular that when the fair was over (December 1915) and the buildings ready to be demolished, some 33,000 visitors begged for its preservation. The trouble was that the "temple" was made for short-term use, having a wood frame encased with plaster of Paris and hemp fiber in a mixture called "staff." The gallery and rotunda, however, were spared, and as they gradually crumbled—as Maybeck once wished —the place became increasingly dear to San Franciscans. Bond issues to save it were put up but agonizingly defeated when, in 1959, Walter S. Johnson, a generous local executive and philanthropist, offered $2

million toward its reconstruction in permanent materials. (Mr. Johnson eventually gave close to $4 million for the project.) This munificence sparked both city and state. Under the direction of William G. Merchant, and, after his death, of Hans U. Gerson—both former Maybeck partners—aided by Welton Becket & Associates, architectural work was begun to rebuild it from the ground up for the ages. The Palace of Fine' Arts, in particular the rotunda and colonnade, can be said to epitomize and terminate Roman opulence in architecture in the U.S.A., a style which had been launched so successfully (but as some say with disastrous results) at an earlier fair, Chicago's Columbian Exposition of 1893. San Francisco's lovingly restored rotunda now rests in Walter S. Johnson Park. Behind it—screened by the spatial intermedium of the colonnade—stands the arced gallery building, which once housed the exhibits of the nations. This large economy building is today filled with highly provocative exhibits of the Exploratorium plus the 1,003-seat Palace of Fine Arts Theater. The 5-acre/2-hectare gallery was divided for the fair into 120 separate exhibition rooms. Having a sturdy steel frame it survived the years (once serving· for indoor tennis courts), and its structure was used in the recent remodeling.

Grounds open daily, Exploratorium open Wed.–Sun. 1–5, Wed. 7–9 P.M.; *Palace of Fine Arts Theater open for cultural events*

---

52   Hallidie Building (1917–18)
130 Sutter Street
San Francisco, California

WILLIS POLK, ARCHITECT

One of the most remarkably advanced buildings of its time, the seven-story Hallidie still stands as a monument to the use of boldly scaled glass. Its facade is *all* glass with the exception of four fanciful bands of superimposed cast-iron decoration and fire escapes. The structure of the building—the concrete columns and girders across the front—is set back 3.3 feet/100 centimeters from the glass wall. Triangular brackets support the thin floor slab next to the glass, the slab increasing in thickness behind the midpoint of the columns. Onto the outer edge of these floor slabs (at every third horizontal mullion) is affixed a mullion which carries the glass. The "curtain wall" was widely

heralded in the 1950s as a new method of construction, the skin being conveniently independent of the bones. However, Willis Polk, almost forty years before, had pioneered the all-glass facade in this country with results that still command the utmost admiration. (There are other curtain-wall antecedents, of course, from Paxton's Crystal Palace, 1851, to Gropius' and Adolf Meyer's Fagus Factory of 1911 and Gropius' Bauhaus of 1925–26.) Wisely the Hallidie Building was declared an Official Landmark by the city's Board of Supervisors in 1971, against the will of the owners. It was the first so designated because of its architectural, as opposed to its historic, significance. The building was sold in 1975 and very carefully restored to its original condition the following year by Kaplan/McLaughlin/Diaz, so that we can once again enjoy this blistering wall of glass, side to side and top to bottom, its admirable speculum set off by festooned nostalgia.

Open during business hours

---

53 Ghirardelli Square Redevelopment (1864–1915/1964)
The Cannery Remodeling (c. 1895/1969)
The Ice House Rehabilitation (1914/1969)
San Francisco, California

Some of the greatest heights of architecture in San Francisco—and the
most pertinent urban and architectural lessons—are not to be found in
the city's new buildings, fine though they may be. They are to be seen
in the revitalization of the old. Until recently our aged structures were
frowned upon as superfluous, non-productive nuisances to be bulldozed as soon as possible. But as San Francisco—and others—have
discovered, much that is old, including such improbable structures as
ancient warehouses, can be transformed into economically viable urban
entities. The Greater San Francisco Chamber of Commerce made a
survey (with federal help) of its aged commercial buildings to deter-
mine their soundness for rehabilitation, a move most cities could with
profit emulate. There are three such projects of note in the city and all
have something to offer:

Ghirardelli Square Redevelopment, North Point, Larkin, Beach, and
Polk Streets. Wurster, Bernardi & Emmons, architects; Lawrence
Halprin & Associates, urban design and landscape architects; graphics
by Barbara Stauffacher. (Open daily and evenings—get Visitors' Map.)
The architects for this, the oldest, largest (and still most successful)
redevelopment—a private undertaking—had as their base the 1915
four-story Ghirardelli ex-chocolate factory (designed by William
Mooser—note the tower), plus a half-dozen other nondescript warehouses, loft structures, and a small apartment house. They then
added a number of suave, low-keyed, and amusing shops, sparked its
center with a fountain (by Ruth Asawa), provided terraces of imaginative planting, developed a series of strolling spaces, put in cheerful
lighting, excavated a three-hundred-car underground garage, and came
up with an engaging, non-regimented center, flowing with spatial and
visual pleasures. Transparency and opaqueness, confined and open,
the near and the far—plus fun throughout—are all there, leading to
shopping and dining and spending. Ghirardelli may seem casual and
relaxed, but there is profound organization behind it, most of it
dependent on clever manipulation of existing space. San Francisco has
always been a city favored by the flaneur, and here enticements to the
stroller reach a level matched only by the famous Tivoli in Copen-

hagen. Moreover it is even more alive by night than by day, so thoroughly has the philosophy of urban development/redevelopment and extended hour-usage been understood. Cities of the world, unite in saving your heritage even if it be gumdrop (or chocolate) factories. The late William Wilson Wurster was architect-in-charge.

The Cannery Remodeling, 2801 Leavenworth Street between Beach and Jefferson streets, near Fisherman's Wharf. Joseph Esherick & Associates, architects; Thomas Church, landscape architect. (Open daily and evenings.) The Cannery, a three-story brick block once owned by Del Monte, presented a different rehabilitation problem from those encountered at the spread-out Ghirardelli, chief among them being how to get people into a nondescript building and up the stairs where two thirds of the shops had to be located. This is an inner-facing problem but with the need to express exterior come-on, especially that of upper-level temptations. First off, the aged brick walls were sandblasted

to their original richness and minor changes made (such as the gable ends of the old roof). Arcades were placed on the upper floors and a smartly designed courtyard was added as the chief street magnet, luring the customers into a half-open, half-closed "patio" where one finds oneself soon seduced and surrounded by tempting shops, boutiques, bars, and restaurants. So that the news of the existence of the upper floors will be telegraphed to those at ground level and onto the sidewalk, a glass-enclosed exterior elevator was prominently placed for all to see, its movement and lights adding to the festivities. An escalator and a broad stair reinforce the upward emphasis. The proliferation of low arches in the new ties to the old. The interior somewhat resembles the souks of Aleppo in its clublike intimacy, but it is full of skillful imagination, particularly considering its humble origin. Peter Dodge was project architect. The firm is now known as Esherick Homsey Dodge & Davis.

The Ice House Rehabilitation, Union Street at Ice House Alley. Wurster, Bernardi & Emmons, architects; Lawrence Halprin & Associates, landscape architects. (Open during business hours.) The Ice House—rather Ice Houses, for they are two separate buildings now connected by an all-glass link—posed entirely different problems from Ghirardelli and The Cannery, which underscores the flexibility of utilizing structurally sound old buildings. As opposed to shopping and

wining-dining, these two sizable ice-manufacturing and cold storage facilities are now used as showrooms for the contract furniture and home furnishings trades. The exteriors were simply sandblasted, a few windows added, and the interiors redone mechanically and subdivided as needed, with, as mentioned, a five-level glass "bridge" connecting the two and emphasizing their native brick quality.

Open as indicated above

---

54 Four Fifty Sutter Building (1928–29)
450 Sutter Street
San Francisco, California

TIMOTHY L. PFLUEGER, ARCHITECT

Four Fifty Sutter is probably the most sophisticated skyscraper of the Art Deco period, a twenty-six-floor building full of elegance and subtleties. The exterior (above the seventh floor) emphasizes via its

chamfered corners that the building is not solely a facade on Sutter
Street but one which wraps around three sides. Note, too, the slight
suggestion of the San Francisco bay window in the fenestration. The
gilded entry with its incised tile extends a lively if compacted welcome.
The lobby more than lives up to the promise of the exterior with a corbeled ceiling, highlighted with touches of gold and silvered elevator
doors, all with rich Mesoamerican motifs. Dark marble walls furnish
the background. The building, moreover, was one of the very first with
an in-house garage, here holding 450 cars. A complete modernization
and upgrading was carried out in 1978–79. From its beginning the
building has been directed to the medical and dental professions.

Open during business hours

55 Golden Gate Bridge (1933–37)
US 101 above the Golden Gate
San Francisco, California

JOSEPH B. STRAUSS, CHIEF ENGINEER: OTHMAR B. AMMANN, LEON S. MOISSEIFF, CHARLES DERLETH, JR., CONSULTANTS

The space experience of traversing the Golden Gate Bridge—especially in a car with the top down (if such can be found)—ranks supreme among bridge-crossings, or any other form of highway exhilaration. Much of this is due to its incomparable setting: the unsullied nature of the winding southbound approach, the intervening hills that permit only snatches of the top-rigging, the capricious veilings by wisps of fog, then the personal confrontation with those mammoth red pylons and their skein of yard-thick cables, the whole transformed from a study in statics into sculpture at 50 mph/80 kph. The George Washington Bridge (1927–31), the Bronx-Whitestone (1937–39), and later the longest span of all, the Verrazano-Narrows (completed 1964) (q.v.,

all in New York)—for all three of which the Swiss-born Othmar Ammann was designer or consultant—are inspired spans, but none carries the sheer intoxication of the Golden Gate and its approaches. Its 4,200 feet/1,280 meters suspension length when completed in 1937 was the longest in the world until 1964 when the Verrazano surpassed it by 60 feet/18 meters. (The Golden Gate Bridge is now second-longest.) Its two steel-plate pylons, 32 x 53 feet/9.7 x 16 meters and slightly stepped back in stages as they rise, are braced horizontally at four spots above the decking, topping off at 746 feet/227 meters above the bay. One of the chief problems in the bridge's erection was the building of the south (San Francisco side) pier in swirling water 85 feet/26 meters deep and over 1,100 feet/335 meters from land. Moreover the bridge, both in construction and after completion, was and is exposed to full blasts from the Pacific, and is often fog-shrouded, while the earthquake belt that has notably tossed the city is only a half-dozen miles (10 kilometers) away. Fortunately the bridge has serenely weathered everything that nature and sometimes man (via ships) has been able to throw against it. It can be crossed on foot or bicycle as well as automobile. One of the greatest sights.

Always open

---

56   140 Maiden Lane (1948–49)
San Francisco, California

FRANK LLOYD WRIGHT, ARCHITECT

Frank Lloyd Wright's career with the helix started with his love for the chambered nautilus. Its architectural manifestation began with his never-built planetarium for Sugar Loaf Mountain (1925) near Frederick, Maryland, sprang from the desert in his Arizona house (1952) for his son David, took off with this fetching bit (until 1968 the V. C. Morris shop), and reached a climax in his Guggenheim Museum in New York (q.v.)—for which this shop/gallery was a miniature prototype. The stimulus of its spaces as one winds up and down its spiral ramp makes the second floor both an attractive prospect and rewarding reality (particularly for its original gift shop client). The circle framed by the ramp—which almost fills the width of the building—is echoed by a two-thirds circle offset at left rear. On both floors services fill the back sections. The ceiling, recently restored to past glories, is composed of a galaxy of plastic circles and half domes—a "female ceiling,"

writes Vincent Scully, surveying its mastoidal forms—from which pours a flood of both natural and artificial light. (The skylight is the only source of daylight.) The solid wall of the facade is of meticulously laid Roman brick. Most merchants would, of course, have insisted on plate glass. Its radiating arch recalls Louis Sullivan's well-known Transportation Building of the Chicago Fair of 1893 with, of course, an entry taken almost straight from H. H. Richardson's Glessner House of 1887. We are enticed into this enigma and giddily treated for our excursion.

Open during business hours

---

57 **Alcoa Building** (1965–67)
1 Maritime Plaza (Washington, Battery, Clay, and Sansome Streets)
San Francisco, California

SKIDMORE, OWINGS & MERRILL, ARCHITECTS AND ENGINEERS

The San Francisco skyscrapers are not as exploratory as those in Chicago nor as assured as those in New York. Several are provocative in parts, especially as regards plazas and landscaping. Several are also

successful in blocking views of the bay. Among the provocative is the Alcoa Building, a 24-story skyscraper which is best observed from the plaza atop its 2-story podium-garage (by Wurster, Bernardi & Emmons). It was designed as a major unit in the 20-acre/8-hectare Golden Gateway Center. Alcoa's most striking feature is, of course, its exo-skeletal structure (used even more dashingly several years later in SOM's 110-story John Hancock Building in Chicago, q.v.). This outside, diagonally braced frame evolved—primarily—from the city's severe seismic conditions. Its twelve X-braced perimeter columns (aluminum-clad over fireproofed welded steel), with vertical tension hangers and inner service core supporting the floors, provide a column-free interior. The resulting exterior scale, while not chivalrous to neighbors, is compelling on the city-scape. But impressive as the structure and its concept be, the prime reward for the building's users and visitors is the almost private plaza on which the building—in aloof fashion—rests. This elevated sculpture "garden" (reached by escalators and stairs), though rigid in its symmetrical plan, possesses some satisfactory spaces and a number of superb works of art. Highlighting this outdoor museum is a hemispheric fountain by Australian Robert Woodward, plus sculpture by Marini, Henry Moore, Charles Perry, and a number of others, to produce one of the most civilized commercial forecourts to be encountered. On the plaza level one also intimately confronts the exoskeleton.

Building open during business hours, plaza daily

58 Bank of America (1968–71)
California and Pine Streets between Montgomery and Kearny
San Francisco, California

WURSTER, BERNARDI AND EMMONS WITH SKIDMORE, OWINGS & MERRILL, ARCHITECTS

Individuality with civility is a rare accomplishment in skyscraper design, but the associated architects—with Pietro Belluschi as consultant—have come up with a dignified yet svelte fifty-two-story tower for the largest bank in the U.S.A. Its personality derives primarily from the unusual angled bays which frame all four sides—and taunt the sun throughout the day—and from the unusual setbacks near the top. Its point of greatest design achievement can be seen in its plaza off steeply sloping California Street, with the Plaza terminated by the low, projecting banking wing on the corner of California and Montgomery. This wing forms a separate but attached square adjunct to the main building, with the whole topped by a boldly structured roof. (The plaza, unfortunately, is in shadow much of the day.) The serrated facades of the skyscraper recall, of course, the famous bay windows which enlighten so much of San Francisco. Note that the single-pane windows are flush with the granite facing, and that the mechanical floors (for air-conditioning machinery, etc.) on the fifteenth and thirty-seventh levels have their greater height prominently framed to lend a keener scale. As one walks around the building the geometric interaction of glass and stone provokes a changing checkerboard. The dark red granite was chosen to lessen the building's apparent size. Garage facilities are underground. Detailing throughout is immaculate. Lawrence Halprin and Associates were the landscape architects; Masayuki Nagare did the plaza sculpture.

Open during business hours

NOTE: Fine as it is as a building, the bank's height and mass are considered intrusive in its neighborhood: subsequent zoning standards rule out more of its size anywhere in the city. The present height limit is 700 feet/213 meters versus 778 feet/237 meters for the bank.

---

59   Student Union (1974–75)
San Francisco State University
Center of campus: W off 19th Avenue via Holloway Avenue
San Francisco, California

PAFFARD KEATINGE CLAY, ARCHITECTS

A madcap building, one perhaps overly concerned with architecture as sculpture, but one jumping with imagination. The exterior is dominated by two shiplike prows poking the clouds, with the stepped

roof at right doubling as a dramatic open-air amphitheater and sunning spot. The angled interaction of the building's geometry sets up spatial tensions as one walks around it. The interior, of necessity, lacks the élan of the outside, and it is also without some of the amenities expected in a student union (adequate assembly room for one); moreover some areas are compromised by the jostling of angles. However, and most importantly, it creates a tempting series of spaces to be explored or to which one can retreat. The Union, in spite of a few shortcomings, adds an enthusiastic note to a mundane campus. It celebrates the student at a college where at times the student did not feel he was being celebrated. It provides him/her with spaces of his/her own, both public and private, and almost literally its architecture flings out a banner of welcome.

Open Mon.–Fri. 7 A.M.*–10* P.M.*, Sat. 10–4*

---

60   Mission San Gabriel Arcángel (1792–1805)
314 Mission Drive at Junípero Serra Drive
San Gabriel, California

Originally the mission was the only edifice in the rolling verdant countryside, and its semifortified appearance was no accident. (Indian attacks on two other missions had already occurred.) Influenced—as all

references point out—by the Spanish-Moorish architecture which Father Antonio Cruzado, the mission's chief designer, had remembered in Spain, the building carries a personality of its own. Today, after earthquakes and nineteenth-century neglect, San Gabriel is romantically impressive, particularly the unusual capped buttresses sustaining the lateral walls and the once vaulted roof (rebuilt in wood after the quake of 1804). In 1908 the Claretian Fathers took over the mission and began restoration, a process which still continues. The foundations of the ancillary buildings around the garden patio were unearthed in 1930. The interior lacks unity, being almost surfeited with decorations and paintings. In its prime the mission was one of the largest wine and brandy producers in California.

Open daily 9:30–4:30, except Thanksgiving and Dec. 25

---

61 San Juan Capistrano Mission (1776–1806)
Three blocks W of IS 5 on CA 74 and Ortega Highway
San Juan Capistrano, California

The stone main church at San Juan was dedicated in 1806 but lasted only six years before an earthquake shattered most of its walls except the transept and sanctuary. Much of the rest of the mission, once the

largest in California, was also flattened. The swallows have made good use of these ruins ever since. However, the adjacent adobe chapel, founded by Father Junípero Serra in 1776 and completed the following year survived in reasonable condition. It is reputedly the oldest building still standing in the state. Its original length of 63 feet/19 meters was extended to 162 feet/49 meters in 1784. The chapel's narrow width (17 feet/5.2 meters) was dictated by the length of beams and rafters available—and portable—for framing the roof. Though the main church had been destroyed, the mission continued until secularization in 1834, and in 1845 all except the ruined church and Serra Chapel were sold at auction. Even then the chapel encountered a parlous life, being, among other things, used for storing hay. Efforts were made to spruce up the mission in the late 1890s, but it was not until the 1920s that major restoration was commenced. It was at this time (1922–24) that the rich reredos or *retablo* was installed (with some pruning) in the chapel; it is a three-hundred-year-old Baroque work from Barcelona that had earlier been sent to grace the cathedral in Los Angeles but was never used. The Junípero Serra Chapel, the towering ruins of the stone church with its great sanctuary arch, and the semirestored cloister (part of which now houses a museum) make this one of California's most evocative settings.

Open daily 7 A.M.*–5* P.M.*: admission*

62   **Huntington Library** (1919–20), **Art Gallery** (1909–11), **and**
       Botanical Garden (1904–   )
       1151 Oxford Road
       San Marino, California

MYRON HUNT AND ELMER GREY, ARCHITECTS; WILLIAM
HERTRICH, LANDSCAPE GARDENER

Henry Edwards Huntington (1850–1927) amassed an enormous fortune, primarily in railroading, and before he died he bequeathed a large
share of his wealth to establishing this Research Library, Art Gallery,
and Botanical Garden. He had determined to "give something to the
public" as early as 1906 and reinforced this in 1919 by setting up a
Board of Trustees who founded the Library and Gallery as a "research, educational, and cultural center." Generosity was matched by
both Mr. and Mrs. Huntington's noted connoisseurship. Mrs. Huntington was responsible for the interest in collecting art: Mr. Huntington
has been called "the greatest figure in the history of American book-
collecting." Their house (now the Art Gallery), the separate Library
building (with one of the world's great collections), and the 207
acres/84 hectares of almost unbelievable gardens provide us with possibly the most sumptuous and certainly the most eruditely endowed estate in the United States. The Newport *palazzi* were exercises in architectural one-upmanship wherein studied opulence was the generator.
Mr. Huntington, on the other hand, sought a landscaped setting of
great beauty and placed his substantial, but not ornate, dwelling amid
it with views unfolding as the site drops down the San Gabriel Valley
thence to the distant Pacific. The house, however, does not fully partake of its setting other than via a somewhat lonely terrace in front.
   Though both dwelling-gallery and library are more than competent
buildings, particularly on the interior, it is the carefully zoned series of
a dozen gardens with "more than 9,000 different kinds of plants"
which provides the greatest rewards. The site, which Mr. Huntington
purchased in 1903, had been a working ranch and orchard. Having
since then been carefully planted and scrupulously tended, the extraordinary variety of trees, plants, and flowers have matured into one of our
greatest horticultural experiences. (Self-guided tour booklets are available.) The Japanese Garden, on the site of a gorge, is outstanding
both for its planting and its "furniture," while its Zen Garden (1968)
is one of the closest approximations of a Japanese temple garden

which one will experience on these shores. The Japanese House came, in part, from Japan and dates from the late nineteenth century. The Desert Garden is also notable: its 12 acres/4.8 hectares contain 2,500 species. Mr. Hertrich, who came on the scene as landscape gardener in 1904, retired in 1949 but served as adviser until his death in 1966.

The architectural specialist will also want to see the mausoleum (1928) in the garden .5 mile/.8 kilometer north of the Library. Designed by John Russell Pope, it served as a semiprototype for Mr. Pope's Jefferson Memorial in Washington (q.v.) of a decade later.

Open Tues.–Sat. 1–4:30, Sun. 12–4:30, except holidays and month of Oct.; advance reservations needed on Sun.

63   College of San Mateo (1967–68)
off CA 92 (19th Avenue) at West Hillside Boulevard, E of IS 280
San Mateo, California

JOHN CARL WARNECKE & ASSOCIATES, ARCHITECTS

A spread-out, formal grouping of college buildings on the hills west of
and overlooking San Mateo and San Francisco Bay. Though somewhat
rigid in its intersecting mall layout—the site-plan actually is reminiscent of Colonial Williamsburg, Virginia (q.v.)—the mutual building
relationships are easy, abetted by informal landscaping. Automobiles
are parked in tree-divided lots on the lower periphery, with a service
road belting the campus. Designed as the first stage (four thousand

students) in the junior college program, the campus will eventually double in size. The architectural module, based on a constant 16-foot/4.9-meter bay for all buildings and the colonnade, tends to the dry side but lends cohesion at the price of piquancy. The theater is placed so that it can also easily serve the community. Landscaping was by Michael Painter of the Warnecke firm.

Campus open during school year

64 Hillsdale High School (1955–56)
Del Monte Street between 31st Avenue and Hillsdale Boulevard
San Mateo, California

JOHN LYON REID & PARTNERS, ARCHITECTS

Hillsdale was a bold, unorthodox—but prophetic—school when it opened. Now, a generation later, it is still impressive. Taking advantage of the gently sloping site, the architects placed the large block of general classrooms at the upper end and developed a sizable court in the center. A three-hundred-seat theater (near entry) and cafeteria close one side of this open space, with workshops on the other, while two top-lit gymnasia and an auditorium seating one thousand align across the bottom. Covered galleries provide weatherproof open-air circulation and also help knit the complex together. Though all units are of one story, the gym-auditorium end is, of course, higher, helping —with the change in grade—to develop a well-scaled rhythm along the 720-foot/219-meter total length.

The most unusual aspect of the school, and one which has been influential in subsequent educational plants throughout the country, lies in the classroom concept whose "loft plan" embraces all general instructional rooms under two almost square, mammoth roofs which are separated by an atrium circulation area. Though all but peripheral classrooms are windowless they are each illuminated by four 6-foot/1.8-meter-square, prefabricated skylights which are finned to admit only north and low south light. The resulting "industrial space," 12 feet/3.6 meters high with a structural module of 28 feet/8.5 meters, can be readily changed by relocating its movable partitions. Questions will of course arise as to the advantages of having a series of classrooms where students cannot see out, but such rooms have wall surface flexibility in themselves and establish a variety of spatial experiences intra alia. Most of the 1,750 students spend three fifty-minute periods in them. Touches of color and, outside, good planting are accents. Burton Rockwell was partner-in-charge; Alexander G. Tarics the structural engineer—note the strongly expressed earthquake bracing on the gym-auditorium end.

Grounds open during school hours

---

65   Mission San Miguel Arcángel (1816–18)
Mission Street (E off CA 101)
San Miguel, California

Founded (1797) as the sixteenth mission, and located almost exactly halfway between Los Angeles and San Francisco in the fertile Salinas Valley—its springtime almond blossoms are famous—San Miguel is

noted chiefly for its mural decorations, above all those on the sanctuary wall. These frescoes were carried out in 1821 by Estéven Munras,
a Catalan artist, who with his capable Indian helpers stenciled and
painted most of the interior. The architectural "motifs" along the side
walls and the folk-art pulpit with sounding board at right are also
good.

In the sanctuary, above the Spanish-carved statue of San Miguel,
note the all-seeing eye of God set in a symbolic triangle; it signifies the
concern of the Lord for mankind. (The eye also appears on the ob-
verse of the Great Seal of the United States—and on the dollar bill.)
Unbelievably, this interior and its art have come down unsullied by nature or man, for after secularization (1836) the premises were used at
one time as a saloon and dance hall with shops adjacent. Most of the
other buildings at the mission were ill-treated, so that some restoration
was begun as early as the 1880s (the church was reactivated in 1878)

with subsequent repairs beginning in 1901. When the mission was returned to the Franciscans in 1928, complete restoration was undertaken, including the cleverly camouflaged insertion of steel beams in
the ceiling to bolster the termite-prone wooden ones. The church
measures 144 feet/44 meters long by 27 feet/8.2 meters wide with
adobe walls 5.7 feet/1.7 meters thick. The unusual arcade across the
front—note the irregularity of the arches—was a welcome feature in
this particulary hot part of the state. The fountain in front dates from
the restoration; the cannon in the arcade was made in Spain in 1697.
The mission now serves as parish church and its facilities are used for
marriages, retreats, *cursillos,* etc.

Mission open daily 10–5; Mission Museum closed major holidays:
donation

---

66   Marin County Civic Center (1959–62/1967–69)
E off US 101 on San Pedro Road, c. 1.5 miles/2.4 kilometers N of San Rafael, California

FRANK LLOYD WRIGHT AND TALIESIN ASSOCIATES, ARCHITECTS

Striding across the landscape like the Pont du Gard, the famous
Roman aqueduct (19 B.C.) in the South of France, with its tiers of
arches (here oblate) marching over hill and dale, the Marin County
Center is the most spectacular civic building in the country. (The Pont
du Gard is prominently shown in FLW's last—and much recommended—book, *Architecture, Man in Possession of His Earth,* Doubleday, 1962.) Mr. Wright's noted solicitude for the landscape has
produced an intimacy between structure and site which fascinates,
the uniform-ridged building increasing its depth in the valleys and
cutting it on the rises, to reflect the waves of topography (both natural
and artificial). The straight "keels" of the roof seem to slash across
the rolling hills of the backdrop. Three "tunnels" for automotive
traffic pierce its base, adding to its spatial passion. The arch over
these roadways is then repeated (with slightly less radius) on the
first or main floor, where its curves leap in series from one end of
the building to the other, shielding as they go a continuous balcony on
each side. (This "outrigging" is suspended from the cantilevered floor
slab.) The second floor is screened by similar arches, but each a third
the span of that below (and again of less radius); the top floor is

marked by a continuous series of circles, two circles for each arc below, and, like the floors beneath, with balconies running along the outside. (The arch springpoints form 60° triangles.) The eave is edged with open half circles, with its prominently haunched blue roof rising behind, itself decorated with circular patterns around its perimeter. A 217-foot/66-meter pylon (with boiler stack inside) punctuates the midpoint of the two arms. Altogether the exterior of the Marin Center is a sight of almost nacreous splendor with its shell-colored walls, blue roof, and pink and gold accents. However, as there is no structural expression in its series of metal-lath-and-stucco bowed and circular "arcades"—this would of course impinge on their rhythm—a slight impression of impermanence results; from some angles they seem thin and temporary. It should be added that the building acts somewhat as a conduit, with little invitation to enter—or even to establish the front door.

The plan concept of the building is based on a long, central, sky-lit corridor lined on both sides with various offices, flexibly partitioned. (The first unit was the 570-foot/174-meter-long administration building: the second—by Taliesin Associates—the 800-foot/244-meter-long Hall of Justice.) A near-continuous acrylic skylight runs most of the length of each wing, sending floods of ever changing sunshine into the balconied corridors below. The upper passageways are narrower than the lower (reflecting their decreased traffic load), hence the open "mall," being wider as it rises, permits maximum sun and light to probe the floors below and to nourish its garden which sprouts richly upward. The space and light of this central spine are architecturally unforgettable.

From the entrance level (a short utility floor) one takes an escalator or elevator to "finances" on the main floor (taxes, auditing, etc.), then to administration, public works, etc., on the second floor, with other departments on the top floor together with the near-circular library under the central dome. All civic functions are placed in this wing, the first to be built, with the courtrooms and Hall of Justice in the new. (The drawings for the first section of the building had been completed just before Mr. Wright's death in 1959. An extensive complex for other municipal functions has been built, including a community theater and two-thousand-seat Veteran's Memorial Auditorium in 1972.)

There are *Arabian Nights,* dreamworld overtones in the Marin County Civic Center—Mr. Wright had planned (1957–58) a large cultural center for Baghdad, Iraq, topped by an abstraction of Aladdin's lamp—and some of the Civic Center's festooned features will not enthrall everyone. But take a look: it is totally extraordinary. William

Wesley Peters of Taliesin Associates was in charge of completing the first stage of the Center and of designing the rest. Aaron G. Green was associate architect.

Sections open during office hours

---

67   San Simeon (1919–47)
on CA 1
San Simeon, California

JULIA MORGAN, ARCHITECT

San Simeon was named for the bay it fronts with little or no relation to Genesis 29:33. William Randolph Hearst himself called his beloved retreat *La Cuesta Encantada,* changing Camp Hill, which had earlier been its prosaic but descriptive designation, to the Enchanted Hill. San Simeon is not so much a unitary house as an incredible collection of elements, most of them of startling quality. This glorious *palacio*— here its parts almost greater than the whole—stands as the crowning refuge of perhaps the last of the prodigal spenders. Besides building his castle, Mr. Hearst spent very considerable sums on embellishing it with works of art. (There is, however, no truth in the rumor that a million dollars a year for fifty years was spent on the art—or that any of it is still stored in warehouses.) Designed—perhaps fitted together would be more accurate—by the noted Julia Morgan (the first woman to enter Paris' École des Beaux-Arts and the first registered female architect in California), the Hearst San Simeon State Historical Monument merits more than a casual look, for one must savor, not skim, its unbelievable richness. (There are several separate tours; all are recommended.)

San Simeon grew organically, like a well-loved garden, around Mr. Hearst's staggering rooms, some of which were from Europe, many by Miss Morgan. The three guest houses were the first constructed (containing some fifteen rooms each), with work on the main house commencing in 1922 and basically finished in 1947: Mr. Hearst died in 1951. The main building's frame is of reinforced concrete which carefully incorporates 115 rooms (38 bedrooms), almost all with priceless furnishings. San Simeon forms a veritable museum of architecture, furnishings, art, and books; it must be experienced to be believed. Almost

equally impressive—and a true index of Miss Morgan's skill—are the terraced grounds and gardens, climaxed by the Neptune Pool with its sweeping stairs and Hellenistic-Style temple which was assembled from genuine Roman elements. As the *Saturday Evening Post* wrote in 1968, "all the pleasures of infinity are to be found here and now." San Simeon was given to the State of California by the Hearst family and corporation, and is officially designated a State Monument. In 1976 it was declared a National Historic Landmark.

Multiple tours daily except Jan. 1, Dec. 25: admission.
Reservations recommended

68   Orange County Court House (1964–65)
700 Civic Center Drive at Flower Street
Santa Ana, California

**RICHARD AND DION NEUTRA IN COLLABORATION WITH
RAMBERG, LOWREY & ASSOCIATES, ARCHITECTS**

The late Richard Neutra (1892–1970) added immeasurably to the architectural development of the U.S.A. The contribution of this Vien-
nese-born maestro is seen at its apogee in his brilliant houses: Lovell
(1929), von Sternberg (1936), Nesbitt (1942), Kaufmann (1946),
and Tremaine (1948)—among others—stimulating a revolutionary
effect on our domestic designing. They number, unequivocally, among

the finest houses in the country. (Unfortunately these dwellings are all in private hands—the superb von Sternberg was destroyed—and are not open to the public.) Among Neutra's larger works the Orange County Court House is the most successful. The building is functionally and expressively divided into a broad, low (two-story) unit for municipal offices routinely used by the public, with a high block (ten stories) for courtrooms and offices projecting at right angles and set back from the street by a particularly well-landscaped garden and pool. The building's exterior is marked by a prominent play of fins and louvers for sun protection (a Neutra trademark), the south side of the high block being almost totally screened by banks of electronically actuated vertical louvers. Would that more buildings were so shielded. The interiors are quietly efficient, with great care taken to make the courtroom atmosphere as sympathetic as possible.

Open during office hours

---

69   Mission Santa Barbara (1812–20)
NE off US 101 on Mission Street, NW (left) on Laguna Street
Santa Barbara, California

The facade of Mission Santa Barbara is suggestive of the chilliness of Philip II's Escorial and—as several authorities have pointed out—of a temple design by Vitruvius (fl. 46–30 B.C.) published in his widely influential *De Architectura*. Santa Barbara's native monumentality—aided by its admirable siting—is also thickened by its two "towers." These almost squat atop the broad plane of the facade which sweeps across the front scarce interrupted by the six engaged Ionic half columns flanking the door. Above rests a curiously detailed tympanum. This insistent width masks the narrowness (27 feet/8.2 meters) of the nave behind—one of the earlier false fronts. The twin cupolas (the second added in 1831–33) thus perch somewhat unincorporated on top. The earthquake of 1925 caused much damage (and restoration), while in 1950 it was found necessary, because of chemical reactions and foundation problems, to rebuild the entire facade utilizing steel, reinforced concrete, and a tougher stone finish, a job completed in 1953. The monastery wing (1811) with its arcaded tempo now serves as a museum and shop, its upper section not added until the 1870s when the boys' *Colegio* was built. The interior, fortunately, remains largely as erected: it was restored in 1927. Note the marbleizing and

the sometimes neo-primitive decorations. The patio or cloister offers a welcome garden retreat; in the 1950s two additional quadrangles (one a restoration) were built for the seminary. The octagonal fountain in front (1808) is fed by an ambitious two-arm aqueduct system impounded by a dam in the hills some 2 miles/3.2 kilometers away.

Open Mon.–Sat. 9–5, Sun. 1–5, except major holidays: admission

---

70 **Santa Barbara County Court House** (1928–29)
1120 Anacapa Street between Figueroa and Anapamu
Santa Barbara, California

WILLIAM MOOSER & COMPANY, ARCHITECTS

After Bertram Goodhue's and Carleton M. Winslow's canonization of the Spanish Colonial in San Diego for the Panama-California International Exposition of 1915–16, architecture in California was never the

same. Like the imported eucalyptus, Iberia invaded the state. Lockard and Sauter designed the nearby, comfortably scaled, Spanish-inspired City Hall (1922–24) in Santa Barbara, De la Guerra Plaza, and a few years later William Mooser—the son of a Swiss-born architectural pioneer in California of the same name—projected the municipal ultimate in this style in the County Court House. It is a handsome building, carried through with stylistic expertise inside and out, "a catalogue and a synthesis of all the things that the Santa Barbarans and their architects were up to" (Charles Moore and Gerald Allen, *Dimensions,* Architectural Record Books, 1976). Though a little heavy around the great arched portal, the asymmetry of roof and the adjoining tower are skillful, as is the building's relation to the grounds. However, it is the interior which carries the greatest imagination. The Board of Supervisors Room on the second floor is, with its rich murals and decorations by Dan Sayre Groesbeck, one of the highlights of its period. But see all of the major chambers, their floor details and their grillwork; they are an accomplished lot.

Recent (1980) research by the indefatigable David Gebhard reveals (in a personal letter) that although Mooser's firm prepared the working drawings for the Court House, the "design was completely revised by Joseph Plunkett of the Santa Barbara architectural firm of Edwards and Plunkett." For the time being, a conundrum will prevail as to the role each architect played.

Open Mon.–Fri. 8–5, Sat. 1–5, Sun. and holidays 9–5: guides available

---

71 University of California at Santa Cruz (1963–   )
Bay Street via High Street, just N of CA 1, c. 2.5 miles/4 kilometers NW of
Santa Cruz, California

JOHN CARL WARNECKE, MASTER PLAN; VARIOUS ARCHITECTS

The University of California at Santa Cruz embarked during the early 1960s upon an exemplary educational and architectural program. The pedagogical philosophy has "likened the campus to a medieval city composed of a number of small villages"—compare the genesis of Collegiate Gothic architecture—creating thus a growing number of individual colleges sprinkled through the trees rather than one monolithic central mass. Each college is residentially self-sufficient with about half of its students living in apartment clusters with their own dining and recreation rooms, together with classrooms and faculty offices. John Carl Warnecke prepared the master plan for this specification, aided by Anshen & Allen, Theodore C. Bernardi, and Ernest J. Kump as consulting architects, and Thomas D. Church as landscape architect. For the design of individual buildings, the university brought in some of the country's leading architects with institutional experience. The site is a gloriously unspoiled rolling embrace of

approximately 2,000 acres/809 hectares, with a wide variety of trees
and shrubs alternating with open meadows. On this a series of eight
residential colleges has arisen, each with some six hundred to eight
hundred students (including non-residents), and fifteen to sixty faculty
members. Total campus enrollment is approximately six thousand students, four hundred of whom are enrolled in graduate programs. The
small size of each college encourages close student-faculty relationships and an altogether human scale of life, yet the central facilities
such as library, performing arts complex, the applied and natural sciences buildings, and health center are, in general, reasonably close at
hand. For the student—as well as the visitor—the most welcome feature lies in the unspoiled, untouched nature which separates each college group. Not an unnecessary square foot of natural topography was
destroyed in this enlightened approach. The architecture which sprouts
amid this forest primeval might be termed, in spite of the luster of its
distinguished designers, very competent but, with few exceptions, not
scintillating. There are a number of good buildings—and some excellent space-modeling—but no inspired results on this inspired example
of land usage.

The major buildings and their architects are:
1) **Cowell College** (1966—411 residents): Wurster, Bernardi &
Emmons
2) **Stevenson College** (1966—433 residents): Joseph Esherick &
Associates
3) **Crown College** (1967—396 residents): Ernest J. Kump Associates
4) **Merrill College** (1968—380 residents): Campbell & Wong
(and Wong & Brocchini)
5) **College Five** (1969—441 residents) *top photo, facing page:*
Hugh Stubbins Associates
6) **Kresge College** (1974—304 students): Moore and Turnbull
(see separate entry)
7) **Oakes College** (1977—310 residents): McCue Boone Tomsick
8) **College Eight** (housed in Clark Kerr Hall—1973): Germano
Milono & Associates
9) **Natural Sciences Buildings** (1965 and 1969): Anshen & Allen
10) **Performing Arts Complex** (1971): Ralph Rapson & Associates
11) **Lecture and Demonstration Building** (1971): Marquis &
Stoller
12) **McHenry Library** (1966 and 1976) *bottom photo, facing
page:* John Carl Warnecke & Associates

13) **Applied Sciences Building** (1971): Reid & Tarics Associates
14) **Cowell Health Center** (1970): John Funk
15) **Central Services Building** (1965): Ernest J. Kump Associates

Campus open daily throughout year

---

72 **Kresge College** (1972–74)
University of California at Santa Cruz
off Heller Drive (west edge of campus)
Santa Cruz, California

MLTW/TURNBULL ASSOCIATES AND CHARLES W. MOORE
ASSOCIATES, ARCHITECTS

A collegiate temenos, architecturally hinting of North Africa, full of excitement, spatial surprises, even dreams. One enters—in the approved Moorish fashion—via a "gate," and penetrates the college's spinal "street." This is approximately 1,000 feet/305 meters long, rises 45 feet/14 meters as it proceeds, and is angled sharply so that the evil

eye cannot see around the corner. Heightened responses greet each new three-dimensional revelation. In many respects the whole suggests a gigantic stage set in the redwoods (with some proscenium thinness); but it is a stage set where each of the 304 resident students (of 650 total) feels an important member of the cast. The resulting sense of belonging—it conjures up almost a secret society—makes Kresge probably the most sought-after college in this extraordinary university. In addition to its challenging unfurlment of spaces, the extensive use of color adds further flair. The backsides of the buildings tend to earth colors, while their street facades are basically white but with bold color accents along the way.

The facilities around the entry comprise offices, provost's house, and some general-activity buildings. Leading from these are the first apartment groups whose buildings, though of equal external dimensions, and all two stories, are subdivided differently within. (Construction is of wood frame and stucco.) Taking a sharp left-hand turn, one encounters the centrally located classroom and local library nexus (major university facilities are in the academic core). Further along stretches another lane of additional apartments (all with individual kitchens) in which students are housed in "flats" for four, "suites" for six to seven, and "sextet" (i.e. community) accommodations. The excursion terminates with a large, roughly octagonal assembly hall, dining room, and cafe. Rigidity has no place in the layout: no building aligns with its neighbor, natural grade meanders throughout, formality is unknown. Charles W. Moore, William Turnbull, Jr., and Robert Simpson were the principals-in-charge. In brief, the most stimulating small campus in the country.

Grounds open daily throughout the year

---

73   IBM Santa Teresa Laboratory (1975–77)
   **Bailey Avenue (6 miles/9.6 kilometers S of freeway on US 101—W
      1 mile/1.6 kilometers on Bailey)
   Santa Teresa (San Jose), California**

MBT ASSOCIATES (McCUE BOONE TOMSICK), ARCHITECTS

IBM has a basic policy of limiting the size of its installations so that they will not burden a community with too much personnel (with need for housing, schools, shopping, etc.) or demands for municipal services

(water, sewage, power, police). Thus this West Coast programming development center or laboratory was located on the site of a former orchard well removed from the more extensive complex which the company had earlier built on the south edge of San Jose. It is IBM's first installation "to be designed specifically for programming activities" and this need determined its highly specialized design.

One of the basic problems was the reconciliation of providing private, individual office "think tanks," where approximately one third of a programmer's time is spent, with areas for accommodating several team members in activities which take up about half of a programmer's time. There must also be proximity to common terminal rooms, conference rooms, and the main computer center, plus, of course, the usual services (library, cafeteria, etc.). Flexibility must be built in, with easy interior circulation throughout. "Outside awareness" and a mind-relaxing environment when away from work were also sought. And although some two thousand employees would be on the scene, a non-institutional ambience was important.

The above demands were met by grouping eight identical four-story office blocks, each cruciform in plan, around a one-story, ground-level computer center. A two-story food service unit abuts at rear. Reflecting the uneven site, the lowest floor, which serves as common link, is partially in the hillside while an enormous terrace—the roof of the computer center—serves as "a garden quadrangle" onto which all office blocks (here three stories) open. This elevated agora forms the visual focus and outdoor circulation area for the complex. The design of the eight blocks began with a meticulous study of the space demands of an office for a single individual. An office module 10 x 10 feet/3 x 3 meters—thoroughly tested with mock-ups—was eventually standardized. Though uniform in size, each work unit has numerous layout options. Every detail of the furniture was studied to mesh with the work space.

After exploring various dispositions of multiples of the basic office—from linear to clustered—a squared U plan was adopted, with four offices on each of the two sides of the U, five across the end, and six inside. The inner ones are variably used as offices or conference centers, etc. The resulting almost square bays of offices, approximately 45 x 50 feet/13.7 x 15.2 meters in size, were then grouped around and plugged into the four sides of a large central service core to establish the cruciform plan mentioned. All buildings connect at ground level while many are also bridged above. Though natural aluminum predominates, color coding, at times vibrant in its positiveness, gives identity to each of the similarly shaped office blocks. This attains striking heights in the semihidden "courtyards" framed by arms of adjacent buildings. Construction is of steel capable of withstanding severe earthquakes. The sleek enclosure of reflective glass flush with bright aluminum makes a highly sophisticated set of buildings. There is a slight "citadel" aspect to the overall complex on the approach but on its private plaza the "campus" quality, excellent scale, and color touches have both individual and collective rewards. Gerald M. McCue was design principal assisted by David C. Boone and Alan R. Williams; the SWA Group were the landscape architects.

Open only by appointment; telephone Public Relations:
(408) 256-1600

---

74   The Sea Ranch (1965–   )
on CA 1, c. 2.5 miles/4 kilometers N of Stewarts Point, c. 11
**   miles/18 kilometers S of Gualala**
Sea Ranch, California

MOORE, LYNDON, TURNBULL & WHITAKER, ARCHITECTS OF CONDOMINIUM; JOSEPH ESHERICK & ASSOCIATES, OF STORE-RESTAURANT; LAWRENCE HALPRIN & ASSOCIATES, PLANNERS AND LANDSCAPE ARCHITECTS

The Sea Ranch enterprise, primarily for second homes, is located a bit over 100 miles/160 kilometers north of San Francisco. The site covers a 10-mile/16-kilometer stretch of rolling, generally lovely land which

rises from the rock-strewn Pacific to meadows and wooded hills. "Dynamic conservation" and careful land stewardship have characterized the philosophy, and initially the practice, of the development of its 5,000 acres/2,023 hectares. Its concern for quality of environment is benevolent (though not as pristine as early on), and the extraordinary research that went into bioclimatic needs, wind and soil studies, etc., which preceded site planning and prompted building design guidelines, is impressive. So that maximum freedom of land would result, no routine strip planning was allowed, only "clusters and commons" of houses grouped together to leave the ground around them open to all property owners. Moreover there are no lineups of houses along the oceanfront blocking the views of those behind, but right-angle emphases, with most groups screened by rows of trees and shrubs from the predominant (and cool) northwest breeze. It is a remarkably well-planned residential development.

The architecture of Sea Ranch, particularly that of the famous seaside condominum (visible from the public center), has exerted a pervasive (when misunderstood, perversive) influence on recent American architecture. Here it represents a back-to-nature school that was logically evolved (wind-tunnel tests among others) and is regionally appropriate. In less capable hands this approach is plucked from the architectural magazines and degenerates into a sawtooth "shack" cliché. Shelter, security, and scale in a wide-open landscape were of prime concern to the condominium's architects, plus "territoriality" and sense of coherence, followed by a hierarchy of spatial experiences from outdoors to in. The ten condominium apartments—redwood town houses on a sea-girt point—form an almost defensively clustered minihilltown. But whereas imagination and the intuitive played their part in design, close technical studies indicated angled or shed roofs to create tranquil leeside shelters. The result is not one of capriciousness. The approach was meticulously developed with a broad entry containing garages, then a smaller sheltered court, and finally one's apartment —with the whole stepping down the hillside as it clutches the topography.

The condominium bears, for some, a curious relation to the wild but magnificent nature about it. This stems from the fact that outdoors is almost an enemy—"The major problem was to get out of the wind and into sunlight." Thus from the interior one observes the sea, maybe the coastline—rarely a glimpse of other units—yet one participates with the surroundings generally through plate glass. The apartment interiors are climaxed by exuberant three-dimensionality with skylights abetting vertically and south views probing the coast laterally. Each unit has a "great room" about which the spaces revolve. Sadly—as the architects point out in their book *The Place of Houses* (Holt, Rinehart and Winston, 1974)—the beautiful, promising beginnings are weakening. Not only is the careful original site-plan for future condominiums ignored, "Its architect [of a new group] appears to be unfriendly"—to judge from a photograph of the result he certainly was. Moreover, some of the recent houses which are scattered around the treeless meadows—a difficult site, to be sure—can be categorized, as was one, as "that excrescence on the grassy slopes." Former design restrictions have in a small measure been eased for more flexibility and profit. However, there is still much to be gleaned from the notable successes of Sea Ranch, and if a few lessons are negative, the overall is very positive—as over 350 families have thus far discovered.

The lodge, restaurant, and store are at their best within, where their natural-finish wood (Canadian cedar), the changes in level, and the play of angles are full of imagination. The dashing graphics are by Barbara Stauffacher. The restaurant and store were expanded (1969) by Alfred Boeke and Louis McLane to include a twenty-unit lodge.

Store, restaurant, and lodge open to public; condominium and houses private

75   **Cable-Car Terminal** (1968)
     **2.6 miles/4.2 kilometers W of CA 89, entry 9.2 miles/15
        kilometers S of IS 80 (near Lake Tahoe)**
     Squaw Valley, California

SHEPLEY, BULFINCH, RICHARDSON & ABBOTT, ARCHITECTS

A well-sculpted cable-car terminal which anchors one end of a spectacular *téléférique* (as well as upgrading the amorphous collection of
buildings about it). The architects have created not only a forthright
terminal, they have seized on the fascination of its machinery and
made of it a glass-enclosed mechanical stage set. Enormous counter-
weights (147 tons/133 metric tons each) flank the entry and rise and

fall 12 feet/3.6 meters as they reflect the cab loads. Inside the towering lobby the whirling cable wheels, the bright orange paint, and the views outward of the peak combine to make a rousing hall. The Swiss-made cable-car system—one of the world's largest—can carry 1,100 skiers per hour (120 per cab) on a 7,000-foot/2,134-meter run with a 2,000-foot/610-meter rise. The dramatically but functionally angled exterior is double-buttressed against earthquakes at three points of each side. Man echoes the mountains. Abraham Woolf & Associates were the structural engineers; T. Genovesi Associates, mechanical engineers.

Open for winter skiing and June–mid-Sept., daily 10–5: admission

76 **Commerce Clearing House** (1970–71)
W off US 101 via Northgate Drive to Thorndale Drive
Terra Linda (N of San Rafael), California

MARQUIS & STOLLER, ARCHITECTS

This smallish, regional corporate headquarters, not far northwest of Wright's Marin County Civic Center in San Rafael (q.v.), establishes sensitive domain on its hilltop location. It achieves this with a scale that states its case but does not offend. Horizontality, sympathetic to the site, is accented, but to keep this from becoming insistent the ar- chitects shrewdly angled the dining room out for a view of San Rafael Bay. The building comprises three floors, the topmost forming the office area, with two decks of parking beneath, half in the hillside. Vis- itors' entrance is at second (i.e. grade) level via an airy three-story court which can be opened in fine weather. The offices, which ascribe a U-shape around the court, open onto this atrium, while on the outside they are surrounded by terraces with views in all directions. Robert B. Marquis and J. Peter Winkelstein were principals-in-charge.

Reception area open during business hours

---

77 **Civic Center** (1972–73)
**401 West Hillcrest Drive; N off US 101, right on West Hillcrest, left
   (N) up McCloud Avenue to Civic Center Drive**
Thousand Oaks, California

ROBERT MASON HOUVENER, ARCHITECT

Comfortably perched and hooded on its hill, where the center over- looks its charges by day and by night, this extraordinarily bold yet sim- ple concept adds new freshness to the prosaic image of city halls. Its design was enthusiastically selected in a national competition that drew 158 entries. From its situation above the fast-growing city of Thousand Oaks (39 miles/63 kilometers northwest of Los Angeles) the offices survey the Conejo Valley and distant hills on a 30-acre/12-hectare plot given the city by a generous local family. So as not to offend this unspoiled, basically residential community, the architect spread out his programmatic requirements in a one-story discontinuous band to fit the land contours. Thus the two (eventually three) buildings are almost invisible from below, becoming more intriguing as one draws near. On approaching, a slight pillbox analogy from the strongly stated concrete carapace might come to mind, but on reaching the upper level, above and behind the offices, only peace and welcoming scale appear. The heavy concrete parapets which overhang and shield the bands of win- dows also hide the rooftop staff parking. The visitor parks his car op-

posite the unit desired, then steps down to a well-landscaped garden court on the uphill side and enters a continuous access hall. Municipal offices fill the northern and larger wing, while the southern, with chamber of commerce and city administration offices, caters to public needs with council chamber at one end.

Reception area open during office hours

Colorado

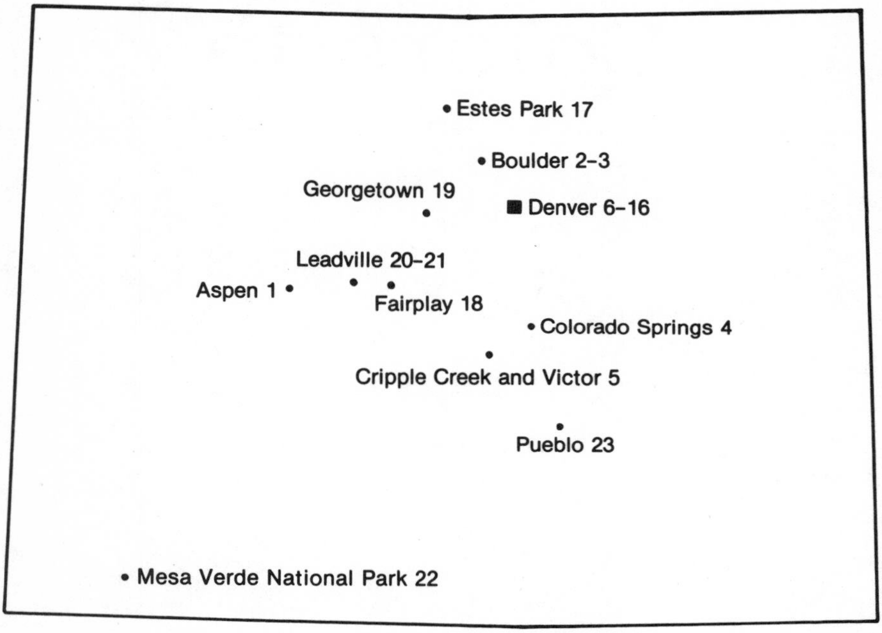

• Estes Park 17

• Boulder 2–3

Georgetown 19   ■ Denver 6–16
•

Leadville 20–21
Aspen 1 •   •   •
Fairplay 18

• Colorado Springs 4
•
Cripple Creek and Victor 5

•
Pueblo 23

• Mesa Verde National Park 22

COLORADO

The buildings in boldface type are of general interest. The others are for the specialist.

Aspen

1 Victorian Buildings (1880–90s)

Boulder

2 **National Center for Atmospheric Research** (1965–66)—I. M. Pei & Partners

3 **Engineering Science Center** (1963–66)—Architectural Associates

Colorado Springs

4 **Air Force Academy** (1956–63)—Skidmore, Owings & Merrill

Cripple Creek and Victor

5 Mining Town Vernacular

Denver

6 Larimer Square (1870s)

7 Trinity United Methodist Church (1887–88)—Robert S. Roeschlaub

8 Boston Building (1889)—Andrews, Jacques & Rantoul

9 **Brown Palace Hotel** (1889–92)—Frank E. Edbrooke

10 **Civic Center Park** (1919)—E. H. Bennett

11 **Red Rocks Amphitheater** (1941)—Burnham Hoyt

12 **Currigan Exhibition Hall** (1968–69)—Muchow, Ream and Larson

13 **The Denver Art Museum** (1968–71)—James Sudler Associates and Gio Ponti

14 **Park Central** (1973–74)—Muchow Associates

D & F Tower (1911)—F. G. Sterner

15 **Johns-Manville World Headquarters** (1977)—The Architects Collaborative

16 **Boettcher Concert Hall** (1976–78)—Hardy Holzman Pfeiffer

Helen G. Bonfils Theater (1980)—Roche/Dinkeloo

Estes Park

17 Visitor Center and Park Headquarters (1965–66)— Taliesin Associates

Fairplay

18 Sheldon Jackson Memorial Chapel (1874)

Georgetown

19 Hotel de Paris Museum and the Town (1874–75)

Leadville

20 **Tabor Opera House** (1879)— Brooke & Brooke

21 Healy House (1878) and Dexter Cabin (1879)

Mesa Verde National Park

22 **Cliff Dwellings** (c. A.D. 1200–1300)

Pueblo

23 Governor Adams Residence (1890–91)—William W. Stickney

1   Victorian Buildings (1880–90s)
Galena and East Hyman Streets
Aspen, Colorado

Aspen achieved fame and considerable fortune in the 1880s when its hills (7,907 feet/2,410 meters base altitude) relinquished an uncommon amount of silver from its seven mines. When the market for white metal collapsed in 1893, the town became almost deserted, remaining thus until it was revived after World War II as a year-round sport and cultural center. Fortunately a few of the town's original buildings have survived, some even have been handsomely restored (Hotel Jerome, 1892, Main and Mill streets, and the Opera House at Hyman and Mill). Another concentration of this hardy mountain Victorian period stands at the intersection of Galena and East Hyman streets. In recent years a vast preservation program has taken place, and Aspen today offers many rewards.

Open during business hours

2 National Center for Atmospheric Research (1965–66)
   **2.5 miles/4 kilometers SW off Broadway (COL 93) on Table Mesa
      Road, then NCAR Road**
   Boulder, Colorado

I. M. PEI & PARTNERS, ARCHITECTS

The Atmospheric Center's setting and the building's relation to it are
highly congenial. The complex rests on the edge of a mesa south of the
city with the Rockies as backdrop, with evergreens on all sides, and
with the flat plains of eastern Colorado fanning out in front. Though
chromatically tied to the mountains by pinkish concrete walls echoing
the hills, the structure asserts itself and its independence by vertical
abruptness and by an emphasis on what might be termed "top thrust"
as opposed to any built-up evolution from the ground. At some angles
the Center, from a distance, appears almost toylike and untethered in
this wild pageant of nature, a lonely bastion against the mountain
gods.

This "community" of buildings—two tall units connected by a lower base—evolved from diffuse program requirements, but with a specific operating philosophy. As space needs at the planning stage could not be precisely defined, flexibility was of utmost importance. The philosophy, in turn, sought a non-dogmatic, non-slick research center where teams of experts could work together on common problems yet each specialist could at will repair to his or her adjacent—and sacrosanct—office. The building thus evolved in clusters with offices, in general, adjacent to central work, discussion, and lab areas.

The Atmospheric Center is reached by a road that allows tantalizing vignettes as one winds up to the summit. One enters past a sculptured "gate" (of some self-importance), to be confronted by two five-story blocks, resembling castellated strongholds, hooded and mysterious. (Some critics feel that the Mesa Verde Cliff Dwellings—q.v.—were of influence here.) The end of the office-laboratory unit faces one, its three "heads" poking from the top like gigantic sentry posts surveying the approaches. Nearest the entry and projecting at right (and at right angles to the other) is a similar unit housing the non-lab-related offices for the Center. These two precisely sliced masses—the dominant elements of the design—are both stunning and disturbing. One is transfixed by their power, yet one wonders what goes on behind those neat, narrow bands of dark windows which run up the center of the broad sides of each "tower," then erupt in wide canopied glass horizontals at top. Offices and labs, one finds, lie behind, and though some sacrifice of natural illumination results, wall space, not window space, was sought, with offices focused on work inside, not views out. Visual infinity and contact with nature await in the top-floor meeting areas and the terraces. Between the two five-story blocks is the service wing common to all. This includes lobby and display area on the ground floor, with cafeteria, kitchen, and dining terrace in the southwest corner and library above. A ramp from the second floor leads directly to the southwest mesa so that the scientists can stroll out and be in direct contact with nature. A third-floor roof terrace also offers relief from office confinement. The other five-story block is connected on the second level (as well as first floor and basement) with the common facilities.

One of the stimuli of the Center is its total three-dimensionality. One can walk completely around it and receive fresh juxtapositions and intergroup relations. Though verging toward the dogmatic in its arsenal character, it is nonetheless highly exciting, and is, one understands, much liked by the four hundred to five hundred scientists who work there. Spaces for future labs and a conference center (near the parking lot) have already been assigned. Dr. Walter Orr Roberts, the head of NCAR, had an active hand in planning the Center. James P. Morris and Robert Lym were associates-in-charge. Dan Kiley was landscape architect.

Reception area open Mon.–Fri. 8–5, except major holidays

3   Engineering Science Center (1963–66)
University of Colorado
Colorado Avenue and Folsom Street
Boulder, Colorado

ARCHITECTURAL ASSOCIATES OF COLORADO: W. C. MUCHOW, PARTNER-IN-CHARGE

The associated architects of this sizable Engineering Center sought to make their complex a good neighbor to the Tuscan hill-town vernacular of the old campus by the late Charles Z. Klauder, a "style" which was established here just after World War I and continued to the

1930s. They also wanted to pay their architectural respects to the Rocky Mountains directly behind. To harmonize with the campus, they employed the local sandstone and red tile roofs which mark the older and adjacent buildings, using this same stone for some walls and raw concrete—as particularly befits engineering character—for others, the concrete being the more successful. As regards the Center's relation to setting, the buildings' angled roof lines recall, somewhat enthusiastically, those tumultuous peaks which leap dazzlingly from the plains that also edge the campus. Moreover they carry, perhaps not inappropriately, an architectural allusion to the mining structures and pitheads which inhabit those mighty hills. The major units of the Center are Aeronautical, Electrical, Civil, Chemical, and Mechanical Engineering, each assuming its space dimensions within an overall module which ties the group together. Included are some 31 classrooms, 250 laboratories, a similar number of offices, and a detached library and auditorium. The office tower provides the central focus and scale buildup with the lower lab buildings radiating about it. The 10-acre/4-hectare complex has been efficiently planned and thoughtfully landscaped, its solids being enlivened by several large and small courts, with fountains playing, plus an imaginative interlock of levels. The concrete walls with their prominent random board formwork are competent; however, one could do without the plethora of hooded windows. But basic design decisions, and above all the excitement of spaces, are very fine. Expansion to the east was anticipated. Architectural Associates included: W. C. Muchow & Associates, Hobart D. Wagener & Associates, Fisher & Davis, with Pietro Belluschi and Sasaki, Dawson & Demay Associates Inc., Design Consultants, the latter firm also in charge of site planning and landscaping.

Open during school year

---

4 Air Force Academy (1956–63)
off IS 25, c. 8 miles/13 kilometers N of
Colorado Springs, Colorado

SKIDMORE, OWINGS & MERRILL, ARCHITECTS

The Air Force Academy presides over one of the most stupendous sites of any major building group in the country, with the Rampart Range of the Rocky Mountains jutting immediately as a backdrop and the Academy itself sharply etched on a podium atop hills which rumble

and fade into the plains to the east. On a part-natural, but fully man-chiseled acropolis, a knife-edge collection of buildings—by the Chi-cago office of SOM—stands at military attention in this setting of grandeur. Harmon Hall, the three-story administration building, defines the upper (i.e. mountainside) limit of the Academy, and is raised on pilotis or stilts so that space snakes through its largely open ground floor to bind site and architecture together. From the terrace in front of Harmon—the Court of Honor—the public can survey the en-tire layout (but proceed no farther than the chapel). This panorama involves a looking-down process which is helpful to the observer, but which does lessen the architectural hauteur of the buildings. Arnold Hall, a large social center, used for festivities, stands immediately at the left of Harmon. It contains an auditorium, two ballrooms, and rec-reational facilities. Vandenberg Hall, six stories high and a quarter mile (1,337 feet/407 meters) in length, projects at the left, providing quarters for 2,640 cadets. Forming a hollow rectangle about two major central courts with cadet rooms lining both sides of its corridors, this building, too, is on pilotis, thus lessening its vast extent as fingers of space penetrate both at ground level and at the "empty" floor between the two top decks and the two lower ones. The field house, with its own road, stands separate northeast of Vandenberg Hall. Across the far (east) side of the campus, parallel to the Court of Honor, and at right angles to Vandenberg, stretches (985.8 feet/300 meters) the Library and Academic Complex, the two in line but not directly joined above ground. The ramp down to the parade ground is adjacent. Mitchell Hall, the dining hall—which can seat all cadets and officers (c. 3,000) at one time—rises at the southwest corner of the class bank, semiframing the "air garden" in front. Carrying the greatest architectural interest of all buildings but the chapel, it boasts an enormous column-free interior, 252 feet/77 meters square, with a ceiling height of 24 feet/7.3 meters. Only four columns per side support this great Warren-truss umbrella whose overall dimensions, with a 22-foot/6.7-meter cantilever on all four sides, measure 308 x 308 feet/94 x 94 meters.

The chapel is the only structure regularly open to the public, and in addition to filling spiritual needs, it provides the architectural marrow of the campus, its heaven-thrusting spires—like the folded plane wings on the flight deck of an aircraft carrier—dramatically relieving the horizontality of its neighbors. Without its serrated verticality mobilizing the group to unity, unity would be diminished. The chapel was the last major building finished at the Academy, and though it is not a church which everyone will like, many will find it fascinating. (A football coach has been quoted as saying, "We don't know whether to pray in it, for it, or at it.") The structure is extremely ingenious technically, being composed of contiguous units of triangulated tetrahedrons, two facing out, one in. These forms, with steel tube structure and aluminum facing, complement each other so that when the two outer ones come to a point, the inner face reaches maximum width, and vice versa. Narrow (1-foot/.3-meter) bands of stained glass mark their junctures. These intriguingly angled forms, seventeen to a side, spring from freestanding, concrete buttresses, leaving a covered passage along both sides and the front of the chapel. The Protestant Chapel occupies the entire upper "platform," and provides pews for 1,200, with a 100-seat choir loft over the entry. The Roman Catholic Chapel, 500 seats, and the Jewish, 100, are placed beneath and half below the grade of the surrounding terrace. There is also on the lower level a tiny, non-denominational Meeting Room. To each his own. The interior of the Protestant Chapel is slightly disturbing to some with its tetrahedral walls "bent" in while the colors of the inch-thick (25 millimeter) stained glass (by SOM) and all the furnishings (*not* by SOM) are disturbing to almost everyone. (The organization of military chaplains played a major role here.) Even the pew details, let alone the altar, pulpit, and lectern, are spiritless. The Catholic and Jewish Chapels are no better.

But regarding the architecture of the Air Force Academy as a whole, we find one of the great undertakings of our time, authoritatively sited to counterpoint the mountains, not blend with them, asserting man's place in nature and in man's guise. Its buildings are obviously—and intentionally—on the mechanistic side, as are the instruments its cadets will eventually fly. Some critics have suggested that the buildings belong more in a metropolitan setting than in wild nature, but this no-nonsense Academy is one of the potent complexes of our century, the epitome of its period. *Sic itur ad astra.*

The 17,878 acres/7,235 hectares of grounds (but not the buildings) are in large measure open to the driving public, but the central architectural emphasis is found, of course, in the Academy buildings mentioned above. Walter A. Netsch, Jr., was in overall charge of design, with Kenneth Naslund structural engineer. Dan Kiley was landscape architect.

Grounds, upper level, and chapel open daily 7–7; apply at Visitor Center, South Gate, for brochure and map

---

5 Mining Town Vernacular
Cripple Creek and Victor, Colorado

These Colorado semighost towns, some 3.5 miles/5.6 kilometers apart and over 9,500 feet/2,895 meters high, nestle in a landscape of eerie desolation. They are surrounded by long-dead volcanoes and the almost sinister detritus of mine tailings—tumuli to the God of Gold. Almost five hundred mines dotted this Dantesque setting in the 1890s —producing over $300 million worth of the stuff (more, it is said, than from California and Alaska combined)—and although an increasing number of mines are in operation today, the fluctuating price of gold versus the high price of labor has closed most of the early ones down. (A few mines are open to the public in summer.) The skyline throughout the area with mining machinery scratching the clouds while it claws the hills makes a spectacular industrial panorama, while "architecture" was not wholly forgotten. Though these two towns never attained the opulence of Leadville (q.v.), Bennett Avenue in Cripple Creek has a few good metal shop fronts, while the Masonic Hall in Victor (illustrated), at North 4th Street south of Victor Avenue, is worth a view for its three richly treated pediments. The town's popula-

tion is now around 500, while in the 1890s it was probably more than 35,000. Today the wild setting and the extraordinary sense of desolation are the heroes.

6 Larimer Square (1870s)
1400 block of Larimer Street
Denver, Colorado

Denver, with reckless urban renewal, has wiped out most of its historic sections (some two hundred old buildings), but fortunately a length of Larimer Street—a century ago one of the main thoroughfares—was spared. Much of this is being restored (by private enterprise) to its

pre-1900 condition, and although overly ambitious paint jobs do occur, the rejuvenation has sparked a series of entertaining shops and restaurants, most of which respect their heritage. Larimer Square was placed on the National Register for Historic Landmarks (1973) and this should ensure future controls and preservation. A series of scheduled festivities seasonally enliven the Square. The nearby Tivoli Brewery (1860–90), at 10th Street and Larimer, is a hoary example of its period. Its future, however, is uncertain.

---

7   Trinity United Methodist Church (1887–88)
Broadway and 18th Street
Denver, Colorado

ROBERT S. ROESCHLAUB, ARCHITECT

An old-line High Victorian Gothic church which takes maximum advantage of its diagonal site. The architect, who came to this country as a child from his native Germany, created a tremendous scale buildup

and acceleration of masses which culminate in a pivotal corner tower 181 feet/55 meters high of fresh design. Note that it carries the rusticated stone through the very spire itself instead of using the more normal and far lighter timber frame and shingles. Note, also, the two smooth bands of stonework in the spire, thus making a Trinity division. The sanctuary, which seats 1,200 and is located on the second floor, is dominated by the large choir and 4,290-pipe organ. The Tiffany stained glass here is very good of its type, representing the Resurrection. Some routineness can be seen in the treatment of the triple portal but most details are superior. An Education Wing was built in 1925, burned in 1966, but rebuilt two years later. Always well maintained, in 1964 the stonework was completely cleaned on the outside and the church spruced up within. As Richard R. Brettell writes in his useful *Historic Denver* (Historic Denver, Inc., 1973), the church "stands across Broadway from Edbrooke's masterpiece, the Brown Hotel, and the two buildings are today the most significant survivals from the greatest building boom in the history of Denver."

Open Mon.–Fri. 9–5, apply at office, plus Sun. service

8   Boston Building (1889)
17th Street at Champa
Denver, Colorado

ANDREWS, JACQUES & RANTOUL, ARCHITECTS

The Boston Building's two-story arched recesses for the windows deliver surprising monumentality to a mere nine-story structure, a technique which R. D. Andrews learned from H. H. Richardson, with whom he had worked before joining Jacques and Rantoul. The architectural firm—and, we understand, the financing—came from Boston, hence the building's name. Note the "expected" coupled half-width windows designating the top floor. The original cornice has been removed for safety reasons and the entry quietly updated.

Open during business hours

9   Brown Palace Hotel (1889–92)
17th Street at Tremont Place and Broadway
Denver, Colorado

FRANK E. EDBROOKE, ARCHITECT

Few voids have ever been as positive as this nine-story, top-lit, 56-foot/17-meter-wide squarish column of properly conditioned air which is the essence and genius of the Brown Palace Hotel. Here, indeed, nothing is everything. For this delightful space—whose most prominent grandchildren are the Guggenheim Museum in New York (q.v.) and the Hyatt Regency Hotel in Altanta (q.v.)—demonstrates what cagily handled, sparklingly illuminated, and people-animated three dimensions can produce. Tracing its origins to the atrium houses

of Pompeii, the *cortile* of Italian Renaissance palaces, and more recently to the old Palace Hotel in San Francisco, 1873–75 (destroyed by the earthquake and fire of 1906, and though rebuilt, not as was), Denver's masterpiece ranks with them all in spatial élan. Note, too, the onyx-lined lower floors, the enormous stained-glass skylight, and the bronze balcony panels, all of which are scrupulously maintained. The exterior of the hotel was influenced, like so many buildings, by H. H. Richardson's now demolished Marshall Field Warehouse of 1885–87. However, as some historians rightly point out, the Brown Palace design also shows a suasion from Adler and Sullivan's Auditorium Building in Chicago (q.v.), begun in 1886. But as Albert Bush-Brown mentions in his *Louis Sullivan* (Braziller, 1960), "Sullivan declared his admiration for Richardson in a series of buildings"—including the Warehouse. Incidentally, the Brown Palace's architect was from Chicago, but stayed to design many of Denver's important works. The hotel's exterior is of moderate architectural concern, but a step into the lobby is *épatant*. Internal changes and modernization (with varying degrees of success) have kept the public rooms, bedrooms, and services up-to-date, but the great lobby has remained largely untouched.

This "ancient" hostel—which was commenced in the heyday of Colorado's mining boom—has been so successful that a twenty-two-story addition was made in 1959 (William B. Tabler Associates, architects), more than doubling the number of rooms.

---

10 Civic Center Park (1919)
Colfax Avenue at Broadway
Denver, Colorado

E. H. BENNETT, ARCHITECT

The city fathers of Denver, with admirable foresight, established a downtown formal park in the early part of this century as a link for its various public buildings. It now forms a welcome disjunction between the aggressive State Capitol (1908—Elijah E. Myers, architect) to the east and the Old Denver Public Library (1910—A. R. Ross, architect) and the City and County Building (1932—Allied Architects Association) to the west. One is introduced into this breathing spot by the well-proportioned Voorhies Memorial Gateway (on Colfax)

flanked by an Ionic arcade on either side (1921—W. E. & A. A. Fisher, architects). The arcade partly embraces and shields a raised terrace which has a shallow oval pool in the center (Robert Garrison, sculptor). Beyond this architecturally organized entry stretch the parterred pleasures of lawn, greenery, and a bit of statuary. The south end of the Park near the Art Museum (q.v.) is "closed" by the less satisfactory colonnade, which, however, does step down on the park side into a fine circular Greek theater (1919—Marean and Norton, architects). Altogether a gracious adjunct to the city as a whole and to the public buildings around it. Frederick Law Olmsted, Jr., and Alfred Brunner made earlier plans for the Civic Center Park, but E. H. Bennett's overall plan was carried out.

Always open

11 **Red Rocks Amphitheater** (1941)
    c. 16 miles/26 kilometers SW of downtown via US 6, then S on
       IS 70, S on COL 26
    Denver, Colorado

BURNHAM HOYT, ARCHITECT

In a setting of palpable grandeur in the red sandstone outcroppings west of Denver, man has tidied up the hillside with seventy quietly regimented curved ranks of seats, installed a stage and related services, and produced the most spectacular outdoor amphitheater in the United States. Downtown Denver vibrates on the distant plain. Cradled between Great Rock and Ship Rock, with Stage Rock as backdrop—their semienclosure producing excellent acoustics—some eight thousand seats have been eased into the wild beauty of this natural bowl, every millimeter of which was preserved where possible by the late architect. Retaining walls are of local stone, the seats of natural wood, and the stepped ranks of concrete. (The rows of seats range in length from 135

feet/41 meters to 230 feet/70 meters.) The stage, altered from its
original design and now a bit intrusive, is double-decked, with services
hidden on the lower floor. Parking is totally out of view. Superb.

Open daily; summer evening concerts

---

12   Currigan Exhibition Hall (1968–69)
14th Street between Champa and Stout
Denver, Colorado

MUCHOW, REAM AND LARSON, ASSOCIATED ARCHITECTS

The weathering steel exterior of Exhibition Hall (in panels 10 x 30
feet/3 x 9.1 meters), is, by its nature, on the somber side—relieved at
the top by the yellowish "cornice" of its structural frame. However,
the interior, with four conjoined space-frames, each covering 170 x 240
feet/52 x 73 meters for a length of 680 feet/207 meters, stops one cold.
This unencumbered space of 100,000 square feet/9,290 square meters
can be subdivided into two 50,000-square-foot/4,645-square-meter
halls, and pyramidal canopy lights in clusters of four can be lowered to
establish proper scale. These lights, which nest in the exposed trusswork, are in bright yellow and red, adding a festive note against the
white of the ceiling even when they are raised. The building's commission was won by three associated firms of architects in a statewide
competition; it comprises a basement, the great exhibition and convention hall above, and a mezzanine with services around its periphery.
Taking advantage of the sloping grade, all service and storage facilities
are accommodated at the lower level. Moreover, because of the building's length (and its sloping site), 13th Street runs through this service
floor and can thus be used for visitor entry in inclement weather. The
loading docks are directly alongside the exhibition floor. The main entrance on 14th Street is set back so that a plaza with trees, planting
boxes, and a fountain would cheer matters up—which they do.
    The interior's unencumbered expanse with its giant inverted space-
frame pyramids upholding the space-frame roof (14.5 feet/4.4 meters
deep) makes, as mentioned, a startling scene. The four roof sections of
double Warren trusses (i.e. based on equilateral triangles) were constructed on the floor, and jacked in stages to final position, the first
"stop" being to attach the pyramidal supporting legs to the frame.
Then the 5-foot/1.5-meter-square reinforced concrete columns (flared

at top as a code requirement) were poured and the legs lowered onto them. There are some 24,000 members in this great structural frame, each 10 feet/3 meters long. The building, as mentioned, can be divided at midpoint to create Halls A and B, with each of its four sections having its own penthouse and air-conditioning system to permit further subdivision. The mezzanine, which lines the exhibition space, is used for administrative offices. W. C. Muchow & Associates were in overall charge, with James T. Ream concerned with design and Dayl A. Larson production. Ketchum, Konkel, Barrett, Nickel & Austin were the structural engineers.

Open during exhibitions and conventions

---

13 The Denver Art Museum (1968–71)
100 West 14th Avenue Parkway
Denver, Colorado

JAMES SUDLER ASSOCIATES, ARCHITECTS, DENVER, AND GIO PONTI, STUDIO PFR, ARCHITECT, MILAN

A museum is a difficult architectural problem, and compounding this native aggravation, The Denver Art Museum (with the finest collection between Kansas City and the West Coast) had to shoehorn its substantial space needs into a tight midtown lot to be near the Civic Center Park and a maximum public. The result is a seven-story building of irregular shape—there are twenty-eight planar facets to its exterior (to mask its mass and to play games with sun and shade)—each plane with its own composition of fenestration à la Mondrian. The building is wrapped in a skin of 1 million gray glass tiles measuring 3 x 6 inches/76 x 152 millimeters. If the startling window development is capricious—as to some it is—it is also compelling: the museum cannot be ignored. But as the remarkable Gio Ponti said, "Architecture must create spectacles." The plan is comprised of two semiseparate, offset towers, roughly 96 feet/29 meters square, which diagonally flank the central elevator-utility core. Each of its seven floors thus carries two separate galleries except the double-height ground floor (the Changing Exhibition Gallery), for a total of eleven. Each provides some 9,500 square feet/882 square meters of display space. The structural pattern was evolved so that the galleries have only two columns hence are readily subdivisible. Artificial light is used throughout, relegating the windows to visual escape hatches for the interior, while from the outside they cast light patterns at night—"nocturnal architecture" said Signor Ponti. A spectacular penthouse roof-garden, abounding in abstract shapes, offers tempting panoramas. James Sudler, Joal Cronenwett—Mr. Sudler's Associate—and the late Gio Ponti collaborated on the design.

Open Tues.–Sat. 9–5, Sun. 1–5, Wed. also 5–9 P.M., *except holidays*

14   Park Central (1973–74)
Arapahoe between 15th and 16th Streets
Denver, Colorado

MUCHOW ASSOCIATES, ARCHITECTS

The genesis of this intriguingly multipartite office building reflects the
tower and lower floor needs of its prime client, the Central Bank and
Trust Company (to the left), with separately defined office sections for
commercial rental. Strict urban renewal demands (heights, etc.) added
their constraints. To arrive at an economic conclusion, the architects
projected a theoretical maximum of zoning possibilities, including
height limitations, then "subtracted"—in a few cases added—a series
of structural modules (30 feet/9.1 meters square) to pare the legally
allowed to the financially feasible. In effect it forms two towers (fifteen
and ten stories high) conjoined by an irregular central section. The
solid-and-void result and the energetic "building-block" profile produce a very smart group. In some respects the tension of closed to
pierced spaces, accented by a skin tightly wrapped in anodized alumi-

num, hints of a squared-off Henry Moore, so strong is its sculptured force. This is furthered by a tantalizing interpenetration quality in the building's relation to site via two passages leading from the sidewalk to an upper brick terrace jostled between the "towers." The most tempting of these is a through-the-building diagonal which, via the terrace, will eventually be connected with a pedestrian bridge over Lawrence Street to the rear.

The lofty banking area occupies most of the lower floor, with shops on the right-hand side. A three-level, 650-car garage lies below grade. Across the main facade (on Arapahoe Street) stretches a narrow block-long landscaped strip designed by Lawrence Halprin & Associates. Though welcome, its geometry and fountain are not totally in synchronization with the architecture. Altogether Park Central forms a stimulating addition to downtown Denver and a very original contribution to the difficult art of high-rise design. George Hoover was chief project designer.

Open during business hours

At the corner of Arapahoe and 16th stands the 21-story tower which formerly highlighted the old **D & F (Daniels and Fisher) Tower** (1911 —F. G. Sterner, architect). The emporium was recently torn down but its fine Venetian-inspired campanile was spared thanks to the sensitive Denver Planning Commission. In 1969 it was entered in the National Register of Historic Places. In 1980 the tower was remodeled into an office condominium, with Gensler and Associates the architects.

---

15   Johns-Manville World Headquarters (1977)
Deer Creek Canyon Road
c. 23 miles/37 kilometers SW of Denver via West Colfax Avenue,
**   S on IS 6/85 to US 6 near**
Denver, Colorado

THE ARCHITECTS COLLABORATIVE, ARCHITECTS

The Colorado topography is the most abruptly dramatic in the United States. After hundreds of miles of eastward plains and prairies, the western fortress of the Rocky Mountains rears suddenly from flatness with Denver clustered at its base. The most impressive man-made ad-

dition to the city's rumpled backdrop is this headquarters for the
Johns-Manville Corporation. (See also the Air Force Academy near
Colorado Springs.) Though of shining aluminum and 1,100 feet/335
meters long, this extraordinary building rests contrapuntally at peace
with its mountain setting, notching into the hillside with a minimum of
cut-and-fill. One's middle-distant impression of the building from the
winding approach road is momentarily disconcerting in that the nearest
(southeast) end rests on two-story-high columns which inject a slight
vertical note into the elegant basic horizontality. However, the road
then leads between the two long office blocks which make up the
building and one is soon surrounded by the grandeur of its structure.
This structural potency is emphasized by the fact that the left unit
(facing the mountains) is elevated on pilotis to mesh with the space.
Two parallel wings, bridged at the second level, were used instead of
one massive building to maintain a sympathetic scale yet not cower before the mountains. The reception area is on the ground floor of the

east building and on entering one enjoys a stunning panorama of a reddish rock outcropping with plains beyond seemingly stretching to infinity. A triangular pool and terrace below entry level ease the transition between the enclosed and the wild. The slope-roofed cafeteria conveniently adjoins.

The interiors—by The Space Design Group of New York—are bright and colorful and employ as many Johns-Manville products as feasible both for their quality and for in-house testing.

The factors involved in the decision to move to this site almost an hour from downtown Denver were, of course, numerous. But the majority of the corporation's 1,700 employees enjoy the inspiring views, pollution-free air, and superb recreation facilities, and many live within a 10-mile/16-kilometer radius.

Open by appointment with Corporate Relations Department; telephone: (303) 979-1000

16   Boettcher Concert Hall (1976–78)
14th Street at Curtis
Denver, Colorado

HARDY HOLZMAN PFEIFFER, ARCHITECTS

Boettcher Concert Hall is part of a comprehensive, interlocked, cultural exhibit, and convention complex known as the Denver Center for the Performing Arts. It possibly has no equal in the United States. The Center is anchored by the 1907 Auditorium Theater which, reputedly, was for years almost unequaled for advanced theater design. In 1976 it was completely updated. The Center then expanded with the Currigan Exhibition Hall (1969—q.v.), the Boettcher Concert Hall, and the Helen G. Bonfils Theater Complex (1980). A six-story garage (1977) by Muchow Associates adjoins. The three newest buildings are connected by an airy galleria 76 feet/23 meters high by 60 feet/18 meters wide, jointly designed by Muchow Associates and Roche/ Dinkeloo. The organization of the entire complex was based on early studies by Kevin Roche.

Boettcher Hall lies at the end of this galleria, which is scheduled to continue to meet the Hall itself to provide under-cover pedestrian access from both sidewalk and garage. In addition, this sparkling glass nexus will widen to make in effect a crystal lobby for both Boettcher and the Center for the Performing Arts. Much of Boettcher's main and boxlike facade thus will be incorporated in the final development.

The interior of the Concert Hall forms a near-square in plan (with lopped corners) and in this rises a startling arrangement of seats in swooping arcs completely surrounding the orchestra. The fourteen tiers and terraces of seats—which hold 2,750—project in irregular "circular" clusters of four to nine rows each, the great majority of them facing the front of the off-center stage. No person is more than 85 feet/26 meters from the stage, most are less than 65 feet/20 meters. The result is a "democratic," intimate, and refreshingly informal concert hall which should go far in attracting Denver's young adult population. (The 360° "surround" layout for orchestral music was pioneered by the late Hans Scharoun in his Berlin Philharmonie of 1963.) The stage is split and hydraulically adjustable and can accommodate 120 musicians. Overhead 106 shallow "bowls" of acrylic plastic form an acoustic canopy as they largely fill the ceiling. These reflector bowls can be adjusted in height to meet varying musical conditions. (There is also an "acoustical moat" under the stage.) The immediate center of

the ceiling is filled with a circular light bridge of prominence. The undulation of the balcony fascias stem from acoustic reasons (but not their gold leaf striping). The seats, which are of natural wood finish and cheerful red cloth, have high backs for sound reflection. The lobby, which flourishes some of the building's mechanics, is overly restricted in size, but when one enters the auditorium one gasps at its warm, almost pulsating space. Christopher Jaffe was acoustician; Jules Fisher/Paul Marantz Associates were lighting consultants; Ketchum, Konkel, Barrett, Nickel & Austin, engineers.

The Denver Center for the Performing Arts was completed in January 1980, with the opening of the **Helen G. Bonfils Theater.** Designed by Kevin Roche/John Dinkeloo & Associates, the complex comprises two theaters and a cinema. As it was not finished when last seen, comment must wait. Knowing the firm's work, the result should be sparkling.

Open for events

17   Visitor Center and Park Headquarters (1965–66)
Rocky Mountain National Park
2.5 miles/4 kilometers W of town via COL 66
Estes Park, Colorado

TALIESIN ASSOCIATES, ARCHITECTS

With ninety-eight mountains over 10,000 feet/3,048 meters—the
highest being Longs Peak at 14,255 feet/4,345 meters—Rocky Mountain National Park offers some of the most spectacular scenery in the
United States. Even the automobile roads are impressive, Trail Ridge
Road—the nation's loftiest major route—attaining 12,183 feet/3,713
meters. The area's beauty was brought to national attention by the
marvelously romantic paintings and enthusiasm of Albert Bierstadt
(1830–1902), while the idea and implementation of reserving it for a
national park was largely the unceasing work of Enos A. Mills. Thus in
1915 Rocky Mountain National Park came into being. It now covers
263,793 acres/106,757 hectares, with the Continental Divide angling
across the Park from northwest to southeast.

The Park Headquarters Building—designed by the successors of
Frank Lloyd Wright—is of dressed local boulders and weathering steel
to create a sympathetic-with-environment center for visitor information and park offices. The entry, on level, provides an information desk
and access to the (lower) two-story, 178-seat auditorium where a

helpful twelve-minute orientation slide/sound program on the park is shown every half hour in summer. The office block extends at right. The unusually handsome stonework, both outside and in, was achieved by utilizing a panel construction whereby carefully selected stones were "composed" face down on horizontal wood frames, smaller stones were scattered as aggregate, reinforcing bars (and in some cases conduits) installed, and the interstices filled with cement. When cured after setting for ten days, the panels, which number over a hundred in various sizes, were lifted into place by heavy cranes. The whole building is quietly and efficiently stated. Edmond Thomas Casey was chief of design.

Open all year, daily 8–5 in winter, 8–9 in summer: admission to Park

18 **Sheldon Jackson Memorial Chapel** (1874)
Hathaway Street at 6th
Fairplay, Colorado

A minuscule, well-preserved, neo-Gothic chapel in a high mining town. The exterior is framed with white boards and battens, topped by a fine belfry. Note that the pattern of the barge boards outlining the gable is repeated over the front door. The interior with its flat dropped ceiling is simple to the point of plainness. Dr. Jackson, a pioneer Presbyterian missionary, went to Alaska when he left Fairplay, becoming an energetic champion of Alaskan Indian rights. The Sheldon Jackson Museum in Sitka is his northern "memorial."

Always open; services on Sun., visitors welcome

19   Hotel de Paris Museum and the Town (1874–75)
411 Alpine Street
Georgetown, Colorado

Georgetown at 8,640 feet/2,630 meters is—so far—one of the least spoiled of the old Colorado mining centers, little having been changed by man or flames after the 1893 crash. It was once, supposedly, "the

greatest producer of silver in the world" and probably the wealthiest city in the state. Now, within sight of Interstate 70 and near several outstanding ski areas, its population of a thousand is quietly awakening and its old buildings are being refurbished and put to active use, while the newer ones are, in general, carefully screened from the old. Architecturally the most ambitious is the two-story Hotel de Paris, built by an outré, arrogant, but immensely clever Frenchman, Louis Dupuy (well-born as Adolphus Francis Gérard), who constructed it mostly himself with, reportedly, a French wood-carver and Chinese laborers. Dupuy ran his establishment like its larger contemporary the Paris Ritz, and ran it so well that a substantial masonry addition was made in 1882. Steam heat and all conveniences were laid on, while the food, often cooked by Louis himself, apparently was sensational. Dupuy died in 1900 and the hotel encountered a checkered career for years, closing in 1932. In 1954 the building and its largely original furnishings were purchased by the National Society of the Colonial Dames of America in the State of Colorado, restored as needed, and opened as a museum.

Museum open May–Sept., daily 9:30–6, Oct.–Apr., Sat.–Sun. 11–4: admission

NOTE: Stroll around the town. There are several good snippets from the past including some startling black and white vernacular.

20   Tabor Opera House (1879)
308 Harrison Avenue
Leadville, Colorado

BROOKE & BROOKE, ARCHITECTS

New York's Metropolitan Opera, the Chicago Symphony, John Philip
Sousa, all touched base at the Tabor, the only opera house in the
country—it is safe to surmise—at 10,152 feet/3,094 meters altitude.
The Tabor was "Cloud City's" claim to culture, an effort to bring "a
respectable place of amusement" to a mining town which entered history as "the most famous in the world." (Much of the Guggenheim
fortune originated here.) Leadville's prosperity seesawed through the
years, first with wealth from gold (1860s), then silver from lead-bear-
ing silver (late 1870s), then near-collapse with the repeal of the Sherman Silver Purchase Act of 1893. (This was legislation which had
been set up to nearly double the amount of silver coinage: it was
repealed because it threatened gold reserves.) Zinc (1900) perked
matters up, and there is now considerable activity in nearby Climax
with molybdenum, a metallic element primarily used for hardening

steel, but Leadville today, with some 4,400 souls, musters only about an eighth of its peak population of the 1890s.

The legendary H. A. W. Tabor—legendary in wealth for a while, and, one gathers, in other matters (e.g. *The Ballad of Baby Doe*)—was the man responsible for building the Opera House, but with the Sherman Act repeal he lost the mortgage in 1893, dying penniless six years later. The building was kept as an opera house and theater—for a while it was owned and run by the local Elks—eventually being used for a cinema. In 1955 Mrs. Florence A. Hollister purchased it, and with tender loving care restored as much as she could. After her death it was taken over by her daughter, Mrs. Evelyn E. Furman. Miraculously, some of the original hand-painted scenery is still intact. The auditorium, which seats 880 including the balcony, is entered from the second floor, giving a fine sweep of the stage, which, like the back stage and lower dressing rooms, is open to the public. The exterior, 60 x 60 feet/18 x 18 meters, has been little changed through the years, nor have the two stores which bracket the entry. The Tabor is a valuable architectural landmark and a social comment on its boisterous times, a building which should be taken under public wing and finances to ensure its future.

Open Memorial Day–Oct. 1; Sun.–Fri. 9–5:30: admission

The Matchless Mine, one of Mr. Tabor's chief sources of income (about $10 million altogether came from it), can also be visited. It lies about 2 miles/3.2 kilometers east of town via East 7th Street. (Open Memorial Day–Labor Day, daily 9–7: admission.)

---

21   Healy House (1878) **and Dexter Cabin** (1879)
Harrison Avenue at East 10th Street
Leadville, Colorado

The plain exteriors of this house and adjacent cabin give little indication of their elaborate interiors. The house, a simple, white clapboard structure, scarce merits a look on the outside (the third floor was added in 1888), but within it carries a full panoply of Victorian furnishings, a few original (the house had two series of owners), some donated by local residents.

The log cabin was built as a hunting lodge and, even more than the house, its rough-hewn, squared-log construction belies the richness within (note the wall coverings and floor). It was moved (1948) to this site after being acquired (1947) by the State Historical Society, which now operates both cabin and house.

Open June 1–Oct. 15, daily 9–4:30

---

22   Cliff Dwellings (c. A.D. 1200–1300)
   **21.5 miles/35 kilometers S of US 160 to Visitors Center (Park
      entrance 10 miles/16 kilometers E of Cortez)**
   Mesa Verde National Park, Colorado

For utmost symbiosis between architecture and landscape, man and nature, one need proceed no further than the Mesa Verde cliff dwellings. One can see circular troglodytic holes in the ground serving as efficient shelter in Tunisia (Matmata), and square ones in China (primarily Honan Province), but one will find more "architecture," more of the creative option of placing stone on stone, in the hundreds of cliff dwellings along the precipitous bluffs of this southwest corner of Colorado. The settlements—the largest and most numerous of their kind in the country—were established by the ancestors of today's Pueblo Indians.

The mesa itself, rising 1,300–2,000 feet/396–610 meters above the plains (8,572 feet/2,613 meters maximum above sea level), offered some natural defense through its heights and thus its top has been occupied and its soil cultivated (beans, squash, and corn) since approximately A.D. 450. Until the mid-eighth century these early people—the Modified Basket Makers (A.D. 450–750)—lived atop the mesa in "pit" houses (i.e. half in the ground), then in primitive, individual mud and stone dwellings. In the mid-eighth century the Indians adopted pole, wattle, and mud to build south-facing arcs of rectangular, attached "row houses," the resulting *pueblos* (i.e. "villages") giving them the name Pueblo Indians. By the year 1000 stone began to replace wooden posts: such construction later developed into complexes as long as 50 feet/15 meters and three stories high. Around 1200 the inhabitants moved off the mesas, and repaired to shelters under the cliff overhangs. It is not known precisely why they moved, for no evidence of unusual violence has been discovered. Defense against their own people has been suggested (clan disputes, etc.), plus theories of overpopulation, or environmental factors such as depletion of soil minerals. In any case many moved into the large "alcoves," almost caves, which had been created from water and frost action on the soft sandstone cliffsides. Hundreds and hundreds of cliff dwellings— five hundred is a frequently used figure (with a maximum of perhaps fifteen hundred rooms)—were then built along the cliff faces of the area, some being tiny affairs seemingly glued to the canyon wall and obviously capable of holding only one agile family's possessions, others virtually of village size. The majority of the population, which some authorities feel amounted to about seven hundred people in this area in the 1200s, lived in the many small cliff dwellings as opposed to the few large ones.

Almost all of the cliff settlements, except the smallest, had kivas or ceremonial subterranean chambers, which evolved from early pit houses, were rounded in shape, and reached only by a ladder via a small hatch in their roof (i.e. the cave floor). Used almost exclusively by the men, they occupied important spots in front of the apartments, each kiva (a Hopi word) being a form of "clan" headquarters and council chamber. Measuring 10–15 feet/3–4.6 meters in diameter, the kivas were approximately 6 feet/1.8 meters tall with a half-dozen ma-

sonry "piers" or pilasters on the periphery forming the vertical structure. On these rested layers of logs, each course angled to the one below until the roof structure was complete: on this mud was packed to seal the roof, which also served as "paving" for the courtyard. In the floor near the center was a fire pit, and as there was only a small opening for ladder access and smoke exit, a clever ventilation shaft fed fresh air to the bottom of the kiva, with a thin slice of sandstone placed upright to block direct draft onto the fire itself. A tiny hole in the floor, called a sipapu, formed the symbolic entrance for the gods of the underworld. In addition to council and religious uses, the kivas doubled as work spaces.

The largest of the Mesa Verde cliff dwellings (and the largest in the country) is the Cliff Palace, *bottom photo, facing page,* which measures 325 feet/99 meters long, has a maximum depth of approximately 100 feet/30 meters, and accommodated 250 to 400 souls at its peak, with some 200 rooms and 23 kivas. (The 110 steps down and the climb up can be strenuous for some at 7,000 feet/2,134 meters altitude.) Spruce Tree House (near the museum), *top photo, facing page,* at 216 x 89 feet/66 x 27 meters is smaller but better-preserved and easier of access. It had 114 rooms and 8 kivas. Architecturally all of them are ingenious, being well ordered in a tightly compacted space, every square foot of which was put to use: "a delirium of man-made geometry" (Vincent Scully, *Pueblo,* Viking Press, 1975). As the Indians lacked all but the simplest tools, the cliffsides themselves were rarely touched, the buildings adapting to the natural morphology of the setting (except for leveling the floor). Some of the "apartments" are four levels high, each being entered by a narrow (16–25-inch/41–64-centimeter) rectangular or T-shaped door. The round towers, incidentally, are most unusual, some authorities feeling that they are a Mesoamerican influence. Almost all exhibit capable masonry work, with the interiors plastered and occasionally decorated. Several stout logs formed the ceiling and roof joists, with smaller logs laid upon them at right angles, then branches and adobe added for finish. A single window, often no more than a peephole, admitted a bit of light and air, the doors being closed at night by a sandstone slab. Most units had a small fireplace. These modest chambers served almost exclusively as sleeping quarters and for storage.

Even more capable work, especially the masonry, can be seen in the semiruins of the nearby Sun Temple, a ceremonial structure superbly situated on a point of Chapin Mesa. This now forms a symmetrical roofless "maze" whose walls, 8–11 feet/2.4–3.4 meters high and 3 feet/.9 meter thick, describe a D-shaped form 121 x 64 feet/37 x 19 meters. Begun around 1270, it was never finished. Except for the reinforcement of the top of the walls no contemporary work has been needed to preserve this tantalizing and mysterious ruin.

The Four Corners area (Colorado, New Mexico, Arizona, Utah) suffered a severe drought from 1276–99—dates established by dendrochronology. It is thought that this, plus soil loss, forced abandonment and emigration southward. The dwellings lay unknown to the white man until Cliff Palace and others were discovered by two cowboys in December of 1888. (Several very small cliff dwellings had been discovered in Mancos Canyon in 1874 and 1875.) In 1906 the area—which had been heavily pilfered over the years—was made a National Park; shortly thereafter scientific measures were taken to excavate the ruins and stabilize the weakened remains to make them safe for visitors.

In addition to the Mesa Verde cliff dwellings built by the sedentary Pueblos, there are other cliff dwellings in the Four Corners region, notably The White House at the Canyon de Chelly National Monument in Arizona (q.v.), and the Montezuma Castle National Monument (q.v.) in the central part of that state. All are well worth seeing; the breathtaking views en route to Mesa Verde alone merit the trip.

Park open all year, Far View Visitors Center from Memorial Day–Labor Day, daily 8–5: admission to Park. The Far View Motor Lodge in the Park is open May 15–Oct. 15: reservations advised

---

23   Governor Adams Residence (1890–91)
Colorado and East Orman Avenues
Pueblo, Colorado

WILLIAM W. STICKNEY, ARCHITECT

A red Colorado sandstone pile, bursting with towers, projections, and arched windows, typical of its period. Used as a school administration building from 1951 to 1978, it became redundant on completion of new educational facilities. However, in 1979 it was purchased by three physicians who are committed to the preservation of the exterior of the building and the grounds. It is a fine example of the self-confident, rugged architectural showmanship of a few generations ago.

Visitable during office hours

Hawaii

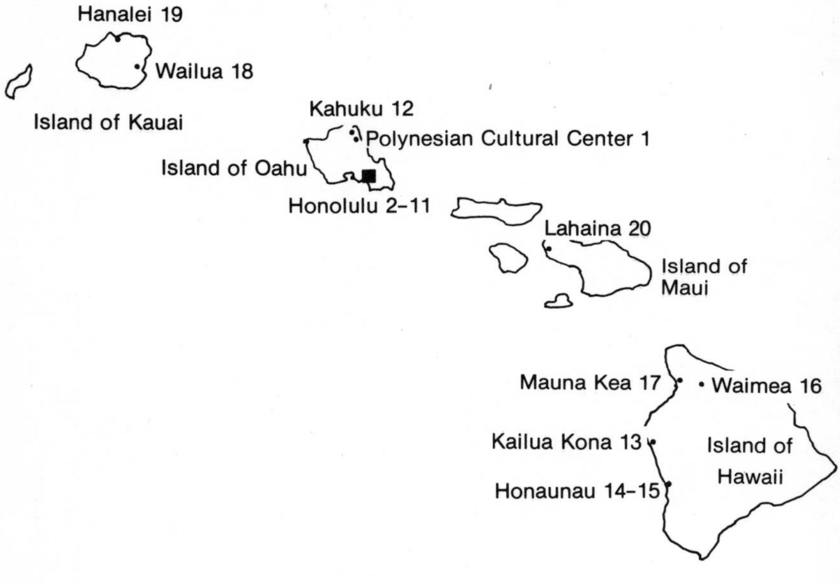

Hanalei 19

Wailua 18

Island of Kauai

Kahuku 12

Polynesian Cultural Center 1

Island of Oahu

Honolulu 2-11

Lahaina 20

Island of Maui

Mauna Kea 17   • Waimea 16

Kailua Kona 13   Island of Hawaii

Honaunau 14-15

HAWAII

The buildings in boldface type are of general interest. The others are for the specialist.

Island of Oahu
   Laie
        1 **Hawaiian Vernacular Architecture and the Polynesian Cultural Center**

   Honolulu
        Grass House, Bishop Museum
        2 **Kawaiahao Church** (1836–42)— Reverend Hiram Bingham
        3 **Mission Houses** (1821–41)
        4 Queen Emma's Summer Palace (Hanaiakamalama—1849)
        5 **Iolani Palace** (1879–82)—T. J. Baker, C. J. Wall, Isaac Moore
        Judiciary Building (1872–74)— Thomas Rowe
        6 **YWCA Metropolitan Headquarters** (1926–27)—Julia Morgan
        7 **Honolulu Academy of Arts** (1926–27)—Bertram G. Goodhue
        8 **East-West Center** (1963)—I. M. Pei & Associates
        9 **State Capitol** (1965–69)—John Carl Warnecke & Associates and Belt, Lemmon & Lo
        10 Queen Emma Garden Apartments (1964)—Minoru Yamasaki
        11 **KuKui Garden Housing** (1969–70)—Daniel, Mann, Johnson & Mendenhall

   Kahuku
        12 Kahuku Sugar Mill (1890)

Island of Hawaii
   Kailua Kona
        13 Kailua Town

   Honaunau
        14 **Pu'uhonua O Honaunau National Historical Park** (City of Refuge— 16th–17th century, restored 1969)

15 St. Benedict's Church (The Painted
    Church—1902)—Father John
    (Velghe)

Waimea

16 Hawaii Preparatory Academy
    (1965–70)—Vladimir Ossipoff

Mauna Kea

17 **Mauna Kea Beach Hotel** (1965–
    68)—Skidmore, Owings & Merrill

Island of Kauai
Wailua

18 Holoholoku Heiau

Hanalei

19 Waioli Mission Hall (1841)
    Mission House (1836)
    Waioli Mission Church (1912)

Island of Maui
Lahaina

20 **The Reverend Dwight Baldwin**
    House (1832–35)

1 Hawaiian Vernacular Architecture and the Polynesian Cultural Center

off Highway 83

Laie, Oahu, Hawaii

There are some twenty islands and over one hundred atolls in the 1,523-mile/2,450-kilometer-long Hawaiian chain or archipelago, a minute and long-isolated fraction of the more than seven thousand islands which pepper the Pacific. Of the former Sandwich Islands only six are substantially inhabited, and although the wide world peoples this half-dozen today, the background of the settlers of our fiftieth state traces to Indo-Malaysian origins. Around 1·500 B.C. a group of these adventurous souls pushed (or were pushed) eastward where they landed in what is now known as western Polynesia, and where they developed the Tonga-Samoan civilization. About A.D. 150 another venturesome band sailed almost 2,000 miles/3,200 kilometers again eastward, in their double-hulled "canoes" (which could hold fifty people plus possessions, and which the early European sailors fortunately described) to what is now the Marquesas, which lie a bit east and far south of Hawaii. From the Marquesas the first migration to the Hawaiian Islands took place (A.D. 500–750). This was followed (around A.D. 1000–1250) by a similar influx of conquering Tahitians from the Society Islands, who themselves had originally come from the Marquesas—some of whom also sailed southwestward to become New Zealand's Maoris. (Places and dates taken from *Resource Units in Hawaiian Culture,* The Kamehameha Schools, 1969, from data adapted from the research of Dr. Kenneth Emory.) Two-way voyages from the Marquesas and Society Islands to the Hawaiian chain were not uncommon, though it is not known how these early sailors made correct landfalls over 2,500 miles/4,000 kilometers of open ocean without instruments—plus carrying provisions for the two- to three-week (or more) journey. (It is 2,742 statute miles/4,412 kilometers from Honolulu to Tahiti, and it is surprising to realize that the "South Seas" island of Tahiti is east of Hawaii, while a slice of mainland Alaska, not to mention the Aleutians, is west of Honolulu.)

The building techniques that all Polynesians, which includes the Hawaiians, developed, and in some cases still employ, were and are based on a thatch tradition over a wood frame—the materials at hand, that inevitable, unfoibled characteristic of all vernacular construction. The most rudimentary form of Hawaiian shelter could be described as an "A-frame" (sometimes bowed) of "grass," while more advanced types have low vertical walls, at times of stone, and reach substantial size with gabled roofs. Framing consists of trimmed posts of hardwood, notched and lashed together, the lashings usually made of braided grasses or coconut fibers, their knottings often of an intricate nature. Reed "rods," or purlins, brace the roof structure horizontally while forming a frame for the thatch, with smaller rods on the sides, strengthened between the structural posts by vertical members, the whole expertly bound together. The thatch used to enclose and make watertight the structure is made of one of several grasses, *pili* being a favorite because of its fragrance, but *pandanus* (whose leaves are flat and broad), sugarcane and *ti* leaves, and banana fibers are also employed. Thatching begins at the bottom and works up to the ridge—whose closure represents the most complicated task and one generally accompanied by a ritual prayer—with one man working outside and a second within. The cord for binding the thatch (and also used for making fishnets, etc.) is of braided coconut fiber or from the bark of the olana bush, a native Hawaiian shrub of the nettle family. When the building is completely thatched it is neatly trimmed. The floors of the better houses are generally of stone covered with mats, others use leaves on tamped earth. A simple fireplace generally occupies the center, bordered by stones, while a single door, closable by a flap or board, forms the sole opening in small dwellings. In an insect-free, subtropical climate, such dwellings were—and are in remote areas today—highly satisfactory. (The white man not only brought in flies, mosquitoes, rats, ants, and a host of other pests—perhaps with some help from the Polynesians—but introduced diseases that ravaged the native population. These scourges—plus intermarriage—reduced an estimated 300,000 pure Hawaiians in 1778 to 44,088 one hundred years later, to 10,502 in the 1960 census, to probably less than half that today.)

Although all of the pre-European buildings have long since vanished, being of short-lived material, even the art of thatch construction fading in the nineteenth century before ferrous tools and sawmills, we nonetheless have highly useful documentation on pure Hawaiian building types. For Captain James Cook, the first European to "discover" (1778) the Hawaiian Islands—and the first to be killed there (1779)·in a lamentable incident—foresightedly took with him an artist (John Webber) and a surgeon with graphic ability, both of whom made numerous drawings of the villages they visited. Their still-preserved sketches have been most helpful to use today in reconstructions such as that at the Polynesian Cultural Center.

The Church of Jesus Christ of Latter-day Saints (Mormon) has had a very active missionary focus throughout much of the Pacific Basin

since 1850. Dedicated to preserving the regional arts of Polynesia, they have brought together in this non-profit Center (on land purchased in 1865) an impressive and authentically reconstructed collection of some two dozen buildings from the major cultural divisions of the South Pacific. There are seven villages representing Tonga, Samoa, Tahiti, the Marquesas, New Zealand (Maori), Fiji and Hawaii, a microcosm which gives valuable insight into now largely vanished eras. Although the structures in all seven villages are of similar "plant" materials, there is an intriguing variation in architectural solutions, all of which are worthy of examination. The diversity of building types is underscored by several hundred students from the nearby and affiliated Brigham Young University—Hawaii Campus (which the Center helps support through scholarships and grant programs), some from each of the above-mentioned islands. They help pay their way through school by serving as guides, entertainers, reservationists, and in numerous other capacities at the Center. Altogether the Center is a revelatory cross-section of Hawaiian and other Polynesian architecture.

A 10.5 x 12.5-foot/3.2 x 3.8-meter authentic **Grass House** can also be seen in the Bernice P. Bishop Museum in Honolulu where it has been carefully reerected and installed. The Museum also publishes a number of highly informative booklets. Its *Arts and Crafts of Hawaii,* by Peter H. Buck, Bishop Museum Special Publication 45, 1957, includes an excellent section on housing. (The Museum's address is 1355 Kalihi Street; it is open daily 9–5, except Jan. 1, Dec. 25: admission.) The architect of Bishop Hall itself (1894) is unknown; Museum Hall (1889), Polynesian Hall (1893), and Hawaiian Hall (1899) were designed by W. F. Smith—with strange disregard for both culture and climate.

The following descriptions of the construction techniques characteristic of the seven "villages" in the Center were thoughtfully provided by the Polynesian Cultural Center. Their notes (here of necessity condensed) give perceptive insight into the variety of shelter responses in the Pacific Basin.

Hawaii Hawaiian huts were made of the wood of trees indigenous to the particular area in the islands where they stood, a common one being the *ohia.* The exterior thatching was made of dried leaves from the *hala* tree (*pandanusodoratissimus*) or *pili* grass. This was sometimes covered with a large fishnet to keep the thatch from curling up from the wind, thus looking untidy. Huts were built on a raised mound of dirt to keep floods from washing through them. Inside, the roof was thatched with *pandanus* leaves and the floor was covered with mats.

Fiji Fijian huts were made out of reed and bamboo, with sugarcane leaf thatching. The high and steeply pitched roof was designed to drain rainwater quickly and effectively. It also allowed for good ventilation and circulation, which were especially important in the warm, humid climate of Fiji. The building was kept cool because the hot air rose and the high roof caught and circulated the breezes. The roof lasted for many years because of the small fireplace in the corner of the room: in most Fijian buildings, such a fireplace was lit every day, thus very effectively smoking the roof and preserving it.

The Marquesas A basic Marquesan architectural feature is the use of the *paepae* or raised stone platform. All structures were built on this, with the chief's dwelling being the largest and the highest-positioned in the village. The Marquesans also built high roofs, which provided good ventilation and ample storage room. The frames for the houses were formed out of *koa* or ironwood; the roof's beams usually were made of hibiscus tree wood. Bamboo also was used as a building material. All structures were thatched with pandanus, coconut, or dried sugarcane leaves. The support poles of the buildings all had carved inscriptions which told the name of the family who lived in it or the purpose of the structure.

Tahiti Most Tahitian buildings were made of bamboo poles lashed together with *sennit,* a strong rope woven out of coconut husk fibers. The roof was usually thatched with leaves from the coconut tree. Supporting poles were fashioned from ironwood. Important buildings, such as community centers or dwellings of royalty, were identifiable by the round-ended architectural style and large size. The floors of these huts were covered with very finely woven mats.

Maori (New Zealand) Typical of Maori architecture was the *Whare Runanga* or house of learning. This was the village center of Maori cultural and tribal activities, where traditional customs and ceremonies were maintained. The *Whare Runanga* was the most important and elaborate building in the village. As with many Maori buildings, it was made of bark and covered on both roof and walls with the split trunks of the *punga* fern which may grow up to 30 feet/9.1 meters high in New Zealand. At the top of the building was the *tekoteko* or gable figure which represents the tribe's common ancestor whose *mana* or protective power was over the entire village.

Tonga In typical Tongan architectural style, the building is supported inside by four large ironwood posts, to which thirty-two coconut palm tree trunks are lashed with sennit rope. No nails or screws are used in this or any other Tongan building. More coconut trunks are split into smaller pieces which are lashed together to make the ribbing which holds up the roof. The roof is thatched with sugarcane leaves. As with most Tongan buildings, there is no furniture. Instead, very fine mats woven out of dried pandanus leaves are spread throughout the building —even lining the bamboo walls. Beneath these mats, dry coconut leaves are placed for extra softness.

Samoa   The construction in typical Samoan architectural style was with a rounded shape, a domed roof thatched with sugarcane leaves, and evenly spaced posts supporting beams in the center. No nails or screws were used; instead, sennit rope braided from the inner fibers of the coconut husk was employed to "tie" the building together. The floor of the house was typically of flat, smooth, round-shaped stones, which were chosen to help balance the temperature in the building. On hot, humid days, the stones helped cool the building, while on cooler days, they helped to keep the building warm.

Open daily except Sun.; village tours 10 A.M. *to dusk. Three shows a day: admission*

---

2   Kawaiahao Church (1836–42)
King and Punchbowl Streets
Honolulu, Oahu, Hawaii

REVEREND HIRAM BINGHAM, DESIGNER

The Kawaiahao Church is a surprisingly competent house of worship, considering that its designer was a Vermont-born missionary and ad hoc architect. The church is the fifth on its site, its smaller predecessors having been of thatch. The tightly trim facade combines a white-painted Classic attached "portico" with a tan and weathered "Gothic"-derived coral tower and walls, but the ambience excuses all architectural naiveté. (Note the entry piers and gates especially.) The simple interior is more accomplished, even though its galleries and small windows reflect New England, not the semitropics. The walls are made up of some 14,000 blocks of coral, or "reef rocks" as they are locally known, cut from the reef that stretches from Waikiki to Pearl Harbor. A Congregational service is held at 10:30 A.M. every Sunday,

in which both the English and Hawaiian languages are used. The building is a National Historic Landmark.

The Reverend Abraham K. Akaka, pastor of the church, very thoughtfully sent me the following excerpts from the diary of Dr. Gerritt P. Judd, written in 1840–42:

July 8, 1840—"Having received the promise of a mano or two (a mano is 10 x 400, equal to 4000) of mamaki kapa and 200 cattle from the king (to be exchanged for shingles for the church), I started for Waialua to hire 100,000 shingles made."

April 27, 1841—"Punihaole (a deacon) went to Ewa to measure timber."

June 12, 1841—"Timber for meeting house being brought."

August 27, 1841—"Wrote contract for roof of church . . . Commenced in good earnest. Sawing going on."

November 11, 1841—"Raised last rafters."

January 10, 1842—"Roof of Hale Pule finished. Paid off the carpenters."

A delightful insight.

Open Mon.–Sat. 8:30–4; Sun. service

3   Mission Houses (1821–41)
553 South King Street
Honolulu, Oahu, Hawaii

Standing a block east of Kawaiahao Church, and also designated Landmarks, are three Mission Houses of which the Frame House is of particular interest in that it was largely prefabricated in Boston in 1819, disassembled and shipped around the Horn. The King having finally given permission, it was reerected on the present site in 1821. Sitting on an excavated basement, which also doubled as dining room, the house, like the church, is of proper New England design with small windows against "northern blasts." (The missionaries and their children suffered as a result.) Additions were made, alterations came and went, then the whole house was restored to its original state in 1935, but with a new inner frame to replace that consumed by termites, and with steel and concrete sustaining the foundations. In 1970, for the Sesqui-

centennial of the missionaries' arrival, only minor repairs and new exhibits were needed. Adjacent to the Frame House stands the erroneously termed "Printing House" of coral, once thought to have been the Island's first permanent building, but recently found to have been built (1841) as additional bedroom space for the Frame House. Printing, incidentally, flourished at this time—most of it concerned with translation of the Bible—and a replica of a Ramage press is displayed in the building to commemorate this. Next door stands the Levi Chamberlain House (1830–31), built like the "Printing House" of coral from the harbor. It served as combined dwelling for the Chamberlains and warehouse for the Mission. Used subsequently as a home and as a school, in 1919 it was completely renovated and now contains offices for the Hawaiian Mission Children's Society, the three buildings together forming an enlightening museum of missionary days.

Open daily 9–4, except major holidays: admission

---

4   Queen Emma's Summer Palace (Hanaiakamalama—1849)
2913 Pali Highway (HI 61)
Honolulu, Oahu, Hawaii

Similar to the plantation houses of its era in Mississippi and Louisiana —and logically so from the heat-humidity standpoint—(note high ceilings and fluted Tuscan columns), this simple summer home bears intimately close connections with the Mainland. All its timbers and woodwork were shipped here from New England, there being at that time insufficient sawmills on the Islands. It forms a cool, "mountain" retreat with most of the furnishings of its time. Purchased by the patriotic Daughters of Hawaii, when its destruction was threatened, the house was fully restored and opened as a museum in 1915.

Open daily 9–4, except major holidays: admission

---

5 **Iolani Palace** (1879–82)
King Street between Richards and Likelike
Honolulu, Oahu, Hawaii

T. J. BAKER, C. J. WALL, ISAAC MOORE, ARCHITECTS

Suggesting the Renaissance gone tropic, plus hints from Second Empire France, the Iolani Palace, though modest in size (100 x 140 feet/30 x 43 meters), is architecturally fascinating. It is, moreover, the country's only Royal Palace. Designed by T. J. Baker, and modified by Wall and Moore "after a serious flaw was discovered in the original plans," the palace, which replaced an earlier one, is constructed of brick stuccoed and numerous well-made columns of cast iron. Two-story lanais embellish each side. Only two monarchs occupied the building: King Kalakaua, who lived there with Queen Kapiolani from 1882 until his death in 1891 (having survived a "revolution" in 1887), and his sister Queen Liliuokalani who ruled only two years, and did not "survive" a revolution when the monarchy was ended in 1893. (Hawaii was annexed as a territory by the United States on August 12, 1898, and the Palace was used as the capitol until the new one—q.v. —was built.) The Iolani, which means "Bird of Heaven," has recently been beautifully restored as a museum. It is an essential document of Hawaii, especially its Throne Room (the original twin thrones are in the Bishop Museum), but also including the other chambers. Many of the artifacts were acquired by King Kalakaua on a trip around the world, the first king, it is said, to make such a tour. (The chandeliers are American.) Stroll, also, through the well-kept grounds with a giant banyan tree (*Ficus bengalensis*) in one corner and an octagonal band-

stand, built (1883) as the King's Coronation Pavilion in the other (and rebuilt, largely of termite-proof concrete, in 1920).

Open Mon.–Fri. 8–4, Sat. 8–12

Directly facing the Palace stands the resplendent Statue of King Kamehameha the Great (1758?–1819), who unified the islands. An American, T. R. Gould, was the sculptor. Behind the statue rises the **Judiciary Building** (Aliiolani Hale), King and Mililani streets, designed by an Australian, Thomas Rowe (1872–74—open during office hours). Perhaps more "correct" in its amalgam of architectural el-

ements than the later Palace (Palladio and Inigo Jones can be detected), the Judiciary lacks the imaginative spark that highlights the royal dwelling. Ironically, it was itself designed as the palace, but official office space took precedence. Its interiors, largely courtrooms, are architecturally unimportant.

---

6 YWCA Metropolitan Headquarters (1926–27) 1040 Richards Street (opposite Iolani Palace) Honolulu, Oahu, Hawaii

JULIA MORGAN, ARCHITECT

The considerable talents of Julia Morgan (1872–1957) fortunately now are being recognized. Her work for Mr. Hearst's San Simeon (q.v.) was outstanding, but in some respects it represented a highly skilled organization of existing parts. This YWCA building totally reflects her design ability and is, many think, her finest achivement. It directly faces the Iolani Palace while on the other side its gardens, designed by Catherine Thompson, once extended to the street behind. Ms. Morgan was the first woman accepted by the Paris École des Beaux-Arts, and the Y's facade and details reflect a restrained semi-classical derivation but one put together with freedom. Its surprise,

and delight, is the unanticipated courtyard in the center of the building, with a sizable open-air swimming pool on one side of the two-story central arcade, and a garden patio, alive with umbrellas, on the other. This latter adjoins the cafeteria which is also open to the public from 6:30 A.M. to 3 P.M. In addition to clarity of organization, note the details and the handsome wrought ironwork. The building serves as metropolitan headquarters, and in addition provides meeting rooms, gymnasium and recreational facilities, and educational functions (arts, crafts, cooking, etc.). Residential accommodations are provided in another building.

Open daily 9–5, except major holidays

---

7 Honolulu Academy of Arts (1926–27)
900 South Beretania Street
Honolulu, Oahu, Hawaii

BERTRAM G. GOODHUE, ARCHITECT

A domestically scaled, quiet building that tactfully encourages exploration of its extensive galleries, its five open-air courtyards, and its sculpture garden. Together they present an outstanding collection of the arts

of China, Japan, Korea, and India (the galleries to left on entering), plus a representative input from America and Europe (galleries to right). In addition to the collections, there are classes in art practice and history, lectures, concerts, films, and a well-stocked library. Note the gentle upturned eaves of the prominent roof and its soft gray tiles, the arc of the individual tiles being echoed in the wall vents at the end. The scale throughout is excellent (except for the exedra in the Central Court with Bourdelle's *La Grande Pénèlope,* 1912, in its niche). The granite paving stones of the Oriental Court reputedly came from China as ballast: sandalwood for incense was shipped back. The Academy was one of Goodhue's last designs (he died in 1924), and was also one where the client and generous donor, Mrs. Charles Montague Cooke, had a contributory hand. The building was finished by Hardie Phillips. The Robert Allerton Library wing, by Albert Ely Ives, was added in 1956 and an educational wing in 1960 by the same architect. The Clare Boothe Luce Wing, designed by John Hara, was opened in 1977 in celebration of the Museum's fiftieth anniversary. This serves largely for the contemporary collection and also includes a 290-seat theater plus administrative offices. The Garden Café (behind the Central Court) is open during museum hours.

Open Tues.–Sat. 10–4:30, Sun. 2–5

8 East-West Center (1963)
University of Hawaii
East-West Road (N of city via University Avenue, E on Dole Street)
Honolulu, Oahu, Hawaii

I. M. PEI & ASSOCIATES, ARCHITECTS

The Center for Cultural and Technical Interchange Between East and West was established by Congress in 1960 for "the promotion of better relations and understanding among nations and peoples of Asia, the Pacific, and the United States." Its main building, Jefferson Hall, authoritatively holds down its site at the top of a curved road with a dramatically cantilevered structure largely made of post-tensioned concrete beams. These are explicitly revealed and their built-up logic gives the building visual potency—and even a hint of Japanese wood construction. The core of the ground-floor level is a two-story lounge, and this is flanked on both sides by six substantial piers with arched heads —almost an arcade. On these piers rest twin continuous beams which

run the full length of the building. At right angles atop these twin beams and their piers are placed a series of closely spaced lateral beams, also of post-tensioned concrete, and not only spanning the width of the lower part but cantilevered 15 feet/4.6 meters beyond the two long sides. Atop this "platform," but set back to create a peripheral balcony, are offices and meeting rooms of the Center with deep fasciaed roof above. The lounge itself, which occupies the whole ground floor except for the stair halls at the two ends, is narrow in width, being actually less than half as wide as the top office level, but its glass-lined sides make an airy room. The off-street side opens onto a quiet terrace overlooking the woods while an oriental garden with stream and large goldfish beckons at the level below. Be certain to see this side of the building: with its landscaping and privacy it is most hospitable. It should be noted that planting for visual pleasure or ornamentation did not occur in the Islands until introduced by the *haoles* ("aliens"), here the Japanese.

The Center is flanked by three dormitories with a capacity of five hundred. Hale Manoa to west (and shown in photograph) is architecturally the most virile. Young & Henderson were the associate architects.

Open during school year

---

9   State Capitol (1965–69)
Beretania Street between Richards and Punchbowl
Honolulu, Oahu, Hawaii

JOHN CARL WARNECKE & ASSOCIATES AND BELT, LEMMON & LO, ARCHITECTS

Architectural symbolism, being elusive, finds rare use today. However in this capitol we find a bowed roof profile with a voluptuous void in the center which hints of the island's volcanic origin, a moat recalling the seas around it, and a towering (65 feet/20 meters high) peristyle of twenty-four columns reminiscent of the palms which line its shores. The large walk-through central court, open to the sky, as mentioned, develops strong architectural forces with its contrast of lateral versus vertical spaces and its sharp chiaroscuro. This courtyard also imaginatively serves as a viewing platform for the two chambers for Senate

and House of Representatives—both ovoid—which occupy lower levels on opposite sides. Their end walls are of glass enabling the public to watch proceedings even when outside the building. (There are, of course, interior spectator galleries.) Senate offices (second floor) and House offices (third) are tucked under and shaded by the larger fourth level which is devoted to departmental offices and is immediately identifiable by its frieze of vertical louvers. The setback executive level occupies the top floor (fifth) and is surrounded by a deck. The square "well" in the center diminishes slightly above the third floor. Parking for 234 official cars is in the basement. Construction is of earthquake-resistant concrete. John Carl Warnecke was architect in charge of design; Cyril W. Lemmon architect in charge of project development. The master plan for the area is now fully developed and the Capitol's grounds flow into those surrounding the nearby Iolani Palace (q.v.).

Grounds and court open daily, tours of building Mon.–Fri. 9–5

---

10 Queen Emma Garden Apartments (1964)
1519 Nuuanu Avenue (HI 61) at North Vineyard
Honolulu, Oahu, Hawaii

MINORU YAMASAKI, ARCHITECT

Three apartment blocks containing 587 units which are located only a short distance from the Capitol and downtown. They are characterized by excellent land usage and mutual disposition, and by calm, almost self-effacing architecture. They do not sing but they hum a civilized tune. Note the window detail whereby a projecting sunshield permits open transoms in rainy weather.

Can only be seen from road

11 KuKui Garden Housing (1969–70)
Liliha Street between North Vineyard Boulevard and Beretania
Honolulu, Oahu, Hawaii

DANIEL, MANN, JOHNSON & MENDENHALL, ARCHITECTS

Decent, low-cost housing is disgracefully absent in the United States but here one can stand up and cheer. This large complex, which houses 630 families, has been compactly but imaginatively planned. Though using the maximum of ground space there is little feeling of confinement, except a small squeeze at rear. This tight land usage was made feasible by confining all parking to the outer periphery and by the injection of occasional six-story duplex units to give volumetric variety to the basic three-story row houses. The latter cleverly combine a ground-floor flat with a duplex above, which is reached by outside stair, the top floor of the duplex having a setback terrace which further

"expands" living space. A community and recreational center act as the focus of the development, somewhat inadequately because of space limitations, while a fifteen-story tower for the elderly marks one corner (at Beretania Street). Housing details such as sun protection, jalousie windows, planting, laundromats, etc., have been cleverly thought out in addition to excellent apartment planning. An extension of the color spectrum beyond white and pale ocher might enliven the scene, and the playground area is not the most imaginative (the buildings framing it not numbering among the best), but all in all this is one of the finest FHA housing developments in the fifty states. Cesar Pelli and Anthony Lumsden were its designers.

Grounds always open

---

12   Kahuku Sugar Mill (1890)
on Kamehameha Highway near NE top of Oahu (c. 30 miles/48
**   kilometers from Honolulu)**
Kahuku, Oahu, Hawaii

Sugar is one of Hawaii's chief crops and exports, and its production facilities give an illuminating insight into—and respect for—the mechanization needed to produce a simple, basic food additive. Sugarcane was probably brought to the Islands by the Polynesians, and it was growing there—mostly as windbreaks—when Captain Cook landed in 1778. Production became increasingly mechanized through the nineteenth century. The present Kahuku Mill commenced operations in 1890 on the site of an earlier plant, but ceased in 1971, its competition having more productive soil, more sunshine, and superior transportation. In 1976 it was transformed into a "mill museum" with the original machinery intact and in some cases in simulated action. Color has been added (in cases perhaps over-added) to code the different processes. An introductory film gives background on sugar-milling and its workers, almost all of whom were imported from China, Japan, the Philippines, and Portugal as native Hawaiians disdained heavy field work. The escorted tour through the mill impresses one with the forces needed—including 1 ton/.9 metric ton of water—to produce 1 pound/.45 kilograms of sugar from stalks of that tall perennial grass known as *Saccharum officinarum*. The raw sugar, generally in 100-pound/45-kilogram burlap bags, was sent to California to be refined. Commercialism is evident in the Mill's twenty ground-floor shops but this can be forgotten in an appreciation of the industrial process concerned with food. There are, incidentally, seven eating establishments on the grounds.

Open daily 10–6 with frequent tours: admission

---

13 Kailua Town
Kailua, Hawaii, Hawaii

Kailua, or Kailua-Kona to distinguish it from the fast-growing Kailua on Oahu, nests in a picture-book bay on the west coast of the Island of Hawaii. Its palms massage the harbor in the foreground while the 8,276-foot/2,522-meter volcanic Hualalai (last eruption 1801) serves as a backdrop. Man is introduced via the spire of the Mokuaikaua Church (an 1837 replacement of the 1826 original with 1937 restorations) and the balconied Hulihee Palace (1838, restored as a museum in 1927 and 1953). The impact of man was particularly important in the history and development of this side of the Big Island. Captain James Cook, who had first "discovered"—at least as regards the West

—the archipelago in 1778, was, as has been mentioned, killed down the Kona coast a year later; the great King Kamehameha I died in his favorite resort of Kailua in 1819; and in 1820 the stout brig *Thaddeus* arrived off Kailua's shore bearing fourteen New England missionaries to "elevate" the enticingly unclad, fun-loving indigenes to the blessings of Christianity. It was not much later, and due largely to the influx of sailing ships and their well-known crews, that approximately three quarters of the local population were dead of the white man's diseases. However, in spite of the machinations of Lucifer, the setting is glorious.

---

14 Pu'uhonua O Honaunau National Historical Park
(City of Refuge—16th–17th century, restored 1969)
on HI 16, S of HI 11, c. 21 miles/34 kilometers S of Kailua
Honaunau, Hawaii, Hawaii

"The cities which you give to the Levites shall be the six cities of refuge, where you shall permit the manslayer to flee" (Numbers 35:6, Revised Standard Version). Although the ancient Hawaiian cities of

refuge obviously differ in detail from those frequently mentioned in the Old Testament, the concept was basically the same. Refuge in a church "sanctuary" was of course carried down to medieval times in Europe and was thus contemporaneous with the Hawaiians. As stern vengeance, often death, was visited on all who broke the complex system of sacred Island *kapus* or taboos (*tabu* itself is a Tongan word), these sanctuaries (*pu-uhonuas*) proved an essential societal cog. Those seeking safety within their sacred confines—often women, children, and old men in time of bitter internecine war—found sanctuary and/or absolution from their misdeeds, the latter at times rendered by the resident priests in a matter of hours after suitable prayers. So important was this haven concept in early Hawaii that "cities" of refuge, sometimes just a designated cave, were found on all islands. The most impressive one remaining is this partially restored example on Honaunau Bay in the Pu'uhonua O Honaunau National Historical Park, not far south of the spot where Captain Cook met his untimely death.

In 1819 King Liholiho (Kamehameha II, who reigned 1819–24)

overthrew the "kapu" proscriptions—which even extended to the type of food women could eat, let alone their not eating with men—and destroyed most of the existing *heieus,* or temples, a startling act of apostasy which undoubtedly facilitated the introduction of Christianity by the missionaries who arrived (providentially?) the following year. Because the bones of King Kamehameha the Great, Liholiho's father, were buried at the Honaunau Temple, or Hale-o-Keawe—plus the remains of other ancestors and relatives—this City of Refuge was spared, only to be razed in 1829. The "City" occupies the end of a small peninsula, and is defined on one side by an angled wall approximately 1,000 feet/305 meters long, 10 feet/3 meters high, and 17 feet/5.2 meters thick, and on the other sides by the sea. The ambitious wall, which dates from around A.D. 1550, is constructed of rough blocks of lava, some weighing between 4 and 6 tons/3.6 and 5.4 metric tons laid without mortar. (The lava came from the 13,677-foot/4,169-meter Mauna Loa, the world's largest active volcano, which lies about 22 miles/35 kilometers east of the City of Refuge. Its last major eruption occurred in 1950 with its lava flowing nearby to the sea; in much earlier blowouts the lava covered the site.) A large platform which once formed the base of a temple, and which also dates from the mid-sixteenth century, stands within the enclosure near the site of an earlier *heieu*—and was probably built with its stones. The highlight of the compound is the third temple, the Hale-o-Keawe mentioned, which served as the Royal Mausoleum. This tent-shaped, thatched structure, built originally around A.D. 1650, was meticulously reconstructed by National Park Service experts in 1966–69 fortunately aided by sketches made by early European visitors. The temple's sacred ground is protected by a stout fence of sharpened pales, with perhaps more effective "protection" afforded by the fearsome collection of *akua ki'i* (literally "god images"), here wooden pole-figures representing the gods buried within, some twenty-three deified kings and chiefs. (Are these pole-figures distant cousins of the totem poles of the Indians of the Northwest continental United States?)

A few hundred yards to the north and near the shore stand two thatched shelters, one left purposefully unfinished to show graphically the complexity of the seemingly simple Polynesian "grass" construction. In sum, the City of Refuge offers a wonderfully enlightening display of old Hawaiian culture. The Park Service has also designed a first-rate orientation building near the entrance.

Park open daily 6 A.M.–midnight, Visitor Center open daily 7:30–5:30; six orientation talks a day

---

15 St. Benedict's Church (The Painted Church—1902)
Middle Keei Road, .3 mile/.5 kilometer NW of HI 16
Honaunau, Hawaii, Hawaii

FATHER JOHN (VELGHE), DESIGNER AND PAINTER

The exterior of this small Roman Catholic church promises few rewards, but on the inside its nave is splendiferous with an elaborate series of neo-primitive paintings. These transform wooden columns into candy-cane palm trees whose fronds wave in the "vaulted" ceiling,

and make its flat chancel wall a Gothic ambulatory in full perspective. (Its architectural design was probably inspired by Father John's studies in Burgos, Spain.) Like medieval stained glass, the painted interior, especially its panels between the windows, shows illustrations of scenes from the Bible. Note, in particular, the panel on the south wall of Eve trying to revive the dying Abel. The interior is, in short, admirable except for an intrusive chancel screen behind the altar and an obtrusive door cut in at right. The church, the work of a Belgian priest who had taught in southern Polynesia for ten years before coming to Hawaii, is one of this country's finest examples of religious folk-art.

Open daily 9–5

16 Hawaii Preparatory Academy (1965–70)
2 miles/3.2 kilometers NW of town at Intersection of HI 25 and HI 26 near
Waimea, Hawaii, Hawaii

VLADIMIR OSSIPOFF, ARCHITECT

For many years Vladimir Ossipoff has designed some of the most sensitive, regionally concerned buildings on the Islands. However, most of this fine work has been in private houses or clubs, hence not open to the public. This preparatory school for boys shows his expertise in site handling, his use of simple materials, and his utilization of the natural flow of air in a series of buildings that step down the grade. Whereas some of the architectural attainment is not signal—the chapel is perhaps overly rustic—the conceptual development and the new classroom units (those nearest entry gate) are first rate.

Open during school year

17   Mauna Kea Beach Hotel (1965–68)
on coast, S of HI 26
Mauna Kea Beach, Hawaii, Hawaii

SKIDMORE, OWINGS & MERRILL, ARCHITECTS

It is not just the stepped terraces of rooms overlooking the views that
make this hotel distinctive: André Lurçat did this at Ajaccio in 1931.
And it is not just the deft planting outside and in—at times it is
difficult to tell outside from in—which gives it so much élan. Such
"landscaping" rightly is found in much sensitive building on the Islands. The above add, of course, to the hotel's very considerable architectural beatitudes, but the greatest impact comes from the unfolding
and interweaving of its inner spaces, both vertical and lateral: these
are almost staggering in their three-dimensional sensuousness. From

the longitudinal spine whose roof is open to the sun by day and the
stars by night (with full-grown palms down its middle probing the
sky), to the stepped-back levels that form the inner gallery-corridors
and overlook the garden courts, the unexpected awaits every step. Such
architectural experiences (by the San Francisco office of SOM) do not
come readily.

The space-forms commence their happy task at the entry, a subtly
innocuous, indeed almost invisible opening (compare Miami Beach)
with a small bridge escorting one to the reception hall where the blue
Pacific lures one forward. All is open. One looks down to the lower
level, out to the ocean, up to the sky, and sideways to the garden
court, with a bouquet of restless palms towering directly in front. Not
even glass is there. Space is. No architectural flabbiness is to be seen,
no ersatz vernacular, no corn, simply an exquisite understanding of
what architecture, not stage-setting, is all about.

The entry level is given over to administration, with the lower floors,
notched into the hillside, occupied by shops, a two-story colonnade,
and bar and buffet, the latter overlooking beach and sea. A 220-seat
auditorium is set in the hillside. The rectangular, wood-framed dining

pavilion lies separate but attached on the ocean side, with a broad terrace onto the Pacific. The main building, with small lateral angling to minimize bulk, contains three levels of bedrooms, half facing the water, half the mountains, each level stepping back as it rises to create tiers of privately screened balconies on both sides. As mentioned, these tiers do not meet at the top, thus the center is open to the sky, while the inner overhangs resulting from the stepped profile provide weatherproof corridors for room access. Cross-bridges at intervals excite the spaces, while the flourishing garden court with full-grown trees down the middle offers peace. The cross-ventilation, incidentally, is so good most of the year that bedroom air-conditioning is rarely needed, both louvered and solid doors being provided. The bedroom furnishings reflect the quiet luxury of a fine home. The extensive artwork, drawn from a wide range of Polynesian culture, is often of museum caliber. It was selected by the architects who also designed the elegant interiors.

The main structure is of reinforced concrete (of excellent formwork scaled with a V-profile) and painted white, with local woods used for many walls. The hotel is named for the Mauna Kea volcano ("White Mountain"—it is often topped with snow, being 13,796 feet/4,205 meters high)—which lies 25 crow miles (40 kilometers) to the southeast. The hotel was built with 154 rooms; 102 more were added three years after opening in a separate building designed by Wimberly, Whisenand, Allison & Tong. A clubhouse with full sports facilities and snack bar is set back on the land side. The landscaping, with considerable cover brought in from other islands because of difficult local lava growing conditions, has been very imaginatively handled, outside and in, by Eckbo, Dean, Austin & Williams. Superb, and, at last, a contemporary building which fully reflects the architectural potentialities of the Islands.

Open year round

---

18 Holoholoku Heiau
Wailua River State Park
on HI 580, .3 mile/.5 kilometer W of HI 56
Wailua, Kauai, Hawaii

This *heiau* and Temple of Refuge is not as impressive as that at Honaunau (q.v.) on the Kona coast of the Big Island, but it will interest the expert. A low, rectangular enclosure of random lava rocks (its

walls were probably higher when first built), a thatched "house" for the priest, small wooden idols (originals in the Bishop Museum), and a large sacrificial rock in the southwest corner mark this sacred enclosure near the spot where by legend the first Polynesians landed more than a millennium ago. The god Ku (in the title) was god of war, and the only one to require human sacrifice, which he generally ordered once a month, usually with war captives. The *heiau* was reconstructed in 1933 by the Kauai Historical Society and the Bishop Museum, undoubtedly aided by a sketch of a similar temple made at Waimea (on the southwest coast of Kauai) by J. Webber, Captain Cook's artist—and the spot where Cook himself first landed on the Islands.

Always visitable

19   Waioli Mission Hall (1841)
off HI 56
Hanalei, Kauai, Hawaii

Surrounded by lanais, this picturesque former church now serves the ex-port of Hanalei as a community center. Because its design so capably solved local problems of a sometimes wet and windy climate by means of wide skirting and sturdy plastered walls, the whole topped by a well-pitched roof, this evolutionary building epitomizes the Hawaiian vernacular. The rainiest spot on earth at 40.5 feet/12.3 meters per annum lies only 12 miles/19 kilometers inland, while the occasional high winds were strong enough to have blown down the original thatched church. The interior is now of little architectural consequence.

The Mission Hall is part of a complete missionary complex which includes the **Mission House** (1836), the first house museum in Hawaii (1921)—open Tues.–Sat. 9–3—and the **Waioli Mission Church** (1912), a Gothic Revival structure.

Open Tues.–Sun. 9–3, except major holidays

---

20   The Reverend Dwight Baldwin House (1832–35)
Front Street at Dickenson
Lahaina, Maui, Hawaii

Lahaina, though offering only a good roadstead and not a good harbor, was one of the busiest whaling ports in the Pacific from 1819,

when it was first visited, until the 1860s. Upward of one hundred ships were often at anchor—the record was 395 in 1846—with their complement of pent-up sailors for whom there was "No God west of the Horn." Conveniently they were oft met by local maidens who delighted in swimming out to the ships and frolicking with the lads. The New England missionaries who sought to bring Christianity to this picturesque village were thus doubly busy in their efforts to save local souls and restrain the sailors. (One sea captain actually shelled the house of a missionary who asked officials to prevent the girls from visiting the ships.) Beyond rowdiness, much of the happy/sad impact of a technologically sophisticated West on islands fresh from the Stone Age took place here. (The Civil War and the discovery of oil, thus lamp kerosene, in the U.S.A., caused the collapse of whaling, and as a consequence Lahaina lost its commercial importance to Honolulu.)

The first Congregationalist to settle in Lahaina (1823) was the influential William Richards who very properly first sought (successfully) to ingratiate himself with the King and Queen. In 1835 the Reverend Dwight Baldwin, a Harvard-trained medical missionary arrived with his young wife, occupying the just-finished house which had been started by their predecessor. As the Baldwin family grew (there were eventually six children), a bedroom and study were first added (1840), then an entire second floor in 1849. Dr. Baldwin also had the nearby building constructed to serve as missionary center, storehouse, the ship masters' reading room (on upper floor), and lookout. The Baldwin House—now the oldest dwelling still standing on Maui—is not of architectural distinction, but it gives useful insight into an early Christian missionary home in the former Sandwich Islands. Moreover this insight reveals a refreshing adaptability to local materials and weather conditions, being constructed of thick coral and stone walls, having a well-ventilated room layout, high ceilings, and wide porches— it is thus at ease with its neighbors. The Baldwin House has been carefully restored and furnished by the Lahaina Restoration Foundation. It should be added that religion was only one concern of these missionaries: reading and writing, mechanical skills, the useful arts, sanitation, etc., were all of consequence. As King Kamehameha II had overthrown (1819), as mentioned, the Islands' rigid taboos only a year before the arrival of the New Englanders, Christianity was of critical influence in establishing "the foundations for the tolerant and progressive State of Hawaii of today."

The village of Lahaina, having been spared the engineering of paradise (e.g. the high-rise madness of much of the Islands), is today seeking to recall its historic identity. On Maui the apartment complexes occupy a distant area unto themselves. Though the atmosphere is more commercial than one would like, some hints from the past still exist. A Historic District Ordinance limits much that would otherwise have gotten out of hand.

Open daily 9:30–5, except major holidays: admission

Idaho

Cataldo 5

■ Boise 1–4   • Ketchum 6

IDAHO

The buildings in boldface type are of general interest. The others are for the specialist.

Boise
1 The Old U. S. Assay Office (1870–71)—Alfred B. Mullett
2 **Intermountain Gas Company** (1966)—Kenneth W. Brooks
3 U. S. Court House and Federal Office Building (1967–68)—Hummel, Hummel, Jones & Shawver; Charles Luckman
4 **Boise Cascade Home Office** (1971–72)— Skidmore, Owings & Merrill

Cataldo
5 **Cataldo Mission** (1848–53)—Father Anthony Ravalli

Ketchum
6 First Security Bank (1887/1967)—Nat J. Adams & Associates

1 The Old U. S. Assay Office (1870–71)
210 Main Street
Boise, Idaho

ALFRED B. MULLETT, ARCHITECT

The old U. S. Assay Office, which in its day processed some $75 million worth of gold, is a stout, two-story structure set in a pleasant park on the edge of the business district (note the granite fence). Measuring 48 x 46 feet/15 x 14 meters, its native sandstone walls are over 2 feet/.6 meter thick. It stands as a more than competent index of century-old frontier government building. Listed in the National Register of Historic Places (1965), its coursed stone facade with ashlar quoins is described therein as "Second Renaissance Revival." In 1933 the interior was remodeled to house the U. S. Forest Service, but at the present time it contains offices for the Historical Society, the State Archeologist, and the Oral History Center.

Open Mon.–Fri. 8–5, except holidays

2 Intermountain Gas Company (1966)
   ## 555 Cole Road at McMullen
   ## Boise, Idaho

KENNETH W. BROOKS, ARCHITECT

"Care, imagination and skill have made what might have been a prosaic utilitarian structure into a fine architectural achievement" (American Institute of Architects upon giving the building a national Award of Merit). Four separate but carefully related units comprise this facility on a bluff on the western edge of the city: the headquarters office block, a service center to west, hospitality house at east, and—greeting one at entry and on axis with the office—a turbine house of putty-gray brick. The turbine house, a truncated cone in shape, was assigned its strategic position to emphasize natural gas as a source of "total energy." The service building and hospitality house are of muted, glazed blue brick which plays an active role in reflecting the sun and clouds. On a beautifully landscaped low podium on the north side sits the trim story-and-a-half administration building both of whose levels overlook the Boise Valley, its all-glass upper walls protected by the wide arcade. The interior of the open main floor is broken by two solid blocks which house workrooms and conference rooms and which are sheathed in the warm gray brick also used outside. The hospitality house is used for lectures, dining, meetings—both company and community—and cooking demonstrations, having two completely

equipped gas kitchens. The location of the turbine house was determined by architect and landscape architect working together. It is set in a moat whose waters are used in air conditioning and for fire protection. Its interior presents an array of color-coded machinery which makes a stimulating functional palette. Using natural gas, the building supplies electricity, heat, and air conditioning for all units. The landscaping, by Lawrence Halprin & Associates, pulls the four buildings together in commendable fashion, and, in the process, carefully hides the eighty-four sheltered parking spaces for the staff behind rows of trees.

Reception area open during business hours

---

3   U. S. Court House and Federal Office Building (1967–68)
West Fort Street at 6th
Boise, Idaho

HUMMEL, HUMMEL, JONES & SHAWVER, ARCHITECTS; CHARLES LUCKMAN, ASSOCIATE FOR DESIGN

A straightforward, well-detailed office building and courthouse. It is given character by its use of its verdant site, the calm framing of the

upper floors, and their overhang beyond the tall, glass-wrapped main floor. One end of the entry level contains an attractive cafeteria with exposure on three sides. A sound achievement in Federal architecture.

Ground floor open during office hours

---

4   **Boise Cascade Home Office** (1971–72)
North 11th Street between Bannock and Jefferson
Boise, Idaho

SKIDMORE, OWINGS & MERRILL, ARCHITECTS

Boise Cascade has always been a downtown corporation and the company wanted to maintain this tradition as well as help stabilize Boise's central business district. The San Francisco office of SOM came up with a dramatic solution to the problem of its mid-urban site. The entire 260-foot/79-meter-square office block of five floors was elevated 40 feet/12 meters above the street, leaving the ground level open except for fire stairs at each corner and an inset glazed central court which rises through the building. Four circular elevators operate from its landscaped center, bridges connecting them with the work areas on each level. Surrounding the court above are the office floors, 72 feet/22 meters wide and glazed on the outside as well as onto the court. There are movable full-height and half-height partitions, but the only fixed elements are the four utility blocks holding fire stairs, toilets, and services. The unexpected spatial transparency of the core with the sun darting inside intensifies the "horizontal communication" which Boise Cascade sought, employee interaction being one reason why a high-rise solution was ruled out. A 250-seat cafeteria occupies part of the fourth floor, along with an auditorium. The structural frame is of steel, as are the continuous spandrels. The court is roofed by an aluminum space-frame with acrylic panes which flood the interior with light. (Compare Yamasaki's Reynolds Metal Building in Detroit— q.v.) Surface parking is accommodated on an adjacent lot which the company owns. The building's lofty open ground level adds substantial sparkle to the downtown area. Morganelli, Heumann & Associates were the interior designers.

Reception area open during business hours

---

5   **Cataldo Mission** (1848–53)
    on IS 90 between Coeur d'Alene and Kellogg just W of
    Cataldo, Idaho

FATHER ANTHONY RAVALLI, DESIGNER

The Jesuits began active missionary work among the Coeur d'Alene Indians in the 1840s, and some forty-five years before Idaho became a state (1890) a site had been selected for a permanent mission. In 1846 Father Anthony Ravalli, who was born in Italy and educated in Europe—his education obviously including some knowledge of architecture—drew up plans for the church of the Coeur d'Alene Mission of

the Sacred Heart, and two years later started construction with the aid of one lay brother plus a band of untutored Indians. Though in partial use by 1850, the church was not completed until 1853: it is the oldest structure standing in the state. The most impressive facet of the building, which measures approximately 40 x 90 feet/12 x 27 meters, lies in its framework and the size of timbers used in its construction. Its beams and columns are huge (some are 22 inches/56 centimeters square), hewn and dressed only with a broad ax, mortised and pegged together without nails, having been hoisted into place by ropes woven from grass! Between the members of the structural frame, grass and mud (i.e. a form of adobe) were placed for walls—probably a French-influenced construction—but it was found necessary to add clapboarding to cover the exterior, plus panels for the interior, to keep out the weather (1865). The inside, like the facade, has an ingratiating primitiveness with enough design competence to hold it together visually. Note, especially, the carved and painted ceiling which, with the Stations of the Cross, was done by Father Huybrechts. The altar and its sculpture were by Father Ravalli. The mission was moved in 1876 and semiabandoned in 1887, falling into gradual dilapidation until rescued in 1928 by concerned citizens from as far away as Spokane. Complete restoration was undertaken (1974) as a state Bicentennial Project. The Mission became an Idaho State Park in 1975, and is listed in the

National Register of Historic Places. The flair of the front—a Baroque-Western-Greek Revival effort—is worth the trip itself.

Open Apr. 15–Sept., daily 9 A.M.–*dusk*

---

6 First Security Bank (1887/1967)
Main Street (US 93)
Ketchum, Idaho

NAT J. ADAMS & ASSOCIATES, ARCHITECTS OF RESTORATION

When the First Security Bank sought a suitable site for their branch in Ketchum, at the instigation of their architect they imaginatively bought an eighty-year-old general store and remodeled it for banking quarters.

They then re-created as much as possible the atmosphere of the 1890s by collecting and utilizing furnishings of the period, both the bank's president and senior vice-president being responsible for much of the research and purchasing. From the cast-iron front, made in nearby Hailey, to the bronzed, wrought-iron teller's cages, including also much of the furniture in between, the interior reflects, only a bit self-consciously, the pioneer days of Ketchum and nearby Sun Valley. Liberties have been taken, but as an amusing exercise in scenography it is full of fun—and it does have some good antiques.

Open during business hours

Iowa

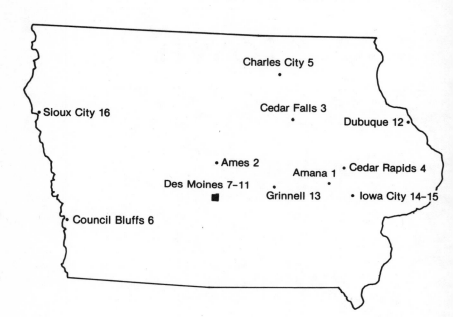

Charles City 5

Cedar Falls 3

Sioux City 16

Dubuque 12

• Ames 2

Amana 1 • Cedar Rapids 4

Des Moines 7-11

Grinnell 13 • Iowa City 14-15

Council Bluffs 6

IOWA

The buildings in boldface type are of general interest. The others are for the specialist.

Amana
1 Amana Colonies (1855–)

Ames
2 **The Iowa State Center** (1969–75)—Crites & McConnell and Brooks, Borg & Skiles

Cedar Falls
3 **University Union** (1968–69)—Hunter, Rice & Engelbrecht

Cedar Rapids
4 St. Paul's United Methodist Church (1913–14)—Louis H. Sullivan

Charles City
5 **Salsbury Laboratories Research Center** (1968–69)—The Perkins & Will Partnership

Council Bluffs
6 General Grenville Dodge House (1869–70)—W. W. Boyington

Des Moines
7 **Terrace Hill** (1867–69)—W. W. Boyington
8 **Iowa State Capitol** (1873–86)—Cochrane & Piquenard
9 **Home Federal Savings & Loan Association** (1960–63)—Mies van der Rohe & Associates
Meredith Memorial Hall (1964–65)—Mies van der Rohe & Associates
10 **American Republic Insurance Company** (1964–65)—Skidmore, Owings & Merrill
11 **Des Moines Art Center and Addition** (1948/1968)—Eliel Saarinen; I. M. Pei & Partners

Dubuque
12 Dubuque County Jail (1857–58)—John Francis Rague
Dubuque County Court House (1891–93)—Fridolin Heer & Son

Grinnell
13 **Poweshiek County National Bank** (1914)—Louis H. Sullivan

Iowa City
14 **The Old Capitol** (1840–42)—John Francis Rague

15 American College Testing Program
Headquarters (1967–68)—The Spitznagel
Partners

Sioux City   16 **Woodbury County Court House** (1916–
18)—W. L. Steele in association with
Purcell & Elmslie

1 Amana Colonies (1855–   )
IOWA 149 and 220, c. 15 miles/24 kilometers SW of Cedar
Rapids
Amana, Iowa

There is more sociological than architectural import in the Amana
Colonies, a group of seven villages established by the Amana Church
Society under Christian Metz. Descended—like many "farm colonies"
—from south German Pietists seeking religious freedom and land in
the New World, the thousand-plus members of the original Amana settlers shared the communal living colonies (separate multifamily houses
but usually joint kitchens, etc.) typical of the concerned-for-all, vio-
lence-eschewing Anabaptists. (See also Ambridge and Ephrata, Pennsylvania, and New Harmony, Indiana.). The uniformity of their quiet
architecture is of interest.

Settling first at Ebenezer, near Buffalo, New York, they then moved
(because of need for more land for new influxes from Germany) to the
fertile fields of eastern Iowa, acquiring 26,000 acres/10,522 hectares.

Their industriousness and dedication have brought them success ever since, though they found it prudent in the Depression (1932) to separate economics from "religious communism." Architecturally the villages of the Community of True Inspiration lack the focus and cohesiveness of the English-generated Shaker groups (see Index), but their farm buildings are expressive and the cemeteries are of interest. As Lewis Mumford wrote, the villages are "the most sturdy and economically successful of religious utopias after those of the Shakers" (*Sticks and Stones,* Dover, 1955). The Heritage House in Amana is a museum (open Apr.–Nov., Mon.–Sat. 10–5, Sun. 12–5: admission) which presents the full background of these God-fearing, hardworking people.

---

2   The Iowa State Center (1969–75)
Iowa State University
Lincoln Way—or US 30—at Elwood Drive
Ames, Iowa

CRITES & McCONNELL AND BROOKS, BORG & SKILES, ARCHITECTS

These four closely knit buildings form a cultural-recreational-continuing-education center for Iowa State University whose campus for 24,000 students lies directly across Lincoln Way. They handsomely complement the University's primary emphasis on science and technology.

The C. Y. Stephens Auditorium (1969) combines theater, concert hall, and auditorium in a structure of architectural virility outside and in. The building, which occupies an uneven parklike corner is tied to its several ground levels by a series of "flying" access bridges, some of which double as unloading shelters for the vehicular approach. Parking for four thousand cars is provided behind the building (a strong facade), and in the lot which the auditorium shares with the nearby coliseum. The exterior, like the interior, is of raw concrete (beautifully poured), the roof with unusual curved soffit of cedar carefully patterned and butted. The weighty "monolithic" cap of the roof, slightly angled over the auditorium and flat over the stage, is the first element to strike one, shades of Le Corbusier's Chapel at Ronchamp coming to mind, though in this case it sits uneasily on the lower section because

the structure is not sufficiently stated. Then the angled bands of concrete and dark glass that frame the sides demand attention, their slope directly reflecting the step-ramps within and the projections of the four stair towers. After dark an inviting glow emanates from the glazed stair-ramps and the front to give the theater its best advertisement. There are exaggerations in the exterior, its roof, as mentioned, appears strangely unsupported, and a lack of three-dimensional cohesiveness is apparent, but the overall impression is one of positiveness.

The interior is far more keenly knit and better coordinated than the outside, from its ample lobbies to its raked auditorium. The ground floor is devoted to ticket offices, coat rooms, and services, and the lobbies above are—for a welcome change—spacious and full of life. The continental seating of continuous wide rows with no interrupting aisles is augmented by three clean-cut balconies, the two lower of which extend along the sides with "toboggan" loges à la Royal Festival Hall in London, total capacity being 2,637. The seats vary slightly in color from tannish in front to darkish red at rear. The natural-finish hemlock ceiling (3 inches/76 millimeters thick) is suspended in scallops over the auditorium, and helps produce superior acoustics. The combination of (1) waves of wood overhead, (2) well-integrated trapezoidal hollow piers of concrete framing the sides (their angled interstices providing exits, their interiors acting as air-conditioning ducts), and (3) the high quality of illumination (floods of it on the walls, downlights over audience) makes this one of the most potent theater interiors in the country. Paul E. Veneklassen & Associates were the acoustical consultants.

The James H. Hilton Coliseum (1971) forms a well-modulated foil to the animation of the Auditorium with its quiet, simply stated semioctagonal form of concrete. The activities accommodated range from basketball to ice hockey to the Boston Pops to graduations. Its 15,000 capacity (12,576 fixed seats upholstered in bright red, the others on portable decks or folding chairs) surrounds a floor area of 101 x 203 feet/31 x 62 meters. Its ceiling was dropped to hide the trusswork, cut heating load, and aid acoustics; it is a singularly good-looking interior for this type of structure.

The J. W. Fisher Theater (1974) is a small-auditorium, large-stage building used for music, drama, dance, and lectures. Its thirteen rows of seats accommodate 424 people. The proscenium measures 36 feet/11 meters wide by 18 feet/5.5 meters high with a 40-foot/12-meter-deep stage. Built of reinforced concrete, the theater's inner walls are of cedar strips, which with the purple carpeting and seats make an intimate setting.

The Carl H. Scheman Continuing Education Building (1975) stretches parallel to Lincoln Way, its three levels helping define the Center's north side. Containing 18 conference rooms, a 440-seat auditorium (on the main floor), and the Brunier Gallery and kitchen (top floor), it offers facilities for seminars, conferences, exhibits, and "for the accommodation and presentation of short-term continuing education and public service programs of Iowa State University."

Open for performances

3 **University Union** (1968–69)
University of Northern Iowa
off 22nd Street near Merner
Cedar Falls, Iowa

HUNTER, RICE & ENGELBRECHT, ARCHITECTS

The nation's colleges abound with new student unions but there are
few conceived in the imaginative mold of this two-level, largely subterranean structure in the east-central part of the state. A strategic midpoint campus location was desired yet it would have been a desecra-
tion to fill the limited spaces between existing buildings. The
architects—like some students—therefore went underground and produced a subterranean cafeteria, meeting rooms, and even a tiny chapel,

with natural light pouring in from four rooftop monitors and from the corners (three of the monitors, incidentally, sheltering stairways). These inner pools of daylight and the clublike atmosphere have made the union enormously successful. On the inside there is an architectural restlessness about the central area, which serves primarily as a dining room, but this is counterfoiled by several off-center, quiet areas, set at half-levels down, one of which shines under its own multicolored skylight. On the lowest level, and with an additional outside entry, are the multipurpose rooms which can be combined to form an auditorium. On top the four projecting light monitors confront each other a bit rigidly, but formalism is softened by changes of levels on the edges and by the play of forms in the built-in seats. The light from the roof monitors at night illuminates the upper "plaza." Altogether a very clever concept for a cold winter, a hot summer, and a crowded campus: it is a street on top and a galleria beneath.

Open daily during school year

---

4   St. Paul's United Methodist Church (1913–14)
1340 3rd Avenue SE
Cedar Rapids, Iowa

LOUIS H. SULLIVAN, BASIC DESIGN

This relatively little-known church consists of a half-round nave, 65 feet/20 meters in diameter, with a social hall beneath. It is attached to a three-story rectangular administration wing, the whole topped by a 108-foot/33-meter-high square tower and a 12-foot/3.6-meter lighted cross. The nave with its banked rows of semicircular pews tends toward the lecture hall in atmosphere, but the church, which ac- commodates approximately nine hundred in sanctuary and balcony, will interest Sullivanites for its unusual plan. All aisles focus on the sanc- tuary. The detailing is inferior because Sullivan himself did not do the working drawings, as the design—including "a dome of many-colored glass"—was too expensive. W. C. Jones, a little-known Chicago archi- tect, pared matters to the bone (Sullivan resigned as architect in 1912) with, some authorities feel, a helping hand from George Elms- lie, Sullivan's old standby. The sanctuary wall was remodeled and vastly improved in 1954, and changed again in 1977 when a new organ was installed. In 1963 the Christian Education wing was added at left.

Open, via church office, Mon.–Fri. 9–12, 1–5, Sun. service

---

5   Salsbury Laboratories Research Center (1968–69)
off IOWA 14, just W of
Charles City, Iowa

THE PERKINS & WILL PARTNERSHIP, ARCHITECTS

A low-keyed, unusually inviting administration and laboratory building in rural Iowa, one of the best new structures in the state. Designed, among other things, to attract top talent to a small town (roughly 10,000 population), the one- and two-story complex projects ir- regularly about a well-landscaped, loosely (but carefully) organized central court. Administrative offices align across the front; an audito- rium seating 250 stands at right off the entry, and laboratories and technical library frame the other sides. On stepping into the entry one is greeted by a glimpse of the garden court beyond, with its several levels, pool, fountain, and trees. Actually, the building was planned so that one rarely loses contact with this refreshing court. The reception area exhibits—as does, indeed, the whole building—a first-rate, chang- ing collection of original art (a welcome foil to the ponderous furni- ture). The offices branch off directly from the reception hall, with au-

ditorium beyond. The laboratories (not open to the public) step back in groups on either side of the library, and enclose the south side of the court. Opening off each lab is a private office for the doctors and technicians, with a small conference room near each bank of labs. There is no assembly-line setup here: the focus is on the individual. Because of the nature of the work involved (poultry and animal disease research), each laboratory is independently air-conditioned. Construction is of cast-in-place concrete with random-width formwork. Production facilities are housed in a nearby plant. Philip Will, Jr., was partner-in-charge. The Franz Lipp/Marvin Wehler Partnership was the landscape architect. Very fine.

Reception areas and garden open during business hours

---

6   General Grenville Dodge House (1869–70)
605 3rd Street at Story Street
Council Bluffs, Iowa

W. W. BOYINGTON, ARCHITECT

Designed by the same architect who did Terrace Hill in Des Moines (q.v.), the Dodge House will be of interest to the specialist. Recently restored, the house is a solid, though not spectacular, example of brick Victoriana. The prominent Mansard roof and the modillion cornice

should be noted, as should the firm statement of the porch, especially its semi-Palladian corner. The dwelling was built for a brilliant Civil War general who later became the chief engineer of the Union Pacific Railroad. "The greatest railroad builder of all time," he laid out and supervised the building of the first transcontinental railroad.

Open Feb.–Dec., Tues.–Sat. 10–5, Sun. 2–5, except Thanksgiving and Dec. 25: admission

---

7   Terrace Hill (1867–69)
2200 Grand Avenue
Des Moines, Iowa

W. W. BOYINGTON, ARCHITECT

Terrace Hill is an epitomization of its period—surprisingly so because Des Moines' population was some 12,000 when this house was built. It bears rewarding comparison with any Victorian mansion in the country. Commissioned by Benjamin Franklin Allen, the state's first millionaire (largely life insurance), the house and extensive grounds

(once 30 acres/12 hectares) are monuments of and to their period. Its superb present state of preservation is due to the fact that it was occupied until 1956 (except for a period when Mr. Allen went bankrupt), generally by presidents of the Equitable of Iowa Insurance Company, the last president leaving a trust fund for its maintenance. Internal changes were made toward the end of the nineteenth century when the kitchen was moved, steam heat installed, stained glass added, and a rock-crystal chandelier of suitable presumption hung in the drawing room, all carried out in the ornate spirit of the time. Upon the death of the last owner—though the trust mentioned was left for upkeep—most of the contents of the house were given to various descendants and the building closed, none of the heirs electing to live there. But interest in the mansion was so substantial that by 1960 a process of refurnishing got under way and today its interior is again sumptuous, some pieces being original to the house, all others of the period. In 1971 it was given to the State of Iowa. The architect of this "country residence in modern French design with Mansard roof" was William Boyington, probably Chicago's most famous practitioner around the time of that city's Great Fire (1871), and chiefly remembered today for his "Gothic" Water Tower (q.v.) in that city. His Terrace Hill is equally memorable, one of the few remaining masterpieces of its giddy era.

Open Mon.–Tues. 10–2, Sun. 12–4, except major holidays

8 **Iowa State Capitol** (1873–86)
East Locust at East 9th Street
Des Moines, Iowa

COCHRANE & PIQUENARD, ARCHITECTS

The architects of state capitols—obviously with the enthusiastic support of their clients—were seemingly as much concerned with the
dome as with office square footage. Walter's 258-foot/79-meter-high
bubble in Washington, D.C. (q.v.), had established an almost irre-

sistible prototype. So it is in Des Moines, where a gold-leafed (23-karat) dome, 275 feet/84 meters high, shines refulgently throughout the day, a lighthouse of politics, so to speak, warning and/or reassuring as the case may be. This, the state's fifth capitol, succeeds doubly, rather quintuply, for its one great dome has a scale-intensifying backup dome at each corner. Splendiferous. On the inside a vast rotunda, decked with appropriate murals, flags, twenty-nine different marbles, etc., introduces one to the glories of the state. The commission for the Capitol was awarded by a competition, with the New Hampshire-born John C. Cochrane teaming with the French-born Alfred H. Piquenard to capture first place among fourteen entries, the second architect's neo-Renaissance expertise playing a decisive role. Cochrane resigned in 1872 and Piquenard died in 1876 before the building was substantially out of the ground. M. E. Bell, who had worked for Piquenard, and W. F. Hackney took over and Bell redesigned the dome. There is an obvious similarity in basic *parti* between the Des Moines Capitol and that which J. C. Cochrane designed for Springfield, Illinois (q.v.).

Open Mon.–Fri. 8–4:30, Sat.–Sun. 8–4; tours Mon.–Fri.

9　Home Federal Savings & Loan Association (1960–63)
Grand Avenue at 6th
Des Moines, Iowa

MIES VAN DER ROHE & ASSOCIATES, ARCHITECTS

Mies, some admirers feel, was better in the singular than the plural, an exquisite exception being his identical-twin apartment houses in Chicago (q.v.). Here in Des Moines he is singularly good. This three-story, prismatic Savings & Loan Association, measuring 121.9 feet/37 meters square in plan and encased in dark glass (upper floors) and dark metal, has been distilled to pure elegance. Much of its delight comes from the fact that the ground floor has been recessed on all four sides so that space is "captured" by the column-framed passages on each flank, allowing a penetration which reaches great intensity at the corners. The building, thus, rests lightly on its setback site, fingers of three-dimensionality intertwining with the structure. The two- and three-module recess of the entry side (on Grand Avenue) also enhances the broad plaza space in front—and vice versa—where trees

(some screening the customers' adjacent parking lot), grass plots, and a subtle bench enter the scene. The ground floor interior forms one well-mannered space 14.7 feet/4.5 meters high, largely clear-glass-walled, and understated in its Attic propriety. Its detailing, like that throughout the building—any Mies' building—is impeccable. A community room, kitchen, and services fill the basement; the first and second floors are taken by the Savings & Loan Association, while the third is let for offices. A drive-in teller's window attaches at rear. Smith-Vorhees-Jensen were associate architects.

Open during business hours

The Mies fan will want to see **Meredith Memorial Hall** (1964–65) at nearby Drake University, University Avenue at 28th Street (entry open during school year). It is curiously heavy and not distinguished on the outside—Mies' buildings must "float" as most of them do—but Meredith (as opposed to the bank) hugs the ground. The inner court, however, is pleasant.

10   American Republic Insurance Company (1964–65)
601 6th Avenue at Keosauqua Way
Des Moines, Iowa

SKIDMORE, OWINGS & MERRILL, ARCHITECTS

Structural, mechanical, and esthetic imagination of a high order mark this eight-story block in downtown Des Moines, designed by the New York office of SOM. The building's east and west sides are bearing walls of solid poured-in-place concrete which thins from a 4-foot/1.2-meter-base thickness as the walls rise. These massive, windowless sides rest on eight prominent steel hinges (four per side) which in turn sit on reinforced concrete, freestanding piers. Notched into these side walls are the ends of prestressed T-shaped girders that span the entire 98-foot/30-meter width of the building, creating a

floor area completely free of internal supports, the only interruption being the central island of elevators, fire stairs, and toilets, which core also acts as lateral bracing. It is a forceful concept, and one directly tailored to the client's need for large, column-free spaces for secretarial pools.

One enters the building via an open, marble-lined court, walled against the nondescript surroundings, and sparked by a strategic Calder stabile and a small yew tree. (Other excellent art will be found inside.) This court, which is partially open, partially roofed, introduces one to the ground-floor lobby, thence to the floor above, which is devoted to the well-glazed dining room and lounge, both inset from the outer edge, and with a terrace overlooking the entry court. Six floors of offices (five clerical, one executive) rise above, all of them with two large (66 x 90 feet/20 x 27 meters) unobstructed areas, mostly secretarial pools, filling the open ends on either side of the central utility core. Junior executive offices lie amidship on these five floors between the ends and facing the service core, their windowlessness being perhaps the building's only shortcoming. (The early model did have token fenestration in this midsection.) The top floor is occupied by senior executives, meeting rooms, and an upper mechanical area. The air conditioning and lighting of all floors is ingeniously wedded to the structure: as the depth of the transverse T-beams which form the floor is 4 feet/1.2 meters deep, the cylindrical air-conditioning ducts (16 inches/41 centimeters in diameter and suitably insulated) are placed between the beam flanges with the fluorescent light tubes affixed to the top of the ducts, where they cast a uniform, indirect light. Paul Weidlinger was the structural engineer.

Reception areas open during business hours

---

11 Des Moines Art Center and Addition (1948/1968)
Grand Avenue at 45th Street West
Des Moines, Iowa

**ELIEL SAARINEN, ARCHITECT OF ORIGINAL BUILDING; I. M. PEI
& PARTNERS, ARCHITECTS OF ADDITION**

Architect Pei has expanded Architect Saarinen's fine old Art Center to project as an almost independent unit beyond the courtyard framed by the older building. A reflecting pool (slightly redesigned from the Saarinen days) emphasizes the separation with Carl Milles' *Pegasus*

and Bellerophon prancing in its waters. The east and west walls of the new wing are blank, so that low sun could be controlled, hence the foci outward are on the pool-courtyard to the north and the rolling park to the south. Across the ceiling, and sending out vibrations of sunshine, extends an inverted-V skylight. Controlled sunlight penetrates at times from above, at other times laterally, but always in context with an art experience, and always subsidiary to the subject. This is a bright setting for art—especially the sculpture for which it was primarily designed.

The play of inner levels and their interaction is as important as that of the game of light, and in the Pei extension there is visual contact between the upper sculpture gallery and the lower—and the outside from each. The large upper "court" connects with the lower (and smaller) both by a straight-line stair and a short bridge to a circular stair. A 240-seat auditorium with small stage shares the lower floor with the gallery. The contrast of this airy extension with the solid-walled, artificially lit museum gives considerable pause for thought—definitely as regards the setting for sculpture.

Open Tues.–Sat. 11–5, Sun. 12–5, holidays 1–5

12 Dubuque County Jail (1857–58)
Central Avenue at East 8th Street
Dubuque, Iowa

JOHN FRANCIS RAGUE, ARCHITECT

"Its design is the finest example of Egyptian architecture to survive the Classical Revival in the United States" proclaims the plaque outside the jail—a claim which the Old Medical College in Richmond (q.v.) and the Downtown Presbyterian Church in Nashville (q.v.) would rightly dispute. Hyperbole notwithstanding, this is one of the few Nilotic-inspired structures to survive from the romantic flings of the last century. Note the wooden "cavetto" cornice atop the limestone walls. The south wing was added in 1875. William J. Wagner, the distinguished architect of Des Moines, and the author-illustrator of the delightful *Sixty Sketches of Iowa's Past and Present,* thinks that Rague, whose father had come from France with Lafayette, had been impressed by New York's very Egyptian (but now demolished) Old Tombs (i.e. jail) of 1838. The jail's designer was also responsible for the Greek Revival Old Capitol in Iowa City (q.v.).

Open during office hours

Take a look, too, at the Beaux Arts **Dubuque County Court House**
(1891–93) adjacent—Fridolin Heer & Son, architects. Neither interior
is recommended.

---

13   Poweshiek County National Bank (1914)
4th Avenue at Broad Street
Grinnell, Iowa

LOUIS H. SULLIVAN, ARCHITECT

Sullivan designed five buildings in Iowa, but the compactly boxed Merchant's National Bank, now the Poweshiek County National Bank, by
far outshines the others. (The other four are the Adams Building in

Algona, 1913; the People's Savings Bank in Cedar Rapids, 1911; St. Paul's United Methodist Church [q.v.] also in Cedar Rapids, 1914; and the Van Allen Store in Clinton, 1915: all but the church are surprisingly weak.) The "strongbox" approach to bank design—epitomized by Sullivan's Security Bank & Trust Company in Owatonna, Minnesota (q.v.)—stands forth vividly in Grinnell, but here as a "jewel box." The building glories in the architect's contrast of plain walls and its "violently superimposed" accent of terra-cotta ornament. The cartouche and circular window surmounting the entry of this bank quiver with geometric interlacings against the quiet, flat brick wall. (Some historians liken this to the symbolic workings of a vault door.) The long side wall directly anticipates Sullivan's People's Savings & Loan Association of 1917–18 in Sidney, Ohio (q.v.), each with a "panel" of ten narrow, clustered windows having plate glass on the outside, marbleized glass behind. Observe, too, the slightly Assyrian terra-cotta frieze around the top. In 1976 a substantial two-story addition was made on the Broad Street side by architects Stewart-Robison-Laffan. At the same time the Sullivan interior was thoroughly restored. The original chandeliers were "reactivated" and even the old fixtures on the check-writing desks, and the brass wall and ceiling lights reproduced. Of all of Sullivan's remarkable buildings, this is probably the most chromatic. Its entrance ornament is unsurpassed.

Open during business hours

---

14   The Old Capitol (1840–42)
University of Iowa Campus
Iowa Avenue at Clinton Street
Iowa City, Iowa

JOHN FRANCIS RAGUE, ARCHITECT

A solid example of the Greek Revival, a building designed as the Territorial Capitol but which became the first State Capitol. It was later the first—and for a time the only—building of the university when the capital was moved to Des Moines in 1857. The building is now a historic museum with the Senate chambers on the second floor continuing to be used for university lectures and meetings. The neat Doric porticos on both front and back are echoed by the two-story-high pilasters beside them. The well-detailed interior is highlighted by its reverse-curve spiral stair. The structure was completely fireproofed in

1921–24, a task necessitating much rebuilding but no design changes. In the 1970s it was totally restored and meticulously refurbished by the Old Capitol Restoration Committee as one of Iowa's contributions to the Bicentennial. There is a marked resemblance of the Old Iowa Capitol to the Old State Capitol in Springfield, Illinois (q.v.), begun in 1837 by Town & Davis, for whom Rague once worked, probably serving as superintendent of the Springfield job.

Open Mon.–Sat. 10–3, Sun. 12–4, except holidays

---

15 American College Testing Program Headquarters (1967–68)
SE off IOWA 1, near junction with IS 80
Iowa City, Iowa

THE SPITZNAGEL PARTNERS, ARCHITECTS

This quiet, civilized building is unpretentious outside, but has an interesting plan and splendid interiors. The plan consists of a series of angled "pavilions" attached to both sides of a hall-spine, curved slightly to match the grade, and expandable against future demands.

The central reception unit is two stories in height, the others one story with basement. The building is of tannish brick, with white cast-stone base and facia, and copper roof. It rests easily on its uneven 17.5-acre/7.1-hectare site by virtue of a curving corridor and excellent landscaping (by Franz Lipp & Associates). The interiors, also by the architects, are of brick and wood, well scaled, and notable for the fine collection of art, including tapestries and decorative tiles, which not only line the corridors but enliven even the rest rooms. Most of the art was personally chosen by the late Harold Spitznagel, largely in Scandinavia. The ACT Building accommodates a staff of 150 who are concerned with research, admissions, guidance, and student financial aid for some 20,000 educational institutions and agencies throughout the United States.

Reception area open during business hours

16 Woodbury County Court House (1916–18)
7th Street at Douglas
Sioux City, Iowa

W. L. STEELE IN ASSOCIATION WITH PURCELL & ELMSLIE, ARCHITECTS

William L. Steele, George Grant Elmslie, and William G. Purcell had worked together in Louis Sullivan's office in Chicago (see Index). This background of Sullivan, with perhaps a touch of influence of the

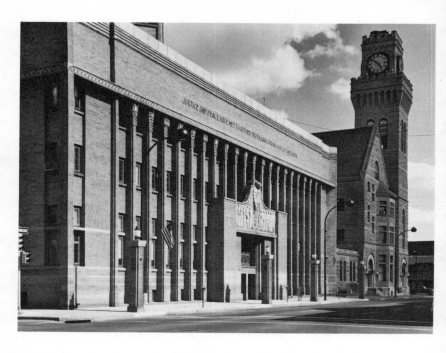

Dutch early modernist Hendrik Petrus Berlage (1856–1934), and a
hint of Frank Lloyd Wright, are fused in this courthouse on the western edge of the state. Steele got the commission—and remained the executive head of the project—but he at once got Elmslie to collaborate
with him and to take charge of overall design. Whatever the influences
and inspirations, the result produced one of our finest public buildings
of the early twentieth century.

The exterior presents a three-story, square block of subdued form,
with an eight-storied tower rising from the center. The detail of the
Roman brick piers that envelop the exterior are accented at entry by
a sculptured group by Alfonso Iannelli. However, it is the interior, illuminated by a glass "dome" (artificially lit), and alive with terra-cotta
decoration, that provides the real glory. The rotunda (square) is, indeed, a triumph of terra-cotta but used with such unity and appo-
siteness that it produces a symphony not a cacophony. Even the genre
painted wall panels (by John W. Norton) contribute their period bit.
One of the finest examples of its architecturally groping time, and, indeed, the present.

Open during office hours

Kansas

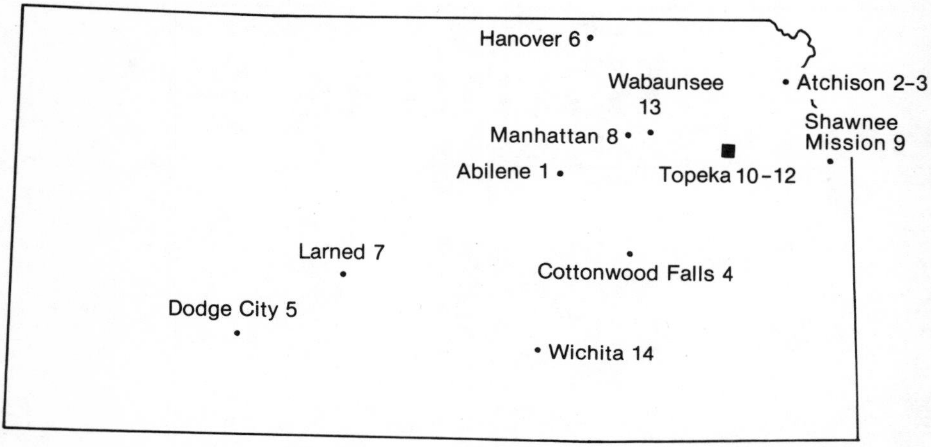

Hanover 6 •

Wabaunsee
13

• Atchison 2–3

Manhattan 8 • •

Shawnee
Mission 9

Abilene 1 •

Topeka 10–12

•

Larned 7

•

Cottonwood Falls 4

Dodge City 5

•

• Wichita 14

KANSAS

The buildings in boldface type are of general interest. The others are for the specialist.

Abilene

1 **Old Abilene Town** (late 19th century)

Atchison

2 U. S. Post Office (1892–94)—
Office of the Supervising Architect,
Treasury Department
Court House (1896–97)

3 **The Mall** (1963–65)—Louis J. Krueger

Cottonwood Falls

4 Chase County Courthouse
(1871–73)—John G. Haskell

Dodge City

5 Front Street Restoration (late 19th century)

near Hanover

6 Pony Express Station (1857)

Larned

7 **Fort Larned** (1866–68)

Manhattan

8 Anderson Hall (1879–84)—E. T. Carr

Shawnee Mission (Kansas City)

9 **Shawnee Methodist Mission** (1839–45)

Topeka

10 Thacher Building (1888)—John G. Haskell

11 **State Capitol** (1866–73/1879–1903)—E. Townsend Mix

12 **Grain Elevators** (mid-20th century)

Wabaunsee County

13 Beecher Bible and Rifle Church (1859–62)

Wichita

14 Farm Credit Bank Building (1972)—Schaefer & Associates

1 **Old Abilene Town** (late 19th century)
off KAN 15 at Kuney Street, S edge of
Abilene, Kansas

With an expanding nucleus of original, century-old buildings, this "reconstruction" well depicts a Western frontier street of a century ago. All of the log structures, the church (c. 1870), school (1874), plus an 1887 Rock Island Railroad station (moved to its present site from across the tracks), have come down intact, though some restoration has been necessary. The planning seems haphazard, and greater documentation would not hurt—moreover the interiors are commercial. Yet the overall atmosphere gives a reasonable account of this famous cow town of one hundred years ago, the terminus of the very active Chisholm Cattle Trail. Note, incidentally, that most of the stores are arcaded against sun and rain.

Open June–Labor Day, daily 8–9, rest of year 8:30–5, except major holidays: donation

2   U. S. Post Office (1892–94)
Kansas Avenue at 7th Street
Atchison, Kansas

**OFFICE OF THE SUPERVISING ARCHITECT, TREASURY
DEPARTMENT, ARCHITECT**

In the 1890s, as increasingly today, the federal government sought high-caliber architectural advice for its buildings. This Post Office obviously stems directly from Richardson, and equally obviously has been "handled in an unusual and creative manner" as the National Register puts it. Note, for instance, that the left-hand tower is taller, the better to "pivot" the corner. The soft, light-colored limestone detail—carved on the site—is showing signs of weathering, and the once lofty interior had its ceiling dropped in the mid-1950s, concealing the inner balcony, but structurally it is as sturdy as when built. The carved oak detailing in the lobby is of particular interest.

Open during office hours

The 1896–97 **Court House,** Parallel Street at 5th, is in the same neo-Romanesque mold.

3 The Mall (1963–65)
Commercial Street between 5th and 7th
Atchison, Kansas

LOUIS J. KRUEGER, ARCHITECT

For a small city (13,000)—pained by declining downtown business and prodded at times by serious flooding from the Missouri and tributary rivers—Atchison has boldly seized the possibility of urban renewal. Suffering "Disaster Area" floods in 1958—a condition and an appellation which brought federal financial help—the city was forced to take action, and the action it took was largely good. After flood-control measures (some twenty-five earth dams) had stabilized the rivers, the Urban Renewal Agency acquired ninety-one parcels of land (only eight needing eminent domain), and redeveloped and modernized the greater part of the central business district. Upon completion of this work, the Agency then sold back much of the property. A two-and-one-

half-block downtown pedestrian mall was created to give focus to the rejuvenated city, an avenue with fountains, small-fry playgrounds, sculpture, uniform signs, and landscaping, while in back of the stores (which are also reachable from the rear) there is meter-free parking for 1,100 cars. The canopy, slightly freestanding, which lines both sides of The Mall, not only protects the pedestrian from the strains of weather, it develops spatial unity, increases the feeling of urban involvement, and enables all the stores, whether old or new, to abut this kindly front. The result has been a firm mercantile success, and—a rara avis for a downtown area—it is especially congenial on warm summer evenings with its lighted fountains and general activity. Some of the details are unimaginative, but the concept and the reality probably have saved the city's commercial life.

---

4   Chase County Courthouse (1871–73)
Village Square, on KAN 177 just S of US 50
Cottonwood Falls, Kansas

JOHN G. HASKELL, ARCHITECT

The seeker of mid-continent architectural fashions for courthouses of a century ago will find gratification in this ambitious and brightly dressed number for a town of 1,000 and its surrounding county. The official bulletin states that "It is built in the Renaissance Style of architecture of the Louis XIII Period," but it would certainly seem more likely that Napoleon III (1808–73) was intended, not the Bourbon monarch. Built of local limestone, with M. Mansart's fashion wrapping the third floor, and topped by a bright red-and-white clock tower rising to a height of 113 feet/34 meters, it forms a jolly addition to the Plains. The most interesting feature within is the black walnut staircase and balustrade. The architect was also active in the design of the State Capitol (q.v.).

Open during office hours

---

5 Front Street Restoration (late 19th century)
500 West Wyatt Earp Boulevard
Dodge City, Kansas

Though a stage set, this 1958 reconstruction of the famous/infamous Front Street in the "cowboy capital of the world" was, however, re-created directly from early photographs. This two-block reconstruction of storefronts thus is basically correct. Dodge City was for a time (1875–84) one of the world's most active cattle shipping centers, and hundreds of cowboys were often paid off at the same time, well earning it its second title of "the Beautiful Bibulous Babylon of the Frontier." Though the street reconstruction is reasonably accurate, the interiors are both conjectural and commercial.

Open June–Sept., daily 8 A.M.*–10* P.M.*, rest of year 8–6*

---

6 Pony Express Station (1857)
Hollenberg Ranch, on KAN 243, 1 mile/1.6 kilometers E of KAN 15E
near Hanover, Kansas

This primitive, weather-beaten cabin—reputedly the only Pony Express station surviving unaltered—is obviously short on architecture. However, it does furnish an understanding of shelter during the surpris-

ingly brief (April 1860–October 1861) but fascinating epoch when the famous Pony Express carried the mail from St. Joseph, Missouri, to Sacramento, California, and back until the telegraph caused its demise. (The distance was 1,980 miles/3,187 kilometers with a change of horses every 10–15 miles/16–24 kilometers, and a change of riders approximately every third station.) Now owned by the state, the station is a museum of the time of its use and a National Historic Landmark.

Open Mon.–Thurs. 9–5, Fri.–Sun. 1–5, except major holidays

---

7   Fort Larned (1866–68)
6 miles/9.6 kilometers W of Larned off US 156
Larned, Kansas

Larned, on the Santa Fe Trail—like many forts built to guard the Western mail, overland trade, and settlers of a century and more ago—was more a military compound or base than a fortified position.

There was no palisade or enclosure at all, only a small blockhouse (though the commissary did have walls 2 feet/.6 meter thick). The Indians (generally) did not dare attack a well-organized detachment of professional soldiers, a fact which permitted some freedom in planning, though all buildings frame a 400-foot/122-meter-square parade ground. Fort Larned, now a National Historic Site, at first (1860) was built of sod but after the Civil War it was rebuilt in stone. The Fort was particularly active during the Indian uprisings in the 1860s—uprisings prompted by the extension of the railroads into their hunting grounds—but it was abolished in 1878 when the various tribes were moved to new reservations and were paid an annuity to keep them away from the Santa Fe Trail! From 1884 to 1964, Larned was in private hands, being converted to substantial ranching and sugar beet operations. Several of the major buildings had their roofs raised (to house more hay), while the others were stripped of porches. However the officers' quarters, barracks, commissary, and ancillary buildings, all of local yellow sandstone, remained sound structurally—the best of any of the Santa Fe Trail posts—and are now being restored to original condition (including the eventual removal of the tin roofs). Displays in many buildings re-create conditions of the Fort's activities and important episodes.

Open daily 8–5, except Dec. 25, with conducted tours

---

8 Anderson Hall (1879–84)
Kansas State University
Vattier Drive, W off Manhattan Avenue
Manhattan, Kansas

E. T. CARR, ARCHITECT

K-State was one of the Land Grant Colleges and Anderson Hall its first major structure. Built in three sections from north to south, its white limestone, slightly restive form dominates the campus. The tower and fenestration comprise the key architectural elements revealing a strange and, at times, questing mixture of roundheaded "Romanesque Revival" windows with pointed "Gothic," all brushed with Victoriana. The interior has been remodeled for contemporary use.

Open during business hours

---

9 **Shawnee Methodist Mission** (1839–45)
3403 West 53rd Street, 1 block N of US 50
Shawnee Mission (Kansas City), Kansas

None of the three remaining structures of this Indian mission is of heroic architectural distinction, but they are surprisingly accomplished.

Because they are among the earliest survivors of the period before Kansas attained statehood (1861), they form a valuable collection. The West Building, which was the first built (1839), looks as though it had been plucked from suburbia U.S.A., while the North Building (1845), seen here, is a comely and capable structure. At one time it had an east end to match the west. The interior of this building has been restored to its 1845–50 condition.

The Mission, which was established to teach up to two hundred Indian boys and girls English, crafts, and agriculture, at one time had sixteen buildings and covered over 2,000 acres/809 hectares (through which ran the famous Santa Fe and Oregon trails, the latter now 53rd Street). During the Civil War the Mission was used as a barracks, then fell into private hands. In 1927 the group was purchased by the state and it has undergone complete rehabilitation, and is administered by the Kansas State Historical Society. Interestingly, there was a contemporary Shawnee Baptist Mission and a Shawnee Friends Mission in the vicinity, both now gone.

Open Tues.–Sat. 10–5, Sun. 1–5, except major holidays

---

10   Thacher Building (1888)
110 East 8th Street
Topeka, Kansas

JOHN G. HASKELL, ARCHITECT

As the Topeka *Daily Capital* described the then new Thacher Building, "The style is a bold and artistic expression of the popular Romanesque, and embraces a combination of some of its choicest features, presenting a magnificent front" (September 30, 1888). Many Midwestern cities have Richardson-influenced commercial buildings from the 1880s and 1890s, but few have come down to us without "modernization." The burly limestone exterior of the Thacher Building, albeit not enhanced by several signs, is remarkably as built. Though scarcely a gem, it is important as an index of the building boom which fueled Topeka for years after it became the capital of Kansas in 1861. (Topeka itself was laid out in 1854.) Originally erected to house a lithographing company, it was acquired by the present owners in 1899 and its interior thus has been partially remodeled. The geometry of the front contrasts the three horizontal waves of arches of the main floor

with four vertical rounded "pilasters" of the top two. Note the triple attached columns with leaf capitals and vine rinceau (and two stone heads) decorating the three major openings. John Haskell was a prominent architect in Kansas at the time.

Open during business hours

---

11 State Capitol (1866–73/1879–1903)
8th–10th Streets at Topeka Avenue
Topeka, Kansas

E. TOWNSEND MIX, INITIAL ARCHITECT

The Kansas Capitol has an unusual architectural background in that it was built in distinct (but coordinated) stages. The East Wing was the first completed (1873) and stood alone and magnificent for six years,

its interior partitioned to house both House of Representatives and the Senate. The West Wing, similar to the East but a few feet/meters longer and wider, was begun in 1879 and finished in 1881, a covered "bridge" joining the two. (The detailing of the second building is inferior to that of the first.) The north and south wings followed, with construction of the central section and dome commencing in 1887 and being finished in 1903. Overall the Capitol's cross-plan measures 399 feet/122 meters north-south by 386 feet/118 meters east-west. The dome, more ambitious than coordinated, rises 304 feet/93 meters. Whereas the exterior is of relatively routine interest, much of the interior is fascinating. The Senate Chamber (East Wing, third floor), designed by State Architect John G. Haskell and L. M. Wood, is a marvel to behold. To quote the official guide, "the Senate Chamber is one of the finest in the United States and was decorated in 1885 at a cost of nearly $300,000. The ceiling is Egyptian architecture and the state imported the Egyptians to do the work." Glorious opulence is carried further by twenty-eight hand-hammered copper columns (for which Italian workmen were imported). It is an interior not to be missed. Take a look, too, at the large mural by Kansas native John Steuart Curry (1897–1946) on the second floor of the rotunda.

Hitchcock and Seale in their *Temples of Democracy* (Harcourt Brace Jovanovich, 1976) claim that "The commission rejected the plan [of Mix's] and ordered Colonel Haskell to revise it completely." However the recent (but undated) *The Kansas Capitol Building* brochure, published by Elwill M. Shanahan, Secretary of State, says that "The building of French Renaissance architecture with Corinthian composite details was designed by E. Townsend Mix."

Open Mon.–Fri. 8–5, Sat.–Sun., holidays 9–4

12 Grain Elevators (mid-20th century)
West Gordon Street (N bank of Kansas River)
Topeka, Kansas

It is perhaps no accident that Kansas' most impressive monuments to its wealth should be found in housing the source of its income rather than in sheltering the recipients thereof. (Kansas is the largest producer of wheat in the United States.) The smaller grain elevators which pepper the state's countryside—as, of course, they do all the Plains States and farming belts—shine encouragingly in the sun as they bulk-handle their grain vertically, while the staggeringly large complexes like those around northern Topeka cannot fail to excite with their interplay of geometric forms. Here is unadorned functionalism—both material and economic—which yet becomes sculpture at a giant's scale. (Reputedly the longest grain elevator in the world—.5 mile/.8 kilometer in length—can be seen at Hutchinson in mid-Kansas.) Would that the buildings by the people and for the people even approached this fundamental excellence. Or as Le Corbusier put it in an article in *L'Esprit Nouveau* of October 1920, then in his memorable *Towards a New Architecture,* "Thus we have the American grain ele-

vators and factories, the magnificent first-fruits of the new age. The American engineers overwhelm with their calculations our expiring architecture." (Translated by Frederick Etchells, published by John Rodker, London, 1931, from the thirteenth French edition: originally *Vers une architecture,* Crès, Paris, 1923.)

---

13   Beecher Bible and Rifle Church (1859–62)
.25 mile/.4 kilometer S of KAN 18
Wabaunsee County, Kansas

A sturdy, neatly proportioned church whose tall windows, well set in the local limestone walls, have character, only slightly marred by their wood storm-door and squat steeple. The church's intriguing name came from the famous Henry Ward Beecher whose Brooklyn congregation, becoming interested in the pioneer community (most of whom came from Connecticut—as did Beecher himself), sent money for fifty-two rifles, appropriately accompanying the sum ($625) with twenty-five Bibles. Deserted in 1927, the church was spruced up for its

centennial—it is one of the oldest in the state—and in later years services have been conducted by the United Church of Christ. Its architect,
if any, is not known. The building is listed in the National Register of
Historic Places.

Generally open only for Sun. services

14   Farm Credit Bank Building (1972)
151 North Main Street
Wichita, Kansas

SCHAEFER & ASSOCIATES, ARCHITECTS

Wichita is the largest and in many ways the most attractive city in Kansas. In recent years it has made a determined effort to maintain its air of progress and urban comity and though not always successful architecturally—what city has been?—its downtown in particular merits attention. One of its better new buildings is this well-designed ten-story block, made commanding by its setback from the lot line, agreeable by its fountain, and convenient by its parking at rear. Though on the formalistic side, with its white marble exterior and recessed dark glass, it is a handsome addition to the business district. Note the setback of the windows to give some sun control.

Open during business hours

Minnesota

Moorhead 21

Collegeville 1–2

Minneapolis 4–20 ■ St. Paul 23–32

South St. Paul 33

Mankato 3

Owatonna 22

Winona 34

MINNESOTA

The buildings in boldface type are of general interest. The others are for the specialist.

Collegeville

1 **St. John's University Church** (1956–61)— Marcel Breuer

Alcuin College Library (1967)— Marcel Breuer

2 St. John's Preparatory School (1961–62)— Hanson & Michelson

Mankato

3 **Behlethem Lutheran Church** (1969)— The Spitznagel Partners

Minneapolis

4 Milwaukee Avenue Historic District (1884–90/1980)

5 **Grain Elevators** (1881–mid-20th century)

6 **Butler Square** (1906/1975)—Harry W. Jones

Hennepin Center for the Arts (1888–89/1978–79)—Long & Kees

7 The Foshay Tower (1927–29)—Magney & Tusler

8 **Christ Church Lutheran** (1949–50)— Eliel Saarinen

9 Southdale Center (1954–56)—Gruen Associates

10 **Tyrone Guthrie Theater** (1962–63)— Ralph Rapson & Associates

11 **Walker Art Center** (1969–71)—Edward Larrabee Barnes

12 Nicollet Avenue Mall (1966–68)— Lawrence Halprin & Associates

13 **The Minneapolis Skyway System** (1962–   )—Edward F. Baker and others

14 Blue Cross Building (1968–70/1976)— Cerney Associates

15 **St. John the Evangelist Catholic Church**
    (1970–71)—Rafferty Rafferty Mikutowski
    & Associates
16 **IDS Building and Crystal Court** (1969–72)—
    Philip Johnson & John Burgee and Edward F.
    Baker
17 **Federal Reserve Bank** (1969–73)—
    Gunnar Birkerts & Associates
18 **Cedar Riverside** (1971–90)—Ralph
    Rapson & Associates
19 **Orchestra Hall** (1973–74)—Hardy Holzman
    Pfeiffer and Hammel, Green & Abrahamson
    Peavey Plaza Park (1977)—M. Paul
    Friedberg
20 **Hennepin County Government Center**
    (1974–75)—John Carl Warnecke &
    Associates
    The Municipal Building (1889–1905)—
    Long & Kees

Moorhead   21 **Church of the Good Shepherd** (1967–68)—
                        Sövik, Mathre & Madson

Owatonna   22 **Northwestern National Bank of Owatonna**
                        (1907–8)—Louis H. Sullivan

St. Paul   23 **The Sibley House** (1835–36) **and**
                        Faribault House (1836–37)
                    24 The Burbank-Livingston-Griggs House
                        (1862–65)—Otis E. Wheelock
                    25 Alexander Ramsey House (1868–72)—
                        Monroe Sheire
                    26 **Landmark Center** (1892–1902/1978)—
                        Willoughby J. Edbrooke
                    27 **Minnesota State Capitol** (1896–1905)—
                        Cass Gilbert
                    28 Cathedral of St. Paul (1906–15)—
                        Emmanuel L. Masqueray
                    29 **Mount Zion Temple** (1950–54)—Eric
                        Mendelsohn
                    30 Bethel Theological Seminary (1966–67)—
                        Hammel, Green & Abrahamson

31 **St. John the Baptist Church** (1968–69)—
Shifflet, Hutchison & Associates

32 Housing for the Elderly (1968–69)—
Freerks/Sperl/Flynn

South St. Paul 33 St. Thomas Aquinas Church (1968–69)—
Ralph Rapson & Associates

Winona 34 **Merchants National Bank** (1911–12)—
Purcell, Feick & Elmslie

Winona National Savings Bank (1914)—
George W. Maher

1 St. John's University Church (1956–61)
**N off US 52/IS 94, c. 12 miles/19 kilometers W of St. Cloud
Collegeville, Minnesota**

MARCEL BREUER, ARCHITECT; HAMILTON P. SMITH, ASSOCIATE;
PIER LUIGI NERVI, STRUCTURAL CONSULTANT

Exuding strength, St. John's Abbey Church presents us with one of the
most intriguing religious buildings in the United States. Its orientation
is north, hence the main facade is sunless for most of the year. This
posed problems of visual vitality which the architects imaginatively
solved by a stupendous—there is no other word—freestanding "bell
banner" 117 feet/36 meters high by 99 feet/30 meters wide, which
rests on four sculpted supports that straddle the entry to the church.
By piercing this trapezoidal banner with an open horizontal rectangle
for bells and a vertical opening for a cross, the sun from the southern
quadrants picks up facets of bells and cross, and with its reflections—
abetted by the positive-negative of solids and openings and the elegant
parabolic curves of the supports—creates a masterful introduction of
the shadowed entry. Moreover the honeycombed concrete and glass facade of the church reflects the sun bouncing from the south side of the
bell banner and brings added life to the front much of the day. The
banner also helps light the church interior through the latter's stained-
glass windows. (Incidentally the final design of the banner—which
suggests the church plan in its shape—represents careful evolution
over Breuer's initial sketches. The rectangular opening with bells was
inspired, we are told, by Greek village churches.)

The shrine is entered via a top-lit baptistry, also trapezoidal in plan,
attached to the front of the building with sunken font symbolically in
center. Directly on stepping into the fabric of the church proper, one
finds oneself under the puissant, freestanding balcony; on moving forward into the nave one encounters the staggering force of the full interior. Its roof is constructed of enormous folded concrete plates which
laterally span the room, their weight and thrusts being carried down to
an edge beam on either side by triangular pleated side walls. (The
influence of the Conference Building in the UNESCO Headquarters in
Paris, designed by Nervi, Breuer, and Zehrfuss—and very similar in
size and shape—can be seen in Collegeville.) An airily suspended baldachino gives focus to the altar and helps define the spaces for clergy
and congregation (1,700 seats).

This enormously powerful room, this spiritual redoubt, does have a

few minor shortcomings. Chief among these is the handling of natural light, for below the great concrete cap are bands of almost unshielded windows along either side, producing a glare which tugs at the eye. Moreover the sanctuary and the Brothers' and Priests' choirs, whose three hundred seats describe an extended semicircle about the altar, seem "unanchored" because of the passages and spaces behind the chancel and the treatment of the reredos. But these are details: the experience of this great church should not be missed. It is perhaps most impressive at dusk.

Open daily 7:30 A.M.–*8* P.M.

Directly facing stands the **Alcuin College Library** (1967), by the same architects, which should also be seen. The interior brandishes two eight-armed "trees" of concrete which uphold—with an intriguing degree of structural arm-flexing—the roof, which measures 200 x 120 feet/61 x 36 meters. These trees make a dynamic room as well as freeing the floor space for maximum flexibility.

2   St. John's Preparatory School (1961–62)
    adjacent to St. John's University, off US 52/IS 94
    Collegeville, Minnesota

HANSON & MICHELSON, ARCHITECTS

A clever adaptation of a classroom complex to a sharply sloping hill-side. The architects established the entrance to the school at the level of the road coming from nearby St. John's University, and let "ter-races" of classrooms step down the grade until the required spaces were achieved. There are four such bands, plus a double-height en-trance hall. The grade was such that each level could have full win-dows looking across the top of the lower rank, with a view of the undulating roof in the immediate foreground and a pine-edged lake be-yond. The vista south ties building to site as one looks outward, while the stepped structure seen from the exterior rests snugly on its small hill. The hill and its dense vegetation protect the building from prevail-ing northwesterly winds in winter, while the cantilevered portions of the roof vaults control solar radiation in summer. The roof vaults are actually of thin-shell concrete but look heavier because of their thick stiffening edge. In plan, classrooms occupy the east half, study halls

the west. The basic classroom module is of three vaults, each 10.7 feet/3.3 meters wide, while the study halls are ten vaults in width.

As the building is only a fragment of a larger complex that was designed but has not yet been executed, it lacks an architectural focus—the auditorium and library have served for this. As a whole, however, the building in concept and adaptation to the site stands out forcefully.

The same architects also designed the nearby dormitory. Val Michelson, the partner-in-charge, was supervising architect for Breuer's St. John's Church, and previously had worked in Breuer's New York office.

Generally open school days

---

3 Bethlehem Lutheran Church (1969)
700 South 2nd Street
Mankato, Minnesota

THE SPITZNAGEL PARTNERS, ARCHITECTS

A sizable (thousand-seat) church replacing an earlier one (since burned) which the congregation had outgrown. Located on the edge of

the downtown business district, numerous architectural problems arose, space and parking among them, which have been solved with skill in the main. The exterior is self-effacing (and because of the budget, of an unfortunately routine brick), but the nave is excellent. As no visual contact with the crowded urban surroundings was desired within the church, daylight enters from a band of low windows which are hidden on the inside by a half-height wall. The diffuse illumination thus produced is augmented over the sanctuary by a direct ceiling skylight. The resulting nave is peaceful and withdrawn in spite of its surroundings, while its plan and pew layout on three sides of the chancel encourage intimacy. The expression of inner structure is direct and handsome. An unusual detail of the interior can be seen in the line of saints painted by the late Cyrus Running directly on the brick on three sides of the nave in lieu of stained glass as decoration, so to speak. This brick (of far finer quality than that facing the building) is of a deep tan color, a happy mate to the natural wood of the sloping upper walls and the white-painted plaster ceiling. Though the saints do not attain museum status as art, their symbolism and color give quiet touches that enliven the room. Simplicity keynotes the well-detailed chancel, as it does the whole church. Choir and organ are placed in a balcony at rear.

Open Mon.–Fri. 8:30–12, 1–5, except holidays, Sun. services

---

4 Milwaukee Avenue Historic District (1884–90/1980)
Milwaukee Avenue from Franklin to 24th Street
Minneapolis, Minnesota

As piquant a collection of small houses—basically for immigrant workers—as one is apt to see. Built speculatively by an entrepreneur to house employees of the St. Paul, Chicago & Milwaukee Railroad, this lineup of near-identical dwellings, gables properly facing the bowered road, their porches nudging the sidewalk, delivers a cohesive ensemble. Individually not distinguished, collectively their caper of triangular roofs produces rhythmic harmony. Milwaukee Avenue (until 1906 termed 22½ Avenue) formed an ethnic, basically Scandinavian enclave where new immigrants could find low-cost housing (often desperately crowded), before moving financially upward, preferably with enough money to purchase a farm. As is obvious, the houses are very much alike—those on one block are almost identical—and very much crowded together. (The lots average 35 feet/10.6 me-

ters wide.) When the forty-eight brick and clapboard residences were threatened with razing to make way for urban renewal, The Seward West Project Area Committee, a neighborhood elected group, the Minnesota Historical Society, the Minneapolis Heritage Preservation Commission, and dedicated volunteers (primarily Robert Roscoe and Jerilee Richtman) persuaded the Housing and Redevelopment Authority that it would be far wiser to save and rehabilitate one of the country's few, largely intact, districts of humble background. The 1,080-foot/329-meter-long avenue is now under intense rehabilitation, with strict facade standards required of all new owners. It was nominated for the National Register of Historic Places in 1974.

Street always open, houses private

---

5   Grain Elevators (1881–mid-20th century)
either side of Mississippi, mostly below 3rd Avenue Bridge
Minneapolis, Minnesota

Much of the considerable wealth of Minneapolis was, and to a certain extent still is, based on flour milling. The city began life in this role, and since the turn of the century a number of the world's largest mill-

ing companies have been located here, their grain elevators ranking among the area's most impressive monuments. It was the Swiss-French Le Corbusier who first gave architectural recognition to these great functionally sculptured forms (although he had never personally seen them). The first mill was not an elevator, but the famous blue limestone, water-powered, Pillsbury "A" Mill built in 1880–81 by L. S. Buffington (Main Street SE at 3rd Avenue SE). Abutting this are mills and elevators dating from 1910–16. These were followed by a succession of those cylindrical silos which proclaim with proud authority their geometric rightness. In the early twentieth century non-flammable concrete superseded wood and then stone in the United States largely due to experiments in France and Germany where combined circumferential and vertical reinforcing was pioneered. Some feel that the earliest example (of concrete) in this country was constructed in Minneapolis in 1900. It was, and is, for it still stands, 25 feet/7.6 meters in diameter and 80 feet/24 meters high. (Steel-reinforced brick for grain elevators was patented in the 1860s.) By the early 1900s concrete was ubiquitous. The first all-metal design was the Pioneer Steel Elevator, designed and erected in 1906 by the William Graver

Tank Works (5th Street at 25th Avenue NE). With a capacity of 500,000 bushels, it is still in use.

Among the most stimulating elevator panoramas in Minneapolis are those shown here off University Avenue between 17th and 23rd streets. But wherever encountered they add a visceral vertical footnote to the cityscape. Unfortunately, the advanced technique of ribless cylinders for housing grain was little explored for housing people or extending other architectural-engineering horizons.

Some mills open to visitors: inquire at Chamber of Commerce

---

6   **Butler Square** (1906/1975)
North 1st Avenue at North 6th Street
Minneapolis, Minnesota

HARRY W. JONES, ARCHITECT; REHABILITATED BY MILLER, HANSON, WESTERBECK, BELL

Stern with authority—and vaguely reminiscent of the Palazzo Vecchio (A.D. 1298) in Florence—this powerfully scaled, dignified structure has, to the benefit of all, been saved. It was spruced up on the exterior, brilliantly remodeled within, and is now enjoying economic life as office space with a hotel planned for its second phase. Built originally as a nine-story, 500,000-square-foot/46,450-square-meter warehouse on what is now the edge of downtown, it had lain empty for a decade until its respectful yet exciting transformation. The architects of rehabilitation carefully preserved the exterior, simply removing the original double-hung windows and extending their openings to floor level, and putting in dark glass for both windows and new spandrels. This enhances the play of stone versus glass and gives more power to the facades. A number of the 14 x 16-foot/4.3 x 4.9-meter bays of the warehouse interior, however, were removed to create two open skylit courts in the center of the block-square building. Like the structure throughout, these are sturdily framed by Douglas fir columns (the lower ones measure 22 inches/56 centimeters square). Their sandblasted wood texture, along with that of the underside of the decking, produces an interior that is airily accented by the glass sliding doors of the surrounding offices. Acrylic skylights flood the atria with illumination. New raised flooring accommodates wiring and air conditioning. Shops occupy the lower two floors, offices the upper seven. A first-rate reha-

bilitation with an inward-centered focus for a cold climate. John R. Miller was principal, Arvid Elness project architect.

Shops and lobby open during business hours

One block away at 528 Hennepin and North 6th Street stands the hoary **Hennepin Center for the Arts** (ex-Masonic Temple) erected in 1888–89 with Long & Kees architects. This downtown fruitcake, also once known as the Merchandise Building, was in parlous condition for years, but in 1978–79 it was totally remodeled by Svedberg-Wermeland into a Center for the Arts. An excellent recycling. Note the cartouches high on both sides.

Lobby open during business hours

7   **The Foshay Tower** (1927–29)
     821 Marquette Avenue
     Minneapolis, Minnesota

MAGNEY & TUSLER, ARCHITECTS

The notion of a habitable obelisk—even a nine-to-five one—is, of course, *divertente:* Sen-Mut, the ancient Egyptian obelisk maestro, would undoubtedly applaud. And though Wilbur B. Foshay wanted his tower to "be accepted as the west's memorial to George Washington," he saw to it that his own name in letters 10 feet/3 meters high appeared on the four sides of the top. This extraordinary excursion in high-rise design was—until the completion of the nearby IDS Building

(q.v.)—the tallest at 447 feet/136 meters for hundreds of miles. But height is secondary to its unforgettable profile (a cachet prominently exaggerated upon in the 1970s in San Francisco). In addition to offices, Mr. Foshay had the twenty-seventh and twenty-eighth floors sumptuously furnished for his own office and apartment, including three bedrooms and three baths with marble tubs and gold-plated fixtures. Alas, the former art student turned utilities magnate was star-crossed and before he could move into his personal pylon, the Depression struck and by December 1929 the tower was in receivership. Shortly thereafter Mr. Foshay and his chief aide were in Leavenworth for fraudulent financial practices. The building itself, though a beacon to the idiosyncratic, was very solidly built. In 1977–78 it was completely updated and refurbished, and being attached to Minneapolis' famous Skyway System, which links the Foshay with buildings of the fifteen-block heart of the city, it offers superior office space.

Open during business hours

---

8 **Christ Church Lutheran** (1949–50)
34th Avenue South at East 33rd Street
Minneapolis, Minnesota

ELIEL SAARINEN, ARCHITECT; EERO SAARINEN, ASSOCIATE

This wonderfully sympathetic church, one of the finest contemporary examples in the country, was among the earlier to break with stultified traditions. The last work of Eliel Saarinen (1873–1950), it bears some resemblance to his First Christian Church, finished in 1942, in Columbus, Indiana (q.v.), but develops more warmth and cohesion than in the Columbus prototype. The nave, which seats six hundred, provides a high central volume with low "expansion" areas on either side. Thus with less than a full congregation the church will not seem sparsely occupied. A thirty-six-seat chapel at the rear, behind the open narthex and placed at right angles to the nave, provides for overflow services as well as accommodating its own conjunctive functions. The choir and organ are placed in a balcony directly over the narthex, while the baptistry is at the forward end of the nave at left. A low curved wood screen at right ties nave to sacristy, enabling direct passage to the chancel for the pastor and also forming a backdrop for the pulpit. Note the slightly angled "panels" of open brickwork high along the right-hand side, where they play both an acoustic and a visual role.

The ceiling is angled for similar considerations. Daylight pours in from tall narrow windows lining the low side aisles, their glazing set on the outer face of the brick piers whose depth minimizes glare. The sanctuary receives a dramatic shaft of midmorning sun from a floor-to-ceiling chancel window concealed behind a projecting louvered wood grille. The chancel wall is angled and curved at the right side to reflect this light and is given emphasis by having its brick painted white and then sanded. Artificial illumination is provided by spoon-shaped indirect fixtures and ceiling downlights.

A courtyard separates the church from an education and fellowship building with administrative offices designed by Eero Saarinen and erected in 1962. An arcade connects the two and provides weather protection. The exterior of Christ Lutheran lacks total coordination but its nave is one of our finest. Hills, Gilbertson & Hayes were associate architects.

Open Mon.–Fri. 9–4:30, Sat. 9–12, Sun. services

9   Southdale Center (1954–56)
off MINN 62 at France Avenue and West 66th Street
Minneapolis, Minnesota

GRUEN ASSOCIATES, ARCHITECTS

This granddaddy of the air-conditioned covered mall has rarely been equaled though it was among the first. Any large shopping complex needs a bright, spontaneous core for orientation, and this is properly furnished at Southdale. Two levels of shopping—difficult to integrate vertically but here cleverly achieved—open directly onto the concourse which is anchored at the ends by Dayton's and Donaldson's, the Twin Cities' large department stores. Lanes of some seventy shops extend from the mall to the parking lots which surround the whole, the parking accommodated on two levels to encourage shopping interaction on the two floors within. Although some of the inner signs have gotten a bit out of hand, the "official" graphics are excellent, particularly the mnemonic animal emblems for the various parking areas.

Open daily

10 Tyrone Guthrie Theater (1962–63)
725 Vineland Place off Hennepin Avenue
Minneapolis, Minnesota

RALPH RAPSON & ASSOCIATES, ARCHITECTS

There are few theaters in the United States which deliver such intimacy between actors and audience as the Guthrie. (The architect worked closely with Sir Tyrone Guthrie in developing the unusual concept.) Accommodating 1,437, no person sits more than 54 feet/16 meters—fifteenth row—from the stage, the audience becoming vicarious participants as they almost engulf the players. It provides a "lively and strangely satisfying" experience as Walter Kerr put it (*P/A,* December 1963). The projected stage derives, of course, from early Greek examples, the most impressive being the almost perfectly preserved hillside Theater at Epidaurus (c. 350 B.C.) by Polyclitus the Younger. The Rapson-Guthrie concept—one also influenced by the Elizabethan stage and the Shakespeare theater in Stratford, Ontario (on which Tyrone Guthrie also worked)—is an asymmetrical variation of the Greek theme which centers on a circular "orchestra" (the stage), with steeply banked seats fanned approximately 200° about it. (Greek plays appear often in the repertory of the Guthrie, and this was a further

factor—in addition to developing greater intimacy—which prompted this theater's thrust design as opposed to the more typical proscenium.) In overall plan the Guthrie tightly fills a rectangular space, with little backstage depth and only a shallow fly loft.

The orchestra seats are supplemented by an asymmetric balcony level, one third of which the architect brings down to the main floor at one end to help erase the "second-class" stigma of the balcony, a move which also "loosens" the entire interior. It is an effective measure. The ceiling consists of multiple and often overlapping rectangular panels or acoustic clouds hung from the roof trusses so that catwalks and light ports can reach any section above and surrounding the stage. The asymmetry, the liveliness of the ceiling, and the rainbow-colored upholstery of the seats all combine to create an exciting milieu. The promenading spaces are reasonably adequate, while the lobby serves both theater and the adjacent Walker Art Center (q.v.) with inspired friendliness. The theater's exterior is slightly arbitrary (at least the large amount of glass behind it attracts the passerby), but as Will said, "the play's the thing," and the interior generates one of the country's great theatrical experiences. Robert F. Lambert was acoustic consultant.

Open during performances

---

11   **Walker Art Center** (1969–71)
Vineland Place at Hennepin Avenue
Minneapolis, Minnesota

EDWARD LARRABEE BARNES, ARCHITECT

The concept of connecting a theater (the Guthrie—q.v.) with an art center by a joint lobby can only create a cultural plus for a city. This pair facing The Parade—a smallish park—greatly enhances the Twin Cities' reputation. The museum, which occupies an important corner site, replaces a 1927 structure which had been outgrown. Years ago the museum established a reputation as one of the most stimulating institutions in the field (primarily) of contemporary art, industrial design, and architecture in the country: this esteem is buttressed by this imaginative building. The museum's understated, almost industrial exterior reveals few of the delights awaiting within: its cubic masses of plum-colored brick are little broken by windows, and it is only when

one approaches the joint entry with the Guthrie Theater that an invitation to enter is extended. Once within, however, its multilevel continuum of spaces, its white walls, floors, and ceilings, and its handsomely installed art make of the museum a provocative exploration. As the architect says "It is flow more than form that has concerned us. The sequence of spaces must be seductive."

The most effective path for the gallery-goer is to take the elevator to the top and to stroll down the broad stairs which interconnect each level, the floors thus doubling as art-viewing platforms (cf. Wright's Guggenheim Museum in New York). This three-dimensional, loosely "programed" progression follows a pinwheel sequence of half floors about a central circulation core, and the variety of perspectives that it develops can be stunning in their impact. There are no dreary corridors or endless cubbyholes stocked with paintings and sculpture but an evanescent flow of spaces. (Fire stairs are placed on and project from the exterior walls.) The seven galleries are spanned by prestressed triple-flanged T-beams of concrete painted white, like the walls, and vary in area and height to create flexibility and lend variety. The high ceilings (10–18 feet/3–5.5 meters) of the exhibition spaces enable the increasingly popular large-scale works of art to be displayed, while movable partitions can be adjusted to make any size group at ease. Lighting relies almost exclusively on flexible spots mounted on tracks between the flanges so that emphasis—or non-emphasis—of illumination can be readily set up. Several unexpected windows lend interest. A series of three roof terraces on the third and fourth floors affords display areas for open-air sculpture, and vantage points overlooking the skyline, either al fresco or from the well-situated fourth-floor restaurant. Off the entry level, in addition to the usual amenities, there are a 350-seat auditorium and a 75-seat lecture hall. Top-notch.

Open Tues.–Sat. 10–5, Sun. 11–5, except holidays

12 Nicollet Avenue Mall (1966–68)
Washington Avenue to 10th Street
Minneapolis, Minnesota

LAWRENCE HALPRIN & ASSOCIATES, DESIGNERS

This ribbon of urban wisdom makes the sidewalk, at least for a good part of the year, not just a pedestrian conveyor belt but an experience. A formerly "endless" downtown shopping street, packed with cars and buses from nowhere to nowhere, has been turned into a sinuous 24-foot/7.3-meter-wide passage for minibuses (plus taxis and emergency vehicles), its sidewalks doubled and tripled in width for strolling and window-shopping. Trees and planting boxes, chosen with the city's demanding winters in mind, have been set up, benches, sculpture, clocks, amusing street lights, and warm bus shelters added—plus electric-heated brick sidewalks that melt the snow—making these eight blocks an exemplary transformation of midtown's prime merchandising street. Public transportation, moreover, is better served, hence more used. The Mall was paid for by a "benefit assessment tax" via a formula worked out with the city and terminating in twenty years when the tax rate will return to normal. Nicollet Mall and The Skyway System (q.v.) have had a pronounced effect in attracting new business to downtown, and there are plans to extend both. Lawrence Halprin & Associates are now known as CHNMB Associates. Barton-Aschman Associates were urban planning and engineering associates for the Mall.

---

13   The Minneapolis Skyway System (1962–   )
Central business and shopping area
Minneapolis, Minnesota

EDWARD F. BAKER AND OTHERS, ARCHITECTS

Classification of circulation, particularly between automobiles and pedestrians, is an acute urban problem, and lack of efficient separation of wheels and feet is one of the factors driving shopping from downtown. The situation is compounded in Minneapolis as it is in most "northern tier" cities with long, harsh winters. For not only can car-people encounters be exacerbated on icy streets, the very chore of shopping under demanding weather conditions can lead to no shopping at all. Minneapolis has set about changing all this and its means of implementation is an ingenious series of midblock "skyways" whose numerous enclosed "bridges" now interconnect the second floors of fifteen blocks in the business and shopping district. There are plans to extend this to a total of seventy-six Skyways by 1985. These bright and airy passageways, heated in winter and air-conditioned in summer, have had a remarkable effect in resuscitating the city (abetted by a splendid

array of new buildings). And instead of taking business away from the ground floor of, say, a department store, they have increased the turnover on the second, and many shops have undergone extensive remodeling to spruce up their upper level with arcades, lunch stands, boutiques, etc. Though most stores do not open until nine-thirty in the morning, they permit passages through them—passages usually marked only by signs and change of floor material—from 7 A.M. with a guard on duty.

The impact of the IDS Building and its Crystal Court (q.v.) gave the system an enormous boost, for the Court not only coordinates a strategic web of four Skyways, it gives a spontaneous focus to the entire net. All of the enclosed bridges constructed thus far were erected with private financing, basically by the owners whose buildings are involved. With the projection of a vast extension of the Skyway System where some owners will not be able to afford their cost, benefit assessment taxes, and municipal or federal grants might become essential, obviously so if civic buildings are involved. The merchants, incidentally, feel that having a Skyway unquestionably pays for its construction and maintenance.

As indicated, the first units of the system were built in 1962 to the design of architect Edward F. Baker following an earlier suggestion of his and of civic leader Leslie C. Parks. Baker Associates also have been subsequently involved with many other units. The designs vary as, of course, do the spans, with the simpler, more "invisible" examples (such as the excellent ones from IDS) being the most successful. A standardization of module would obviously effect economies but this has not yet been done or desired. Widths usually run between 16–18 feet/4.9–5.5 meters. With Nicollet Mall adding much to the spring-summer-fall pleasures of downtown Minneapolis, and the net of Skyways helpful in summer and almost essential in winter, the city's shopping and business core is one of the healthiest in the nation. It has become, indeed, "the weatherproof city," and the presence of these amenities will probably be a key factor in activating plans for new downtown housing and apartment projects. As Mr. Baker—a joint venture architect of the IDS Building—is careful to point out, such a system is not automatically applicable to all cities: here it works wonders. Moreover it has stimulated many building projects which would have "escaped" to other locations.

It was announced in April 1980 that St. Paul, Minneapolis' "Twin City," would also construct a downtown skyway system.

Open daily

---

14   Blue Cross Building (1968–70/1976)
off MINN 13, c. 4 miles/6.4 kilometers S of Mendota Bridge
Minneapolis (Eggan Township), Minnesota

CERNEY ASSOCIATES, ARCHITECTS

A ruggedly positive, low office block a few miles south of the Twin Cities. Situated on a hillside across the Mississippi River from the airport, it enjoys good communications and a fine view. Approach and parking are from the upper level via Red Cross Road, and entry to the building, because of grade, is from the top floor. The exposed frame is of weathering steel, the reddish color of which is set off by the blank end walls of purplish brick. This makes for a hard, tough building on the outside, but one eased by window walls which are set back from the roof edge to provide sun protection and covered outdoor circulation. On stepping within one finds an admirable play of spaces, especially in that the long wall on the river side rises an unobstructed full two stories in height inside the building—the top floor being narrower than the lower—thus creating a three-dimensional whirl of space and association between the upper and lower clerical levels, both being vis-

ible at once. At the far end of the entry hall stands a five-story tower used for vertical circulation, president's office, meeting rooms, and, at the enlarged base, a restaurant. In 1976 a sensitive two-story addition was added, doubling the size of the building. The quality of illumination, detailing, and colors is excellent.

Lobby open during business hours

15 **St. John the Evangelist Catholic Church** (1970–71)
1428 Preston Lane at Interlachen Road
(S off Excelsior Avenue, just W of Meadowbrook Golf Course)
Minneapolis (Hopkins), Minnesota

RAFFERTY RAFFERTY MIKUTOWSKI & ASSOCIATES, ARCHITECTS

An unusual, complicated, intriguing church in a western Minneapolis suburb. There is no immediately graspable entity here, but spaces flow into spaces, turn corners, secrete, and explode. This adventure is augmented by the canted ceiling planes and by the natural illumination

which derives primarily from dramatic skylights in several separate roof angles. Some indirect light emphasizes spatial separation. The baptistry occupies an appropriately central spot near entry; the congregations's seven hundred seats are grouped on three sides of the chancel with proper liturgical closeness. The chancel wall, projected a few feet in front of the rear wall of the church, is emphasized by a thin steel cross set into and stretching the width and height of its white-painted brick. The bishop's chair is placed directly in front, while the plainest of pulpits and an irreducible stone altar stand on either side, a group of growing plants rising behind the pulpit. The altar, of reddish-gray granite, is devoid of trappings, a simplicity as admirable as it is rare (only the organ at left intrudes). A thirty-seat chapel, though separated from nave and chancel, remains in visual contact with each.

The walls of the nave are of white-painted brick, while the sharply canted ceilings are of natural finished wood. The brick in the circulation areas and on the exterior has a tawny color. On the outside, an energetic play of roof angles, low at outer edge rising toward center to keep the domestic scale of the neighborhood, carries out (with some exaggeration) the multifaceted spaces of the interior. A large community room and priests' offices occupy the unit at right on entering. A previously existing school takes up the rear part of the lot. George E. Rafferty was the designer; Frank Kacmarcik, liturgical consultant. The firm was formerly known as Progressive Design Associates.

Open Mon.–Sat. 7:30–6, Sun. services

---

16 IDS Building and Crystal Court (1969–72)
Nicollet Mall, 7th Street, Marquette Avenue, 8th Street
Minneapolis, Minnesota

PHILIP JOHNSON & JOHN BURGEE AND EDWARD F. BAKER,
ASSOCIATED ARCHITECTS

Though the Investors Diversified Services tower in no way resembles
the Campanile in the Piazza San Marco, in function this elegantly
sheathed fifty-one-story skyscraper polarizes the city much as does the
Venetian fulcrum. It forms a beacon, figuratively and literally, on the
city's profile, while close up its Crystal Court acts as a spontaneous
magnet for much of the activity of downtown Minneapolis—as, of
course, does the Piazza for Venice. Thus vertically and horizontally the
impact of each quickens the city and the citizen. Moreover this block-
square complex also contains a 285-room hotel (the nineteen-story
Marquette Inn, at the corner of Marquette and 7th), an eight-story
office block (on Marquette) with an underground garage for 526 cars,
and along Nicollet and 7th Street—a key shopping corner—a two-
story Woolworth plus numerous smaller retail facilities. The chief generating factor in developing the plan was to have these four units embrace and define the central Crystal Court and do so not just on one
level but two, the second one tying into and expanding the city's extraordinary network of elevated pedestrian Skyways (q.v.), a series of
air-conditioned bridges which interconnect fifteen downtown blocks.
(See also Nicollet Mall description.) Thus after leaving one's car in an
underground garage, one can work, lodge, shop, wine, dine, and play
throughout the city's center without once having to face the chill blasts
of winter or summer's downpours.

The 775 feet/236 meters of the IDS skyscraper are more than 50
per cent higher than the next tallest building (Magney & Tusler's singular Foshay Tower of 1929, q.v.), and this profile "responsibility"
was not lost on the architects. To keep its bulk from urban abruptness,
even intrusiveness, they "stepped in" each of the four corners with
seven uniform vertical setbacks—"zogs" Johnson calls them—so that
the two ends of the building are precisely half as wide as the midsection. By this means the greenish-blue mirror glass which encases the
building is not one "boring" mass but a series of faceted facades that
catch and enjoy the sun. In addition further exterior interest is created
by the spacing of the muntins, hence window width, which are approximately twice as close as normal, being 30 inches/76 centimeters on
center: "more the aspect of a birdcage than a glass box" (PJ).

The Crystal Court forms one of the most spirited, attractive mid-city

crossroads which one will see. Vaguely pentagonal in plan, it is an irregular cube in three dimensions topped by a startling roof—almost
constructivist sculpture—which rises in deeply coffered tiers (note
structure) to a maximum height of 121 feet/37 meters. Through the
pyramids of plastic and glass which roof this animated concourse
streams the sun—and below the populace. Its marked lack of rigidity,
horizontally and vertically, is emphasized by the second-level "balconies"—reached by escalators—which wrap around almost three
quarters of the *cortile* and afford festive viewing platforms for observ-
ing the flow of people. Planting boxes, ample benches, banners, an
"outdoor" cafe on the balcony, a tempting variety of shops on both
levels, and an overall atmosphere of pleasure, even glamor, have been
skillfully created. In a way it suggests a glazed-in Rockefeller Center
Mall. Four Skyways, carefully not aligned, lead from the upper level to
tie the Crystal Court to the city's two most important department
stores and two office buildings, and also to afford major access to the
hotel. The street-level entrances to the Court are directly underneath
the mid-block Skyways.

On the exterior of the IDS complex there are some awkward junctures
between tower and hotel, and the facades of the latter are not
overwhelming, but altogether this is a brilliant contribution to urban
design, one which carefully embraces downtown Minneapolis and
stitches its space into the very fabric of the city instead of walling it
off. As a result it has become an urban umbilicus, the delight of
shoppers winter or summer—and long after 5 P.M. It is in this new dimension of civic integration and welcome that its prime significance
lies.

51st Floor Observation Deck open daily, Sun.–Thurs. 10–10,
Fri.–Sat. 10–midnight: admission. Crystal Court open daily

---

17   Federal Reserve Bank (1969–73)
250 Marquette Avenue (Plaza off Nicollet Mall)
Minneapolis, Minnesota

**GUNNAR BIRKERTS & ASSOCIATES, ARCHITECTS; SKILLING
HELLE, CHRISTIANSEN, ROBERTSON, STRUCTURAL ENGINEERS**

Veering near the obstreperous as regards structure, the Federal Reserve
Bank veers toward necromancy as regards experience, particularly on
its terrace side. It is at once both improbable and stunning. The ra-

tionals for its structural swoop (i.e. the catenary expressed in its facades) arose from the necessity of creating column-free floors underground—where all the bullion is stored—because a grid of vertical supports would compromise the movements of armored cars and complicate related storage problems. Moreover routine offices and high-security areas were to be separated. The architect therefore concentrated his loads at two points 275 feet/84 meters apart, ran two great piers up eleven floors above a plaza, connected and braced them with a 28-foot/8.5-meter-deep roof truss plus rigid frame facades, slung cables from the tower tops, then tied his floors onto these cable supports. It is the same simple notion as multidecking a suspension bridge. A not inconsiderable additional advantage is that the suspended office floors thus are columnless. (Floor access is via a central semidetached elevator tower with emergency exits and toilets at each end of the building.) To underscore vividly the drama of the catenary, the architect detailed the tawny reflective glass which sheathes the building in two planes, putting all below the curve flush with the outside edge and all glass above the catenary a few inches inset to reveal the vertical mullions.

A broad sloping terrace rises from Nicollet Mall—giving further importance to this urban spine—flows beneath the building, and terminates 20 feet/6.1 meters above Marquette Avenue. It is carefully landscaped, fitted with numerous clever benches (note their concealed lights), and accented with several excellent pieces of sculpture and a fountain. The terrace, however, can be a rootless space in which to linger. Personnel entrance, and a quiet entry it is, is off Marquette with two truck ramps, closed except when in use, along this same street. Underground employee parking uses the two side streets. The bank is planned so that a 50 per cent addition in office space can be realized by adding six floors at the top, floors which in this case would be suspended from an arch on either side, the reverse, thus, of the catenary.

Though rationalized, this is one of the most imaginative buildings one will see.

Conducted tours Mon.–Fri. except holidays: inquire for hours

---

18   Cedar Riverside (1971–90)
Cedar Avenue between South 4th and 6th Streets
Minneapolis, Minnesota

RALPH RAPSON & ASSOCIATES, ARCHITECTS

The Cedar Riverside project—the country's first New-Town-in-Town —is a magnificently ambitious plan "to build a high-density quality environment that will provide the setting for healthful and rewarding living within the central city" for 30,000. It occupies a once-depressed area a dozen blocks from downtown Minneapolis and almost adjacent to the West Campus of the University of Minnesota. Its land usage and architecture are full of expertise and sympathetic social concern, and the project could be a bellwether for much urban redevelopment if its full program is carried to completion. The "if" is, however, a large one and legal action—some seemingly malicious—has been brought by those who claim that the basic "high-rise, high-density design" is "socially destructive," etc. In any case, as of this writing, the second phase of Cedar Riverside (named for two prominent streets) is in abeyance. To build on expensive land obviously demands a high-rise response, and if mothers won't let junior "go down 39 floors to play" they should not have moved in in the first place—or should go down with him. As Mr. Rapson has said, "I don't advocate high-rise housing for everybody and every situation. But to house so many people in this area with its pressing need for shelter, what is the alternative?"

Cedar Square West (1971–73), the first unit of Cedar Riverside, is probably the finest large-scale housing in the U.S.A. Its great variety of heights combines—without perceptual identification—upper-bracket rental apartments with subsidized low-income units in a complex group, yet there are no indications of municipal "do-goodness," few

vistas without rewards, and less than a hint of architectural ennui. This alto plano of midcity shelter for some 3,600, occupying 8 acres/3.2 hectares and not far from the Mississippi River (and Interstate 94), is made up of interconnected buildings clustered about a central plaza and containing a total of 1,299 apartments in buildings ranging in height from 4 to 40 stories. Of these—all 100 per cent rented—222 are semiluxury, 960 medium-range, and 117 low-income, each with options as to basic type in their studio to four-bedroom sizes. An 860-car garage lies under the plaza, or is attached, with automotive access using different levels from pedestrians. Most living rooms have floor-to-ceiling glass doors which visually expand the smallish quarters while opening onto narrow balconies. By judiciously contrasting the various building heights, and by vivid use of colored panels (red, yellow, blue) an interest results which is intertwined with a provocative interaction of spaces and scale build-up. The complex is of economic necessity tightly compacted, and the lack of shopping and related facilities—all anticipated in the as yet unbuilt community "centrum"— is unfortunate. But if Cedar Riverside is brought to its full development, Minneapolis, Minnesota, and the United States will have a central-city housing development of which we can all be justly proud.

Barton-Aschman Associates were the technical coordinators for site planning, traffic, and engineering; Sasaki, Walker & Associates, environmental design; and Gingold-Pink were the associate architects. Heikki von Hertzen—the Finnish backer of Helsinki's famous Tapiola —was consultant on community development.

Grounds open daily

---

19   **Orchestra Hall** (1973–74)
1111 Nicollet Mall
Minneapolis, Minnesota

HARDY HOLZMAN PFEIFFER AND HAMMEL, GREEN & ABRAHAMSON, ARCHITECTS

The exterior of Orchestra Hall is understated by day but glows brightly by night. Its facades are almost self-consciously utilitarian, but step inside the lobby and the magic begins. The open tiers and "bridges" of the 50-foot/15-meter-high lobby sing with bright colors and revel in ample strolling spaces. The fully exposed ventilating ducts, painted a bright yellow, lace through the green-painted steel structure and the

blue pipework, with blue-red carpeting underfoot (and running up one side of the balustrade). The "wells" of space allow spectator viewing not only laterally but up and down the various levels, adding to the visual excitement of the oft-neglected intermission period of concert- and theater-going. Nesting cocoonlike within this animated embrace, and totally insulated structurally and aurally from it, rests the striking auditorium. (A double wall, the outer of steel frame and brick, the inner of concrete, effect this.) But far more important than looks, "Tonally it is one of the most remarkable concert halls in the world" (New York *Times,* October 23, 1974). Moreover this fantastic acous- tic and visual setting helps establish great liaison with the orchestra. Both sound and looks are based on a wave projection directly con- trolled by the startling arrangement of "cubes" which poke out from the stage wall (behind the orchestra) and proceed to march over the entire ceiling to the rear of the house, diminishing in size and angle but increasing in number as they go. The three-quarter cubes behind the orchestra evolve into flattened geometric shapes at rear. Almost en- croaching at first sight, these acoustic measures soon become friends. It is pertinent to point out in regard to acoustics that the first planning decision insisted on a rectangular-shaped room, one common to most of the great traditional concert halls of Europe. The cubes (of heavy plaster) replace the openings and ornaments of the nineteenth century. The rest of the stage is slightly marred by the dangles of spotlights and by the treatment of the side panels. But aside from these details, the 2,573-seat auditorium is unequalled acoustically, while it—and the lobby—are visually remarkable. Dr. Cyril M. Harris was the acoustical consultant. Hammel, Green & Abrahamson are St. Paul based, Hardy Holzman Pfeiffer from New York.

Open for performances

M. Paul Friedberg & Partners were the landscape architects for the adjacent **Peavey Plaza Park** (1977). Measuring 150 x 350 feet/46 x 107 meters, the park focuses (somewhat busily) on the terraced waterfall at one end. Small group entertainment is often scheduled, and in winter the pool is used for ice skating.

---

20   Hennepin County Government Center (1974–75)
South 3rd–4th Avenue between 5th and 7th Streets
Minneapolis, Minnesota

JOHN CARL WARNECKE & ASSOCIATES, ARCHITECTS

The exterior of this twenty-four-story county office block is clad in South Dakota reddish granite, but there is no granitic heaviness within. For the architect has taken the two administrative functions of the building—the courts and municipal offices—and housed them in two near-identical parallel slabs which he then separated by a 60-foot/18.3-meter-wide atrium, X-braced for wind stability, glazed at the ends, and roofed with glass to make a covered garden concourse. The resulting inner space is commanding. It rises 350 feet/107 meters through most of the height of the building and is transversed by seven airy bridges. "Glamor space" is becoming more common on the architectural scene—the nearby IDS Crystal Court (q.v.) is a brilliantly airy example—and the impact of the Hennepin Center adds a new chapter. The interior of the Court's unit is carefully zoned for separate circulation by public and the judiciary. The Center rests astride 6th Street which also provides conveniently covered automobile access. A

420-car garage is placed underground. The Government Center is the key unit in an eighteen-block renewal area. The new building's atrium precisely focuses on the clock tower of the old City-County Municipal Building (see below); it also connects with it by underground tunnel. Peterson Clark & Associates were associate architects for the Government Center: Ketchum, Konkel, Barrett, Nickel & Austin were the structural engineers.

Open during office hours

The **Municipal Building** (1889–1905) stands across the plaza from the Government Center (open during office hours). Long & Kees were its architects, winning the competition for its design in 1887 (cornerstone date is 1891). Romantic in its concept of medieval towers, turrets, and oriels, the granite bulk of the City Hall is antiromantic in its formal, symmetrical massing. Though it bears an obvious relationship to Richardson's Allegheny County Building in Pittsburgh (q.v.), it

carries its own strong stamp. In coordination of elements, especially the relation of towers to main bulk, it is possibly better knit than the latter. Occupying a full block—its circumference is 1,232 feet/375 meters—it is topped by a handsome clock tower which rises 345 feet/105 meters and is carried on its own foundations. Though at times altered within, occasionally regrettably, it has been well maintained. Most of the building is now occupied by Minneapolis city offices.

21 Church of the Good Shepherd (1967–68)
16th Avenue South at South 6th Street
Moorhead, Minnesota

SÖVIK, MATHRE & MADSON, ARCHITECTS

A Lutheran church of dignity and simplicity located in a city across the Red River from Fargo, North Dakota. Framed in concrete and enclosed in well-patterned brick, there is a forthrightness of materials which attains a high level in the worship room especially. The natural wood of the ceiling, altar, pulpit, and pews (whose imaginative slat backs recall the louvers of the windows along the left side) adds a satisfying tactility and contrast to the masonry. The church room comprises one total area, with nave (seating 504) and chancel inti-

mately grouped together under an angled ceiling. The sanctuary stands modestly at one end of this rectangle, raised only slightly above nave floor and freestanding in front of the rear wall, furthering the close relation between minister and congregation. The baptismal font stands at right, facing the chancel and inset between two columns of the well-expressed structural frame. The church tower rises above the font, its open quality adding a vertical spatial outlet and an indirect play of daylight. The artificial illumination comes from downlights set into the ceiling. Choir and organ are placed in a balcony at rear. Classrooms and pastor's office line the street side. A restlessness can be seen in parts of the exterior, but within all is very serene.

Open Mon.–Fri. 8–12, 1–5, except holidays; Sun. service

22   Northwestern National Bank of Owatonna (1907–8)
Broadway and Cedar Street
Owatonna, Minnesota

LOUIS H. SULLIVAN, ARCHITECT

Few buildings—of any period of architecture—measuring a mere 67 feet/20 meters on a side hold down a corner site with more authority than this masterpiece. Formerly the National Farmers' Bank (and the

Security National Bank), it was the first—and remains the finest—of a small but glorious series by Sullivan after he unfortunately left Dankmar Adler (1895) with whom he had enjoyed fifteen wonderfully productive years. Troubled by a nervous breakdown, this "founder of Modern Architecture" spent his last ten years ill, divorced, and virtually without work until his death in 1924.

In Owatonna, Sullivan's well-known arch motif set in a rectangle is employed on each of the two facades which are virtually identical except for entry on the west. As will be recalled, Sullivan used a more elaborate form of an arch in a rectangle in his famous Transportation Building at Chicago's World's Exposition of 1893. However, as regards the bank Hugh Morrison writes that "the idea of the single great arches of the facade" was George G. Elmslie's (*Louis Sullivan*, Norton, 1935). Elmslie himself claimed not only "every last detail of decoration, inside and out, but the main motif as well" (ibid.).

As regards the 36-foot/11-meter half-circles of the arches (and the square windows below them) here they are sharply incised in the two flat planes of brick, not set back in radiating bands as in the 1893 Fair building. The faces of the bank, abutting each other decisively, rest on a firm sandstone base (at the spring-line of the arches) and are crowned on top by a boldly corbeled cornice. A running terra-cotta and glass mosaic decorative band frames each "panel" of the facades, with two monumental cartouches per side, giving a pharaonic imprimatur to the upper corners. The windows that fill each arch are of opalescent glass. Sui generis, these facades are unmatched. Fortunately they are exactly as Sullivan (and Elmslie) created them, including the low office wing along the south side.

The lofty, square, and colorful interior is highlighted by decorated arches (structural mirrors of the exterior) which support the well-tended ceiling. Four wrought-iron chandeliers of intriguing complexity, and painted to match the green carpeting, hang in the middle. The bank's interior, which had been ill-used for years, was remodeled with great sensitivity (and some simplification) in 1956–58 by Harwell H. Harris, thanks to the enlightened attitude of the president, Clifford C. Sommer, who showed the same foresight which a previous president, Carl K. Bennet, exhibited when he bravely commissioned Sullivan to design the bank in 1907. One of the great delights of its era, it constitutes a milestone in the development of a banking architecture that had hitherto sought refuge in monumental imitations of ancient Rome. The entire interior was cleaned and flat surfaces repainted in 1979.

Open during business hours

---

23   The Sibley House (1835–36) **and Faribault House** (1836–37)
**1st Street, just NE of intersection of Mendota Bridge Road and
   MINN 13**
St. Paul (Mendota), Minnesota

Though the Sibley House was the first stone dwelling in the state, it is no primitive bunkhouse but a reasonably sophisticated example of domestic architecture. It was built at the junction of the Mississippi and Minnesota rivers at Mendota, which means "meeting of the waters" in Sioux. The nearby Faribault residence, built shortly afterward, is even more formally "correct." The former, erected by the first governor of the state, General Henry H. Sibley, and the latter, built by a fur trader, Jean-Baptiste Faribault, both reflect the eastern background of these two men, primarily Pennsylvania, though Sibley was born in Detroit and Faribault near Quebec. The Sibley walls, of stone quarried on adjacent Pike Island, are over 2.5 feet/.76 meter thick against possible Indian attack. The last uprising occurred in 1862, with forces under General Sibley himself putting it down. By the late nineteenth century, both houses were lying empty and had been vandalized, the governor's residence having served as a warehouse, among other uses, hence few of the interior furnishings are original. The house, however, was

rescued, and in 1910 was opened to the public and refurbished of the 1850–60 period. The Faribault—which has a fine collection of Indian artifacts—was restored and opened in 1937. Nearby stands the Sibley Tea House, built as a residence in 1854 by Hypolite Dupuis, the secretary of General Sibley: remodeled in 1928, it is owned, like the two houses, by the Minnesota Daughters of the American Revolution.

Open May–Oct., Mon.–Sat. 10–5, Sun., holidays, 1–6, closed Mon. June–Aug.: admission

24 The Burbank-Livingston-Griggs House (1862–65)
432 Summit Avenue
St. Paul, Minnesota

OTIS E. WHEELOCK, ARCHITECT

A belvedere of almost Hindu complexity crowns it, and bracketed eaves, running in the fashion of the day around every available roof edge, encircle this limestone Italianate-Victorian mansion. It provides one of the highlights of the sumptuous array of dwellings—the others

are private—along the famous Summit Avenue. The century-old exterior is as built except for a wing added to the west side in the 1920s, but the interior was almost totally transformed in the 1930s into a veritable museum of ten basically eighteenth-century French, Italian, and English rooms, each elaborately furnished. Dismantled from their original moorings and shipped to Minnesota, they were capably shoehorned into the Victorian frame; and though obviously not pure Architecture U.S.A., the house well merits a look. The Art Deco amusement room has a piped-in sound system, and indirect lighting—advanced techniques for the 1930s. The mansion was given to the Minnesota Historical Society in 1968 by the daughter of Mrs. Griggs, the last owner.

Open Mon.–Fri. 10–4, Sat.–Sun. 1–4:30, except holidays: admission

---

25 Alexander Ramsey House (1868–72)
265 South Exchange Street at Walnut
St. Paul, Minnesota

MONROE SHEIRE, ARCHITECT

A limestone Victorian mansion built in the French Renaissance Style with a Mansard roof silhouette, bunched brackets, and porch across the entire front. The house is solidly and prosperously Victorian, with

carved walnut woodwork, decorative marble fireplaces, crystal chandeliers, and Brussels carpeting. It is one of the few century-old residences in the state whose furnishings are still well preserved and whose grounds are well kept. The reconstructed wooden carriage house serves as a visitors' center, an exhibit space for carriages, and a Victorian gift shop. Since 1964 it has been the property of the Minnesota Historical Society.

Open Mar.–Dec., Mon.–Fri. 10–4, Sat.–Sun. 1–4:30, except holidays: admission

---

26 **Landmark Center** (1892–1902/1978)
Old Federal Courts Building
75 West 5th Street
St. Paul, Minnesota

WILLOUGHBY J. EDBROOKE, ARCHITECT

Sprouting a multiplicity of towers, turrets, and sharply angled roof lines on the exterior, and harboring within a splendid four-story-high skylit *cortile,* the old Federal Courts Building adds needed architectural richness to downtown St. Paul. At one time headquarters for all federal offices in the region, the building became redundant when new and larger governmental quarters were completed in 1967. Threatened with demolition, a Mayor's Committee was established and recycling was highly recommended. The Minnesota Landmarks organization was created (1970) to take charge of the building and supervise its restoration. The lower three floors—the most important—have been thoroughly spruced up and serve as fine exhibition space, as cultural center, and for offices of five cultural and civic groups. The most interesting single room—other than the airy court—is the Butler Room (✻326), a former courtroom outstanding for its plaster ceiling and its fireplace. The Center was opened to the public in 1978. W. Brooks Cavin, Jr., was project architect for the early restoration 1972–74; Perry, Dean, Stahl & Rogers were design architects 1974–78, with Winsor/Faricy Associates.

Open Mon.–Wed. 8–5, Thurs. 8–8, Fri. 8–5, Sat. 10–5, Sun. 1–5, except major holidays

27   Minnesota State Capitol (1896–1905)
Aurora and Park Avenue
St. Paul, Minnesota

CASS GILBERT, ARCHITECT

Other states have their dome-bedecked capitols, and some boast interiors of no small grandeur, but it is doubtful if any can equal the Roman-bath splendor of the upper halls and grand stairways of this one in Minnesota. It was designed—via a double and curiously conducted national competition—by an Ohio-born, Minnesota-educated (with one year at MIT) architect. Later Cass Gilbert went on to greater fame with his "Gothic" Woolworth Building in New York (q.v.), then regressed, some feel, with his Supreme Court Building

(1935) in Washington, D.C. (no q.v.); but overall the St. Paul Capitol ranks high among those strange structures surfeited with political megalomania. The dome itself, a scaled-down copy of Michelangelo's atop St. Peter's—the last epistle of the Romans to St. Paul— dominates the countryside as domes are wont to do. (Note the quadriga at its base.) The building's length is 434 feet/132 meters. Inside, the executive offices fill, with only moderate inefficiency, the first floor, while Supreme Court, House, and Senate occupy the second. "The Capitol has never been well adapted to carrying out the functions of modern government" (*A Century of Minnesota Architecture,* The Minneapolis Society of Fine Arts, 1958).

Unfortunately Interstate 94 cuts a swath (at least sunken) across the front edge of the capitol complex where it tends to isolate government from downtown. Obvious to all except the Bureau of Public Roads, it would have been far better located north of the capitol—as a distinguished planner long ago recommended.

Open Mon.–Fri. 9–4, Sat. 10–3, Sun. 1–3, except holidays: guided tours hourly

---

28 **Cathedral of St. Paul** (1906–15)
Summit Avenue at Dayton
St. Paul, Minnesota

EMMANUEL L. MASQUERAY, ARCHITECT

One would be hard put to find a church as triumphantly Beaux Arts as this. Its architect was born and educated in la belle France and came to the United States at the suggestion of his classmate, John M. Carrère. Masqueray, after working in several New York offices, subsequently designed a series of churches throughout the Midwest, of which this granite cathedral is the largest. At 381 feet/116 meters long by 216 feet/66 meters wide it is also one of the biggest in this country, accommodating almost four thousand worshipers. The prominent siting has been handled so that the church's function of urban fulcrum is powerfully taken care of. The unusual facade combines an arched opening topped by a gable and flanked by towers with belfries of Spanish Baroque influence. Note the extraordinary richness of the carving at entry and above the arch. Behind, the great copper dome with cross above rises to 280 feet/85 meters—but with some lack of

coordination with the other major elements. The dome, which measures 96 feet/29 meters in diameter on the interior, gives centrality to the worship space with the main focus provided by the exedra of the chancel. Here a Baroque baldachino by Whitney Warren and seven stained-glass windows (representing the sacraments) by Charles J. Connick add proper accents. Whitney Warren and Maginnis & Walsh were contributing architects. Though open for worship in 1915, the interior was not fully completed and decorated until 1953.

Open daily 6–6

---

29   Mount Zion Temple (1950–54)
Summit Avenue at South Hamline
St. Paul, Minnesota

ERIC MENDELSOHN, ARCHITECT

The late Eric Mendelsohn (1887–1953) led a peripatetic and at times frustrating architectural life. He first startled the world with a series of superlative sketches which he began in the trenches of World War I.

Though tiny affairs they have a power and expressionism that still grip. (Some of these sketches, it is proper to add in discussing Minnesota, were of grain elevators.) His boundless imagination took concrete shape in 1920 with the expressionistic Potsdam Observatory, which still stands southwest of Berlin, a building that skyrocketed him to prominence, and enabled him to enjoy a very active practice in his native Germany until the Nazis entered the scene. Going to England (1933–36 and 1937–39), and back and forth to Palestine (1934–38), and in 1941 to the United States, Mendelsohn finally was able to get considerable work in this country, primarily designing synagogues. Yet none, good though they be, live up to his work abroad. Mount Zion is, many feel; the finest in this country, being particularly notable on the exterior for the relation, indeed the spatial tension, set up between the large sanctuary and the smaller chapel placed separately at right angles to it. These copper-clad, almost windowless boxes, enjoy an exquisite relation to each other as they project boldly above the brick walls which form a pinkish base tying the center together. (Mendelsohn's first sketches were for two accordion-pleated forms; the simple rectangular ones finally used are much more potent.)

The interiors of both main sanctuary and chapel lean to the spartan, even claustrophobic, due to the tight enclosure and to the fact that the only windows are behind and above the congregation, but as a group in space it sets up vibrations. Beside the two worship halls there is a large community room (with small stage and kitchen), which can double as an extension of the main chapel on High Holy Days. There are also administrative offices and, at a slight angle, a classroom wing. After Mendelsohn's death, the Temple was completed by his associates, Bergstedt & Hirsch.

Tours upon request: telephone for information: (612) 698-3881

30   Bethel Theological Seminary (1966–67)
W off MINN 51, S of IS 694 at Valentine Lake
St. Paul, Minnesota

HAMMEL, GREEN & ABRAHAMSON, ARCHITECTS

The materials are simple: several shades of red brick, copper roof, black-painted sash, and, within, natural wood and white-painted plaster. But they have been discerningly put together in seven buildings on a 214-acre/87-hectare new campus for Bethel College. There is some mannerism in the roof treatment, but the relaxed Nordic quality of the group, its excellent relation to its wooded site, and its details are commendable.

The seminary buildings are at the north central area of the campus and should not be confused with the main college buildings, which are at the south.

Grounds open during school year

31   St. John the Baptist Church (1968–69) .
812 1st Avenue NW, near IS 694 Interchange with IS 35W
St. Paul (New Brighton), Minnesota

SHIFFLET, HUTCHISON & ASSOCIATES, ARCHITECTS

Almost fortified in external appearance—the tradition of Albi?—this
Roman Catholic church in a northwest suburb of St. Paul outwardly
displays little hint of the exciting play of spaces and natural light
generated within. The walls are formed by a series of squared, U-
shaped "towers," slightly separated, and of uniform height but varying
width. On the inside these open U-shapes form a periphery of recesses
that enclose the church and serve (on the main wall) for chapel, chancel, shrines, and sacristy, with shallower U-shapes defining the other
sides. A passage, which at times becomes dramatic, surrounds most of
the interior between the outer walls and an inner half-height partition
that envelops the congregation, the inner "wall" framing the 1,450-seat
nave which rests detached and "private" within the overall space. The

pews, divided into groups on three sides of the altar, slope down to the underplayed chancel which projects like a thrust stage into the congregation. The "towers" rise above the nave ceiling and are topped by inner-facing roof monitors which throw a curtain of indirect light onto the circumferential enclosure, with a large roof skylight pouring a dazzling emphasis onto the chancel. No direct light is visible. Three tall, narrow banners add colorful notes. Structural expression in the ceiling is vague and the inner columns are redundantly wrapped in brick, but these are merely questionable details of an extremely original concept with a vibrant nave and superior natural lighting. Marlin D. Hutchison was project architect.

Open Mon.–Sun. 6 A.M.*–4:30* P.M.

---

32   Housing for the Elderly (1968–69)
Front Avenue at Grotto Street, W off Como Boulevard
St. Paul, Minnesota

FREERKS/SPERL/FLYNN, ARCHITECTS

Placed in an active family neighborhood, this twenty-story apartment for the elderly is distinguished by its planning and its astute use of economical and upkeep-free concrete. Accommodating 152 double units (minimum age for women sixty-two, men sixty-five), its architects have given the building a friendly scale by dividing it into two "slabs" of dwelling units, each floor having four apartments per side, with small core for circulation and service between them. Overall mass is thus broken down and internal circulation reduced. At the ends of the service core are a series of balconies, creating social areas and identity for the occupants. An unusual detail can be seen in the precast, bolted-on sunshade over the windows combined with a flat band under them to hide future air conditioners (or their absence). The Community Day Center projects as a one-story wing at left opening onto a small garden.

Ground floor open daily

---

33 **St. Thomas Aquinas Church** (1968–69)
9th Avenue at Ashland
South St. Paul, Minnesota

RALPH RAPSON & ASSOCIATES, ARCHITECTS

A startlingly "primitive" structural expression characterizes this Catholic church in a south suburb, reveling in a direct statement of beam on beam, member on member, laid up atop each other in almost Japanese temple fashion. The vertical frame of the church is formed by twelve reinforced concrete columns, six per long side (23 feet/7 meters on center). On top, connecting them laterally, rest double plates of laminated wood. Spanning these at right angles—an intercolumniation of 97 feet/29 meters but with an overall length of 155 feet/47 meters— are deep, slightly bowed laminated roof beams, the longest wood members ever used in the state. Resting on top of these eight beams (two at the edges in a double cantilever) are the purlins and roof decking. Each element is placed atop the one below with a directness recalling a lad's building blocks. A stuccoed base with several glass areas encloses the lower part of the outer walls, with a continuous clerestory about the upper rectangular periphery. The off-center nave, which seats 1,000 on two sides of the sanctuary, also has a roof monitor to give added light to the chancel. (Because of wide overhang there is only a slight glare facing the congregation.) A small chapel, softly wrapped by a stuccoed wall of the same height as that on the exterior, stands at right, baptistry at left, with confessionals behind chancel wall. All fittings from altar to candles reflect the spartan simplicity of its one-room atmosphere and its extremely economical "stick on stick" construction. The church's religious atmosphere is, perhaps, non-conformist but its structure gives us an unusual new dimension.

Open daily 6–6

---

34   Merchants National Bank (1911–12)
Lafayette Street at 3rd
Winona, Minnesota

PURCELL, FEICK & ELMSLIE, ARCHITECTS

Though Purcell and Elmslie worked with Louis Sullivan, they were always in his shadow—and sometimes Wright's—even after they had left to set up shop for themselves (1909). Elmslie, as has been mentioned (Owatonna Bank—q.v.), was at one time Sullivan's right hand and often personally drafted the master's intricate ornament. The two architects were of the same mind, favoring broad, plain wall surfaces highlighted by decorative accents of power and color, e.g. the "Static"

and the "Dynamic." It is thus with this bank—the firm's finest non-domestic work—a building beautifully preserved and in 1972 thoroughly restored. Note the superbly expressed "lintel concept" above the enormous windows of the two facades, with each broad brick facia or panel resting on two brick piers that are carefully glass-separated from the adjacent wall spurs. In the center, between sharply cut lower windows, stands the entry surmounted by an exquisitely designed and produced "motif"—"the play work in the architect's day, his hour of refreshment" wrote Elmslie. Square in plan, the bank's interior is as elegantly simple as the outside. It was sympathetically expanded (1969–70) by Dykins & Handford. One of Minnesota's great buildings.

Open during business hours

Take a look also at the **Winona National Savings Bank,** Main Street
at 4th, designed (1914) by George W. Maher, a Wright disciple.
(Open during business hours.) It combines scale and formalism with
the stretched-out eaves of Wright's prairie houses topped by ancient
Egypt's cavetto cornices.

Missouri

MISSOURI

The structures in boldface type are of general interest. The others are for the specialist.

Ironton	1 **St. Paul's Episcopal Church** (1870–71)
Jefferson City	2 Central Motor Bank (1962)—Skidmore, Owings & Merrill
Kansas City	3 Twenty West Ninth Building (1887–90)—McKim, Mead & White
	4 Boley Clothing Co. (1908–9)—Louis S. Curtiss
	5 Country Club Plaza (1922–25/1925–74)—E. B. Delk and E. W. Tanner
	6 **The Liberty Memorial** (1924–26)—H. Van Buren Magonigle
	7 **Business Men's Assurance Company Building** (1962–63)—Skidmore, Owings & Merrill
	8 **Kansas City International Airport** (1968–72)—Kivett & Myers
	9 **Crown Center** (1967–83)—Edward Larrabee Barnes
	10 H. Roe Bartle Exhibition Hall (1974–76)—Convention Center Associates
	Municipal Auditorium (1934–36)—Alonzo H. Gentry; Voscamp & Neville; Hoit, Price & Barnes
	11 Kemper Arena (1974–75)—C. F. Murphy Associates
St. Louis	12 Old Cathedral (1831–34)—Joseph C. Laveille and George Morton
	13 **The Old St. Louis Court House** (1839–45/1851–62)—Henry Singleton, Robert S. Mitchell, William Rumbold
	14 Chatillon-DeMenil House (1848/1863)—Henry Pitcher
	15 **The Campbell House** (1851)—William Fulton (?)

16 **The Eads Bridge** (1867–74)—James B. Eads

17 Grand Avenue Water Tower (1870)— George I. Barnett

18 **Raeder Place** (1874/1978)—Frederick W. Raeder

19 **Old Post Office** (1872–84/1984)— A. B. Mullett

20 **Wainwright Building** (1890–91)—Adler & Sullivan

21 The Wainwright Tomb (1892)—Louis H. Sullivan

22 **Union Station** (1892–94) **and Aloe Plaza Fountain** (1940)—Theodore C. Link; George H. Pegram; Carl Milles

23 Powell Symphony Hall (1925/1968)— Rapp & Rapp

24 Terminal Building, St. Louis Airport (1957/1965)—Hellmuth, Yamasaki & Leinweber, architects

25 **The Climatron** (1960)—Murphy & Mackey; Synergetics, Inc.
Tower Grove (1849)—Barnett & Peck

26 **The Priory of St. Mary and St. Louis** (1962)—Hellmuth, Obata & Kassabaum

27 McDonnell Planetarium (1962–63)— Hellmuth, Obata & Kassabaum
Forest Park (1876–1904)—George E. Kessler

28 **The Gateway Arch** (1962–68)—Eero Saarinen & Associates; Severud-Elstad-Krueger Associates

29 Forest Park Community College (1967–69)—Harry Weese & Associates

30 Community Federal Center (1977)— Hellmuth, Obata & Kassabaum

Ste. Genevieve

31 **Bolduc House** (c. 1787)
Amoureaux House (c. 1770)

1 St. Paul's Episcopal Church (1870–71)
East Reynolds Street at Knob
Ironton, Missouri

Epitomizing the small-town, all-wood, Victorian Gothic Episcopal church of a hundred years ago, St. Paul's remains refreshingly untouched in the twentieth century. Its steeply pitched roof—unexpectedly decorated with a large chevron pattern—its white, vertical batten sides, and its unspoiled interior with hand-carved pews combine to make the church an architectural autograph of another era. A locally prominent judge donated the land and, apparently, the design, though it is doubtful that he drew it up himself. There were, of course, the usual English and American architectural handbooks and magazines which all builders could—and did—turn to and copy from. Wooden Village Gothic was popular for churches from New England (there is a fine one in Ipswich, Massachusetts) to the South (Talbotton, Georgia —q.v.), thence irregularly across the country, but this beautifully preserved exemplar in an eastern Missouri town ranks with the best. It was listed in the National Register of Historic Places in 1969.

Open daily

2   Central Motor Bank (1962)
500 Madison Street
Jefferson City, Missouri

SKIDMORE, OWINGS & MERRILL, ARCHITECTS

A superior building, setting, and landscaping (by the architects), with clear emphasis on this as a Motor Bank as opposed to one on a street front. Actually the architects made trees, flowers, and pool so prominent that the glass shell of the building almost disappears amid them, a decision which has paid dividends. The simple rectangle of the bank proper comprises two floors and basement, the upper floor cantilevered over the lower, with a large "spatial well" or opening near the center which visually ties the banking area to the computer, etc., floor above. An employees' lounge is also placed on the upper floor, while there is a roof garden on top. The main vault and security facilities are located in the basement. Structure is of welded, rigid-frame steel. Two drive-up

teller windows directly serve motorists, supplemented by four auto-tellers in a freestanding, canopy-protected island (right in photo-graph), which is connected underground with the bank proper, all six being computer-controlled to direct the motorists to the next available facility. There is a special parking lot for customers needing ex-machina attention and another lot for employees. Wedemeyer & Hecker were associate architects.

Open during business hours

---

3 **Twenty West Ninth Building** (1887–90)
20 West 9th Street at Baltimore Avenue
Kansas City, Missouri

McKIM, MEAD & WHITE, ARCHITECTS

In 1886 the New York Life Insurance Company decided to construct a building in Kansas City having the then unheard-of height of ten floors, the local maximum at that time being an elevatorless three. They therefore contacted the rising Stanford White of McKim, Mead & White and in due time had the design for their palazzo well in hand. Mr. White planned an H-shaped building with two identical and parallel wings, properly separated, and joined at the ground floor by a sumptuous, barrel-vaulted hall. Above the great arched entry perches a bronze eagle, with a 15-foot/4.6-meter wingspread, by Louis Saint-Gaudens, Augustus' younger brother. Elevators, stairs, and services are grouped toward the middle, leaving the two office wings surrounded by windows, and open in plan except for a single line of columns down the middle of each. The well-windowed bearing walls are of local stone with floor beams of steel, then an innovative structural system in the city. Recently threatened with destruction, 20 West 9th has been thoroughly rehabilitated and adds a fine note to downtown KC.

Open during business hours

NOTE: Stanford White—and bird-watchers will be interested to know that architect and artist—produced a near identical building in Omaha, Nebraska, 1620 Farnham at 17th, for the Omaha National Bank (1887–90). When the bank moved across the street (1970) into new quarters in the twenty-nine-story Woodmen of the World Tower, designed by the Leo Daly Company, the mascot eagle went with it. The old bank was remodeled in 1976.

---

4   Boley Clothing Co. (1908–9)
12th and Walnut Streets
Kansas City, Missouri

LOUIS S. CURTISS, ARCHITECT

Though not sensational considering today's architectural developments, this six-story building is nonetheless an extraordinary but too little-known pioneer. Its walls (except at the corners) are enclosed by continuous bands of glass, accented slightly by glazed French doors, alternating with painted steel spandrel strips. This is probably the world's first expression of steel-mullioned strip-windows and uninterrupted metal spandrels forming a facade. (Gropius and Meyer's Fagus

Factory dates from 1911–13; Willis Polk's glass-sheathed Hallidie Building in San Francisco—q.v.—from 1918.) The continuous glass was made possible by a 5-foot/1.5-meter cantilever beyond the columns. Although the lower floor has been savagely handled, the building remains a landmark in our architectural development. The original research on the work of Louis S. Curtiss was undertaken by Fred T. Comee, of U. S. Steel Corporation. It is listed in the National Register of Historic Places.

At present not open

---

5 Country Club Plaza (1922–25/1925–74)
Broadway at 47th Street or J. C. Nichols Parkway
Kansas City, Missouri

E. B. DELK AND E. W. TANNER, ARCHITECTS

Claimed to be the country's first fully rounded suburban shopping community, this well-organized grouping still seduces its middle- and upper-bracket clientele. It was developed by the famous J. C. Nichols

as a natural adjunct to his very successful, early-twentieth-century Country Club District of private houses. The shopping center's architecture—all under strict controls and maintenance—obviously calls on Old Spain for its inspiration, in particular Seville, the "sister city" of Kansas City. (Note the scaled-down Giralda at the northwest entry.) Those essential ingredients of proper ambience—good architecture, parking, landscaping, fountains, statuary, and striped awnings—are all there. A far-seeing pioneer. Over 150 shops and stores will be found. Edward Delk was architect for the initial phase, Edward Tanner the second.

Open during business hours

---

6 The Liberty Memorial (1924–26)
100 West 26th Street
Kansas City, Missouri

H. VAN BUREN MAGONIGLE, ARCHITECT

One of the finest memorials to the American dead of World War I is located atop the hill beside Crown Center. Terminating a bluff, the Memorial—a national competition winner—presents an enormous inscribed flat wall (488 feet/149 meters long by 48 feet/15 meters high) to the city side (north). Behind and above this rises a towering shaft with a low exhibition building at each side and a broad terrace in front. It makes a particularly impressive sight from the doughty Union

Station almost at its feet. (The near vestigial station, 510 feet/155 meters long, was built in 1910–14 with Jarvis Hunt architect.) On the main approach side of the Memorial a landscaped allée, 600 feet/183 meters long, develops a proper introduction, leading to a low podium guarded by two sphinxes, their eyes covered against the shame of warfare. The semirounded shaft of the Memorial rises 217.5 feet/66 meters above, with flat facets alternating with curved ones that climax in four slightly abstracted figures at top. (There is an elevator to the observation platform.) An eternal flame—"the Flame of Liberty"—burns above. The side buildings, their "shaved classic" architecture far ahead of its time, contain a Museum at left and a Memory Hall to right. The top-lit Museum contains memorabilia of World Wars I and II, while Memory Hall is noted for a series of gigantic murals—that on the north wall being 69 feet/21 meters long—painted by Daniel Mac-Morris. The *In Memoriam* on the east wall was done by Jules Guerin, the French artist whose murals can also be seen in Washington's Lincoln Memorial (q.v.).

Park always open, Museum Tues.–Sun. 9:30–4:30, except major holidays

7   Business Men's Assurance Company Building (1962–63)
Penn Valley Park, Southwest Trafficway at 31st Street
Kansas City, Missouri

SKIDMORE, OWINGS & MERRILL, ARCHITECTS

Crowning with authority the highest hill in the city, the nineteen-story
BMA (by the Chicago office of SOM) numbers among a handful of
vigorous skyscrapers in the United States. One will find imitations of
its basic exo-skeletal grid and dark glass—some copies indeed by the
same firm—but this is in a class by itself. One of the key elements in
the BMA's excellence lies in the fact that the ground floor is not
enclosed, except for small entry and vertical circulation core, in effect

putting the building on stilts or pilotis. Thus the park setting and the distant city can be seen in and around and through the structure, while the building itself orbits on its hilltop. This ground-floor disposition also suggests the office layout above with central services surrounded by largely column-free desk space. In addition to lightness at entry level, there is from the second floor upward a spatial penetration at the corners due to the insetting of the window-walls from the marble-reveted frame. This 6-foot/1.8-meter setback helps shield the glass from sun and weather and also establishes a vibrant contrast between shadowed glass and white structure. The interiors—often open for guided tours—are up to the distinguished SOM standard. Note, on entering, the detailing of the red brick floor and the travertine for the walls. An employee's dining room under the plaza level opens onto a landscaped terrace. There is also a 180-car underground garage. Bruce J. Graham was partner-in-charge.

Open during business hours

---

8   Kansas City International Airport (1968–72)
c. 18 miles/29 kilometers NW of city via IS 29
Kansas City, Missouri

KIVETT & MYERS, ARCHITECTS

An efficient, civilized, low-keyed airport, one of the simplest to use—and one of the handsomest to be found. The plan provides three (eventually four) separate, three-quarter round buildings, each 1,000 feet/305 meters in inner diameter and each serving one major and several feeder airlines. Fifteen to nineteen planes can be parked on the outer periphery of each of these enormous circles with cars within. The inner road is raised 13 feet/4 meters above basic ground level so that the terminals are two stories (actually a story and a half) on the passenger approach side and three on the apron side. An in-building service road (on Terminal B) encircles the apron (i.e. lower) level where airline operations take place.

   To reach one's terminal and departure gate, one proceeds, if arriving by car, around the inner lane of an access road to one's flight gate. Color-coded gate information, with departure and arrival times, is posted on automatic indicators along the four-lane drive so that one can arrive at proper flight position without difficulty. One checks one's baggage at the curb (at most airlines), parks the car in the capacious

(short-term) central lot, and walks a maximum of 400 feet/122 meters to the check-in counter and flight station. If arriving by cab or limousine, one enters the terminal directly. When one lands, baggage claim in most cases is directly adjacent to egress from the plane; thus all that arriving passengers have to do is pick up their luggage and cross the

75-foot/23-meter-wide terminal to board private or public transportation. The passage, it should be emphasized, is on one very convenient level, a blessing made possible by the differential in exterior ground levels mentioned. Inexpensive color-coded buses provide interterminal communications and access to long-term parking.

Architecturally the buildings are first-rate (except the 219-foot/67-meter-tall control tower, which had to be enlarged). The spaces in the double-height passenger areas carry a fully glazed balcony on the field side with lounges, snack bar, and services. The warm-tone concrete structure is well designed and expressed, while the use of wood and colors adds the proper complementary note. But it is the terminal's one-level passenger flow-through which gives it outstanding clarity and distinction: its circulation is unsurpassed.

There is, however, a serious shortcoming at KCI—the present lack of undercover parking. Missouri's and Kansas' summer and winter months are not charitable, and it was short-sighted to have omitted this amenity. There are active plans to construct six-story garages in the central areas of each terminal but these will not add to the notably hospitable scale that now exists. Roof parking as at Tampa and Houston (q.v.) was impossible with narrow buildings 2,300 feet/701 meters long, but coordinated garages should have been incorporated from the beginning. As "this meant a lot more money immediately," it was vetoed by the city and the airlines. Thus a short-term advantage (ready cash) lost to a long-term, more expensive, and more inconvenient solution. But one cannot fault the airport's distinguished architects for this. Clarence Kivett was partner-in-charge; Albert F. Rhoads associate for terminals and central facilities; Burns & McDonnell engineers; Sasaki, Walker Associated landscape consultants.

---

9   Crown Center (1967–83)
Pershing Road between Main Street and Gilham Road
Kansas City, Missouri

EDWARD LARRABEE BARNES, PLANNER AND COORDINATING ARCHITECT; OTHER ARCHITECTS AS NOTED

The Crown Center complex—privately financed and built by the Hallmark Corporation—is one of the country's most ambitious and successful mixed-occupancy downtown rehabilitations. Occupying an 85-acre/34-hectare hilly, almost unbuilt-on site (just nineteen families

had to be relocated), it is situated only a block from the still imposing Union Station. The Center consists of a coordinated office, hotel, shopping, printing, and residential minicity which, hopefully, will not only germinate activities beyond the workaday clutch that leaves most business areas deserted at sundown, but will also, as Joyce C. Hall, the founder of Hallmark, put it, "bring interesting people back downtown." The previously existing Hallmark headquarters and production facilities (1955, Welton Becket, architect) occupy much of the upper part of the site, with the new hotel, shopping, and office buildings along north and east sides, and housing on the hillside to west.

The dominant structure is the fourteen-story, 728-room Crown Center Hotel, rising behind a five-story "reception-function block"—and imaginatively designed by Harry Weese & Associates. On the interior, part of the hotel's natural limestone hill site was left exposed—with some stones reset—to form a dramatic indoor waterfall (with recirculated water) and a garden backdrop for the towering skylit lobby. Attached to the hotel on the far side—and also open to the plaza—is an unusually sprightly and attractive three-level series of over forty shops and eateries by the Barnes office (with individual shop designs) which should by all means be seen.

Zigzagging at right angles up the 75-foot/23-meter grade step five interlocked six- to seven-story units comprising the highly sophisticated and assured office group also designed by Edward Larrabee Barnes. Their height was kept purposefully low and their horizontality emphasized to lend keener scale buildup to the overall complex. Garaging for 2,300 cars is provided beneath the offices. Hotel, shopping block, and offices frame Crown Center Square, also designed by the Barnes office. This plaza steps in landscaped terraces down to a cobblestone area where a fountain with forty-nine jets, seven on a side, springs directly from the pavement, each spout controlled individually both as to height (up to 25 feet/7.6 meters) and, at night, as to color. A perky red Calder stabile, giant umbrella-like shelters, and good planting add their contribution. Unfortunately the four lanes of Grand Avenue cut across one side of the plaza, and though traffic is generally light, for some observers it is disconcerting to have so little separation between cars and strollers. (There is a bridge over the road.) Along the upper Main Street (west) side of the site stretches the long-range residential development, presided over by the thirty-story, 437-apartment condominium designed by The Architects Collaborative. It is hoped that the total permanent population of the Center will eventually reach 8,000.

Well thought out, well planned, and well executed, Crown Center has already sparked the rehabilitation of much of the surrounding area.

Marshall & Brown of Kansas City were associate architects for the hotel; Norman Fletcher was the TAC principal; Landscape Associates of Little Rock designed the waterfall and garden in the hotel; Peter G. Rolland & Associates and The Office of Dan Kiley were the landscape architects. The initial land use program was developed (1961 +) by Gruen Associates.

Hotel always open; shops and offices open during business hours

---

10   H. Roe Bartle Exhibition Hall (1974–76)
12th–14th Streets, Central and Broadway
Kansas City, Missouri

CONVENTION CENTER ASSOCIATES, ARCHITECTS

Principally used for trade fairs and industrial exhibitions, the two-block-long Bartle Center rounds out the rich variety of facilities which Kansas City offers: commerce, culture, sports, and entertainment. The hall spans 13th Street and thus also provides sheltered entry. The two lower levels are of reinforced concrete on a 30-foot/9.1-meter structural module, and provide support facilities for the enormous exhibit room on top. This superstructure has a clear span of 309 feet/94 meters, with a length of 720 feet/219 meters. Each of the eight, 90-foot/27-meter-wide, triangular steel frames supports six Warren-design roof trusses, 21 feet/6.4 meters deep, which were shop-fabricated in three sections and field-connected with high-strength bolts. The building is enclosed with 2-inch/5-centimeter-thick insulated and enameled metal sandwich panels. It was designed as a joint venture of Seligson Associates; Horner and Blessing; Howard, Needles, Tammen & Bergendoff; and C. F. Murphy Associates.

Directly across Central Street stands the **Municipal Auditorium** (1934–36), Alonzo H. Gentry; Voskamp & Neville; Hoit, Price & Barnes, architects. It is a classic example of the large-scale, limestone-sheathed Moderne auditorium of its period. Note the excellent Art Deco detailing. The carving on the friezes depicts "the intellectual and social purposes for which the building is used." Combining music hall, arena, Little Theater, and exhibition hall, the Auditorium is a synopsis of an era and its architecture. There is an underground connection with the Bartle Exhibition Hall.

Both open for events

11   Kemper Arena (1974–75)
17th Street and Genesee (via 12th Street Viaduct)
Kansas City, Missouri

C. F. MURPHY ASSOCIATES, ARCHITECTS AND ENGINEERS

The exterior of the Kemper Arena is one of the most dramatic structures of its kind in the United States. Its white metal skin is dominated by eight sensational steel tube space-frames that embrace the sides and uphold the roof. Walking under its trusses almost suggests Le Corbusier's book *When the Cathedrals Were White,* so powerful is this outrigging of "flying" buttress trusswork. In plan the upper half of the building forms a rectangle with tightly rounded corners: the lower (i.e. entry) half is, however, amply rounded to reflect the ovoid seating pattern within. As the entrances are at the four corners, the overhang of the top gives some shelter below. Crowd flow is smooth. The interior, partly below grade to facilitate seating, is visually passive after the structural dynamism and bright "purity" of the exterior—but then any room would be. The Arena accommodates the full panoply of events with basketball, circuses, rodeos, ice hockey, and rock concerts. It seats up to 17,600 for concerts, while the lowest ranks of seats can telescope under the upper ones to make a larger floor area.

Kemper is located in an old, largely ex-stockyard and industrial section of the city and its shining whiteness is purposefully attention-compelling in its plebian neighborhood. It is also a catalyst for upgrading many of its warehouse neighbors, some of which are sturdy examples of their period and well worth notice.

Open for events

---

12 Old Cathedral (1831–34)
2nd and Walnut Street off Memorial Drive
St. Louis, Missouri

JOSEPH C. LAVEILLE AND GEORGE MORTON, ARCHITECTS

Near the south leg of the Memorial Arch (q.v.)—in an area once crowded with aged buildings—stands the Basilica of St. Louis, King of France, the fourth church on this site, and the first major example of the Greek Revival in the state. (The style was more seriously explored five years later in the nearby Old Court House—q.v.) Most of the

church's classical "Revivalism" resides in the tawny, chaste Doric portico at the entry. Several details in the cornice are elementary, as are the sides of the church, but note the 135-foot/41-meter-high, well-proportioned steeple. The interior was brightly renovated (1958–64) by Murphy & Mackey, who removed a great number of accumulated statues and a weighty altar and reredos. His Holiness, the late Pope John XXIII, elevated the church to a basilica in 1961. The Old Church Museum is attached to the highway side (open daily 10–5: small admission).

Open daily 8–6

---

13   The Old St. Louis Court House (1839–45/1851–62)
11 North 4th Street
St. Louis, Missouri

HENRY SINGLETON, ROBERT S. MITCHELL, WILLIAM RUMBOLD, ARCHITECTS

The Classical command of the Greek Revival Old Court House visually vanquishes the hurly-burly of its neighbors on every side, while on the interior the prodigality of its polychromed central hall and lunettes takes care of the visitor. Its presence adds luster to the downtown scene, lending episodic counterpoint to Saarinen's Gateway Arch (q.v.), which it faces. The Court House experienced a series of construction periods and, as might be gathered, a series of architects. The rotunda and west wing were dedicated in 1845 to the design of Henry Singleton—who won the 1839 competition—aided by George I. Barnett. The next major figure (1851) was that of Robert S. Mitchell, who with his brother John F. had moved to St. Louis from their native Ohio. Mitchell was primarily responsible for the final shape of the building, adding three other wings to match that on the west, thus creating its Greek-cross plan. The old dome was then (1857) razed by one architect, T. D. P. Lanham, and rebuilt by another, William Rumbold, who engineered its cast- and wrought-iron framing (1862), a ticklish task at the time, for which Rumbold received a patent. This dome, which measures 57.3 feet/17.4 meters in diameter with a height of 42.5 feet/13 meters, predates Thomas Ustick Walter's similarly constructed iron dome on the Capitol in Washington, D.C. (q.v.) by two years. The building was last used as a courthouse in 1930, when new and larger quarters were opened, and it lay largely quiescent until

the National Park Service acquired it in 1940 and commenced partial restoration under the direction of Charles E. Peterson and Ralph Emerson. It has since been carefully adapted to be a museum dedicated to St. Louis' history and its role in the western expansion of the nation. The paintings in the dome, mostly by Karl Wimar, are reputedly the first murals west of the Mississippi.

Open daily 8:30–5, except major holidays

---

14 Chatillon-DeMenil House (1848/1863)
Cherokee Street at DeMenil Place, 1 block W of Broadway
St. Louis, Missouri

HENRY PITCHER, ARCHITECT

The simple 1848 farmhouse which represents the first stage of this mansion was dwarfed in the early 1860s by the Greek Revival "addition" by Henry Pitcher. (Victorian details also appear.) Though the first section still stands, it is the nine rooms of later date, along with their Ionic porch facing the Mississippi, which carry most interest. (Note, too, the iron railing and fencing, possibly made locally.) Whereas the rooms have few of their original furnishings, they have been excellently restored in the 1840–70 period, and opened to the

public in 1965. Refreshments, incidentally, are served in the Carriage House. The city is fortunate to have the house at all, for Interstate 55 originally was planned to cut right through it. The cooperative Highway Department, being alerted to the house's value by the Landmarks Association of St. Louis, then altered its routing.

Open Tues.–Sat. 10–4, Sun. noon–5, except major holidays: admission

---

15   The Campbell House (1851)
1508 Locust Street
St. Louis, Missouri

WILLIAM FULTON (?), ARCHITECT

The unprepossessing exterior of this town house is highlighted only by a minimal touch of the Greek Revival frame of its front door plus the bay window onto the garden side. Behind this, however, is lined an array of sumptuous rooms filled with their original furniture. Few houses can claim such total inner preservation as the Campbell: it well merits a visit from all interested in its Victorian period for its lush but uncluttered harmony. Built for John F. Hall, it was purchased

by the wealthy Robert Campbell three years later. After the death of Campbell, then that of his wife, their three surviving sons lived in the house as semirecluses until their death (one in 1890, two in the 1930s). Nothing, apparently, was touched for over seventy years. The double parlor, immediately at left on entering, is the most elaborate room—note the twin chandeliers and the mirror (from Philadelphia)—but all are worth a visit, including the bedrooms upstairs. The dwelling was probably designed by William Fulton, a St. Louis architect (c. 1802–68); John A. Bryan, Charles Nagel, Verner I. Burks, and William Peckham have at various times been concerned with its restoration. It is now owned and operated by the Campbell House Foundation.

Open Tues.–Sat. 10–4, Sun. 12–5, except holidays: admission

16   The Eads Bridge (1867–74)
foot of Washington Avenue
St. Louis, Missouri

JAMES B. EADS, ENGINEER

The Eads—the Great Illinois and St. Louis Bridge—represents one of the supreme developments of America's technical know-how. It opened, on July 4, 1874, a new phase of spanning then unheard-of spaces (center arch 520 feet/158 meters, the two adjacent arches 502 feet/153 meters each). By so doing it hastened the demise of the river steamboat while enormously accelerating the Pacific push of the railroads, thus the opening of the West. The struggles which James Buchanan Eads (1820–87) went through—he had never built a bridge before (!), let alone an "impossible" one of this scope—make fascinating reading. In its design, Eads immediately recognized that its foundations would have to be based on bedrock (in places 103 feet/31 meters deep), and these footings in a powerful, swift (up to 12 mph/19 kph), arbitrarily shifting river proved no simple matter. However, Eads at the age of twenty-two had invented a diving bell (to recover—highly successfully—cargo from sunken river steamers), so he had a certain working-under-water expertise which served him well when he had to devise the large caissons necessary to protect workmen building the bridge's foundations. (Eads pioneered caisson use in the United States on this job.) Moreover he had *walked* over much of the bottom of the Mississippi with his diving apparatus, hence knew its forces and treacheries at first hand. He also knew iron, steel, its producers, and metal-skilled labor from building a series of remarkably successful armor-plated river warships for Union use in the Civil War, his first being launched a year before the *Monitor* slid down the ways.

However, Eads was only a self-trained engineer, and for him to attempt to design and construct the then longest bridge in the world was a staggering undertaking. (The three combined arches of his bridge made it longest: Telford's Menai Straits Suspension Bridge of 1826 in Wales spanned 580 feet/177 meters, while Ellet's suspension bridge —at Wheeling, West Virginia (q.v.)—covered 1,010 feet/308 meters in 1849.) Moreover Eads determined to build the bridge largely of steel, a material whose economical production by Henry Bessemer was barely ten years old and very much untried as a major structural element. This was, indeed, the first structural use of rigid steel members (not cables) for bridges in the country—"one of the great calculated

risks of engineering history," as Joseph Gies put it in his *Bridges and Men* (Doubleday, 1963). (Cast iron and wrought iron, including wrought-iron wire cables, had, of course, been earlier employed.) For his bridge Eads used steel tubing, 18 inches/46 centimeters in diameter and .25 inch/6 millimeters thick for the enormous supporting arches; and by erecting scaffolding atop his previously constructed masonry piers, he was able to cantilever his tubed trusses foot by foot from each side of the piers until they met heroically in the center of their spans. (The mean high water clearance was 55 feet/17 meters.) The two decks of the bridge (the top for vehicles and pedestrians, the lower for railroads but no longer used for them) are supported on double-tube arches by multiplane, Warren truss triangulations which anticipated the space-frame so popular today. The Eads Bridge is one of the signal monuments of the evolving technical ability— "the innocent daring" (Gies)—of the United States. Its esthetics are also potent. The spidery, lattice lightness of the supporting members against the Roman aqueduct grandeur of the granite-faced limestone piers, plus the fact that the center arch is slightly wider than the other two (to give more visual life), combine to make this the outstanding non-suspension bridge in the country. It is appropriate that one of the significant contributions of nineteenth-century engineering lies only a few hundred feet away from one of the most poetic of the twentieth —the Gateway Arch (q.v.), also of steel. Colonel Henry Flad was Eads's constant assistant; Charles Pfeifer and Professor William Chauvenet of Washington University were structural consultants. The bridge was declared a National Historic Monument in 1965.

17   Grand Avenue Water Tower (1870)
East Grand Avenue at 20th Street
St. Louis, Missouri

GEORGE I. BARNETT, ARCHITECT

There have been several noted uses of the isolated, single Classic column. Phocas, an obscure Roman emperor, had one put up in his honor (A.D. 608) which still stands in the Forum (he was hanged two years later); a M. de Monville, a French nobleman, erected for his residence at Marly, just west of Paris, a "broken" or "ruined" fluted column six stories high and 45 feet/14 meters in diameter (c. 1785); and as recently as 1922 Adolf Loos (1870–1933), the great Austrian modernist, proposed to house the Chicago *Tribune* in a 400-foot/122-meter-high Doric column! Rarely, however, has the idiom been used so grandiosely as here in St. Louis, where it served (until 1912) as a water tower and equalizer: it kept the pump flow uniform for the City Water Works down the hill. Its 154-foot/47-meter hollow height (of brick stuccoed) is capped by a florid cast-iron Corinthian capital. When built it stood alone on the hillside: it now polarizes the neighborhood. The British-born Barnett and his architect sons were active for years in the St. Louis area. The tower is listed in the National Register of Historic Places.

---

18   Raeder Place (1874/1978)
727 North 1st Street (Laclede's Landing Area)
St. Louis, Missouri

FREDERICK W. RAEDER, ARCHITECT; KIMBLE A. COHN &
ASSOCIATES, ARCHITECTS OF RENOVATION

Siegfried Giedion, the late Swiss architectural historian, whose book *Space, Time and Architecture* (Harvard University Press, 1941 et seq.) opened the eyes of the contemporary world to the meaning and contribution of the buildings of the past, described the St. Louis waterfront area and its cast-iron architecture as "a witness to one of the most exciting periods in the development of America. Some of its commercial buildings—fur and china warehouses, Pony Express offices, ordinary business blocks—exhibited an architecture far in advance of the ordinary standards at the time of their erection." Hundreds and hundreds of cast-iron-fronted and -supported buildings were put up following the great fire of 1849 (which started in Laclede's Landing Area), the city seeking a quick recovery to maintain its position as the Gateway to the West. The California gold rush also took place in 1849. The speedily erected, more or less fireproof, cast-iron facades and framing were ideal for the job. Alas, today only a pitiful few remain, the great majority having been destroyed, ironically, for

the Jefferson National Expansion Memorial and its arch. Among the best is the six-story Raeder Place which was originally built as the Christian Peper Tobacco Company Building. Possessed of good scale and resolute detail, it is a century-old structure of great value in the history of the city. Note the roundheaded windows of its well-lit east facade. Laclede's Landing Area underwent a startling "rediscovery" in the late 1970s, and many of its sturdy but shabby structures have been brightly rehabilitated into a variety of tempting shops, offices, and restaurants. Raeder Place was renovated in 1978 into a restaurant on the ground floor with office and showroom space above, by architects Kimble A. Cohn & Associates.

Open during business hours

19 Old Post Office (1872–84/1984)
Olive Street between 8th and 9th
St. Louis, Missouri

**ALFRED B. MULLETT, ARCHITECT; HARRY WEESE & ASSOCIATES
AND PATTY, BERKEBILE, NELSON ASSOCIATES, ARCHITECTS OF
REHABILITATION**

Designed by the doughty architect of the old State, War and Navy Building in Washington (now the Executive Office Building, q.v.), with "War and Navy" and the then recent Civil War possibly influencing its "stronghold" aspect, this robust number has only recently been reprieved from a fate worse than a parking lot. Though it might faintly suggest a fortified building, the 30-foot/9.1-meter-deep areaway surrounding it is *not* a moat but a light well; and the inside iron shutters were for fire protection, *not* against mob violence, their circular holes being for pressure release (in case of fire), not gun ports. Moreover there is no truth to the rumor that there was a well in the basement to slake defenders in case of attack. (However, it was expected that gold bullion would be stored there.) Actually little short of an 8-point Richter Scale earthquake could harm its granite walls, so substantially was it built. Erected partially on quicksand, some 4,400 Missouri pine pilings 34 feet/10.4 meters long, topped with 4 feet/1.2 meters of concrete, were needed for its foundations. But this solidity, which fills an entire downtown block, was realized with eminent architectural skill in scale buildup and an almost Sansovinian play of light and shade (plus a share of local scandal). Built as a combined Custom House and Post Office, its design reflects Second Empire France—appropriate in a city dedicated to that country's Louis IX, or St. Louis (1214–70). Note on the 8th Street pediment the statues of *Peace and Vigilance* by Daniel Chester French.

The federal courts having moved out in 1935 (the Post Office in 1913), the building was declared surplus and its future commenced to be in doubt, particularly as local real estate interests eyed its site. But concerned citizens, led by the late Austin P. Leland and buttressed by the indomitable George McCue of the St. Louis *Post-Dispatch* (now retired), and backed by the National Trust, the American Institute of Architects, and the Society of Architectural Historians, effected its saving. The General Services Administration, which owns the building,

has been most solicitous regarding its future, conducting a limited competition for its adaptive use. This was won by Patty, Berkebile, Nelson Associates of Kansas City in a joint venture with Harry Weese & Associates of Chicago. The ex-Post Office (officially the St. Louis Custom House and Post Office) will house both federal offices and commercial tenants. It is scheduled to be finished in 1984, the hundredth anniversary of its opening. It is, without question, one of the finest of its period in the country and high among the fifty or so structures designed by Alfred Butt Mullett when Supervising Architect to the Treasury Department (1866–74).

Under renovation and restoration: opening scheduled for 1984

20 **Wainwright Building** (1890–91)
Chestnut Street at 7th
St. Louis, Missouri

ADLER & SULLIVAN, ARCHITECTS

The problem of the tall building—that uniquely developed American building type—had been solved in technical terms a few years before the Wainwright. However, the first metal-framed "skyscraprs" (roughly twelve stories or more), involving as they did drastically new design problems, were almost an embarrassment to their early architects, who proceeded to drape them with confused historic trappings of timidly neutral disposition. William LeBaron Jenney is generally credited with the first high-rise use of skeletal metal construction in his famous but now destroyed Home Insurance Company (1884–85) in Chicago, an eleven-story pioneer of cast and wrought iron and steel, but no gem to gaze upon. Holabird & Roche's far more advanced Tacoma Building (1886–89), also in Chicago and also destroyed, had

thirteen floors, all marked by a daring use of glass, but it was a lumpish, layer-cake building to view. Sullivan, however, the designer of the Wainwright, asked "what is the chief characteristic of the tall office building? And at once we answer, it is lofty. This loftiness is to the artist-nature its thrilling aspect . . . It must be in turn the dominant chord in his expression of it, the true excitant of his imagination. It must be every inch a proud and soaring thing, rising in sheer exultation that from bottom to top it is a unit" (Sullivan's essay on "The Tall Office Building Artistically Considered," reprinted in his *Kindergarten Chats,* Wittenborn, 1947). And so it is. Just as Sullivan himself has been rightly called "the father of modern architecture," so the Wainwright in its expression of verticality and unity is the progenitor of the skyscraper as it was subsequently to develop—the first "to pay attention to the voice of steel" (Nikolaus Pevsner in his *Pioneers of Modern Design,* Museum of Modern Art, 1949). Or as Fiske Kimball put it, in the Wainwright the "wall surface was abandoned for a system of pier and spandrel" (*Architectural Record,* April 1925).

For more than a generation this cohesive, nine-story plus "attic," U-shaped structure influenced the tall buildings of the world. (In plan it measures 127 x 114 feet/39 x 35 meters.) Sullivan wanted it to express on the exterior precisely what went on inside (though he fudged in making his non-structural piers as heavy as the others). Thus the two lower floors state their commercial character, the ground level being largely plate glass for the shops which occupy it, and the second being primarily for walk-up offices and stores. Above the first and second floors, which are sheathed in reddish-brown sandstone, a pronounced stringcourse emphasizes the separation of the commercial from the seven floors of professional offices above, the whole boldly capped by a tenth-floor utility level with small circular windows peeking from its fantastic cornice. (The building's many copiers transmuted these logically expressed elements into a "classic" column of base, shaft, and capital.) The Wainwright's verticality stands strongly expressed by the corner columns (of exaggerated size), and by the seven-story-high, red brick piers between the ranks of windows. Prominence is given these piers by their smoothness, in contrast to the intricately ornamental spandrel panels between them, by their elegantly rounded "rope" edges, and by the fact that the spandrels are set back from the pier face so that, from an oblique view especially, verticality is the dominant impression. (The piers from acute angles actually recall a parade of classic-derived pilasters: Sullivan's experience in the Paris Beaux-Arts?) The red terra-cotta spandrels were not culled from historical antecedents, which most subsequent skyscraper architects espoused, but grew from Sullivan's incredibly facile pencil and Celtic imagination. Note that the panel design differs on each floor. The Wainwright even at ten stories dominated downtown St. Louis for years, and its basic design was shortly afterward (1894–95) used by Sullivan himself for the Prudential (ex-Guaranty) Building in Buffalo, New York (q.v.). The latter shows more finesse than the Wainwright, its entrances for one thing being better integrated, and it attains finer overall proportions because of the increased number of "office" floors (ten versus seven) between the two-story "base" and elaborately corniced roof. It does, however, have decorated piers, which, for many, does not represent an improvement. But the simpler, sturdy Wainwright ranks among the country's greatest buildings of the nineteenth century. As Hugh Morrison wrote, "In the Wainwright Building, Sullivan gave esthetic form—for the first time in America—to the comparatively new problem of the tall office building" (*Architectural Record*, June 1956).

In 1974 the building was purchased by the State of Missouri, which also sponsored a national competition for the rehabilitation of the entire block for a state office complex. The competition was won by Mitchell/Giurgola of Philadelphia, with Hastings & Chivetta of St. Louis as associates. Renovation is scheduled to be completed in early 1981. A three-story Court of Appeals and Division of Family Services will adjoin.

Open during office hours

---

21 The Wainwright Tomb (1892)
**Prospect Avenue, SE corner of Bellefontaine Cemetery, entrance at
    4947 West Florissant Avenue**
St. Louis, Missouri

LOUIS H. SULLIVAN, ARCHITECT

Ellis Wainwright, whose famous building we have already seen, lost his lovely wife at a tender age (he outlived her thirty-three years). Deep in sorrow, he asked Sullivan to design her (and eventually his) tomb. Sullivan complied with one of the country's most sensitive mausoleums, one forming almost a cube in shape, topped by a dome stepped back at its springing. In front, to soften the transition of its almost Ledoux geometry to the landscape, he extended a "porch" with seats at each end and four low steps in front. A rinceau of exquisite plant-

form details traces across the front, outlining the form of the limestone mass while emphasizing the door. There is quiet, even peaceful eternity here. Its entombment of death has few equals.

---

22   Union Station (1892–94) **and Aloe Plaza Fountain** (1940)
Market Street between 18th and 20th
St. Louis, Missouri

THEODORE C. LINK, CHIEF ARCHITECT; GEORGE H. PEGRAM, ENGINEER; CARL MILLES, SCULPTOR OF FOUNTAIN

A picturesque pile, the design of which was won by invitation competition, a terminal that for a short time reigned as the largest railroad station in the world. On the exterior some influence of H. H. Richardson's Romanesque Revival, plus other French touches, are evident in a facade which stretches over 600 feet/183 meters, its turrets bristling bravely upward with what the late Carroll L. V. Meeks aptly termed "romantic scenery" (*The Railroad Station, An Architectural History,*

Yale University Press, 1956). E. A. Cameron may have had an early hand in the design but he resigned before construction began. There is some thought that the elusive Harvey Ellis also made contributions. The barrel-vaulted Grand Hall, or waiting room, on the second floor drips with architectural nostalgia, weeping today perhaps at the paucity of people who now use it. Behind stretches a seemingly endless train shed, designed by Pegram. The original thirty-one rows of tracks, plus ten more added in 1929–30, once efficiently handled up to 260 mostly long-distance trains a day. Pegram's shed uses a low-profile, five-arch roof to span its width, hence the space lacks that overwhelming impact delivered by several of the dramatically vaulted stations in London and on the Continent. But the St. Louis shed at 606 feet/185 meters wide by 700 feet/213 meters long still achieves an awesome expanse of roof. The future of the station (as of early 1980) is uncertain. Hopefully it will be recycled.

Carl Milles (1875–1955) was the master of the play of urban waters and a pioneer in injecting spray, in addition to "solid" jets, into fountains. Here in the **Aloe Plaza Fountain,** representing the allegorical marriage of the Mississippi and the Missouri—whose union some 15 miles/24 kilometers to the north sired St. Louis—we have a civic celebration. (The village was founded in 1764 below the river junction because of higher ground.) This Meeting of the Waters could also be described as the marriage of bronze and H_2O, so intimately conceived are the statues and their spray. When seen with the water off, the group stands disjointed and kithless. The angles of the jets and their grouping are complemented by the figures which range from the fish-size to the more than life-sized couple. The seriousness of the demure bride (the Missouri) and the eagerness of the groom (the Mississippi) are offset by several outlandishly gleeful sea scoundrels, a total cast of fourteen. One of the few great urban fountains.

---

23   **Powell Symphony Hall** (1925/1968)
718 North Grand Boulevard at Delmar
St. Louis, Missouri

RAPP & RAPP, ORIGINAL ARCHITECTS; WEDEMEYER-CERNIK-CORRUBIA, REMODELING ARCHITECTS

Wrapped by cream walls and ceiling (one flows into the other), radiant with highlights of crystal and gold, and emblazoned with turkey-red carpeting and seats, the Powell sets an opulent new stage for the

famed St. Louis Symphony. Considering its origin as a movie palace, the building stands as a tribute to its original designers and its sympathetic yet imaginative restorers and, even more important, to the concept that the old can often serve the present. Rehabilitation—here the first cinema recycling—has won a glamorous victory and at a small fraction of the cost of a new concert hall. It is a success throughout, though the stage treatment behind the orchestra, with its five panels, carries insistence. St. Louis was wise—and is culturally and pecuniarily richer—in having salvaged this ex-cathedral of the silent cinema to be the new home of the country's second oldest symphony orchestra. They even rescued and reinstalled the bar from the old New York Metropolitan Opera House. Acoustics are excellent, "a delight to the ear" (New York *Times,* January 26, 1968). The outside forms a good period piece but cannot equal the interior. Ben Schlanger was theater consultant and associate architect; Cyril M. Harris, acoustical consultant; David Mintz and Lewis Smith were the lighting designers.

Open for performances

24   Terminal Building, St. Louis Airport (1957/1965)
NW from downtown on IS 70 (Mark Twain Expressway)
St. Louis, Missouri

HELLMUTH, YAMASAKI & LEINWEBER, ARCHITECTS

The day it opened the airy, spacious concourse of the Lambert-St. Louis Terminal won deserving acclaim. Its three groin vaults, each 110 feet/33 meters on a side, form one of the country's first thin-shell dome constructions. Their interplay creates an airy, sprightly interior. Moreover the vistas out are excellent as they partake of the field and its activities. However, the lower level is less than appealing, walking is a chore, as is parking, while, to the specialist, the exterior supports for the vaults are curiously concealed. Minoru Yamasaki was original

partner in charge of design. Hellmuth, Obata & Kassabaum were the architects of the expansion and for recent improvements of baggage handling, as well as the replanning of ground access and parking.

Always open

---

25   The Climatron (1960)
Missouri Botanical Garden (Shaw's Garden)
2315 Tower Grove Avenue at Flora Place
St. Louis, Missouri

**MURPHY & MACKEY, ARCHITECTS; SYNERGETICS, INC.,
STRUCTURAL ENGINEERS**

A wondrous web of simple plastic panes and intricate aluminum struts providing an ideal canopy over a prodigal array of plants. Buckminster Fuller's geodesic principles have been put to maximum advantage in creating this shelter, which is 175 feet/53 meters in diameter and 70

feet/21 meters high, forming a low vault that rests on five concrete piers. The components which make up the hexagonal exoskeletal framing of the Climatron are composed of aluminum tubes in two planes, approximately 30 inches/76 centimeters apart, connected by aluminum rods to make a triangulated truss. The weather skin of some 4,000 triangles of .25-inch/6-millimeter acrylic plastic (Plexiglas) is hung about 1 foot/30 centimeters below this frame. Plexiglas is not only one third as heavy as glass, it permits photosynthesis and is unbreakable in a hailstorm. The air conditioning is almost fiendishly ingenious, for it produces—under one partitionless roof—four major meteorological zones and nine minor ones, ranging from hot tropics to cool uplands, from 60° to 90° F (15–32° C) and 50–100 per cent humidity. One can command electronically cool days and warm nights for some plants, or warm days and cool nights for others. There is even a waterfall. The trees and plants are so fond of their new home that their growth approaches the obstreperous; because of this the Climatron was possibly more graspable architecturally five years after opening than it is today when its cobweb structure is almost hidden. (The ghost of the outside framework forms an effective background to the inner triangular panes.)

A peripheral walk encircles the gardens, permitting a "bird's-eye" view of the whole. There is also, even in this limited area, a keen sense of exploration as one moves into and through the various groves and up and down its clever levels: anticipation has everywhere been developed. A *temple d'amour,* from the original garden, provides a nostalgic touch. At night flood-lights, their effect enticingly visible from the outside, vary from moonlight on one side to midday on the other. Dr. Frits W. Went, the Director of the Garden in 1960, developed the plan and the air-conditioning zoning with the architects. For the building's design, Murphy & Mackey was the first American architectural firm to receive the R. S. Reynolds Memorial Award in Architecture (1961). The office of Murphy & Mackey is now known as Murphy, Downey, Wofford & Richman.

Open May–Oct., daily 9–6, Nov.–Apr. 9–5, except Dec. 25:
admission

Nearby stands **Tower Grove** (1849) by Barnett & Peck—open the same hours as Climatron, separate admission. This was once the country home of the English-born Henry Shaw, a keen businessman turned botanist, whose researchers formed the initial basis of the Missouri Botanical Garden. Its Victorian furnishings are notable.

26   **The Priory of St. Mary and St. Louis** (1962)
        St. Louis Priory School
        c. 18 miles/29 kilometers W of downtown on US 40, N .4 mile/.6
        kilometer on Mason Road (c. 3 miles/4.8 kilometers W of
        IS 244)
        near St. Louis (Creve Coeur), Missouri

HELLMUTH, OBATA & KASSABAUM, ARCHITECTS

The Baptistry of Nocera,. Italy, was probably the first (A.D. 350) to espouse a circular plan for a Christian religious building. But San Stefano Rotundo (A.D. 470) in Rome gets credit for being the first precisely cylindrical church (210 feet/64 meters in diameter). Later architects, from the sixteenth-century Bramante in Rome to the twentieth-century Bartning and Böhm in Germany, have designed circular, altar-centric churches. In general they have not been satisfying essays. And in spite of the commanding and photogenic exterior of this church near St. Louis, we encounter the faults that plagued its historic prototypes: the priest has his back to a section of the congregation (here

1,000 maximum), while spatially there is little buildup, and little architectural climax or concentration of light. One inescapably faces a window. The result is that the admirably simple altar floats under the eye of the "dome" with the same parade of windows behind it as in front. This central position of the sanctuary does, it should be pointed out, encourage liturgical intimacy—the rationale of its shape—with the faithful grouped about and the monks in the retro-choir.

The exterior is intriguing in itself and is a masterful exposition of sprayed concrete, both in design and in execution. Twenty parabolas, 21 feet/6.4 meters high, form the lower periphery which is 138 feet/42 meters in diameter, with a second tier of arches, 12 feet/3.6 meters high, above, and a 32-foot/9.7-meter arched steeple-belfry topping all. The interior cross section reveals a stunning organization of complex geometry, whose "ribs" neatly cascade from the compression ring at top and are tied by a horizontal tension ring between upper and lower tiers. The windows are of plastic laminate, black on the outside yet sufficiently translucent to admit satisfactory illumination. The exterior at night glows from its inner light. A screen of colored glass by Emil Frei gives a quietly colorful yet largely transparent background to the Celebrant's seat, and also semiconceals the monks' entry. The surrounding school was also designed by the same architects. Gyo Obata was principal in charge of design; Paul Weidlinger was structural engineer; Pier Luigi Nervi, the famous Italian architectural engineer, was structural adviser.

Open daily 9–5 during school year

---

27   McDonnell Planetarium (1962–63)
off Clayton Road, SE corner of Forest Park, exit off US 40 at
**   Hampton Avenue**
St. Louis, Missouri

HELLMUTH, OBATA & KASSABAUM, ARCHITECTS

The bold geometry and strategic site of this 408-seat planetarium make it one of the city's landmarks. However, its dome is nestled atop and within the hyperbolic outer form; the exterior, thus, does not "announce" what goes on inside. In puristic terms this concealment is questionable, but the finesse of the whole and its powerful profile do much to make it mnemonic. The outward splay at top of the hyperbola provides a moon-viewing platform above the planetarium's half-dome.

Exhibition spaces line the inner periphery, with an internal ramp taking one to the observation deck. Gyo Obata was in charge of design.

Open Tues.–Sat. 10–5, Sun. 12–6, plus some evenings, except major holidays: admission

The Planetarium rests in **Forest Park** (1876–1904), the nation's third largest city park with 1,374 acres/556 hectares. The St. Louis World's Fair (The Louisiana Purchase Exposition) of 1904 took place here: some of its almost fey buildings are still to be seen. The Fair also occasioned the overall landscaping of the Park by George E. Kessler, little formal organization having been done until that time.

---

28   The Gateway Arch (1962–68)
Jefferson National Expansion Memorial
foot of Chestnut, Market and Walnut Streets
St. Louis, Missouri

**EERO SAARINEN & ASSOCIATES, ARCHITECTS;
SEVERUD-ELSTAD-KRUEGER ASSOCIATES, STRUCTURAL
ENGINEERS**

Flaming in sun, disappearing in mists, ghostly by the light of the moon, and, above all, proclaiming that here verily was the country's gateway to the West, the Gateway Arch ranks with the greatest monuments of

world architecture. In an ethos that feels uneasy with a monument, here will be found a monument of an age's potential, a mighty parabola of polished steel astride the path to half the nation. This incredible monumentality and its symbolism were achieved by the slenderest of catenaries, by honed geometry, not the earth-bound massiveness seen in most architectural heroics.

The arch, which rises to 630 feet/192 meters, has a span to match its height. Its structural cross section forms an equilateral triangle 54 feet/16 meters wide at the base, with a flat side facing out and the "point" facing in. It was constructed by placing one triangular section atop another by a traveling "creeper" derrick, which marched (simultaneously on each arch arm) slowly up its sloping flank on a special demountable track, lifting the sections in place, then filling their double walls with concrete (for stabilization) to the 300-foot/91-meter level. When the arch was closed—fantastic precision was needed so that the two arms would align—the cranes lowered themselves (and their tracking) to the ground. The lower steel triangular sections are 12 feet/3.6 meters high and, as mentioned, 54 feet/16 meters on a side;

the upper ones are 8 feet/2.4 meters deep by 17 feet/5.2 meters laterally, 142 being used altogether. The sections are all double-walled, the two faces separated by 3 feet/.9 meter. The outer skin is of stressed stainless steel .25 inch/6 millimeters thick, the inner face of carbon steel .37 inch/9.5 millimeters thick. Passengers ride to the top (highly recommended) in self-leveling "gondolas" or capsules, attached in tandems of eight, each holding five passengers. There are two of these "trams," one in each leg. An emergency stair (1,076 steps) descends each side. A Museum of Westward Expansion (well worthwhile) occupies the underground Visitors' Center.

The Saarinen Arch ranks among the supreme achievements of the United States, a euphoric summation of architecture, engineering, and sculpture working together. It almost seems alive. Erected with uncanny exactness—even the cinema of its construction is electrifying—it stands as a realization, perhaps *the* realization, of what late-twentieth-century man can do when his eyes look high and his hand is true. The arch (in spite of insufficient but improving landscaping) has helped spark the renaissance of downtown St. Louis, with new buildings, a new stadium, new shops, and new apartments filled with ex-suburbanites. (Unfortunately too much of the character of old "levee" St. Louis was eliminated in the process.) Of all the structures in this book, the Gateway Arch, it is safe to say, will be the one most admired when the country celebrates its Tricentennial. The MacDonald Construction Company was the prime contractor, with the prefabricated steel sections made by Pittsburgh-Des Moines Steel Company.

Open Memorial Day–Labor Day, daily 8 A.M.*–10* P.M., *rest of year 9–6, except major holidays: Visitors' Center free, charge for tram ride to top*

29 Forest Park Community College (1967–69)
W on US 40, S at US 67, W on Oakland Avenue
St. Louis, Missouri

HARRY WEESE & ASSOCIATES, ARCHITECTS

Designing an urban junior college for 5,000 students (maximum 7,000), largely in a one-building matrix, without creating a monster poses questions on both educational and architectural levels. The architect has solved his program's problems well, housing the classrooms

in one stretched-out, four-story unit with the other functions in a right-angle wing. The design elements which prevent this from becoming ponderous can be seen in the lightness and the penetration of the ground floor, and the four double stair and utility towers which interrupt its almost 500-foot/152-meter length. The administration block is attached behind the classrooms by a spatially active three-tiered open "walkway" (one of the campus highlights). The gymnasium taps onto the class block at the far end.

Open during school hours

---

30 **Community Federal Center** (1977)
Ballas Road at Manchester
take US 40 W to Ballas, S on Ballas to Manchester
St. Louis, Missouri

HELLMUTH, OBATA & KASSABAUM, ARCHITECTS

An unusual suburban office block approximately half occupied by a savings bank with the rest rented to an upper-bracket series of corporations, often as regional headquarters. The concept for the building evolved not only from Community Federal's functional and design requirements, but also from a sensitivity to the surrounding suburban community. Though seemingly built up in almost random "building block" fashion, the Greek-cross plan of the Center is structurally symmetrical about its two axes and there are interesting facades in all directions. The size of the floor areas is gradually reduced as the building rises. The module is a 30-foot/9.1-meter bay of reinforced concrete arranged and alternated both vertically and horizontally to produce dynamic facades. Note, on entering, the high lobby and its space-frame structure. As the building is well set back on its site, there is ample parking on two sides. The area to the north, nearest the residential zone, was landscaped with emphasis on preservation of existing trees. Gyo Obata was principal in charge of design.

Open during business hours, including Sat. morning, except holidays

31 Bolduc House (c. 1787)
South Main Street between South Gabouri and Market
Ste. Genevieve, Missouri

The French, working first as explorers, then as fur traders, moved from Canada (and Wisconsin) down the Mississippi in the late seventeenth century, claiming the land for France (LaSalle in 1682). By the early eighteenth century they had established at Ste. Genevieve their first permanent base (1732) in what later became Missouri, settling in St. Louis in 1764. The Spanish then acquired all of what was then called "Louisiana" (1763) but secretly retroceded it to France in 1800. In 1803 through Jefferson's far-sightedness the great Louisiana Purchase was put through and the entire area (roughly to the Rocky Mountains) came to the United States, more than doubling the then size of the country. French influence, however, continued for years—as it did in New Orleans—and we still find souvenirs of their culture.

The small town of Ste. Genevieve, some 50-odd miles (80 kilome-

ters) down-river from St. Louis, is one of the most rewarding of the French-dominant centers, and the Bolduc House one of the finest Creole examples. The dwelling was constructed around 1787, utilizing sections (possibly only large beams) of a nearby house, erected in 1770. Behind the mandatory palisade, which not only kept out stray cattle but stray eyes, the typical angled hip-roofed, wide-galleried house was built of massive oak timbers placed vertically and close together on a stone foundation, a system called *poteaux sur sole*. Straw mixed with clay and animal hair (*bouzillage*) filled the spaces between the uprights. A heavy oak-trussed roof, reflecting Norman regionalism, covers the 48 x 82-foot/15 x 25-meter house with the original roofing probably of thatch. A simply supported veranda—probably enlarged around 1846—encircles it on three sides to provide protected open-air work and rest areas, plus preserving the whitewashed walls. The house was acquired by the National Society of the Colonial Dames of America in the State of Missouri (1949), and carefully restored (1956–57) outside and in, along with outbuildings and garden, by Dr. Ernest Allen Connally. Outstanding of its type.

Open Apr.–Oct., daily 10–4: admission

The Amoureaux House (c. 1770), south on St. Mary's Road (US 61—open daily 10–5, except Dec. 25: admission), is similar to the Bolduc and will interest the specialist. The earliest part was constructed of sharpened, rot-resistant, red-heart cedar. Unfortunately today it wears a tin hat, but the interior, now an antique shop, has been restored. There are plans afoot in Ste. Genevieve to undertake a long-range restoration of the entire town. *Bonne chance!*

Montana

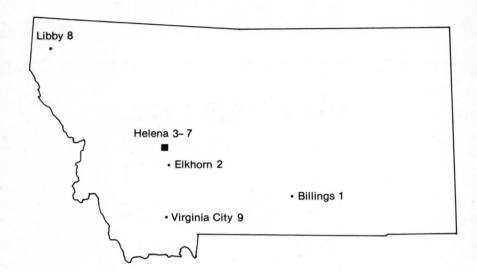

Libby 8

Helena 3– 7

• Elkhorn 2

• Billings 1

• Virginia City 9

MONTANA

The buildings in boldface type are of general interest. The others are for the specialist.

Billings   1 **Fortin Educational Center** (1968–69)— CTA

Elkhorn   2 Ghost Town (1880–90)

Helena   3 **Last Chance Gulch and Its Buildings** (1880s)

4 Lewis and Clark County Court House (1886–87)—Hodgson & Stem

5 Templeton Hotel (1887)—T. F. Mathias and Fred Heinlein

6 Civic Center (1920)—Link & Haire

7 Diamond Block Building (1889/1975)— Shaffer & Stranahan; Richard I. Shope and Herbert L. Jacobson

near Libby   8 **Libby Dam** (1964–75)—U. S. Army Corps of Engineers; Paul Thiry

Virginia City   9 Madison County Court House (1876) and Town

1   Fortin Educational Center (1968–69)
Rocky Mountain College
off Rimrock Road, E of 17th Street West
Billings, Montana

CTA, ARCHITECTS-ENGINEERS

The Fortin Center houses a complicated series of functions in an expressive architectural massing. The program required space for a 2,400-seat gymnasium, a smaller gym, AAU-size swimming pool, small auditorium, group of classrooms, health clinic, and administrative offices. Early studies proposed a single, large structure, but the architects quickly realized that a block of the required size would ill serve the scale of the campus, as well as being offensive to the domestic quality of the neighborhood. They therefore eased the gymnasium and

pool—by far the largest cubic-space users—into the slope on the north side, providing them with separate access and parking to suit their semipublic nature. Then they developed on the south side an intriguing collection of forms, their shapes internally generated by the space requirements of separate facilities. The geometry here might be a bit solid (there are few windows), but it is stimulating. A multiplicity of functions has been brought together with excellent scale and fine play of light and shade. Larry Keller was project designer under the direction of Ed Jones, principal-in-charge.

Open during school year

---

2 Ghost Town (1880–90)
12 miles/19 kilometers NE off MT 281
Elkhorn, Montana

The off-the-highway ghost town buff will be rewarded by a visit to mile-high (1,600 meters) Elkhorn (though the road can be dusty). Elkhorn was developed in 1875 by A. M. Holter, and its first buildings

were a mill (1884) and smelter (1885) to process the ores. The railroad was then completed (1887) to haul out the huge amounts (some $14 million) of gold, silver, and lead which the district produced. At one time 2,500 hopefuls labored here, many with their families. The boom collapsed in 1897, but there were short revivals in the early part of this century and there is some activity at present. What is left of the oft-vandalized buildings forms a cogent, albeit somnolent, image of those plank outposts where so much of the history—human, material, and even architectural—of the West was written. Fraternity Hall, now owned by the Western Montana Ghost Town Preservation Society, is the most outstanding single building. The Society also owns two others of importance, all of which have been stabilized. The "town" is now situated in the Deerlodge National Forest, complete with picnic tables.

---

3 Last Chance Gulch and Its Buildings (1880s)
Helena, Montana

Toward the end of the nineteenth century, before U.S. architecture became timid, there existed a handful of gutsy practitioners, the most accomplished of whom was Frank Furness of Philadelphia (see Index). These men, some influenced by Richardson, produced many of the most powerful—if at times outlandish—buildings which this country has spawned. Among the lonely nuggets in the northwest are the burly examples along Last Chance Gulch, the capital city's main street—so named because the weary prospectors took one last poke (1864) into the stream and came up (eventually) with some $20 million worth of gold. Sudden wealth erupted, as did sudden death, and in 1888 it is said that Helena was the richest city per capita in the United States. The city in its early days sought to attract a variety of businesses and settlers from the East to lessen its mining dependency. It concentrated on substantial, in some cases exotic, commercial buildings to act as bait, and which also filled local needs. A scattering of these hoary delights remains, and the city today, under the skilled architectural eyes of Herbert L. Jacobson and Richard I. Shope, among others, is embarking on a constructive, long-range Urban Renewal Program, one which seeks to preserve intact these several blocks, rehabilitating when needed. If all goes well this could be one of the West's great "period" streets. (Most of the following information is due to the kindness of Messrs. Jacobson and Shope and to Professor Willard B. Robinson, whose advice and writings were of great help.)

Ingloriously, the most fascinating structure in the city, the Novelty Building (1888), John Paulsen, architect, is no more. Heavy rains in 1975 undermined the rear, which collapsed, then in an act of official vandalism the still-standing facade—almost a history of architecture by itself—was torn down. Admittedly the building was in parlous condition, but with foresight instead of neglect it could have been saved. Among the principal buildings of interest (remaining), listed by street number, are:

Atlas Block (1888), #7–9. Shaffer & Stranahan, architects. Although one of the tamer numbers, its ground floor boasts a stout arch—reminiscent of a Richardson library—while on a platform that rises above the eave a determined metal salamander does battle with unlikely reptiles. The building was built for an insurance company, hence its name—with a small statue of Atlas at midpoint. The fire-resisting myth of the salamander is expanded by the stylized flames of the cornice.

Power Block (1889), #58, 60, 62. Shaffer & Read, architects. Architecturally the Power Block is the most accomplished building along

the Gulch, a six-story pile of rusticated granite that holds down its corner site with authority. Its design stems largely from the upper half of Richardson's Marshall Field Wholesale Store (1885–87—now destroyed). Its march of windows is set in roundheaded reveals, topped by a stringcourse, and finished with an "attic" band of small windows, also roundheaded (the corresponding ones at Marshal Field were squared). The expression of the large-windowed shops of the ground floor versus those of the offices above recalls Sullivan. The interior framing is of heavy mill (timber) construction. Marred by signs, ₦58 Last Chance Gulch is a worthy mountain cousin of the Chicago School. Fortunately it is in good structural condition.

A smaller example of the same Richardson ilk that will interest the specialist will be found in the **Securities Building** (1886) at 101 North Main Street at Grand; Hodgson, Wallingford & Stem, architects. Though now bereft of its tower, it possesses some good detailing, along with free-wheeling fenestration.

Open during business hours

4   Lewis and Clark County Court House (1886–87)
Broadway at Ewing
Helena, Montana

HODGSON & STEM, ARCHITECTS

This subdued late-nineteenth-century block has subtleties of design
that will appeal to the specialist. Note, incidentally, the excellent
stonework. Until 1935 the building sprouted a prominent tower, but
this was taken down following the series of earthquakes of that year;
the heavy coping was also removed. The interiors are of minor interest.

Open during office hours

5 Templeton Hotel (1887)
415 North Main Street
Helena, Montana

T. F. MATHIAS AND FRED HEINLEIN, ARCHITECTS

The cast-iron-front seeker will find here a well-detailed, at times poorly maintained, example of the building technique that once swept the country. When assembled from facade elements manufactured in Helena by the John Stedman Foundry, the Iron Front Block, to use its original name (it was built for offices), must have been one of the town's finer structures. It has been said that it "quite possibly represents the most extensive use of iron in Montana." Note that the parade of roundheaded windows on the second floor eases into arced lintels for the top two.

6   Civic Center (1920)
Neill Avenue at Benton
Helena, Montana

LINK & HAIRE, ARCHITECTS

Those who incline to Mecca at the proper five times a day will be struck by this "mosque" which now houses the City Government. One of the few Islamic-inspired buildings in the country, it is one of the most ambitious, its design being based (freely) on Iranian prototypes. Built as the Algeria Shrine Temple by the Shriners, it was acquired by the municipality during the Depression. The interiors are of little architectural interest.

Open during office hours

7   Diamond Block Building (1889/1975)
North Park Avenue at 6th Avenue (opposite old Post Office)
Helena, Montana

SHAFFER & STRANAHAN, ORIGINAL ARCHITECTS; RICHARD I. SHOPE AND HERBERT L. JACOBSON, ARCHITECTS OF RENOVATION

This small office block was begun late in the last century and suffered the inevitable decline when more up-to-date facilities later challenged it. It has been skillfully and sympathetically updated. The architects—known for their work in preserving and restoring the city's gutsy building heritage—have maintained the statement of the granite wall while sprucing the upper two floors with metal bay windows (note spandrel detail), all with character. The large windows of the ground floor push the scale a mite, but altogether Diamond is a very fine rehabilitation.

Open during business hours

8   Libby Dam (1964–75)
18 miles/29 kilometers E of town on MT 37
near Libby, Montana

U. S. ARMY CORPS OF ENGINEERS, ENGINEERS; PAUL THIRY, ARCHITECT

The Army Corps of Engineers has designed over fifty dams in the United States, making it the creator of the largest number of hydro-electric power plants in this country. High among its output in archi-tectural-engineering terms is Libby Dam, stretching 2,200 feet/670 meters to close—almost regally—the rocky cleft gouged by the Kootenai River. Most dams are impressive, but Libby (420 feet/128 meters above the stream bed) attains grandeur by its close respect for nature and by the elegance and precision of its concept down even to details. As the architect put it, "carelessness with minor detail detracts from the whole." Moreover it represents the first time that the Corps has used an outside architect from inception, a close associationship that benefited every aspect, from master plan (by Paul Thiry) to the knife-sharp designing of barricade, overspill, and visitors' facilities.

The T-framed powerhouse, adjacent to the spillway, can be reached from the dam top by elevator. Its carefully illuminated all-concrete interior forms "a great cavelike space" of dramatic force. The most prominent feature of the top of the dam—which, incidentally, is open to automobiles—is the Treaty Tower. The attached bas-relief (won by competition) is not quite of the caliber of the beautifully coordinated architecture and engineering. The views are magnificent.

As the Kootenai rises in Canada (42 miles/67 kilometers to the north), environmental concerns were doubly important, prompting in 1964 a formal diplomatic treaty. (While in office, former President Ford dedicated the dam.) A small landslide caused the denudation above the east embankment with the unexpected effect of extending the visual geometry of the dam complex partially up the mountainside. The river itself is "the consciousness of the total problem," and Paul Thiry and the Corps of Engineers are seeing to it that its new banks and the nature about them—plus, of course, the extensive public facilities along the 117-mile/188-kilometer lakeshore—will be properly attended to. Sydney Steinborn, chief of the Engineering Division, U. S. Army Engineer District, Seattle, was engineer-in-charge.

Guided tours May–Oct., daily 10–5

---

9   Madison County Court House (1876) **and Town
Main Street (MONT 287)
Virginia City, Montana**

Virginia City—like its sister in Nevada (q.v.)—erupted in the gold-rush period which stampeded much of the West in the last century, here in 1863. When placer mining (mining by means of panning or hydraulic sluicing) was no longer productive, the town lapsed into a "semi-ghost" condition, remaining partially deserted until 1946, when rehabilitation was commenced. A farsighted "holding action" had been previously (late 1930s) organized by Mr. and Mrs. Charles A. Bovey, who founded the Historic Landmark Society of Montana and donated funds to acquire a substantial clutch of century-old buildings in Virginia City, structures which otherwise would have ended up as firewood. After World War II, restoration was undertaken on over two dozen buildings, including the newspaper office (the state's first), brewery, general store, etc. Today this tidy village (population less than two hundred) enjoys a flair of its former days with only a modicum of

commercialism. Its gabled and bracketed brick courthouse, remarkably well preserved after more than a century of Montana winters, would find favor in most communities. The interior was badly injured by fire in 1972 but has been completely restored. The courtroom on the second floor is well worth inspection. The additions at the rear are routine but altogether the Court House forms an excellent example of its time and remote location. It has, indeed, been called "the most sophisticated building in Montana."

Open during office hours

Nebraska

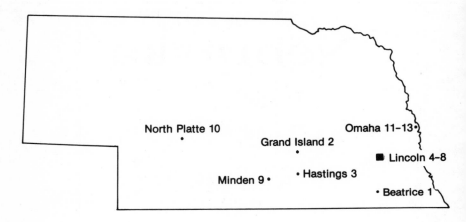

North Platte 10

Grand Island 2

Omaha 11–13

■ Lincoln 4–8

Minden 9

Hastings 3

Beatrice 1

NEBRASKA

The buildings in boldface type are of general interest. The others are for the specialist.

Beatrice	1	**Palmer-Epard Cabin** (1867)
Grand Island	2	**Stuhr Museum of the Prairie Pioneer** (1966–67)—Edward Durell Stone
Hastings	3	**The Nebraskan Grain Elevators**
Lincoln	4	**Thomas P. Kennard House** (1869)—John K. Winchell
	5	**The Citibank** (1893/1969)—The Clark Enersen Partners
	6	**The Nebraska State Capitol** (1922–32)—Bertram Grosvenor Goodhue
	7	**Sheldon Memorial Art Gallery** (1962–63)—Philip Johnson
	8	**Lincoln East Educational Complex** (1967–68)—Davis & Wilson
Minden	9	Pioneer Village (mid-19th century)
North Platte	10	Buffalo Bill Ranch (1886/1909)
Omaha	11	**Archbishop Bergan Mercy Hospital** (1966–67)—Leo A. Daly
	12	Central Heating and Cooling Plant (1968)—Leo A. Daly
	13	**W. Dale Clark Library** (1975–77)—Hellmuth, Obata & Kassabaum and John Latenser & Sons **Central Park Mall** (1978–80)—Bahr, Vermeer & Haecker

1   Palmer-Epard Cabin (1867)
Homestead National Monument
on NEB 4, c. 4 miles/6.4 kilometers NW of
Beatrice, Nebraska

The Homestead National Monument and this tiny cabin—in which, reputedly, a family of ten once lived—illustrate a revelatory chapter in
the opening of the West. The Homestead Act, which President Lincoln
signed in 1862, gave to any adult citizen or citizen-to-be a "quarter
section [160 acres/65 hectares] of unappropriated Government land"
if he or she built a house, lived on the land, and farmed it for five
years. At the end of that time the title (for a small fee) passed to the
homesteader. The Act had many shortcomings. Monopolists got too
much and many settlers were underfinanced and ill equipped to deal
with raw, unfenced land. (Only about one third survived the five years
to make their claim.) However, it was responsible for stimulating the
settlement of much of the westernmost Prairie States, and attracted

many unemployed Easterners, European immigrants, Civil War veterans, and ex-slaves who were lured by the prospect of free land. As it turned out, there was in many cases just enough acreage "to lure farmers to their doom," and it is worth noting that the Act peaked early in this century, not the nineteenth, when over four hundred thousand homesteaders successfully acquired land from the public domain.

The Homestead National Monument was established (1939) to commemorate this legislation which was so important to the development of the West, and the site chosen is one of the first farms claimed under the Act. The house of the original settler and his family has disappeared, but the Palmer-Epard story-and-a-half cabin, built (1867) nearby a few years after passage of the Act and moved to this site in 1950, is illustrative of the bedrock simplicity in which the early Nebraskans lived. Be sure to see the slide show and exhibits in the adjacent Park Service Visitor Center.

Open daily, Memorial Day–Labor Day, 8–6, rest of year 8–5, except major holidays

---

2   Stuhr Museum of the Prairie Pioneer (1966–67)
Junction of US 34 and US 281
4 miles/6.4 kilometers N of IS 80 (Grand Island exit)
Grand Island, Nebraska

EDWARD DURELL STONE ASSOCIATES, ARCHITECTS

A not unfamiliar palazzo, square in plan and resting on a circular island surrounded by a circular moat. Its columned, shaded, and inviting form is reached by a short bridge. The interior is full of sunshine—as are most of the late architect's buildings—and the sight and sound of fountains add to the pleasures. The exhibit space on the ground floor is largely for circulating and temporary exhibitions, while the upper level, which opens onto the airy two-story central court, has an interpretive display of pioneer artifacts.

Of parallel interest is the nearby outdoor, coordinated collection of regional structures, arranged as a middle-late-nineteenth-century Nebraskan village along a spur of railroad track complete with operating steam train and 1895 station. A series of appropriate retail shops faces the railyard, while a short distance away are cottages, houses, church (1888), and barns. Altogether this is a valuable index of early Nebraska architecture. Edward Durell Stone, Jr., was the landscape architect.

Open Memorial Day–Labor Day, Mon.–Sat. 9–6, rest of year 9–5, Sun. 1–5, except major holidays: admission

---

3   The Nebraskan Grain Elevators
off US 6, SE of
Hastings, Nebraska

Grain elevators, the cathedrals (and Stonehenge) of the Prairies, rise everywhere throughout the Great Plains where they form the architectural-engineering muscle of this vast area between the Mississippi and the Rockies. The elevators provide storage for corn and grain—here for the Cornhusker State—and vary from small rural examples of wood or metal with pent-roofs to magnificent rows of reinforced concrete with rectangular head house topped by conveyors. Handsome and functional at any size, they are extraordinarily powerful as architectural-engineering sculpture, some with almost the potency of an Egyptian hypostyle hall. Although every farming community has its elevators, Hastings, Nebraska's fourth-largest city, has along its southeast edge several particularly impressive groups. (This part of the state is located near the top of the winter wheat belt that begins in western Oklahoma and covers much of Kansas.) Note especially the cluster belonging to the Morrison-Quirk Grain Corporation, forming not only a right-angle grouping but utilizing the newer, more efficient hexagonal

design instead of the routine, conjoined concrete cylinders. The "hex bins" can be more easily slip-formed (and their forms more often used) than the circular. Their shape, it is enlightening to know, stemmed from studied observation of the hexagonal tiles seen so often on the floor of the smallest room in most houses. The reinforced-concrete walls vary from 6–7 inches/15–18 centimeters in thickness, depending on whether the wall is interior or exterior. The Morrison-Quirk facility, incidentally, holds 8 million bushels/281,912,600 liters.

Along the edges of Lincoln, also, there are strong masses, many off US 77 and NEB 2.

4   Thomas P. Kennard House (1869)
1627 H Street, 1 block SE of Capitol
Lincoln, Nebraska

JOHN K. WINCHELL, ARCHITECT

Considered the oldest house still standing in the region, this Italianate Victorian residence furnishes a good mid-continent example of the style which spread from coast to coast in the twenty or so years beginning in the 1850s. Set in a well-treed lot, surrounded by picket fence, it is sturdily built of brick painted pale yellow, with wood trim of white, and overwindows of galvanized metal—a spirited facade. (Many Nebraska farm buildings also boasted architecturally ebullient details.) Note the rich detailing of the cornice and the square cupola. The exterior underwent alterations through the years, but accurate restoration to its original condition was made possible by means of a tack-sharp "aerial" photograph taken in 1871 from atop the nearby first capitol. The interior, which also suffered, has been carefully re-created to the period with original furnishings from Nebraska homes.

In 1965 the house was made a Statehood Memorial and hence is beautifully maintained as a branch of the Nebraska State Historical Society. The house emphasizes the interpretations of the Nebraskan social history with frequently changing exhibits depicting events or customs characteristic of the period and region. The era of interpretation centers on the 1870s. Thomas Kennard, incidentally, was largely responsible for selecting Lincoln as the capital of the new (1867) state.

Open Mon.–Sat. 8–12, 1–5, Sun. 1:30–5, except major holidays

---

5 The Citibank (1893/1969)
20th Street at O
Lincoln, Nebraska

**ORIGINAL DESIGNER UNKNOWN; THE CLARK ENERSEN
PARTNERS, ARCHITECTS OF RESTORATION**

With imagination for concept and with strict architectural regard for reality, this ancient Rock Island Railroad station has been transformed into an efficient drive-in bank. The old brick walls were cleaned and

repointed, and the fittings, hardware, and other details carefully restored. Even roll-top desks and a pot-bellied stove were installed. Old
railroad souvenirs and posters, abetted at appropriate times (i.e. large
deposits) by piped-in train sounds, decorate the walls of the banking
(ex-waiting) room. This is a wonderful use of a discarded relic: would
that the concept of rehabilitation and utilization of our other bypassed
railroad stations, great or small, were more widespread. It is listed in
the National Register of Historic Places. (See also the Choo-Choo Inn
in Chattanooga.)

Open during business hours

---

6 The Nebraska State Capitol (1922–32)
14–16th Streets between H and K
Lincoln, Nebraska

BERTRAM GROSVENOR GOODHUE, ARCHITECT

Bertram Grosvenor Goodhue (1869–1924) was one of the last of the
great romantic and eclectic architects, and this capitol is his greatest
building. Goodhue began architectural life at fifteen, worked for
James Renwick (q.v.) for six years in New York (he never went to
college), then moved to Boston where he worked with Ralph Adams
Cram. The pair eventually teamed up to "revolutionize ecclesiastical
architecture." In 1914 he withdrew from Cram, Goodhue & Ferguson,
and for a while from Gothicism, to set up shop on his own in New
York. Having received a firm schooling in the Gothic under Renwick,
and Byzantine and even Spanish commissions with Cram and Ferguson, it is extraordinary that Goodhue could come up with such a
total break in the competition for this State Capitol. (There are suggestions of Eliel Saarinen's Helsinki Railroad Station, 1906–14, in the
design.) For Nebraska, Goodhue wisely wanted a lofty building, "a
Tower on the plains," that would soar above the flat landscape. The
notion of another of the domes from Rome that dot most states was
anathema. (Incidentally, his first sketches were far more Classic than
his competition winner. The competition was primarily to select an
architect from the ten competitors, not a final design.) The result is a
beacon—literally and figuratively—of a building, 400 feet/122 meters
high, surmounted by Lee Lawrie's 19-foot/5.8-meter bronze figure of
a sower.

The significance of the Capitol lies not only in its advanced architectural quality, but in the fact that it constituted a magnificent, pioneering break with a long-outworn tradition. Moreover it integrated architecture and sculpture, particularly in its buttressed piers, to a degree rarely seen since the Gothic. (The figures in the Capitol's great piers are, however, non-medieval in their rigidity.) In overall concept, Goodhue's design created a low mass, 437 feet/133 meters on a side, its periphery efficiently double-lined with offices, pierced at midpoints by four entrances. These entries connect to form a Greek cross within the square framed by offices, with open courtyards filling the four corners. The majestic (95 feet/29 meters high) main entrance hall (north side) occupies one arm of the cross, the legislative chambers the east and west, while main offices fill the south. The tower rises skyward on piers which mark the central crossing. Goodhue had originally planned to utilize much of the tower for the library stacks, hence the smallness of the windows. But working offices, not books, were substituted after his death. There is a slight dryness in the exterior, but considering that the competition for its design was won in 1920, the

Nebraskan Capitol is one of the key forward-looking buildings in America. There is, one hastens to add, no dryness in the interior. Every square inch boasts symbolic mosaics, murals, paintings (most of them by Hildreth Meière), multicolored tiles, and hanging lamps, all coordinated with magniloquent scale. The building is extraordinary both in its daring and in its intimate coordination between architect and artist. Goodhue died in 1924 and the Capitol was completed by his associates.

Open Mon.–Fri. 9–5, Sat. and holidays 10–5, Sun. 1–5, except Dec. 25

---

7   Sheldon Memorial Art Gallery (1962–63)
University of Nebraska
North 12th Street at R
Lincoln, Nebraska

PHILIP JOHNSON, ARCHITECT

The impeccable box approach to the display of art stems from Karl Friedrich Schinkel's "Old Museum" in Berlin (1824–28) and is climaxed on these shores by John Russell Pope's National Gallery in Washington (finished in 1941). The Sheldon Gallery, an adjunct to university teaching, proclaims a lineal form of classicism. This begins on the exterior with the travertine-encased piers (exquisitely detailed and made in Italy) which lead amidship to the double-height Great Hall, precisely as wide as the wings which frame it. The 30-foot/9.1-meter-high hall, which bifurcates the building, is dominated by a bronze-faced bridge staircase—inspired, says the architect, by Eisenstein's movie *Potemkin*—acting both as "liaison" between the top-floor galleries and as a space-playing feature. "You are above everyone here. You are also going from one dark place to another dark place, out into the exposed air . . . See the great sense of mystery" (*Arts & Architecture,* August 1963). This results in a compartmentalization of one group of galleries on one side of the hall and another on the other which contrasts with Johnson's sinuous "progression of spaces" that highlights so much of his other work.

All the galleries are windowless and artificially illuminated (for maximum flexibility), and many of them have off-white, cotton-pile "rugs" on the wall as a mar-proof surface and an excellent background for paintings. A three-hundred-seat, sharply raked auditorium fills most of the main floor at left. A pleasant sunken sculpture garden has been added at the south end. Hazen & Robinson were the supervising architects.

Open Tues. 10–10, Wed.–Sat. 10–5, Sun. 2–5, except major holidays

---

8   Lincoln East Educational Complex (1967–68)
N off A Street on 70th
Lincoln, Nebraska

DAVIS & WILSON, ARCHITECTS

This large "one-building" educational enterprise is basically a high school for a maximum of 2,400 students. But it is also designed to be used as an adult continuing-education and vocational-training plant twenty-four hours a day, year round. The building is comfortably placed on a substantial (160-acre/65-hectare) site to utilize best the uneven terrain, with the divisions jointly used both by students and

adults occupying the high central ground. The one-story public "core" includes administration, adult center, and shops (also used for adult vocational training), with the taller auditorium (1,200 seats) in their center. The three-story class block attaches at left (west), while the high double gymnasium (boys' and girls') stands at right and can be reached by the public without going through the school. Structural framing is of reinforced concrete with walls of a special 1-foot/.3-meter-long brick which varies in color from ocher to deep red. The school was planned so that parking for the nearby stadium could serve throughout the week for faculty and students. Athletic fields adjoin. Aside from a minor confusion of entry, and a lack of shelter for either of its front doors, this educational plant is as capable in architecture as it is forward-looking in community philosophy.

Open during school hours

---

9   Pioneer Village (mid-19th century)
NEB 10 at US 6 and 34
Minden, Nebraska

In spite of being a commercial enterprise, there are several rewarding architectural examples among the reputedly thirty thousand items in this "village." Chief among them because of its rarity is a reproduction

of a sod house or "soddy" that the pioneers in the nearly treeless Plains areas very often erected. There are probably fewer than a dozen left out of perhaps a million\ built. This one was constructed in 1954 with modern timber-frame roof. With thick walls of earth, these houses had good insulating ability; for regionalism, they verily could not be equaled. Sod was usually cut in blocks, roughly 1 x 3 feet/.3 x 1 meter in dimension, and laid like outsize bricks, grass side down, in a modified English bond (two rows of stretchers alternating with one of headers for stability). The walls were then smoothed with a spade outside and in, the inner face generally being plastered when the owner could afford it or lined with newspapers when he could not. The roof was framed by using several tree trunks to uphold the ridge (another trunk), with trimmed branches and brush forming crude "rafters." (A framed roof was used when the owner could afford one.) This primitive skeleton was then covered with more sod and earth and planted with grass to reduce erosion. In addition to the insulation mentioned, a soddy, which generally required 10 acres/4 hectares or more of sod to build, had the delightful advantage of often bursting into bloom following a spring shower. (A two-story soddy, built in 1884, still stands near Broken Bow.) Other architectural items worth noting in

Pioneer Village include an 1869 "fort" (modern roof), a land office, railroad depot, church, and school.

Open daily 8 A.M. *to sundown: admission*

---

10   **Buffalo Bill Ranch** (1886/1909)
3 miles/4.8 kilometers W of US 83 via Buffalo Bill Avenue
North Platte, Nebraska

No triumph of the architectural world, this house nevertheless gives a reasonable impression of a nineteenth-century western rancher's dwelling, here used as home and a Scout's Rest Ranch. Of elementary Victorian inspiration, designed by Buffalo Bill's sister, it has been restored throughout, unfortunately simplified in the process. Though relatively few of the furnishings belonged to Colonel William F. Cody, they are all authentic. Be sure to see, also, the barn and the cedar-log cabin at the rear for more memorabilia of the time and place. The cabin was one of Cody's line shacks from the headwaters of the Dismal River Ranch. The ranch is now a State Historical Park.

Open Memorial Day–Labor Day, daily 9 A.M.*–8* P.M.: *rest of year by appointment*

11 Archbishop Bergan Mercy Hospital (1966–67)
7500 Mercy Road (off Center Street)
Omaha, Nebraska

LEO A. DALY, ARCHITECT

A well-analyzed and—to judge from staff reactions—smoothly operating five-hundred-bed hospital (recently added to) located on the western edge of Omaha. With its clearly expressed functional divisions, and its facades sheltered against the sun by adjustable, vertical louvers, it makes an efficient package. The four-story patient block rests atop the entry-administration floor, each clearly expressed, as is the entry itself. Behind extends the ground-floor one-story complex containing surgical wing, laboratory, radiology, etc., with a self-care wing with single-bed rooms at rear. An obstetrical nursing unit is placed on top of this. The louvers, operating in automatic banks, form an outrigging shielding almost all fenestration, and though they sometimes "protect" solid brick walls, they develop much-needed sun control in Omaha's scorching summers. When they are closed, their shape allows low-level light to enter the patients' rooms. The interiors of the hospital, from patients' rooms (primarily two-bed) to public areas, are satisfactory in a relatively standard plan of hospital layout. The only unhappy note is the quality of the "art" on the walls, over which the architect had no control.

Public areas open daily

12   Central Heating and Cooling Plant (1968)
22nd and Howard Streets
Omaha, Nebraska

LEO A. DALY, ARCHITECT AND ENGINEER

An unusual example of industrial architecture for an unusual requirement, a need which might well gather momentum with our rightful
concern about pollution. The plant, on the edge of downtown Omaha,
is a central heating and cooling facility for approximately forty buildings in the business district. Whereas central steam plants for heating
have been well known for years (though with air conditioning not as
popular as previously), the concept of piping chilled water (c.
$40° F/4° C$) for major building air conditioning is relatively new.
Such a plant of course eliminates the necessity for putting heating/
cooling facilities into individual structures. The architect has here
made a showcase of the complicated machinery and its piping, the latter functionally color-coded in eight bright hues. Heat is produced at
the left (west) end of the building, chilled water at right, with the
lower half-floor taken up by the steam and refrigerant returns. The
public is welcomed.

Open during business hours

13 W. Dale Clark Library (1975–77)
215 South 15th Street
Omaha, Nebraska

**HELLMUTH, OBATA & KASSABAUM AND JOHN LATENSER &
SONS, ARCHITECTS**

A downtown library which though formal in elevation is light and airy
within. Basically square in plan, the building is clad in striated limestone across the front and back and with mirror glass walls on the two
sides. The five-story, 122,000-square-foot/11,334-square-meter library
utilizes both open and closed stacks, its books organized according to
subject departments. A major design feature of the interior is an open
well which breaks up the horizontal character of the floor areas and
makes users more aware of the collections and the services of other

floors. This is topped by forty-eight acrylic domes, radiating light into the core. The stacks on each floor are in different muted colors. The building is set back from the property lines and moated on three sides; thus the bottom floor is not a basement but opens onto a planted area. Parking for forty-eight automobiles is also provided here. Altogether, this is an accessible, hospitable "cultural anchor" for Omaha's central business district. Gyo Obata was principal in charge of design.

Open Mon.–Fri. 9–8:30, Sat. 9–5:30

The **Central Park Mall,** 14th Street between Douglas and Farnam (1978–80), abuts the rear of the library. Bahr, Vermeer & Haecker were the architects with Lawrence Halprin landscape architect. The Mall's flow of waters, a symbolic river, its multilevels and its banners add sparkle to the business district. Hopefully it will eventually extend to the Missouri River itself (beyond 8th Street), a stream that rightfully encouraged the incorporation of Omaha as a city in 1857, but which has been largely neglected in urban terms since then. The river area, it should be noted, has a splendid collection of elderly warehouses.

Nevada

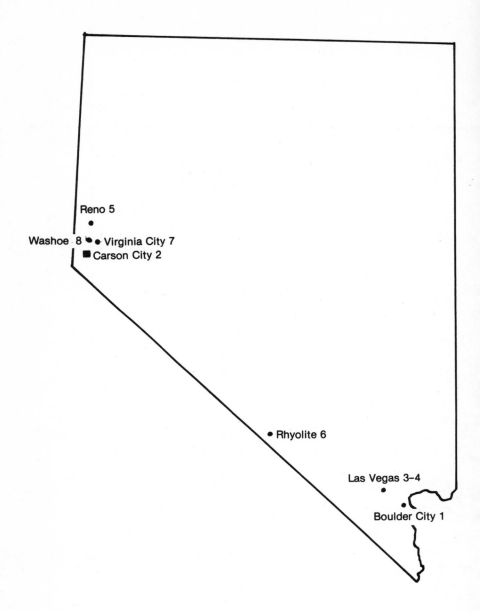

Reno 5
•

Washoe 8 •• Virginia City 7

■ Carson City 2

• Rhyolite 6

Las Vegas 3–4
•

•
Boulder City 1

NEVADA

The buildings in boldface type are of general interest. The others are for the specialist.

Boulder City   1 **Hoover Dam** (1931–36)—U. S. Bureau
                        of Reclamation

Carson City   2 State Capitol (1870–71)—Joseph Gosling

Las Vegas   3 **The Strip** (late 20th century)
                      4 Southern Nevada Vocational-Technical
                        Center (1966–68)—William Blurock &
                        Partners, Julius Gabriele, and James Brooks
                        McDaniel

Reno   5 **Washoe County Library** (1966)—Hewitt C.
                        Wells

Rhyolite   6 **Rhyolite Ghost Town** (1905–8)

Virginia City   7 **Virginia City** (late 19th century)
                        Storey County Court House (1876)

Washoe County   8 **Bowers Mansion** (1862–75/1967)

1 Hoover Dam (1931–36)
US 93, on Nevada-Arizona border, c. 7 miles/11 kilometers E of
Boulder City, Nevada

U. S. BUREAU OF RECLAMATION, ENGINEERS

Hoover Dam rises in a wild, intractable landscape, spun overhead with a gossamer net of high-tension wires. It comprises one of the country's greatest achievements of man harnessing nature to the advantage of each. Floods which once ravaged California's Imperial Valley and some of our other rich farmlands have been contained and water shortages largely eliminated by the controlled release from the dam's reservoir, the 110-mile/177-kilometer-long artificial Lake Mead. The lake also serves as a key recreation facility for the region. In addition to the stabilized irrigation which the dam and lake make possible, a process augmented by the Parker and Imperial dams downstream, some 1 billion gallons/3.8 billion liters of water a day are supplied for domestic

and industrial uses to Southern California (via a 242-mile/389-kilo-meter-long aqueduct and five pumping stations to lift it over the mountains). Moreover, its hydroelectric production, created from the non-polluting force of gravity, was for ten years (1939–49) the greatest in the world. At 1,344,800 kilowatts generating capacity it is still one of the largest.

Hoover Dam itself measures 726.4 feet/221 meters in total height above stream bed, with a crest length of 1,244 feet/379 meters and a bottom thickness of 660 feet/201 meters of solid concrete. (Figures are from a U. S. Department of Interior folder.) 1-inch/25-millimeter pipes with a total loopage of 582 miles/937 kilometers were embedded throughout the great mass to cool the concrete so that in pouring —which began in June 1933—it would cure properly and speedily. There are also five inspection galleries laced through it to monitor the dam's behavior, a feature subsequently adopted for most large-scale dam construction. Clamped on the rocky vise of restless hills, its smooth mathematics relay stunning splendor to the beholder. Moreover the architectural-engineering aspects of powerhouse and substations (with the exception of some details) are good. Altogether, dam and setting are enormously impressive. John Lucian Savage was the brilliant chief engineer as he was for the Bureau of Reclamation up to World War II.

Conducted tours daily of dam and powerhouse, Memorial Day–Labor Day, every 15 minutes, 7:30 A.M.–7:15 P.M.; rest of year, 8:30–4:15: admission

---

2   State Capitol (1870–71)
Carson Street (US 395) between 2nd and Musser
Carson City, Nevada

JOSEPH GOSLING, ARCHITECT

A relaxed atmosphere, part Classic Revival, part Victorian, characterizes Nevada's century-old State Capitol: it is pleasantly low-keyed throughout. There was, as would be expected, influence from architectural developments on both coasts—its designer hailed from California—with its stylistic expression delayed by the rough journey over the mountains, the Rockies on the east and the Sierra Nevada on the west. Modest in size—the Capitol measures 148 feet/45 meters

long by 98 feet/30 meters wide—it suggests an "oversized courthouse." The roundheaded paired windows, earlier popular elsewhere, should be noted, along with the prominent quoins. The hexagonal cupola is capably handled. The rooms at each end of the second floor which once housed the Senate and Assembly—functions recently moved to a new building down the street—are restrained chambers. Inside, a 400-foot/122-meter-long frieze (first-floor corridor) proclaims the resources of the state, its mineral accent blazoned by the mining picks which uphold its swags. A. V. Higgins of Reno was the artist. An octagonal annex for the State Library was added at the rear in 1905, and the wings at both ends were extended in 1913–14 by architect F. J. De Longchamps. The Capitol was thoroughly renovated and restored on the interior in 1980.

Open during office hours

3   The Strip (late 20th century)
    Las Vegas Boulevard South (US 91 and 466)
    Las Vegas, Nevada

The "vulgarity" of several areas of the U.S.A. is so blatantly prepos-
terous as to assume a valid index of twentieth-century folk culture.
New York's Broadway once reveled in a make-believe of improbability
and delight, but Broadway has fallen on sordid days and more sordid
nights. Vegas' Strip—a word that adroitly defines—now reigns as
queen, a bawdy queen brandishing aerial signs which engage from dusk
to dawn in uninhibited battle to lure all comers to the dens that line
this boulevard. The resulting neon Armageddon, as one drives the
gauntlet between flashing phalanxes (including plaster warriors), lays
siege to the senses in a mind-boggling campaign that almost always
succeeds. One finds oneself with defenses down, willingly trapped, en-
gagingly shilled, so electric are the forces and so imaginative the
means. And the structures behind these aerial fireworks—which, of
course, constitute their goal—are almost invisible, so subdued are they
in scale. One casino is dwarfed by a sign over 200 feet/61 meters
high: "When is a building a sign and when is it a symbol?" This is one
of the world's most successful "playgrounds for adults."

In 1968 the thought-provoking Robert Venturi took fifteen of his
Yale School of Architecture students to examine The Strip, an excursion which led to the book *Learning from Las Vegas* (MIT Press,
1972) that he wrote with his wife, Denise Scott Brown. It is
a challenging book and one which can perhaps be encapsulated in his

statement: "Architects who can accept the lessons of primitive vernacular architecture, so easy to take in an exhibit like 'Architecture Without Architects' [by Bernard Rudofsky], and of industrial, vernacular architecture, so easy to adapt to an electronic and space vernacular as elaborate neo-Brutalist or neo-Constructivist megastructures, do not easily acknowledge the validity of the commercial vernacular" (*Forum,* March 1968). Perhaps we should look again at The Strip.

24 hours a day

---

4 Southern Nevada Vocational-Technical Center (1966–68)
Maple Avenue at Russell Road, SE edge of town
Las Vegas, Nevada

PHASE I—WILLIAM BLUROCK & PARTNERS AND JULIUS GABRIELE, ASSOCIATED ARCHITECTS
PHASE II—WILLIAM BLUROCK & PARTNERS AND JAMES BROOKS McDANIEL, ASSOCIATED ARCHITECTS

"The controlling purpose of vocational-technical education is to provide organized instruction that will enable students to participate suc-

cessfully in our society" (SNVTC booklet). To this end an ambitious, trades-oriented campus has been built on the outskirts of Las Vegas, complementing Clark County's general education facilities. Courses range from automobile mechanics, refrigeration, and cosmetology to electronics. The site is an exposed plateau formed by a lava flow; the building response is compacted but offers extensive views. A space-radiating interior, centered on a brightly top-lit "mall," gives the school an architectural quality not suggested by its more routine exterior. From this inviting two-story core, a generous and spontaneous gathering spot, classrooms radiate on both levels. The first phase of the master plan, accommodating one thousand students, was completed in 1966; the second phase, with facilities for six hundred more, was finished in 1968.

Open during school hours

---

5   Washoe County Library (1966)
Center Street, between East Liberty and Ryland
Reno, Nevada

HEWITT C. WELLS, ARCHITECT

It is difficult to know whether to classify this building as a library or a botanical garden. In either or both cases the interior provides a highly inviting space for the perusal of books and periodicals. One is welcomed, on entering, by a forest of levels and a profusion of greenery instead of being confronted by escalators, card catalogs, and control desks. The luxurious planting, which includes full-grown trees plus several small fountains, is doubly appreciated in this semidesert region. The atmosphere resulting sets the stage, which is amplified by projecting disc-shaped platforms for reading perched among the leaves. Stacks are located at each end with a one-hundred-seat lecture room at the lower level. The exterior is not spectacular, but the atmosphere within is great. Mitchell J. Serven was the landscape architect who carried out Hewitt Wells's "garden" concept.

Open Mon.–Fri. 9–8:50, Sat. 9–5:50, Sun. 1–5, except major holidays

---

6   Rhyolite Ghost Town (1905–8)
c. 6 miles/10 kilometers W of Beatty and US 95 via NEV 58
Rhyolite, Nevada

Nevada's main source of natural wealth lies in the minerals in its desolate but often stunning hills and mountains. At the end of the last century and the beginning of this one, a number of rough, tough mining towns sprang up, mostly to desiccate when veins ran out. A surprisingly competent architecture, much in masonry, was evident in some of these now all but abandoned "ghost towns." Among the more "poignant," and one which is readily accessible, is Rhyolite, just east of Death Valley National Monument. A few shattered walls—this is an earthquake zone—are all that remain of a city which once held eight thousand, but for the ghost-towner this short detour will be worthwhile. Note the paths radiating to the mine-tunnel openings which dot the hillsides. Nearby one can see tracks made some 150 million years ago on very warm lava by a high-stepping dinosaur.

---

7 Virginia City, Nevada (late 19th century)

Virginia City, folded in ore-burdened hills, enfiladed with short-order tourists, collapsed here, spruced there, desolate yet active, genuine but artificial, gives a tantalizing if commercialized impression of an Olde West mining town. Silver and gold are still there, difficult to reach economically now that Henry Tomkins Paige Comstock (1820–70) and successors have worked it over, but the shaftings are very visible from almost any point, and some are in operation today. Architecturally in "the richest place on earth" there are several buildings that echo a few of the facilities and fortunes dug, generally by hand, from the most generous hill of silver and gold yet discovered. The visitor should survey the entire town. In addition to the sometimes amusing bar-spattered main road (C Street: NEV 17) there are the Storey County Court House (1876) uphill on B Street (see below), the Savage Mining Company Office (1862), bracketed, bold, and recently restored, downhill at 146 D (open daily), with the handsome Mackay House close by (129 D Street, open daily in summer), plus a smattering of others from that period in the 1860s and 1870s when the Comstock was king and thousands of tent-housed prospectors combed every inch of Sun Mountain, pick in hand. In 1869 a railroad was pushed through, rather up (the city's altitude is 6,250 feet/1,905 meters), and heavy machinery brought in which enabled miners to get at the Big Bonanza of the Lode (1873), a strike 1,200 feet/366 meters deep that reputedly produced over a hundred million dollars' worth of silver and gold in a half-dozen years before it was exhausted. It is claimed

that a billion dollars altogether was taken from the area. A fire in 1875 destroyed much of the town, and though it was immediately rebuilt—with enthusiasm—by the end of that decade the accessible minerals were working thin and decline set in. Virginia City is now down in population from perhaps 33,000 in the 1870s to 600 today—its bars from 110 to 20. To preserve its important remaining buildings, the town's center has been designated the Virginia City Historic District and placed in the National Register. The Comstock Historic Preservation Committee aids in preserving one of the West's most important boom towns.

The **Storey County Court House** (1876), on B Street, effuses a rich mixture of elements, mostly in cast iron. Outstanding are the round-headed windows of the ground floor—reflecting the arched entry—and the flatheaded windows with angled pediment above, the whole topped by a strong cornice. Though the architect, if one, is unknown, the builder was one Peter Burke; he was a capable man.

Apply at Visitors' Bureau, C Street, for map and information

---

8   Bowers Mansion (1862–75, restored 1967)
on US 395, c. 10 miles/16 kilometers N of Carson City
Washoe County, Nevada

The Bowers Mansion faces a verdant plain, a lake, and the mountains that produced the famous Comstock Lode whence came the Bowers' wealth. Surrounded by poplars and evergreens, this unexpectedly sophisticated house occupies a dulcet niche in an oft-inhospitable landscape. Its architecture—a bit of the Georgian in its symmetry plus the Italianate in the brackets and double roundheaded window on axis—is restrained. It is given a certain cachet by the three balustrades which wrap the sides of the lower porch and the second-floor deck, with the top one encircling a flat roof. The rhythm of the ocher balusters which demark these levels delivers a slight wedding-cake impression but also a certain style. On top sits an octagonal cupola. Everything in this U-shaped mansion was to be of the finest. It was built for a prospector and his sparsely educated wife, whose adjacent claims triggered their union, shortly to be followed by enormous wealth. The total cost of house and furnishings was said to be over $200,000, but like many get-rich-quick tales, this too ended in sadness. Sandy Bowers died of silico-

sis in 1868, then, six years later, Mrs. Bowers began to add the third
floor to provide facilities to turn the house and grounds into a resort
hotel. Unfortunately, a civil suit was brought against her (1875) and
she lost not only the case but the property. Dilapidation eventually set
in and the mansion slipped into near oblivion. Its collapse was
prevented when the Reno Women's Civic Club was joined by the
Washoe County Commissioners, the two groups raising the money to
buy it (1946), and making the estate a County Park. In 1967 Edward
S. Parsons was commissioned to undertake complete architectural restoration of the house (including the removal of the Mansard), plus the
assembly, through donations and purchases, of representative furniture. The house may not be as fascinating as the saga of its owners, but
what could be?

Open daily May 15–Oct., daily 11–12:30, 1:30–4:30: admission

New Mexico

● Aztec 3

Taos 13
●
Chaco Canyon 4   Ranchos de Taos 8 ●
●   ● Las Trampas 7
                            Chimayo 5 ●
        San Ildefonso 9 ●
                               ■ Santa Fe 10–12

        Laguna 6
             ●   ● Albuquerque 2
        Ácoma 1

NEW MEXICO

The buildings in boldface type are of general interest. The others are for the specialist.

1   Ácoma and San Estévan (1629–42)
13 miles/21 kilometers SW of IS 40 at Casa Blanca exit via
  NM 23
Ácoma, New Mexico

The acropolis of Ácoma, verily a city on a hill, is the most dramatically situated pueblo in the country. Surveying a terrain of wild, petrific desolation, its height and steep escarpments have offered protection, hence encouraged settlement, for perhaps two millennia, making it probably the oldest continuously inhabited town in the United States (a distinction which the now crumbling and semiabandoned Oraibi disputes). Moreover, it is readily accessible to motorists via good gravel roads, including of late one to the top, and it welcomes visitors graciously. (However, be certain to get permission—for a fee—to take photographs or to sketch.)

Ácoma's soilless sandstone mesa, roughly 70 acres/28 hectares in extent, rises some 357 feet/109 meters above the plains and 7,000 feet/2,134 meters above sea level; it is appropriately called "The Sky City." The village's natural defenses are strengthened on the north side by a near-solid lineup of contiguous houses of one to three stories in height which stretch approximately 770 feet/235 meters near the edge of the bluff. These are (or were originally) windowless on the side facing out. Two other rows of stone and adobe cellular dwellings, in roughly parallel lines but more casually dispersed, made up the rest of the urban pattern until 1629. Then the Spanish, who had discovered the village in 1540, commenced the first church (on the south edge), setting up an antipodal contrast of buildings for conqueror and conquered on opposite sides of an invisible line. The Spaniards did not want their building to impinge upon the village. There is, however, a lack of spatial organization, or even proper plazas for ritual dancing, in the basic layout of Ácoma. In addition to the three lanes of houses there are seven rectangular kivas for the men. Many dwellings have been semiabandoned as inhabitants have moved to farms on the plain to return mainly for summer or for festivals. All material for building, from adobe and stone to the great beams for the church, had to be lugged to the top via precipitous paths, as the mesa itself offers only bare rock, defense, and views to its inhabitants.

As the Indians had few tools to dress stone, and lacked the skill (and wood for formwork) to construct arches and vaults, the churches of the region developed into a series of thick-walled, narrow, flat-

roofed buildings with few windows (and these, as at Ácoma, at times changed), plus, occasionally, a high transverse transept window illuminating the sanctuary. In construction, the Indians kept building procedures simple, sticking to adobe for walls, roofed by trunks, branches, and packed earth. Arches and domes were never used in early New Mexico or by American Indians anywhere except with bent reeds. (Compare the much later vaulted churches in Texas and California.) There is, peripherally, a men-women work division in pueblo construction, the men traditionally charged with the woodwork while the women built the walls—"a disgraceful occupation" (Kubler).

San Estévan epitomizes these characteristics, and with its front "yard," its "raised" cemetery, and its attached *convento* for its resident Franciscan friars, it attains a rough grandeur on the outside and offers a regional treat within. Its nave is long (126 feet/38 meters) and narrow (31 feet/9.4 meters) and without transept but with pronounced taper at the chancel, culminating in a painted reredos. As the vigas, here undressed trunks some 37 feet/11 meters long, had to be hauled from forests 20 to 30 miles/32 to 48 kilometers away—and, for religious purposes, not to be touched to the ground—"a sacrilege" (*Acoma, The Sky City,* Mrs. W. T. Sedgwick, Harvard University Press, 1927)—a restricted nave width was inevitable. These beams were placed atop the stone and adobe walls—how such weights were lifted is not precisely known—and given added bearing by outsized corbels, often fancifully painted. The walls themselves are of great thickness (up to 7.8 feet/2.4 meters, writes Kubler), tapering at the top. It is a plan which under the circumstances was inevitable, having the same ancestry and reflecting the same rationale as village churches in Old Mexico, a tradition which was carried by the padres up the Rio Grande to find expression in New Mexican examples. (New Mexico was so called in the sixteenth century: after Florida it bears the oldest state name.)

San Estévan underwent repairs and small changes through the generations (two windows in the apse at one time having been put in then subsequently walled up, etc.), but for much of the last hundred years it has needed more attention than it has received. Undoubtedly parts of the first church (1629) are incorporated in the one we see today, for beams and stone brought to place with such travail were not lightly to be thrown away. The Pueblo Revolt of 1680–92, during which many churches and Spanish buildings were ransacked and incinerated, seemingly left it largely in peace. In 1924 the Committee for the Preservation and Restoration of New Mexican Mission Churches undertook major repairs, including an invisible concrete roof. Restoration has been very active of late. One of the great chapters of American Indian life and Spanish religious influence, Ácoma is, of course, a National Historic Landmark. (George Kubler in his admirable book *The Religious Architecture of New Mexico,* 1940, reprinted by Rio Grande Press in 1962, offers expert background on all the Hispanic churches in the state. Also recommended is *The Missions of New Mexico, 1776,* translated by Adams and Chavez, University of New Mexico Press, 1956.)

Open daily from one hour after sunrise to one hour before sunset: admission

2   La Luz Development (1967–74)
W of city on IS 40, 2.6 miles/4.2 kilometers N on NM 448 (Coors Road exit)
Albuquerque, New Mexico

ANTOINE PREDOCK, ARCHITECT

The La Luz Community consists of ninety-two attached houses—town houses in the country—fanned in irregular groups. Most of them enjoy views over the Rio Grande, the city, and the distant Sandia Peak (10,678 feet/3,255 meters high). Though it is a private development, and its condominium houses are not open to the public, enough can be seen from the road for one to appreciate what imagination can produce in compact land usage in the open country. Spanish and

pueblo influences are obvious: the architect spent almost a year study-
ing in Spain. This, however, is no historical rehash but an up-to-date
distilling of lessons of the past. These concerned meeting the demands
of nature (intense heat and cold and with spring dust storms), plus
using the past's millennium-tested local material, adobe, here 16 inches/
41 centimeters thick and cement-stuccoed for greater permanence.
Though clustered together like blank-walled ramparts (on approach
sides), the houses enjoy inner privacy, most having walled patios, plus
sweeping views of an unspoiled open mesa to the east, where along the
river flood plain 200 of the 500 acres/81 of 202 hectares are left wild
and wooded. The west walls of the houses are largely solid against low
sun and high winds. There is good separation of pedestrian and
vehicles with inner plazas and walkways. Altogether the development
is very imaginative, very much at home on its tawny desert setting.

Only visible from the street

---

3   Aztec Ruins National Monument (A.D. 1111–15/mid-13th
      century)
Ruins Road, .7 mile/1.1 kilometers N of US 550
Aztec, New Mexico

Erroneously called "Aztecs" by early Europeans, the builders of this
substantial settlement—whose precise dates come from dendrochronology—were the Pueblo (i.e. "village") Indians. Their ancestors moved
into this San Juan River area about two thousand years ago, and toward the end of the eighth century A.D., began to develop the connected flat-roofed communities the Spaniards called pueblos. (Nomadic
hunters had traversed the region probably ten thousand years ago.
Some historians think that the Pueblos were driven from Mexico by
the warlike Aztecs.) Besides providing us today with an intriguing ruin
in the northwest corner of the state, the complex is important in both
urban and architectural terms. First, this was a geometrically planned
community, built as a squared-U to form an open rectangle, approximately 278 x 360 feet/85 x 110 meters in size, focused on a circular
Great Kiva. Its site, being relatively defenseless, indicated peaceful,
sedentary conditions. The Aztec ruins, moreover, comprise a "megastructure" that is one interconnected block of five hundred cellular
dwelling and storage units. These housed some 450 people in two- and
three-story "apartments," each roughly 10 x 12 feet/3 x 3.6 meters in

size. On the base level across the back, the pueblo is as much as six rooms deep, and four to five along the sides. The windowless inner rooms were used for storing food against the winter months and for personal possessions. Finally, like Pueblo Bonito in Chaco Canyon (q.v.) but unlike New Mexico's score of other pueblos, it is constructed totally of dry sandstone, not adobe. Its workmanship, considering that the cutting and dressing tools themselves were of stone, is astonishing. Note the alternation of wide and narrow bands. The quarry, incidentally, lies 1 mile/1.6 kilometers away.

Aztec is also distinguished by its Great Kiva (there are twenty-nine smaller ones) which projects half above ground and has been carefully reconstructed (1934) on the foundations of the original. This startling room—which was probably used by the whole community—should by all means be seen, for it forms one of the few extant or restored examples of monumental interior space of the Indian era in this country. Measuring 48.3 feet/14.7 meters in inner diameter, its center section is upheld by four piers made of alternating layers of log sections and stones, with beams across them and other logs on top radiating to the periphery. Surrounding the central section, which is set 8 feet/2.4 meters below grade, are fourteen small chambers (for sacral storage, perhaps) with two doors each, a small one to the central arena and one to the outside. (These latter were sealed during one of the alterations.) An altar, or fire pit, stands opposite the entrance with two mysterious, rectangular pits, or "vaults," on either side. These are held by some to be sudatories, or sweat baths, while others consider them "foot drums" when covered with hides. A circular stone bench rings the whole. (The restored, somewhat smaller kiva at Ocmulgee, near Macon, Georgia [q.v.], forms an interesting, less sophisticated parallel.)

This splendid kiva and town were abandoned around A.D. 1150, thus not very long after completion, it is surmised because of rainfall failure and/or the shifting of the Animas River, a tributary of the nearby San Juan. However, it was reoccupied and in part remodeled by others around 1220–60. These people—probably Chacoan—closed the open side of the pueblo and reroofed the kiva, only to abandon the site permanently during the great drought of 1276–99—the period of the High Gothic in Europe.

Open late May–Labor Day, daily 8–6, rest of year 8–5, except Jan. 1 and Dec. 25: admission

4   Pueblo Bonito (A.D. 828–1126)
Visitor Center 30 miles/48 kilometers S of NM 57 (or 64
miles/103 kilometers N of US 66 on NM 57)
Chaco Canyon National Monument, New Mexico

Pueblo Bonito represents the meridian of Indian architectural achievement in what is now the United States. Yucatán by the Mayas and Machu Picchu by the Incas far outstrip Amerindian work in both scope and technical know-how, but this long-deserted settlement in the Chaco Canyon is still prodigious. And though its ruins may not be as dramatic visually as those at Mesa Verde, Colorado (q.v.), the architectural sophistication of Pueblo Bonito is far superior to the cliffside adaptations by the Colorado Anasazi. Moreover, Pueblo Bonito was not a monument erected for religious rituals (as in Meso-America), but an active four- to five-story "town" for as many as 1,000 souls (possibly 1,200 maximum), occupying approximately eight hundred rooms spread over 3 acres/1.2 hectares. Until the development of the American apartment complexes of recent years it was indeed the largest megastructure on these shores.

Bonito was planned in a D-shape with its high, almost windowless arced back confronting the cliffs behind. Its contiguous tiers of southerly facing apartments step down in curved terraces to focus, almost like a contemporary stadium, on a central "plaza," the whole closed by a low wall across the straight side near the Chaco Wash. In front of the apartments are the underground kivas, thirty-two clan kivas and two great kivas, the larger 52 feet/16 meters in diameter.

Not only was there a "town plan" for Pueblo Bonito (and other settlements of the Chaco), construction techniques were very advanced. The high curved wall which enfolds much of the complex is an outstanding example of stonework of any ethos. This perimeter enclosure, measuring approximately 800 feet/244 meters long, is faced on both sides with beautifully dressed and fitted small stones, while rubble fills the center—an advanced veneer technique called emplecton and common especially in ancient Greek and Roman architecture. Wide foundations were laid with walls properly narrowing toward the top, and doorways were often placed in line, reflecting a definite layout of room arrangement. The stonework of the short domestic divisions, where wall meets wall and openings occur, can only be described as elegant. It should be pointed out that not all masonry was of this exactness: earlier sections were of crude stone.

Pueblo Bonito, as indicated, was neither the earliest nor the only settlement in the canyon. It was, indeed, one of a system of "satellite communities." Man had been dwelling and farming, as opposed to nomadic hunting, along the Chaco River at least since the sixth century A.D. (hunters since, perhaps, 7000 B.C.), and around a dozen sizable communities were strung along its course. Many of their ruins are visitable today. Remote sensing techniques have outlined an extensive network of uniform, straight roads connecting each pueblo with resource areas beyond the canyon's escarpment. The wheel, of course, was unknown. Bonito was simply the largest and architecturally the most sophisticated in its vision of overall concept and in its skill of detail execution. The settlement was largely abandoned around A.D. 1200–50, but not, it is thought, because of the terrible late-thirteenth-century drought. Increased population, which led to land-exhaustion, then alkalization and lowering of the water table are mentioned as causes. But what a monument the Indians left!

Check in first at the Visitor Center for a self-guiding pamphlet and to see the small museum with reconstruction of the pueblo. A number of sites will merit a visit, with the Great Kiva at **Casa Rinconada** (opposite Pueblo Bonito) rating especially high. Built around A.D. 1150, this restored (1933–35) but now unroofed kiva is, at 63.5 feet/19.3 meters in diameter and a maximum height of 12.1 feet/3.7 meters, one of the largest in the country. It is furthermore characterized by excellent stonework which was originally plastered and probably painted. Precise orientation can be seen in the four holes which once held its roof posts: they align with the cardinal points. It is probable that Casa Rinconada (Corner House), unlike most kivas, was an isolated place "of public assembly" (Gordon Vivian and Paul Reiter, *The Great Kivas,* The School of American Research, 1965).

NOTE: The road into Chaco Canyon National Monument can charitably be described as poor: in wet weather it is virtually impassable for a two-wheel-drive vehicle. No tourist facilities exist except for rest rooms and a non-fee campground.

Visitor Center open daily 8–5, except Jan. 1 and Dec. 25;
interpretive talks and campfire programs June–Labor Day

5 El Santuario de Chimayo (1814–16)
off NM 4, 1 mile/1.6 kilometers S of junction NM 4 and 76
Chimayo, New Mexico

A remote Spanish-American village church, one marked by bucolic setting, an ingratiating parvis, an almost quaint brace of wooden towers
(added early in this century along with the gable roof), and a most unusual nave. The light level is low, and always has been, with no contemporary fixtures to mar its integrity. Built as a private thank-offer-
ing, the church remained in the family for over a hundred years until it
was acquired (1929) by friends and given to the Roman Catholic Diocese of New Mexico. The thickly vigaed nave is decorated with four
reredos, two per side and measuring almost 13 feet/4 meters high,
along with numerous *bultos* or images of saints. However, the climax is

the sanctuary retable (of complex iconography), its framing, and its 6-foot/1.83-meter-high crucifix, the latter reputedly a near-duplicate of one in Esquipulas, Guatemala. There is an appealing primitive quality to the whole design. Just off the sanctuary to the left is a small sacristy with, some hold, a *posito* of healing mud capable of curing or ameliorating a panoply of diseases.

Open daily 8–5

Not far away stands the **Plaza del Cerro** (c. 1730), virtually fortified by its ring of buildings. It lies 1 mile/1.6 kilometers northwest of the Santuario in Chimayo proper. The Plaza, like the Santuario, is listed in the National Register of Historic Places.

---

6   The Mission Church of San José de la Laguna (1699–1706)
on hillock, W edge of
Laguna, New Mexico

San José's exterior massing recalls the softly molded, white-stuccoed architecture of the Mediterranean, while its interior is spiced by energetic wall decorations. The mission and its small church (105 feet/32 meters long by 22 feet/6.7 meters wide) rank high in our inheritance of Spanish-Indian architecture in the United States. Note the integration of the twin bells on its planar facade—typical of the Balearics. Though of the same "standard" plan as, say, the larger church at nearby Ácoma (q.v.), the Laguna mission both in siting and architecture is more intimately scaled, and having been reasonably cared for in this century, is also in finer condition. A simple walled courtyard with a few trees forms an introduction to the mission, with the priest's house to left and small baptistry to right having an inner door to the nave. The church itself is constructed of rough stone covered by whitewashed plaster worn by the elements to a tactile smoothness.

The long, darkish interior, with three windows on the south wall plus a smaller one over the entry, reaches a climax at the chancel with its beautiful *retablo* (1804–5, restored by E. Boyd in 1950). The splayed side walls adjacent to the reredos were at one time also decorated, mostly with scrolls, but they have since been whitewashed out. (See Kubler's illustration.) The ceiling over the chancel is also ornamented. The lower walls of the nave convolute with boldly primitive paintings, rich in symbolic color and designs to represent the elements affecting

crop growth. They were probably added some fifty years after the dedication of the church itself. The ceiling of the nave is spanned by the usual vigas, here debarked tree trunks on simple corbels, covered with herringboned branches brightly painted. Father Antonio de Miranda supposedly designed the church and supervised its construction. The mission was in a badly deteriorated condition in the middle of the last century but was eventually stabilized. A new roof was added in 1923 by the Committee for the Preservation and Restoration of New Mexican Mission Churches. In the 1930s and 1940s further restoration was carried out under the supervision of the Franciscan priest.

Open daily 8–5

---

7   San José de Gracia (c. 1760–76)
Village Plaza, off NM 76
Las Trampas, New Mexico

This ingratiating village church, at one time known as Santo Tomás Apóstol del Río de las Trampas, has been carefully restored (1967) by the Las Trampas Foundation. Set approximately 8,000 feet/2,438 meters high in the Sangre de Cristo Mountains, and surrounded by a low

adobe wall, the church and its somewhat amorphously defined "plaza" form the civic focus for its tiny—and once fórtified—village (population c. 50). This clutch of buildings creates a valuable and elsewhere vanishing Spanish Colonial-Mexican subculture, little spoiled (except for utility wires) by the late twentieth century. Restoration included new exterior surfacing of its 4-foot/1.2-meter-thick adobe walls, a new roof, and interior rehabilitation. (The Committee for the Preservation and Restoration of New Mexican Mission Churches had carried out roof repairs in 1923.) The interior with its usual choir loft, white plaster sides, corbeled beam ceiling, and rough, unpainted wood floor establishes the background for the folk-art furnishings. Among these rewards note the pulpit perched on a single twisted and carved column and reached by a short ladder. The reredos is "almost certainly" the work of a local craftsman. Note, in plan, the two small transepts, and, above, the transverse clerestory which washes the chancel with light. The side windows were probably put in subsequently. The not-unusual balcony across the facade, bracketed between the wall ends which double as "towers" (tops restored), was at one time used by the choir when outdoor services took place. Fortunately the entire village has been given National Registered Landmark status—it forms an almost unique example of its kind.

Open daily 8–5

8   San Francisco de Asís Misión (c. 1813)
center of village, off US 68
Ranchos de Taos, New Mexico

The buttressed apse of this aged church stands as a stalwart synthesis of structural demands and sculptural fascination. One almost shakes in its presence. However, it is important to realize that the buttresses seen here and sustaining other adobe buildings in the Southwest differ totally from those which ingeniously transmit to the ground the roof and vaulting thrusts of the Gothic cathedrals of Europe. The medieval flying buttresses were from the beginning of the church's design an essential and highly sophisticated element in the architectural-engineering of load handling and weight transmittal. The buttresses that render lateral support to adobe walls in New Mexico are of bulk, not empiric mathematics, and squat about their buildings sometimes as ad hoc additions. This is not to imply that they are not in their own right singularly impressive; they are simply another form of buttressing. The supports which cluster about the apse of San Francisco were at times reinforced; hence their mighty structural and esthetic impact is, in small part, fortuitous; they form, however, some of the greatest abstract architectural sculpture one will encounter: it is probably the most photographed end of a church in the United States. The rest of the exterior, the whole wrapped in a low adobe wall to create a parvis, is agreeable but not overwhelming, there being an out-of-character, al-

most Victorian quality about the two belfries and the too-sizable "Gothic" front door (which was originally square). The outside measures approximately 35 x 125 feet/11 x 38 meters.

The interior is of structural interest with its closely spaced vigas and corbels, but because the major source of light comes from two windows opposite each other halfway down the nave (both probably added later on), the sanctuary and transepts are gloomy in spite of a small (and original) transverse clerestory between nave and higher transept roof. (A new roof was added in 1930–31.) The strong contrast of light versus gloom suggests the violence and passion in architecture seen in Hispanic life and land: one has only to compare the clinical daylight-flooding of the New England meeting houses. The fine painted wood panel in the east transept of San Francisco should be noted but the stations of the cross and the other works of art are not recommended. The church was hard-plastered in 1967, making upkeep much easier but hiding the soft adobe texture of the walls. (In 1979 mud plaster was again used.) The nineteenth century was especially troublesome for the church, but fortunately San Francisco survived. Its apse alone makes a trip today memorable.

Open Mon.–Sat. 10–4, Sun. masses 7, 9, and 11—closed after last mass

9　San Ildefonso Pueblo (c. 1300–　)
4.5 miles/7.2 kilometers W of US 64/84 on NM 4, then 1 mile/1.6 kilometers N at marker

San Ildefonso, with its loosely defined main plaza, highlighted by a circular (and elevated) kiva near the center, has been occupied since around 1300, being near the juncture of two rivers. Though buildings have come and gone, this village of approximately two hundred still maintains a sense of urban focus unusual to most pueblos. Its use of occasional cottonwoods as delimiters (unfortunately rare) is welcome. The quietly dispersed one- and two-story buildings framing the plaza establish a relaxed scene. For the general tourist San Ildefonso is after Taos and Ácoma one of the most revelatory of pueblos, but do not anticipate urban magnificence. It is listed in the National Register of Historic Places.

NOTE: The local pottery, made from basaltic Black Mesa clay, is famous.

10   Palace of the Governors (1610–12)
The Plaza
Santa Fe, New Mexico

Santa Fe, founded in 1610, is the second oldest continuously inhabited city in the United States. (St. Augustine, Florida—q.v.—was established in 1565; Jamestown, Virginia, was settled in 1607 but abandoned late in the seventeenth century.) Santa Fe is also our oldest state capital and at 6,990 feet/2,131 meters above sea level it is the highest. Spaniards from Mexico City, with Don Pedro de Peralta governor, founded the city, which they called La Villa Real de la Santa Fé de San Francisco de Asís. They immediately commenced construction of a large presidio or military compound—Casas Reales—containing "Palace," barracks, chapel (possibly later), administrative offices, and services. The presidio's overall measurements were approximately 400 x 800 feet/122 x 244 meters. The Palace itself measures 240 feet/73 meters long by 36 feet/11 meters wide. (In the late 1860s it was shortened a bit for a road program.) The rooms on the front of its stretched rectangular plan overlook the historic plaza; those on the rear open onto an enclosed patio. The building originally formed one corner of the presidio, now long since vanished. The one-story facade did not initially have the sheltering *portales,* and it is not known precisely when this peristyle was added. Several eighteenth-century maps indicate, roughly, an arcade, but the only definite knowledge starts with the Mexican period (1821). It is likely that the first building looked somewhat like today's Old Spanish Governor's Palace of 1749 in San Antonio, Texas (q.v.).

During and after the Pueblo Revolt of 1680 all of the Casas Reales was heavily damaged and the Spanish forced to flee southward. However, in 1692 the town was retaken and the buildings repaired. Upkeep, however, seems to have been uneven and the Palace itself was once (1731) termed "a mess." Governor Bustamante had it practically rebuilt in 1731. (See *The Missions of New Mexico, 1776,* translated by Adams and Chavez, University of New Mexico Press, 1956, for excellent background on the whole area.) A series of governors—Spanish, Mexican, and Anglo (after 1846)—occupied the building in spite of its sometimes poor condition. In 1909 the ancient and much repaired structure was given to the Museum of New Mexico—itself created that year—and major (and questionable) repairs undertaken (1911–13). Since then a thorough, long-term restoration has taken place under the museum's auspices and the splendid result today shows the Palace in its evolution from Colonial structure through its Victorian period.

Although there is little architectural distinction in the Palace of the Governors, as an index of very early Spanish-Pueblo building it gives valuable insight into the primitive conditions of some 370 years ago. And it is, of course, our "oldest surviving non-Indian building" (Hugh Morrison in his *Early American Architecture,* Oxford University Press, 1952). Its construction traditions go back, perhaps, to a thousand years, adobe—earth—being the basic wall material. The Indians had applied adobe in layers until the Spanish showed them the more efficient brick form. Vigas—tree trunks which could be handled by two men—formed roof beams. As is obvious, these often project beyond the eaves. The adobe-viga tradition became so strong that in Santa Fe today there are architectural ordinances to maintain "traditional" building appearances.

Be certain to see the Museum of New Mexico (adjacent to the Palace) with its excellent exhibits; the Hall of the Southwest Indians is particularly recommended. Incidentally, the museum allows Indians only (mostly Pueblos) to sell their handmade jewelry and other artifacts in the arcade of the Palace.

Open mid-Mar. to mid-Oct., daily 9–4:45; rest of year, Tues.–Sun. 9–9:45, except holidays

11   The Santa Fe Opera House (1967)
c. 6 miles/9.6 kilometers N of city off US 64, 84, 285
near Santa Fe, New Mexico

McHUGH & KIDDER, ARCHITECTS

The concept of summer opera under the stars, particularly at the
sparkling elevation of 7,000 feet/2,134 meters and in a spectacular
mountain setting, was a stroke of genius. The architectural response
meets the delight of site with a semi-open-air solution that combines
excellent views and acoustics in a two-section, well-sculpted structure.
This has been realized by making the stage house and its mechanism a
detached unit, and fanning the 1,366 seats up the slope in front. As a
hedge against inclement weather approximately half of the seats at the

rear are covered by a cantilevered roof, while several of the front rows
are sheltered by the projecting overhang of the stage roof. (Rain is so
unlikely at the time of year when performances are given that it seems
almost regrettable to have any cover.) However, all the audience,
whether under projecting cover or not, feel a contact with the stars
above (plus those on the stage) and the distant lights of Los Alamos.
A tension develops between the geometric timber roof over the rear
part of the audience and the almost expressionistic stage house (which
recalls the early work of Eric Mendelsohn). Some details might be
questioned, but the basic thinking is commendable. Because the opera
is limited to a short summer season, the stage mechanism had to be
both ingenious and economical, a mandate well carried out.

An earlier and smaller house on the site burned in 1966. Opera
began here in 1957 under the renowned John Crosby. His directing
and efforts (down to scene-painting), the quality of the company
(largely young and capable), and the "festival operation" of its often
exploratory programming (four world premieres, fifteen American,
etc.) have, with the architecture, made this the well-termed "miracle in
the desert."

Open for performances July–Aug. at 9 P.M.: *admission*

---

12   Outdoor Theater (1970)
Institute of American Indian Art
Cerrillos Road (US 85) at Teseuque Drive
Santa Fe, New Mexico

PAOLO SOLERI, ARCHITECT; PACHECO & GRAHAM, ASSOCIATES

Paolo Soleri, whom the sentient Ada Louise Huxtable calls a "prophet
in the desert," is America's most fascinating architect. Although less
than a handful of his designs have been built, his incredibly imaginative projects and his staggering draftsmanship (and models) have ex-
cited an entire generation. The Corcoran Gallery in Washington and
the Whitney Museum in New York (among others) circulated (1970)
a spellbinding show entitled "The Architectural Vision of Paolo
Soleri," much of which has also been published in his book *Arcology:
The City in the Image of Man* (MIT Press, 1969). This city, it might
be added, fashions the man-made as working hand in hand with nature, a fusion of ecological tenderness with habitat needs in what Soleri

calls "arcology." The resulting metropolis, or metropoles, some of which are underground, resemble fantastic beehives, "snorkled mega-structures" (Huxtable) of unbelievable complexity, yet with no occupant more than a fifteen-minute walk from the unspoiled Mother Earth around it. Fortunately a small prototype is now being built north of Phoenix. (See Arcosanti Buildings, near Dugas, Arizona.)

Of the buildings constructed by Soleri and his disciples, this theater is one of a precious few, but its realization and details—not by the designer—leave him unhappy. It creates, however, an intriguing series of forms with strange overtones of magic and the mythological. (Minoan Crete seems to lurk in the background.) Soleri excavated one area of the flat and unpromising "backyard" of the Institute, and using this earth to produce a berm, he sculpted the landscape in sympathetic echo of the mountain background while producing an extraordinarily flexible theater where anything can happen, and probably does. The stage can be entered from a variety of levels and approaches, which hint of the unexpected, yet the amphitheater serves equally well for outdoor commencement exercises. The long lateral approaches are primarily for traditional Indian ceremonies. Earth and concrete, the prime ingredients, have been manipulated and handled in a strange but curiously impressive fashion.

Open Mon.–Fri. 10–5: check in with administration office

13   Taos Pueblo (pre-16th century)
2.6 miles/4.2 kilometers N of Taos on Pueblo Road
Taos, New Mexico

Wheeler Peak, New Mexico's highest mountain (13,161 feet/4,011 meters), forms the backdrop, a small grove of cottonwood rustles nearby, and a mountain stream gurgles through: it is no wonder that this spot has been continuously settled for over a millennium. And, further, it is no wonder that its Tiwa-speaking Pueblo Indians, like the ancient Greeks siting their temples, have treated the land religiously, parts indeed being sacred (Blue Lake in the hills). Some seven hundred years ago at the beginning of the so-called Pueblo IV Period (c. 1275–1598), the ancestors of the present Indians, having long mastered basic agriculture, moved into the Taos region and commenced building their famous cellular communal houses of adobe, simple prototypes of which trace back to, perhaps, the eighth and ninth centuries. The "apartment" complexes we observe today are probably little changed from those seen and described (as "pueblos" or villages) by the first Spanish explorers under Coronado in 1540. Some experts,

John P. Harrington among them, feel that the very word Taos is "probably a Spanish variation of the native name Tua, meaning house, houses, or village" as quoted by Stanley A. Stubbs in his *Bird's-Eye View of the Pueblos* (University of Oklahoma Press, 1950). The present buildings were largely constructed and slightly relocated around 1700 following the Pueblo Rebellion of 1680–92 and the fire of 1694. Because of their extent and height (up to five stories) they are unique in the Western Hemisphere for adobe construction. (Abroad, one finds more daring in the pisé "skyscrapers" and fortified towns in the Hadramaut and in the Dadés Valley of Morocco, but in these arid spots rain is almost non-existent. In New Mexico, it—and snow—must be contended with seasonally. The word "adobe," incidentally, can be traced back to Egyptian hieroglyphics via Coptic, Arabic, and Spanish versions. This sun-dried brick construction was introduced to the Spaniards by the Moors: its origin extends to Neolithic times.)

The plan of the Taos Pueblo, officially San Gerónimo de Taos, is puzzling, a strangely open "square" with a stream dividing the town into North and South Houses. Each covers roughly the same area but the north unit (at left from the church) favors one- to five-story construction, while the other is primarily one to two stories. The irregular plaza in the center was for ceremonial and propitiatory (mostly for rain) dances. But whatever side of Taos Creek, which flows from Blue Lake, one lives on, egalitarianism of living quarters seems in order for its approximately one thousand inhabitants. There is shelter democracy here without hierarchical distinction even for the governor (annually elected) and the *cacique,* or high priest (a lifetime appointment). This shunning of domination, even passivity—characteristics which, we are told, still remain—at one time tempted incursions by nomadic Apaches, Comanches, and Utes, who lived largely on pillage. To protect themselves from raids the Taoseños erected a wall (mid-eighteenth century) around their pueblo, to which, in times of danger, the neighboring Spanish were invited. It was the only settlement so defended. The reservation land was "communally held," while the farm land and the dwellings could be individually or "clan" owned, but generally "under informal community control." The kivas at Taos are grouped in the northeast and southeast corners.

It is the extraordinary cellular living and storage units at Taos which most excite the visitor: the piling of cube on cube coalescing with the splendor of abstract geometry to produce a scale buildup that echoes the hills. Here is a unique measure of ancient American vernacular: "the greatest aboriginal communal dwelling in the United States" (Earle R. Forrest in his *Missions and Pueblos of the Old Southwest,*

Rio Grande Press, 1929, 1965). Moreover, the near-solidity of the adobe walls gains emphasis from the contrast with the tenuous wooden outrigging of the shelters in front and by the ladders used to reach the upper terraces. The open-sided frameworks are used for drying and to help protect the domical ovens where daily and ritual bread are baked. Most of the wall openings, that is the doors and "large" windows seen today, date from the last half of the nineteenth century, when depredations ceased and glass became available. Previously walls had been near-solid, except for smoke holes, and access was only by hatches in the roof in kiva fashion. The church (c. 1848—not distinguished) is one of several on the site, the first of which was destroyed in 1680. The ancient mission of San Gerónimo, 1706, stands in ruins in the northwest corner of the pueblo, shelled into oblivion by American troops in 1847.

Detailed inspection of the pueblo will reveal a certain unkemptness, particularly following rain or snow, and the whole is finer than the parts, but this whole is so strangely *encantada* (especially in the late afternoon) that the Taos Pueblo will mesmerize most observers. Fortunately, 48,000 acres/19,425 hectares of land, seized by the United States Government in 1906, was returned to the Taos Indians in 1970. Thus they are once more in possession of their sacred preserve —"our church and our school. It is filled with life given by God." Along with the earlier but ruined Pueblo Bonito (q.v.) and the largely ruined cliff dwellings at Mesa Verde (q.v.)—all tribally related— Architecture U.S.A. obviously began with Pueblo Indian culture.

With the attractions of late-twentieth-century accommodations, it will probably not be long before the pueblo itself will be kept strictly as a non-inhabited "museum."

Open May–Oct., daily 9–5, Nov.–Apr., daily 9–6: admission plus fee for photographing or sketching

North Dakota

Fort Totten 5

Riverdale 8

Blanchard 4

Medora 7

Mandan 6 ■ Bismarck 1-3

NORTH DAKOTA

The buildings in boldface type are of general interest. The others are for the specialist.

Bismarck 1 **North Dakota State Capitol** (1933–34)— Joseph Bell de Remer and W. F. Kurke; Holabird & Root

2 **Annunciation Priory** (1959–63)—Marcel Breuer

3 **Mary College** (1967–68)—Marcel Breuer

Blanchard 4 **KTHI Television Tower** (1963)—Kline Iron & Steel Company

Fort Totten 5 **Fort Totten** (1868–71)

Mandan 6 **Slant Indian Village** (c. 1650–1785/reconstructed 1938)

Medora 7 Château de Mores (1883)

Riverdale 8 **Garrison Dam** (1959)—U. S. Army Corps of Engineers and Charles T. Main, Inc.

1 North Dakota State Capitol (1933–34)
Capitol Park
Bismarck, North Dakota

**JOSEPH BELL DE REMER AND W. F. KURKE, ARCHITECTS;
HOLABIRD & ROOT, ASSOCIATES**

The North Dakota State Capitol ranks among the more daring and more successful buildings of its time in the United States. It is the outstanding governmental structure of the 1930s. As the official leaflet states, "The average visitor to North Dakota's state capitol is not immediately impressed with the exterior, for it is different. It is not what he expected, after viewing other state capitols. The building has a style of architecture entirely its own. No other capitol building in all the world approaches it in such considerations as simplicity, practicability and usability." The folder adds that the building cost $2 million at 46 cents per cubic foot, an extraordinarily low figure.

The early 1930s were a difficult time for architecture both philosophically and financially. The beginnings of "contemporary" architecture were being seen in the United States, generally expressed by

what we now call the Moderne or even Modernistic, the latter with its jazzed game of angles. It was a searching-out process with little background material to bolster the exploration. And the Depression of course ended almost all major construction. Thus when the architects evolved the design for the Bismarck Capitol, replacing one destroyed by fire in 1930, it was probable that a businesslike efficiency rather than glamour would result. The Capitol measures 389 x 173 feet/ 119 x 53 meters and is accented by an eighteen-story office tower. There is perhaps a profile influence from Goodhue's famous Nebraska Capitol (q.v.), but the influence—except in bravery for both—is slight. The low section at left contains legislative chambers, the Senate with 52 seats and the House with 116. These rooms are restrained but elegant, and are particularly noted for their fine wood paneling. A Memorial Hall 150 feet/46 meters long by 40 feet/12 meters high stretches across the entry. Steel-frame construction is used throughout with limestone facing. Strangely, there is no art in the building—no murals, mosaics, or sculpture. Although De Remer from Grand Forks and Kurke from Fargo are listed as the principal architects, it is likely that Holabird & Root had more than an "associates" role. The North Dakota Capitol is a key building of its period.

In 1980–81 a Judicial Wing and State Office Building were added to the Capitol. To judge from an official rendering, it is not of the caliber of the original building. Ritterbush Associates and Foss Engelstad Foss were associated architects and engineers.

Tours Mon.–Fri. on hour 8–11 A.M., *1–4* P.M., *also from*
Memorial Day–Labor Day on Sat. 9–4, Sun. 1–4

---

2 Annunciation Priory (1959–63)
c. 7 miles/11 kilometers S of downtown via 9th Street, past airport
   on ND 1804
Bismarck, North Dakota

MARCEL BREUER, ARCHITECT; HAMILTON P. SMITH, ASSOCIATE

The Annunciation Priory of the Sisters of St. Benedict, plus its nearby affiliate Mary College (q.v.), constitute one of the major and best architectural groups in the country concerned with Roman Catholic religion and education. Located near the top of a rolling site overlooking the Missouri River, the two establishments occupy opposite sides

of a hill, out of sight of each other but only a few minutes' walk away. They are powerful, assertive buildings, striding the landscape rather than emerging from it, but affiliated with their setting by their judicious incorporation of local stone.

The priory is marked by a beautifully three-dimensional, 100-foot/30-meter-high bell banner which recalls the one by the same architects at Collegeville, Minnesota (q.v.). It gives a needed vertical accent to the landscape and to the long, low building mass, and was designed to be seen from any angle. The basically symmetrical priory rises behind, its four main units set parallel to each other, forming a modified H-shape connected across top, middle, and bottom by passages. The long three-story residence wings (the vertical legs of the H) frame and enclose the compound on the two sides, that for the nuns (at west) containing 72 private rooms and a dormitory for 62 younger sisters, a similar one at east providing a dormitory plus classrooms for 118 girls. In between these wings stand the tall block of the chapel, the priory's spiritual and physical center, and another unit containing dining hall, services, and a small student chapel. The three courtyards between the four independent but attached buildings are paved to serve as sheltered, outdoor sitting areas. All four buildings are connected by a central transverse "hall" (the bar of the H-plan) wide enough to contain also lounges and offices, while across the front, and connecting

the ends of the two residence units, marches a covered walk whose V-supports produce considerable rhythm.

The public enters the chapel via a court between this "cloister" and the transverse hall mentioned. The chapel's interior is dominated by the strong geometry of its split hyperbolic white-painted concrete ceiling, while its side walls toward the front are of colored betonglass (thick chunks of glass set in mortar) and white-painted stone (at rear). Focus is given the chancel by a gold-leaf reredos and a double-curved canopy (of plywood) cantilevered from the wall behind the reredos. An unusual feature of the chancel is the enclosure at left for infirm sisters to attend mass yet remain out of sight. The front pews are placed at right angles to the axis of the chapel and are divided into facing halves to facilitate the responsive chanting by the sisters. The other pews are supplemented by seats in the balcony to accommodate a total of five hundred. The community and recreation room for the sisters, projecting from the northwest corner, is particularly satisfactory.

Keen recognition of an often severe climate can be seen in the sheltered courtyards, covered walkways, and deeply recessed windows. Details, especially the use of color, are first-rate throughout. Traynor & Hermanson were local associated architects.

Chapel open daily: tours available—telephone: (701) 255-1520

3   Mary College (1967–68)
**Apple Creek Road, c. 7 miles/11 kilometers S of downtown via
   9th Street, past airport, on ND 1804**
Bismarck, North Dakota

**MARCEL BREUER, ARCHITECT; HAMILTON P. SMITH AND
TICIAN PAPACHRISTOU, ASSOCIATES**

Mary College, a growing coeducational institution, which moved to its
present quarters in 1968, is related to and controlled by the Annunciation Priory (q.v.) but forms a separate entity. Founded (1955) as a
junior college, it is now a fully accredited, four-year institution. Its
dormitories accommodate at present 207, but there are approximately
300 day students in addition, all enjoying a high faculty-student ratio.
Some third of the student body is non-Catholic. The buildings are interconnected—much like the priory—to form a cluster on the hillside.
The dominant unit is the three-story administration-classroom-labora-
tory building whose four exterior walls are shielded by vertical concrete louvers. An L-shaped, two-story residential block at one end,

roughly matched at the other by the student center, cafeteria, lecture halls, and library, make an open U about the taller main structure. All of the lower units are enclosed by precast concrete wall panels with splayed openings and ends, a Breuer trademark and one often copied but rarely with the scale and finesse shown here. Many of the windows in these frames are opaque; behind every third stands a column. The public rooms and lounges enjoy spacious views over the Missouri River Valley.

Grounds open during school year

---

4 KTHI Television Tower (1963)
11.5 miles/18 kilometers S of Mayville on ND 18, just SW of Blanchard, North Dakota

KLINE IRON & STEEL COMPANY, ENGINEERS AND ERECTORS

Any structure that is nearly as tall as the combined height of the Empire State Building (1,250 feet/381 meters without TV mast) *and* the Eiffel Tower (984 feet/300 meters) is of architectural-engineering significance in that it pioneers a technology that can lead to advanced shelter. (Roebling's bridges, for instance, opened new space-conquering dimensions by utilizing wrapped steel cables; Saarinen's Dulles Airport [Virginia—q.v.] with its cable-supported roof was a lineal descendant.) The 2,063-foot/629-meter-high tower shown here, stayed with 40,125 feet/12,230 meters of guy wires, has to withstand height, wind, and torsional forces in addition to extreme climatic onslaughts. (Its top sways 10 feet/3 meters in a 70 mph/113 kph wind.) Located about 25 miles/40 kilometers NNW of Fargo on the wheat and flax fields of North Dakota, the tower represents a daring step forward in our engineering and eventually our architectural capabilities. Almost unbelievably, it was put up in thirty-three working days. Furman Anderson was the design engineer.

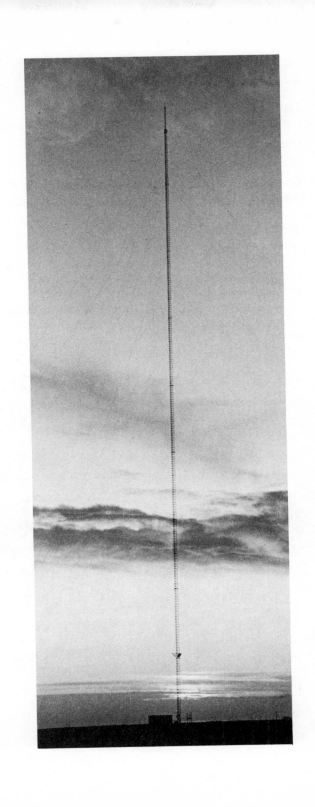

5   **Fort Totten** (1868–71)
    off ND 57, c. 12 miles/19 kilometers SW of town of Devils Lake
    Fort Totten, North Dakota

"The best preserved military post of the Indian war period in the trans-Mississippi West" proclaims the brochure on Fort Totten, and rightly so, for all nineteen of its buildings are original. Much of this structural integrity stems from the fact that, unlike most Western outposts following Indian "pacification," this was turned over to the Bureau of Indian Affairs in 1890 for use as a boarding school. Fort Totten—created to protect communications between Minnesota and Montana—was initially (1867) constructed of logs, but the following year it was moved 800 yards/731 meters to the south and all buildings were built in brick made of local clay. In the usual military fashion, the quarters, mess hall, hospital, commissary, etc., frame an open pa-

rade ground. The buildings of chief architectural interest are those along Officers' Row on the west side of Cavalry Square. Though there are no gems, reasonable touches of the Greek Revival appear in some porches with a bit of Victoriana in others. The State Historical Society took charge of the fort in 1960. A museum gives enlightening background. The fort originally stood on the edge of Devils Lake (to the Indians "Spirit Lake")—named because its mineral content makes it unpotable—but the water has receded.

Open May–Oct., daily 8–6

---

6   Slant Indian Village (c. 1650–1785/reconstructed 1938)
Fort Lincoln State Park (near museum)
Custer Memorial Road 4.5 miles/7 kilometers S of
Mandan, North Dakota

All of the settlements of the sedentary Plains Indians now exist only as archeological sites, their full images preserved in the sketches and paintings of artists·like George Catlin, Charles M. Russell, and the Swiss Karl Bodmer. Catlin's magnificent "Bull Dance" (in the National Collection of Fine Arts in Washington) shows the ingenious circular domed dwellings, which Catlin likened to enormous inverted kettles, of the Mandan Indians, who gave their name to the nearby city. (Incidentally Frederick Remington's famous paintings were almost all of nomadic Indians such as the Sioux.) The Mandans lived in fortified villages, located on the first high terrace above the Missouri River, and spent their time in raising crops and hunting. Such terraces were 40–60 feet/12–18 meters above the flood plain, with bluffs rising as much as 200 feet/61 meters behind. They moved to the river bottoms for the winter season. The reconstruction of five Mandan earth lodges at Fort Lincoln Park, four residential and one ceremonial, was carried out (1938) by the Civilian Conservation Corps under the supervision of the State Historical Society of North Dakota. These earth lodges, however, were not raised on actual excavated sites.

The stalwart inner framework of these shelters consists of four trimmed tree trunks some 8–10 feet/2.4–3 meters high stepped in holes in a square formation and braced at top by horizontal tree beams to form in effect an open cube. The outer and lower peripheral frame, roughly 6 feet/1.8 meters high and more or less circular in plan, describes the circumference of the lodge with medium-size rafters slanting from this edge to rest on top of the inner structural "cube."

The diameter for a residential lodge ranged from 20–60 feet/6–18 meters, while the ceremonial lodge reconstructed here is 84 feet/26 meters in diameter. On top of the angled roof rafters were laid willow branches which were then packed with sod or earth, creating an almost domical effect. The roofs are sufficiently strong to support groups of people. The low exterior walls of the Mandan lodges in their depictions by Catlin (1796–1872) and Bodmer (1809–93) were generally vertical but in the reconstruction here these man-high walls take on a slant only a bit less pronounced than that of the rafters, the whole earth lodge giving the effect more of a mound than an "inverted kettle." (Catlin's depictions are not reliable for Slant Village, as he arrived forty-five years after it had been abandoned.) A vestibule, closable with hides, gave entrance—somewhat like an Eskimo igloo—with a squarish hole at the top of the main room to permit smoke to escape and light to enter. The central section was excavated to increase height and form a fire basin. The settlement at Fort Lincoln State Park was abandoned about 1781–85 as the direct result of a smallpox epidemic which decimated the Mandans. Originally there were sixty-eight earth lodges on the site with a palisade of sharpened logs surrounding the village.

Because of the deterioration of the original reconstruction, the State Parks and Recreation Service is now undertaking another rebuilding of Slant Village. The date of completion of this is not yet known.

Open June–Aug., daily 9–9; May, Sept.–Oct., 9–5: admission

7   **Château de Mores** (1883)
    1 mile/1.6 kilometers W of town, off US 10 and IS 94
    Medora, North Dakota

Though no more than a wood-frame summer house and built as such, this "château" of twenty-six rooms gives some insight into the modest regional architecture of its time. Put up by a French marquis so that for part of the year he could supervise his nearby packing plant (whose operation failed four years later, and burned in 1907), the house has survived largely as constructed. Used for a while as a hotel (1929–35), it remained in the family until given to the state (1936) by the marquis' son. Most of the furnishings are original and are, indeed, far more impressive than the simple residence itself. The town of Medora—named for the marquis' wife—has several restored buildings worth investigating.

Tours daily 8–5, except in bad weather: admission

8   Garrison Dam (1959)
ND 200, W off US 83 at Gateway
Riverdale, North Dakota

**U. S. ARMY CORPS OF ENGINEERS AND CHARLES T. MAIN, INC.,
ENGINEERS**

Like the stupendous TVA undertaking (q.v.), this dam has transformed an entire region by controlling and utilizing waters for irrigation, power, and recreation. Previously, and often devastatingly, the river had run unused out of the state. However, the Garrison Dam is not the relatively short, often steep type characteristic of much of TVA's work, but what is known as a rolled-earth fill dam. Moreover it is one of the longest in the world, measuring 11,300 feet/3,444 meters at crest, over a half mile/.8 kilometer thick at base, with a maximum height of 210 feet/64 meters. The flattish topography and the

modest gradient of the Missouri River made a long, earth-filled dam by far the most economical form. Near the left bank stands the concrete powerhouse. The spillway over which one can drive, ND 200, is located on the right bank. Whereas the spillway has an interesting and unusual "double-decking" on the downstream side, the intake structure and powerhouse do not attain the architectural-engineering design level seen at TVA. But the whole enterprise is so far-reaching—and the earth dam itself so well landscaped (it literally disappears in the countryside)—that it well merits a look. Power production is 430,000 kilowatts.

Lake Oahe, which the dam created, is almost 200 miles/322 kilometers long with a 1,600-mile/2,575-kilometer shoreline. On its shore near Mobridge is a statue of Sakajawea, the Indian woman interpreter who guided Lewis and Clark in this region in 1805.

Powerhouse open daily 9–6, free guided tours June–Aug.

Oklahoma

Bartlesville 2–3 •

Sand Springs 10
Guthrie 5   • • Tulsa 12–14

Oklahoma City 6–9   Fort Gibson 4

Anadarko 1 •   Shawnee 11

OKLAHOMA

The buildings in boldface type are of general interest. The others are for the specialist.

Anadarko   1 **Indian City U.S.A.** (Reconstruction)

Bartlesville   2 **H. C. Price Tower** (1954–55)—Frank Lloyd Wright
                          3 Phillips Petroleum Building (1963–64)— Welton Becket Associates

Fort Gibson   4 Old Fort Gibson (1824–57/1866–89/ 1935–36)

Guthrie   5 Guthrie Historic District (1889–1907)

Oklahoma City   6 Hopewell Baptist Church (1953)— Bruce Goff
                          7 **St. Patrick's Church** (1962)—Murray Jones Murray
                          8 **Oklahoma Theater Center** (1969–70)— John M. Johansen
                          9 **McGee Tower** (1973) **and The Robert S. Kerr Park** (1975)—Frankfurt-Short-Emery-McKinley
                             Metro Concourse System (1974) Sorey, Hill & Binnicker

Sand Springs   10 Hissom Memorial Center (1962–63)— Murray Jones Murray

Shawnee   11 Santa Fe Railroad Station (1903)

Tulsa   12 **Boston Avenue United Methodist Church** (1927–29)—Rush, Endacott & Rush
                         13 Cities Service Building (1969–71)— Stevens & Wilkinson
                             Center Plaza Apartments (1970)—Murray Jones Murray
                         14 **Central Tulsa Pedestrian System** (1976–78)—Hudgins, Thompson, Ball & Associates

1 Indian City U.S.A. (Reconstruction)
off OK 8, 2.3 miles/3.7 kilometers S of
Anadarko, Oklahoma

The Indians of North America, whose ancestors for some fifteen thousand or more years poured across the Bering Strait until the breakup of this land passage (12,000 B.C.?)—and who also possibly arrived via southern seas—developed an ingenious variety of shelters. These range from all-stone, permanent settlements (see Pueblo Bonito, New Mexico), to the standardized, prefabricated, portable, bark- or hide-covered (later canvas-covered) tepee. The wigwam, incidentally, has been at times confused with the tepee, but the former was not readily demountable, as its poles were driven deep into the ground, and it was often covered by an intricate arrangement of bark, or reed thatch, but rarely hides. Moreover the wigwam characteristically took on a

domed or vaulted shape, with two parallel lines of poles bent over, tied in the middle, and then covered. Some were large enough for communal needs.

Oklahoma was called Indian Territory from 1834 to 1907, when it received statehood, and until this latter date its five gratuitously termed "Civilized Tribes" each maintained its separate government and proper diplomatic relations with the U.S.A. Oklahoma today has the largest number of Indians of any state.

Reconstructed here at Anadarko under the direction of the University of Oklahoma Anthropology Department and with the expert help of the Indians themselves stands a cross section of dwelling types traditionally built by the Plains Indians. They represent the Apache, Caddo, Kiowa, Navaho, Pawnee, and Wichita tribes. Their variety underscores the different life-styles prevalent even in one general locale, some being shelter for migratory tribes who used tepees (Kiowas, etc.) and the wickiup (a brush- or bark-covered frame favored by the always restless Apache), others for sedentary tribes such as the Caddoes,

who constructed stockadelike permanent homes of vertical logs chinked with clay and grass, much as the early French did along the Mississippi. Some of the most interesting examples at Anadarko are the swamp-grass houses of the Wichitas. All are ingenious "architectural" solutions, created with the simplest of "found" materials, and altogether they form an illuminating chapter in our earliest shelter history.

Open May–Aug., daily 9–6, Sept.–Apr., daily 9–5, except major holidays: admission

A **Southern Plains Indian Museum and Crafts Center** lies just east of Anadarko on US 62. (Open June–Sept., daily 9–5; Oct.–May, Tues.–Sun. 9–5, except major holidays.)

---

2   **H. C. Price Tower** (1954–55)
East 6th Street at South Dewey Avenue
Bartlesville, Oklahoma

FRANK LLOYD WRIGHT, ARCHITECT

The late Mr. Wright's dream of a mile-high skyscraper (5,280 feet/1,609 meters) for Chicago never, alas, got further than his inimitable drawings; nor did the 1929 plan for the twenty-story St. Mark's Tower, a prototype for Price, which he proposed for New York. However, in 1955 he finished his first and, unfortunately, his last skyscraper, a nineteen-story combined office and apartment block which invigorates the undulating prairies of northeast Oklahoma in no small fashion. It is an enigmatic work by a gyrating genius, a building not easily understood or readily forgotten. Among other attributes, it stands as a manifesto against the smooth-skin, curtain-clad high-rise— a not unpopular trend today. And in spite of the Price's complicated appearance, its plan basically forms a square broken on each side by angled projections.
    The structure of the building, which can be partially grasped on the ground floor, consists of a spine, a "tap-root foundation," of four vertical "fins" of concrete set in a squared four-vaned windmill formation but not touching at the center, thus leaving core spaces for the lobbies. These 18-foot/5.5-meter-long "arms," each with one elevator "attached," are rotated at 60° to the outer skin of the building and are contained within this skin. From each pair of their right-angled

arms the floors are boldly cantilevered, eliminating completely the need for exterior columns. The facade treatment was therefore liberated from the typical grid of steel or concrete imposed on almost all tall buildings. The rotating of an X-shaped structural core within a square exterior, then the cantilevering of hollow floor slabs from the arms, is technologically ingenious (and expensive), and Wright made the most of his non-moduled facades. (Rotated-plan buildings are today favorably regarded by several prominent architects.)

The Price Tower provides for three offices and one duplex apartment per floor (a number of the originally eight apartments have been changed to offices). As mentioned, the arms (fins) of the structural core do not project beyond the building's face; however, the cantilevered floor slabs do, that of the living rooms in the southwest corner of the tower forming the largest of the five angled protrusions from the building's square shape. The apartments (some with fireplaces) are immediately identifiable by their double-height vertical louvers, which give a feeling of freedom within and provide sun-protection in the afternoon. The projection of the apartments' kitchens abuts that of the living quadrant, with fire stair on the "windmill diagonal" on the opposite side of the building. The two other projections are minor, and contain, on either side, lavatories for the offices, which offices are marked by copper louvers placed horizontally against sun and sky glare. The glass is gold-tinted (among the first so treated), and the masonry tan, so there are, along with the 20-inch/51-centimeter-wide copper finning and sculpted spandrels, chromatic touches. The overall exterior nourishes a whirlwind of activity considering that it spans only some 45 feet/14 meters per side, with hyperactivity (and some indelicacy of detail) at the top, which also sports roof terraces. Some find this architectural nervousness fascinating, by day as well as night, others consider it excessive. Many, however, regard the Price Building as both a structural and an esthetic triumph. In any case it is the only skyscraper—non-skeletal at that—by our greatest native-born architect and the more one analyzes its rationale, the more one understands Wright's "romantic" rejection of what he termed the "fascist derived" typical skyscraper.

Lobby open during business hours

---

3 **Phillips Petroleum Building** (1963–64)
West 5th and South Keeler Streets
Bartlesville, Oklahoma

WELTON BECKET ASSOCIATES, ARCHITECTS

A nineteen-story, bran-colored, and textured office block which sets high marks for precast concrete panel construction for tall buildings. All of its 1,800 frames were not only precast (and meticulously so), they were, except at the solid corners, also preglazed with amber-colored solar glass. With this technique of fully finished wall components, a floor could be enclosed every three days. The standard window "frames" are 4.7 feet/1.4 meters wide by 13 feet/4 meters high, each weighing 4,000 pounds/1,814 kilograms. Those on second and top floors are taller and heavier. All were craned into place then bolted and welded to the structural frame. The ground floor of the building is inset to give visual lightness and to provide a covered passage, with an extra-width inset on one side for protected automobile loading. Highly advanced technically, it is also a handsome office building.

Lobby open during business hours

4   Old Fort Gibson (1824–57/1866–89/1935–36)
c. .6 mile/.9 kilometer N of town
Fort Gibson, Oklahoma

Gibson was the earliest fort in the Territory, and when founded was the farthest west in the nation. It served as a frontier post for the tribes, many of which had been transplanted from the East, that then made up Indian Territory. During the period of "Indian Removal" (1825–40) the fort also protected the bewildered newcomers from the resentful Plains Indians who, of course, were native to the area. The 55-acre/22-hectare site is dominated by the fort itself, which forms a palisaded square with three sides framed by one-story arcaded buildings and the fourth closed by two two-story buildings, that to east of the entrance having served as officers' quarters. All of these structures were of logs. The parade ground was in the center. The fort was abandoned (1857) just before the Civil War but was reactivated 1866–89, and it was in this latter period that the nearby stone buildings were constructed. (These are now largely in ruins.) In 1890 Fort Gibson was permanently decommissioned. During the Depression, the state of Oklahoma and the War Department reconstructed the original log fort and its palisade, and it is this restoration that we see today. It forms an illustrative chapter in the development of the Territory and state and is listed in the National Register of Historic Places.

Open Apr.–Oct., Mon.–Sat. 9–7, Sun. 1–7; Nov.–Mar., Mon.–Sat. 9–5, Sun. 1–5, closed Dec. 25

---

5   Guthrie Historic District (1889–1907)
14th Street, College Avenue, Pine Street, Lincoln Avenue
Guthrie, Oklahoma

Guthrie, "the birthplace of Oklahoma," was first territorial capital (1890–1907), then state capital (1907–10) until the government was removed to Oklahoma City some 30 miles/48 kilometers to the south. The city—like several in the former Indian Territory—was created literally overnight. On April 22, 1889, the townsite consisted of several tents and two wood-frame buildings, the depot, and the U. S. Land Office. By nightfall of the next day Guthrie was a tent city with an estimated twelve to fifteen thousand inhabitants. Within the year the territorial government was organized, speculative building flourished, and the first brick and stone commercial structures were completed. When its political importance dried up, Guthrie was quietly forgotten, and though it did lose some citizens, it has remained almost unchanged to this day. Thus, uniquely, it gives us an insight into a relatively

unspoiled Midwestern town at the turn of the century. About four out
of five houses and stores have survived and "The entire city within its
1907 limits (7 blocks) has been placed in the National Register of
Historic Places as the only intact territorial and state capital remaining
in America" (*Historic Preservation,* October–December 1975). A
Guthrie Preservation Trust has been established to rehabilitate its commercial buildings, for although the two upper stories are almost unde-
faced, the ground floors have often been "modernized." A Belgian-
educated architect named Joseph A. Foucart designed a number of
Guthrie's fancifully bracketed and corniced "Victorian" structures.
Many of the office blocks and stores are helpfully dated and identified.
In 1974 the Logan County Historical Society was organized to further
promote local preservation. For more information the Society can be
contacted directly in Guthrie; telephone: (405) 282-3706.

Best seen from street

6 Hopewell Baptist Church (1953)
8 miles/13 kilometers W of US 77 (Broadway Expressway) via 3rd Street West in Edmond, which is a northern suburb of Oklahoma City
Oklahoma City (Edmond), Oklahoma

BRUCE GOFF, ARCHITECT

The admirers of Bruce Goff have rightly lamented that his architecture is so extremely personal that his commissions are mainly limited to private houses of sympathetic friends. This small church (three hundred seats) is one of only several non-residential buildings available to the public. (See also the Boston Avenue Methodist Church in Tulsa.) The Baptist Church here seeks an architectural symbolism to tie the religious activities of its parishioners to their working life—one largely connected with oil wells—a successful enosis, but one no easier in architecture than in daily living. In addition there was probably in the back of the architect's mind the indigenous tepee form that once dominated this landscape.

Bruce Goff is adept at utilizing inexpensive, often surplus material, and here he employed reconditioned 2.5- and 4-inch/6.4- and 10-centimeter pipes used in the oil industry for the supporting trusses of his twelve-sided church (note their refinement), with simple corrugated aluminum for the sides. The pastor then corralled the pipe fitters and riggers from his flock and put the whole piece together for an unbelievable twenty thousand dollars. Windowless against the road noises outside, the interior basks in light from a clerestory at peak. In addition to the intimate nave, there are an assembly room plus meeting rooms in the half-basement. Some fussiness can be seen around the sanctuary, and a few awkward junctures occur on the exterior (and more upkeep is needed), but this is a *multum in parvo* achievement by a too-little-understood architect.

Often open in addition to Sun. services

---

7   **St. Patrick's Church** (1962)
2021 North Portland Avenue
Oklahoma City, Oklahoma

MURRAY JONES MURRAY, ARCHITECTS; FELIX CANDELA, STRUCTURAL ENGINEER

Inspired by a bold and unusual basic concept, St. Patrick's is one of the few churches of our time with an idea, and it is an admirable one. The concept first involved creating a religious "palisade" with 30-foot/9.1-meter-high exterior walls of concrete, panels (those on the two sides separated by narrow redwood louvers) completely surrounding the church and shutting out the distractions of its mid-urban neighborhood. A glass-walled church was then placed within this temenos, with a 29-foot/8.8-meter-wide ambulatory—sheltered by roof overhang —encircling the nave. The inner face of the high peripheral wall is decorated by a continuous band of fifty-two near-identical angels, arms somewhat rigidly upraised as they encircle the church. The street face displays a geometric pattern. These precast elements were designed by Frank Kacmarcik. The ambulatory—between palisade wall and church —serves as introduction to the sanctuary, as a "cloister" and place of peace, and as a substantial overflow for the congregation in temperate weather. (The glass sides of the nave are partially openable while the public-address system serves both inside and out.)

The entrance to the nave, which seats five hundred, is, appropriately, via the baptistry, a veritable room in itself (even to having its own foundations), a block which faces one somewhat abruptly on passing through the door of the outer palisade. Symbolically this black box form underscores "our separation from the Church until we are baptized," and through baptism we reach the light of the Church. The appropriateness of this symbolism is matched by the uplift which one encounters on stepping into the nave: the effect is electric. Daylight floods in from the peripheral open space between roof overhang and the outer compound wall (the two do not touch), and the resulting play of light is most satisfactory. Artificial light comes from behind the glazed bands separating the edges of the rectangular concrete umbrellas which form the structure of the church roof. A freestanding dossal screen of gold-leafed cinder blocks, designed by Josef Albers, marks the sanctuary. There is, perhaps, not enough visual peace at this important end of the church, with angels (on outer ambulatory wall), a dossal within, and stick "ciborium" above being somewhat in competition. Moreover on the exterior there is a touch of rigidity. These details, however, fade in the joy of the nave—Huxley's "stone-roofed greenhouse"—and in the private, walled retreat that nave and its in-spired ambulatory produce. Much of the construction of the church was done—as in medieval France—by men, women, and children of the parish. Felix Candela, the brilliant Spanish-Mexican structural en-gineer, designed the ten hyperbolic paraboloid "umbrellas" of the roof.

Open daily 9:15–5

8   Oklahoma Theater Center (1969–70)
400 West Sheridan, between Hudson and Walker Avenues
Oklahoma City, Oklahoma

JOHN M. JOHANSEN, ARCHITECT

Let it be said immediately that this former Mummers Theater (now an adjunct of Oklahoma City University) is one of the most exciting build-ings in the country. It is not, nor was it intended to be, "a thing of beauty," and it might well puzzle more than it endears. Bogglingly different on the exterior—"without formal intent"—its logic and its peculiar delight grow upon one. As the architect, somewhat esoteri-cally, put it, in likening its design process to the field of electronics, there are "three 'components' with 'subcomponents' attached, plugged into one 'chassis' or 'gate,' and then connected by four 'circuiting systems,' superimposed at separate levels to avoid cross-circuiting . . . And these components are connected by interlaced circuiting systems—ramps, stairs, bridges, and ductwork. It matters little, once the organ-izing idea is determined, what the actual number, or forms, of these elements may be" (*Architectural Forum,* May 1968). He thus takes the thrust-stage theater, the arena theater, and the administrative block with children's theater and rehearsal space on top, and gives each component its freedom and ability to assume its optimum shape, lacing them all together by mutually needed services. Moreover most buildings in these days of our pampered ethos devote some 40 per cent of their space and expense to circulation and to the mechanical (air conditioning, electricity, elevators, etc.). Johansen, instead of "absorb-ing" these "non-productive" elements within the fabric of the structure to produce a pristine cover-up, has dramatically "flung" the mechanical and circulatory functions into and onto the spaces atop each of the three units, producing perhaps an "anti-building," but one logically generated and enormously stimulating to use. Color (only on the steel) adds no little to this milieu. Blue is used for the three "gang-

planks" from the street, red for the outside stairs and "people tubes," ocher for the lobby projections around each unit, white for the cooling towers and air-conditioning machinery (where detached placement minimizes motor noises), black for the corrugated supply ducts from them, and natural concrete for all structures. A Léger-like impression results.

The 592-seat main theater is circular in plan with a thrust stage that pokes its angles into the audience. It seemingly disappears *under* it, for the seats which surround the acting arena are gigantic balconies in form, cantilevered lightly over the stage, hovering in space with actors appearing and disappearing in any of a dozen vomitoria. A certain "bear pit" relationship between actors and audience might be noted, but the place is alive with action. The intimate 240-seat arena theater, ovoid in plan, simply has four rectangular ranks of seats which frame and rise from stage level, entrances for all being at the open corners. Tickets and administration occupy the street level of the smallest unit, with a children's theater and combined rehearsal hall above. The central space between the three buildings doubles as a fair-weather intermission piazzetta. There is even a pool (of dubious need) underneath. Interior finish throughout is at times minimal, but so was the cost. Altogether a fantastic complex. As the Honors Jury of the American Institute of Architects wrote, "it is an extraordinarily fresh and provocative work of architecture—rational, but wonderfully witty; mechanistic but joyfully humane" (*AIA Journal,* May 1972). Charles A. Ahlstrom was associate in charge; David Hays was stage designer; Seminoff-Bowman-Bode were the supervising architects. Only the main theater and the arena are now open.

Open during performances

---

9   McGee Tower (1973) **and The Robert S. Kerr Park** (1975)
123 R. S. Kerr Avenue
Oklahoma City, Oklahoma

FRANKFURT-SHORT-EMERY-McKINLEY, ARCHITECTS; PIETRO BELLUSCHI, CONSULTANT

Two features distinguish the McGee Tower in the Kerr-McGee Center: its relation to the street and its fenestration. As regards the former, it is well set back from the property line so that a "garden" entry, complete with trees, plants, and fountain, welcomes the user—a gracious introduction to a skyscraper. And because this space is "given" to the sidewalk, the thirty-story slab of offices could rise without setback. (Unfortunately the low buildings on either side of the forecourt—one vertically determined, the other horizontally—do not compliment the entry.) The fenestration, above the airy two-story ground level, employs multiples of a one-pane module, with a single-pane opening or bay for the lower seven floors, two-pane windows for the next nine floors, and three-pane bays for the top ten. Utility floors separate the three divisions. Though there is arbitrariness in this window arrangement, the design is carried through with style. It will be recalled that H. H. Richardson, among others, frequently doubled the mullion module as the building rose—the reverse of McGee.

Open during business hours

The Robert S. Kerr Park lies across Kerr Avenue from the Kerr-McGee Center. Measuring 260 x 100 feet/79 x 30 meters, it utilizes an 8-foot/2.4-meter dropoff in grade to create a three-hundred-seat amphitheater. This steps down the slope to a moat with free-running waters and a 40-foot/12-meter circular stage which often is active with entertainment in seasonal weather. A small waterfall and pool occupy the northeast corner, and one can stroll under the falls. Granite is the main material, with magnolias and honey locusts the chief trees. John Bozalis was overall park architect; Warren Edwards, landscape architect.

Much of downtown Oklahoma City is linked by an extensive series of underground pedestrian "avenues," the **Metro Concourse System** (1974), which has proved to be remarkably successful. Commissioned by nine private local business firms, and totally paid for by them, it is a much-used urban asset (over ten thousand people daily), lacing the central business district together in cheerful, weatherproof fashion. It is both heated in winter and air-conditioned in summer. There are plans for its extension, so effective has it been. (Compare the similar system in Dallas.) Sorey, Hill & Binnicker were the architects and engineers, with Grossman & Keith consulting engineers.

10   **Hissom Memorial Center** (1962–63)
      N off OK 51, 3 miles/4.8 kilometers W of Sand Springs (c. 10.5
          miles/17 kilometers W of Tulsa)
      Sand Springs, Oklahoma

MURRAY JONES MURRAY, ARCHITECTS

Goethe wrote that the measure of a nation's civilization can be seen in
its treatment of prisoners. The same, alas, can be said of its care of
those who cannot care for themselves. In both penology and the field
of mental health, all fifty states have made such dismal records of non-
achievement that most of Europe wonders if the United States is not in
this regard a medieval backwater. This memorial center for the men-
tally retarded child stands out in contrast, its friendly campus of sixteen one-story "cottages" accommodating seven hundred children from
six to eighteen years of age. Active therapy being essential, there is a

fully accredited school, a vocational training center, arts and crafts building, and hospital. Approximately one third of the children "graduate" back to their communities. The others, when reaching eighteen, are transferred to adult facilities. There are a few architectural exaggerations (roof of cafeteria), and circulation in the administration building gets confused at times, but in the main the architecture, like the philosophy behind it, is very fine. McCune & McCune were associate architects.

Visiting hours 1–4 daily

---

11 **Santa Fe Railroad Station** (1903)
Main Street and Minnesota Avenue
Shawnee, Oklahoma

The dedicated dowser in the Richardsonian ripples that traveled westward will relish this step-gabled, bravely turreted, red sandstone castle. Note the half-round, arcaded entrance end with its small, freestanding "gables," their steps recalling the major ones on track side. The navelike waiting room should also be seen. The depot is listed in the National Register of Historic Places as a "Rare surviving SW example."

Open Mon.–Fri. 8–5

12 Boston Avenue United Methodist Church (1927–29)
    South Boston Avenue at 13th Street
    Tulsa, Oklahoma

RUSH, ENDACOTT & RUSH, ARCHITECTS

One of the country's most daring churches when it was opened over fifty years ago, the Boston Avenue Church continues to command respect. With a faint architectural reference to Gothic aspirations and a touch of Art Deco, there is sturdy architectural forcefulness in proclaiming faith, while its 255-foot/78-meter tower, topped with copper and glass, creates a dramatic urban focus. The three large figures over the north entrance represent Susanna, John, and Charles Wesley. (Susanna was the mother of the two brothers and a strong influence on their lives.) John Wesley (1703–91) in 1784 founded the Methodist Church (though he had initially sought to stay within the Church of England). Above the south entrance is carved a circuit-riders' group. A series of abstracted praying hands crown the tower and educational wing as they "point to the receptivity of divine grace." Robert Garrison was the sculptor.

The plan of the building consists of a semicircular auditorium symmetrically attached to a rectangular four-story educational-social-office block. The worship room, which seats 889 on the main floor and 461 in the balcony, carries out with commendable consistency the motifs of the exterior. Its semicircular raking pews focus on the pulpit "which signifies the centrality of the preaching of the Word," with a vaguely gothicized but effective rood screen and a symbolic mosaic behind. The educational wing with nursery and preschool facilities was completed in 1965. It was designed by M. Murray McCune of McCune McCune & Associates.

The design of the church has been credited in many publications solely to Bruce Goff, then a twenty-two-year-old member of the firm. However, a personal letter from the church (September 1979), in referring to early documents, states "that Miss Adah Robinson, artist and art teacher, was asked by the Building Committee to present designs for a Church which would express definitive modern Christianity in mid-America . . . that Rush Endacott and Rush was contracted on Miss Robinson's recommendation because Bruce Goff, a former student, worked as draftsman for the firm. She thought he could best translate her drawings into architectural terms." Miss Robinson is mentioned in the architectural contract of June 1926, as being responsible for "all artistic features interior finish exterior design." The church also adds that "Apparently Mr. Goff became a partner in the firm in 1929 or 1930 when the name was changed to Rush Endacott and Goff." In any case, the Boston Avenue Church is a landmark of its kind. In 1978 it was listed in the National Register of Historic Places.

Open daily 9–5, except holidays

---

13   Cities Service Building (1969–71)
110 West 7th Street
Tulsa, Oklahoma

STEVENS & WILKINSON, ARCHITECTS

A quietly positive, twenty-eight-story skyscraper that does much for Tulsa. The building is set back on its 300-foot/91-meter block-square site, with pools and breathing space on two sides and a garage for 587 cars (less satisfactory) to the east. It forms the first phase of a down-

town plaza. Overall relation to the street—a facet of design often not properly attended to—is excellent, aided by the ground- and second-floor setbacks which provide a sheltered arcade around the entire building. The computer-designed construction is unusual in that a Vierendeel truss of post-tensioned concrete was used to provide wind resistance in a rigid frame and so minimize internal bracing. The interior space is columnless, with a 35-foot/11-meter span from service core to exterior walls, all based on a 5-foot/1.5-meter module. Gray solar glass was used in the near-square, inset windows. Occupied 94 per cent by Cities Service, the building stands as a distinguished company headquarters. William H. Barnett was principal-in-charge; James F. Kortan, project designer; Black, West, and Wozencraft of Tulsa, associate architects.

Open during business hours

Almost next door at 100–200 7th Street (and visible in the background of the photograph above) rise the two parallel but offset twenty-story apartment houses of **Center Plaza** by Murray Jones Murray (1970). (They can only be seen from street.) Offering 379 apartment units, each with a balcony, and 17 town houses all located within a block of the new Civic Center (which has good planning but not sufficiently coordinated architecture), they provide superior, well-landscaped quarters for back-to-the-city living. There are plans to erect six more towers.

---

14   Central Tulsa Pedestrian System (1976–78)
Main Street and 5th Street
Tulsa, Oklahoma

**HUDGINS, THOMPSON, BALL & ASSOCIATES,
ARCHITECTS-PLANNERS**

Downtown Tulsa has undertaken an extensive series of street-level pedestrian malls. These stretch for seven blocks, cheering the active
while furnishing the weary with well-designed shelters, benches, kiosks,
and planting. Trees and grass grow on Main Street. Appropriately the
system was conceived, planned, and financed by privately raised funds
from the property owners, retailers, and businessmen who front on or
overlook the mall. (Some private moneys were also contributed for
earlier feasibility studies.) Main Street's three blocks of the system are
closed to all traffic except emergency vehicles, while limited (mostly
cul-de-sac) access is provided for automobiles on parts of 5th Street.
A 1,027-car garage is located at 4th and Main streets. The intersections of the two right-angle pedestrian ways is marked by a fountain
and small park. Brick (replacing concrete) has been used throughout
for paving, lending good texture, identification, and handsome looks.
Tul-Center Inc. reports that acceptance and approval of the Pedestrian
System has been "overwhelming and has exceeded all expectations."
There are plans for its extension: let us hope that it will connect with
the city's new River Parks. HTB Inc. were also the landscape architects in addition to being architects-planners for the project.

Always open

Oregon

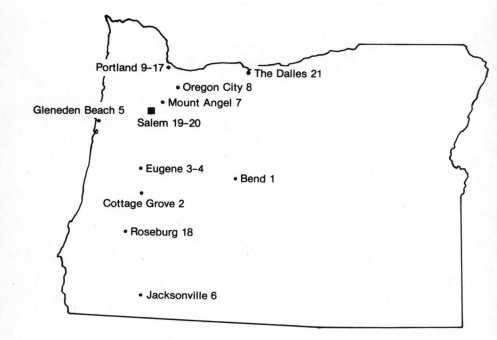

Portland 9–17
The Dalles 21
Oregon City 8
Mount Angel 7
Gleneden Beach 5
Salem 19–20
Eugene 3–4
Bend 1
Cottage Grove 2
Roseburg 18
Jacksonville 6

OREGON

The buildings in boldface type are of general interest. The others are for the specialist.

Bend

1 Sunriver Lodge and Community (1969–   )—George T. Rockrise & Associates

Cottage Grove

2 **First Presbyterian Church** (1950–51)— Pietro Belluschi
Zion Lutheran (1952)—Pietro Belluschi
Central Lutheran (1951)—Pietro Belluschi

Eugene

3 Deady Hall (1873–76) and Villard Hall (1885–86)—W. W. Piper; Warren H. Williams

4 City Hall (1962–64)—Stafford, Morin & Longwood

Gleneden Beach

5 **Salishan Lodge and Residences** (1962–65) —Skidmore, Owings & Merrill; John Storrs; Barbara V. Fealy

Jacksonville

6 **Jacksonville Historic District** (mostly 1860–84)

Mount Angel

7 **Library, Mount Angel Abbey** (1967–70) —Alvar Aalto

Oregon City

8 McLoughlin House (1845–46)

Portland

9 **Pioneer Post Office** (1869–75)—A. B. Mullett

10 **The Old Church** (1882–83)—Warren H. Williams

11 First Presbyterian Church (1886–90)— William E. McCaw and Richard Martin, Jr.

12 **Late 19th-Century Downtown Buildings**

13 Commonwealth (ex-Equitable) Building (1947–48)—Pietro Belluschi
U. S. National Bank (1917)—A. E. Doyle

14 **Portland Center Project** (1966–68)—
Skidmore, Owings & Merrill
Boise Cascade Building (1968)—
Skidmore, Owings & Merrill
Blue Cross Building (1969)—Skidmore,
Owings & Merrill
Lovejoy Park and Fountain (1966)—
Lawrence Halprin & Associates

15 **Auditorium Forecourt Fountain** (1970)—
Lawrence Halprin & Associates

16 **Portland Community College** (Phases I and
II, 1967–69)—Wolff-Zimmer-Gunsul-
Frasca-Ritter

17 Neighborhood Bus Passenger Shelters
(1974)—Skidmore, Owings & Merrill
Transit Mall (1979)—Skidmore, Owings &
Merrill

Roseburg   18 Douglas County Museum (1969/1979)—
Backen, Arragoni & Ross

Salem   19 **Ladd & Bush Branch, U. S. National Bank**
(1869/1967)—John Nestor

20 Bush House (1877–78)—Wilbur F.
Boothby

The Dalles   21 Surgeon's Quarters (1857)

Sunriver Lodge and Community (1969–)
2.5 miles/4 kilometers W of US 97, c. 15 miles/24 kilometers S of Bend, Oregon

GEORGE T. ROCKRISE & ASSOCIATES, ARCHITECTS OF LODGE

The abandon with which most developers despoil the countryside, bulldozing the trees and erasing the hillocks, has brought a reaction in the marketplace, and the discerning resort-community seeker will not now tolerate such shortsightedness. A few developers have from the beginning sought optimum land usage and architectural advice, and among the finer examples is this 5,500-acre/2,226-hectare community at Sunriver, a year-round settlement at an altitude of 4,200 feet/1,280 meters, surrounded by carefully preserved forests, laced with lakes, and lining the Deschutes River, whose banks will never be built upon. The bicycle is the favorite means of transportation. The 211-room

lodge of lava and wood was designed by George T. Rockrise & Associates, with various other architects responsible for the adjacent condominiums, houses, and shopping center. "Clean" light industry is being invited and it is hoped to have a population of up to fifteen thousand by the mid-1980s. Sunriver was conceived by John D. Gray, who also created Salishan at Gleneden Beach (q.v.), Oregon's superbly planned resort on the coast. He seeks "to use this land better, to set an example": long may he continue. James J. Amis was partner-in-charge; Royston, Hanamoto, Beck & Abey, landscape architects.

Always open

---

2   First Presbyterian Church (1950–51)
216 South 3rd Street at Adams Avenue
Cottage Grove, Oregon

PIETRO BELLUSCHI, ARCHITECT

The relaxed neighborhood atmosphere of the First Presbyterian (also known as United Presbyterian) commences at the sidewalk with a simple wood fence and gate establishing domain. The great locusts and oaks in front escort one to this gate whose open vertical slats merely suggest enclosure, letting the eye into the temenos where it is greeted —both from sidewalk and within—by a magnificent boulder directly on axis. This huge mossy stone carries an inscription from Psalm 122: "I was glad when they said to me, 'Let us go into the house of the Lord.'" One makes a short left-hand turn, then a right—both under a covered walk—past the rock and a small but careful planting area. A wood bell standard, simply carved at top (by the pastor), holds down the far end of this forecourt. The manipulation of progression, the trees outside and in the enclosure, the stone and planting, the band of gravel and small rocks along the nave, the understated bell mount—all against the background of the natural fir boards and battens of the church itself—make an extremely sensitive introduction to the church. It is a prelude that provides both an esthetic experience and a religious transition when approaching or leaving the church.

The nave is entered directly from the narthex, and faces due north as it overlooks the garden. A high, large louvered window (with the famous Belluschi scale handling in the grille design) gives an accent of slightly tinted light to the chancel which receives further emphasis from the fact that the spruce ceiling swoops gracefully up at this end.

The natural-finish wood on the ceiling and on rear and "garden" walls gets fine contrast from the white plaster on walls at front and left. Note the pattern of downlights in the ceiling. The chancel is slightly marred by the half-height projection of the vestry wall at left with puzzling vertical louvers behind (not apparent on exterior), but this is only a detail of an otherwise worshipful and in-touch-with-nature nave. And, it is important to realize, religious ambience was attained without traditional religious trappings: the cross alone may be said to be the only element from the past. Emphasizing this freshness, the choir is placed on one side of the congregation at nave level to underscore the Presbyterian non-structured "family" approach. A parish hall, juniors' room, Sunday school, small chapel, and minister's office (separately enterable from Adams Avenue) wrap around the nave on three sides. The church is listed in the National Register.

Open for Sun. services; on weekdays inquire at church office

Pietro Belluschi designed several other distinguished churches contemporary with this one in Cottage Grove (notably **Zion Lutheran,** 1952, 1015 Southwest 18th Avenue, and **Central Lutheran,** 1951, 2104 Northeast Hancock Street, both in Portland), but this local-wood Presbyterian example with its inspired, stepped-up profile as it rises toward the chancel, its simple, dedicated nave, and its incomparable parvis lift it very high among the "early" modern churches of the United States.

Belluschi's use of wood, whether as here in a simple "barn" tradition, or with sophisticated laminated wood arches (which he greatly helped to popularize) as in the two Portland examples mentioned, was very influential in church design throughout the entire country.

3   Deady Hall (1873–76) **and Villard Hall** (1885–86)
University of Oregon
East 13th Avenue on Mall, just W of University Street
Eugene, Oregon

W. W. PIPER, ARCHITECT OF DEADY HALL; WARREN H. WILLIAMS, ARCHITECT OF VILLARD HALL

Deady was the first building on the University of Oregon campus, for a time accommodating all its functions. When Villard was completed ten years later, a Second Empire-influenced pair was created which will appeal to the specialist. Entwined with ivy and engulfed with trees, they make a picturesque campus twosome. Both are of brick stuccoed. Villard was not helped by the awkward addition of a theater wing (1949) to one side, but its Mansard roof conquers all. The interiors are of minor architectural interest. Each is listed in the National Register of Historic Places.

Open during office hours

---

4   **City Hall** (1962–64)
Pearl Street between 7th and 8th Avenues
Eugene, Oregon

STAFFORD, MORIN & LONGWOOD, ARCHITECTS

An ingenious proposal for its midtown site won the architectural competition for this city hall. The program specified that the great ninety-year-old walnut tree just off-center on the lot be preserved and that open-air parking be provided for some two hundred cars, conditions which the other competitors met by designing a high-rise for the edge of the block, forfeiting the rest of the area to a parking lot. Stafford, Morin & Longwood took a totally different approach, creating a block-square, well-elevated plaza 315 feet/96 meters on a side, on which they freely developed a periphery of municipal offices. A glass-enclosed council chamber "floats" in a pool in the center, while the "open air" parking is accommodated underneath the terrace, screened by planting along the sides. Each department in this "rain country" has its covered parking. And the walnut tree? It rises majestically from the ground through the open-center elevated platform where it lends focus to the council chamber—and pleasures to the plaza. Though some of the architectural details are questionable (such as the design of the screen), the concept, land usage, and planting are ingenious. Altogether a provocative concept—and reality—for an official building. Lloyd Bond & Associates were the landscape architects. Andy Vincent did the mural.

Open during office hours

---

5 **Salishan Lodge and Residences** (1962–65)
on US 101
Gleneden Beach, Oregon

SKIDMORE, OWINGS & MERRILL, MASTER PLAN; JOHN STORRS, ARCHITECT OF LODGE; BARBARA V. FEALY, LANDSCAPE ARCHITECT

The lovely Oregon coast was first attacked by loggers and is now being gnawed at by speculative builders and by little-zoned, mushrooming resorts. To show what can and should be done a local industrialist, John D. Gray (see also Sunriver Lodge), has created, with top-level professional advice, a 600-acre/243-hectare community with gratifying concern for setting. The site, fronting 3 miles/4.8 kilometers of the Pacific, was homesteaded by the Sijotas and the Rajeskis until its purchase by Mr. Gray. The basic program for developing the area was to create a private residential section on the ocean or westerly side of the highway (which bisects the site) and public accommodations on the east, with an eighteen-hole golf course split but conjoined between

them. There are also houses in the hills above the Lodge. Altogether there are almost six hundred living units on the beach, facing Siletz Bay, or atop the several ridges, and, it is important to point out, many of these lots and even their vegetation are under leasehold, not direct private ownership, so that maximum protection to overall development can be maintained. Even lawns are frowned upon as smacking of suburbia: the natural world rules. All utilities are, of course, underground. Moreover, the houses (by various designers) must meet strict standards of the architectural review committee in siting, harmony with environment, and design (this last not always brilliant). It should also be added that road access to the residential area is solely by a keyed, automatic gate.

The highly acclaimed Salishan Lodge with its superior accommodations for guests and conventions rests on a hillside with fine views in three directions. It provides the public facilities for the 150 guest rooms which radiate in clusters from the main building. (It is, of course, also much used by those with adjoining residences.) Each unit of the Lodge is provided with covered parking in front, so that the automobile is almost invisible, and, within, each offers an open fireplace and a balcony. Every tree, where possible, was saved, while the area cut over by loggers (spruce mainly) is now the eighteen-hole golf course. Rough-cut board-and-batten planks encase both Lodge and residential buildings. All is discreet, immensely respectful of setting—and full of lessons.

Lodge only open to public

6   Jacksonville Historic District (mostly 1860–84)
Jacksonville, Oregon

Jacksonville, in the southwest corner of the state, prospered briefly
(1851 to the 1860s) as a gold-mining town. Though some gold continued to be mined into this century, the town's real strength developed
as a retail trade center for the surrounding agricultural area. It reached
a peak from 1860–80, when much of what we see there today was
built. However, when the Oregon & California Railroad bypassed Jacksonville in 1884, decline set in. Though some of the population moved
out, few buildings were demolished, many simply being reworked or
recycled. As a result, Jacksonville today has the best-preserved collection of pioneer buildings in the state, most of them—fortunately for
their preservation—of brick. A number of these houses and stores,

refreshingly uncommercialized, are open to the public, and the best procedure for the visitor is to get a free—and excellent—guide at the Chamber of Commerce (open 10–4 on weekdays from Memorial Day to Labor Day) on Oregon Street, just north of California. With the exception of the Italianate-style museum at 206 North 5th Street (formerly the Jackson County Court House—1883, G. E. Payne, architect), few of the buildings exhibit architectural pretensions, but the overall impression—in spite of utility wires—is cohesive and little spoiled.

California Street, highlighted by the **Beekman Bank** (1863) and the **United States Hotel** (1880—corner shown in photograph), offers the richest lode, having more than a solid block of largely intact buildings dating from 1854 to 1884, but others of modest note will be found, including three surviving churches (**St. Joseph's Roman Catholic Church** of 1858 being the best), plus, of course, the **Jacksonville Museum** (the courthouse mentioned earlier), on 5th Street, whose collection offers a good display of the era. (The museum is open Memorial Day–Labor Day, Mon.–Sat. 9–5, the rest of the year Tues.–Sat. 9–5, Sun. all year noon–5, except major holidays.) The United States National Bank, whose office is sympathetically installed in the hotel, played a substantial role in the rejuvenation momentum of the town by thoroughly sprucing up the old hotel and locating their offices in it instead of erecting a shiny new model down the street. (See also their bank in Salem.) Other restoration funds came from individuals, foundations, and local clubs.

Open as indicated

---

7   **Library, Mount Angel Abbey** (1967–70)
    c. 20 miles/32 kilometers NE of Salem, on hill E of
    Mount Angel, Oregon

ALVAR AALTO, ARCHITECT; DeMARS & WELLS, ASSOCIATES

An amicable building, but one which is almost timid on the exterior. It is only the second structure in the United States by the great Finnish architect (1898–1976), a man who early—and continuously—injected humanism into the development of modern architecture. (Aalto's other building on these shores is his Baker Dormitory for MIT in Cambridge, Massachusetts—q.v.) One of Aalto's first designs to electrify the international scene was his library for Viipuri (1930–35), a town

ceded to Russia by Finland in 1944. Badly damaged in the war, the building is now properly restored. In this Oregon grandson of that still unexcelled masterpiece can be seen some of the maestro's compassionate scale and handling of interior space, light, and detail. The Mount Angel library, which is used by the Benedictine Abbey's high school, college, and seminary, faces south onto the central college mall, forming a low-keyed, brick closure between its Romanesque-derived neighbors. One story high at the entry level, it takes advantage of its hillside site to develop three floors, two of stacks with one work level, dropped below on the north side. This frontage is the most dramatic and photogenic elevation, but because of the sharp grade differential it is difficult to see.

The building in plan forms a long, basically rectangular block stretched out on the edge of the hill with fan-shaped block of stacks and reading rooms "attached" at rear. As one enters, a one-hundred-seat conference and rare-book room stands to the right (note its ceiling), with staff and technical rooms to the left. One then steps forward from the low lobby to survey, indeed command, the curved asymmetric sweep of the two levels of stacks pulsating with space before and below one. It is in this all-white interior that Aalto's mastery of three dimensions, and his talent for manipulating light via skylights, roof monitors, conventional windows, plus, of course, artificial lights (which emanate from the same areas), are most evident. The illumination concept and detailing are potent contributions from this late northern giant. (Note the radiating slat fixture over the control desk.) Aalto was preoccupied (perhaps overpreoccupied) with the fan plan since his German experiments with his famous apartment house in Bremen (1962) and Cultural Center for Wolfsburg (1963), but here at Mount Angel it works with spatial come-on and unobtrusive logic, the angles of all stacks, for instance, radiating from the control desk for complete surveillance. There is open stack space for 75,000 volumes, with expansion allowance for 225,000 more. Study carrels line the perimeter of the four-angled faces of the "fan," those on the lower level being lockable. Fortunately, the furnishings, including important hardware and lighting fixtures, are also of Aalto's design. Erik T. Vartiainen, a young American architect, worked with Aalto on the project. Architectural humanism is not dead.

Open daily during school year

---

8 McLoughlin House (1845–46)
713 Center Street
Oregon City, Oregon

This simple, clapboarded house was probably designed by the owner using lumber from his own mill. There is little stylistic ancestry evident other than a vague Colonial, but this was nonetheless a substantial pioneer house for its time and region, one of the few still standing in the Northwest. Threatened with destruction at the beginning of this century, the dwelling was saved by the McLoughlin Memorial Association (1909) and moved to this city-donated present location overlooking the Willamette River. In 1935 it was carefully restored and furnished in the mid-nineteenth-century style. It is now a National Historic Site. Dr. John McLoughlin, incidentally, was a major figure—virtually a czar as a fur factor—in the development of the Northwest Territory.

Open June–Sept., Tues.–Sun. 10–5; Oct.–May 10–4, except holidays: admission

---

9 **Pioneer Post Office** (1869–75)
520 Southwest Morrison Street, between 5th and 6th
Portland, Oregon

ALFRED B. MULLETT, ARCHITECT

Century-old government buildings are a vanishing species in the United States, and this—the oldest standing federal structure in the Northwest—is of value partly because it is still there, but more so because of its capable architecture. Designed in Washington, it was begun only ten years after Oregon attained statehood. Mr. Mullett was later (1888) responsible for that gutsy exaltation in Washington known as the Executive Office Building (q.v.), but here in Portland he moved more timorously with a subdued Classically girdled rectangle topped by a slightly malaprop cupola. The Post Office's two upper stories, neatly divided by Tuscan pilasters, rest on a slightly "rusticated" ground floor; its projected pediments on the long sides and chaste detailing all combine to produce a patrician structure. Note the usual diminution of the windows with the rising floors. A wing was added to the west side (1903–5) to create greater square footage, primarily for the Post Office. The building is also used for the Federal Court House, but the Custom House moved to its own quarters in 1901. Once threatened as "surplus" because of the completion of new facilities, the Pioneer Post Office has been carefully remodeled (1973) for judicial use by Allen, McMath & Hawkins. The large, very dignified court-

room on the second floor for the U. S. Court of Appeals is the finest single room.

Open during office hours

---

10 The Old Church (1882–83)
1422 Southwest 11th Street at Clay
Portland, Oregon

WARREN H. WILLIAMS, ARCHITECT

The Old Church, originally constructed as the Calvary Presbyterian Church, is one of the best late-Victorian Carpenter Gothic examples in the state of Oregon. Its exterior, which has been kept in first-rate con-

dition, enjoys more than the usual minuet of gables, brackets, steeples, buttresses, tracery, barge boards, and chimneys (note these especially), all jostling oyster-colored, board-and-batten walls and dark roof. The three-hundred-seat interior is less consistent stylistically and combines Gothic, Renaissance, and Baroque elements. Note the vaulted ceiling, stained-glass windows, and the Hook & Hastings organ, shipped around the Horn and beautifully restored. A non-profit corporation now administers the building which is used for a variety of community events. It is a National Historic Landmark.

Open Tues.–Sat. 11–3

11   First Presbyterian Church (1886–90)
1200 Southwest Alder Street
Portland, Oregon

WILLIAM E. McCAW AND RICHARD MARTIN, JR., ARCHITECTS

With its hammer beams almost audibly hammering away, and with its gallery flaring into a swoop to echo the curved ranks of seats and the bowed lateral arches, the interior of this church is one of the most spirited of its High Gothic Revival period. (The balcony was added in 1892 to increase seating to fifteen hundred.) Squarish in plan, the better to hear the minister, it sets a theatrical scene. Except for the change in the lighting fixtures, the interior fortunately remains intact as built. The exterior, of black Oregon basalt with sandstone trim, which an early church bulletin says was "patterned after a railway station [unnamed] in Massachusetts," is architecturally not up to the interior. Note, however, its 150-foot/46-meter-high steeple and the carriage porch. The church is listed in the National Register of Historic Places.

To visit apply to church office at 610 Southwest 13th Avenue

12   Late 19th-Century Downtown Buildings
Portland, Oregon

The older section of downtown Portland, especially that near the
Willamette River, still has—in spite of fires and destruction—a number of buildings of the last century which are of considerable architectural and historic merit. They contribute definite zest to the local
scene. It is to Portland's credit that some of this heritage, though almost always commercial in character hence subject to opportunistic
machinations (if not mastications), has been preserved, restored, and
put to viable use. A number of these buildings will be seen on a stroll
through the city's two historic districts—Skidmore Old Town and
Lower Yamhill Street. The following three are thought to be of
greatest interest to the non-specialist. It should be added that an increasing number are being restored. Though not all are open to the
public, it is their exteriors which are of general moment. They are, in
chronological order:

New Market Theater (1872), 50 Southwest 2nd Avenue; W. W.
Piper, architect. This three-story building, which once combined a
second-floor theater of twelve hundred seats with a ground-floor market
and a third-floor cafe—it now serves primarily as a garage—provides
a fecund if schizoid facade of no small pretension. The street level presents a startlingly rich mixture of cast-iron columns and fancifully
carved wood cornice, all shining in white paint, with the two upper
floors (of Italian Renaissance inspiration) in red, deeply modulated
brick. It is, many feel, the finest example of its era in town. The New
Market Annex (1889), 58 Southwest 2nd Avenue (architect unknown), shows well-handled H. H. Richardson influence, especially the
upper floors.

The Bishop's House (1879), 219 Southwest Stark Street; P. Heurn,
probably the architect. A high-flying, three-story Victorian Gothic
structure of cast iron and brick, monumentally attended to on the top
floor, but done with flair. Following its sale by the diocese on moving
to other quarters, the Bishop's House underwent various commercial
uses until it was purchased in 1965 and thoroughly restored outside and
in to serve as attractive office space. (Open during office hours.)

Blagen Block (1888), Northwest 1st Avenue at Northwest Couch
Street; architect unknown. Designed as a four-story wholesale building
and still serving this purpose, the Blagen Block boasts a mélange of

Baroque cast-iron columns. Note also the close-cropped upper floors—
all three slightly different—which burst into a double pedimented and
balustraded "cornice" across the top, the two pediments emphasizing
the structural division into halves down the center of the building.
Though composed of freely drawn elements, the module of the window
bays and the rhythm of the double pilasters which frame them hold
this ambitious front together.

For fuller information on Portland's nineteenth-century inheritance
—what was and what there is left of it—see William John Hawkins
III's very thorough *The Grand Era of Cast-Iron Architecture in
Portland* (Binford & Mort, 1976).

Variously designed and open

---

13   Commonwealth (ex-Equitable) Building (1947–48)
Southwest 6th Avenue between Stark and Washington Streets
Portland, Oregon

PIETRO BELLUSCHI, ARCHITECT

The innovations of the Equitable Building influenced subsequent skyscraper design throughout the country, yet many of its contributions
have not been sufficiently appreciated. Four years before Lever House
in New York City, for instance, it used, probably for the first time, a
flush curtain-wall skin whereby the structural frame, spandrels, and
glass are virtually in the same plane (maximum difference ⅞ inch/22
millimeters). Moreover, the doubling of the plate glass and its sealing
in a fixed frame were both innovative measures. (The bay proportions
of two large panes and three spandrel divisions are superb.) In addition, the subdued but effective use of color revived a skyscraper note
which had been largely dormant since the late Raymond Hood's ex-
McGraw Hill Building (q.v.), 1931—on New York's 42nd Street. In
Portland, aluminum-covered concrete—another first—was used with
light-brown cast aluminum spandrels and combined with blue-green
glass to produce a quiet, sophisticated twelve-story building. (A thirteenth story was subsequently added.) The building was recently sold
and renamed, but the basic suavity is still there (except in the remodeled
lobby). As an innovative skyscraper the Equitable/Commonwealth
ranks very, very high.

The Roman Revival building at right is the **U. S. National Bank,** designed by A. E. Doyle (1917). Its four-story-high Corinthian columns and pilasters are topped by an unusually rich entablature and balustrade (and bear a more than casual resemblance to McKim, Mead & White's slightly smaller Knickerbocker Trust Building of 1902–4 in New York City—now demolished). Note the bronze front door. The main banking room is one of the city's finest of its period. Pietro Belluschi worked with the Doyle firm from 1927 to 1943, becoming a partner in 1933.

Both open during business hours

14   Portland Center Project (1966–68)
Southwest Harrison Street at 1st Avenue
Portland, Oregon

SKIDMORE, OWINGS & MERRILL, ARCHITECTS

Urban renewal is being attempted in many cities of the United States, too often with depressing results. However, the three rental residence towers here plus adjacent shopping mall, garage, and related functions provide a generic model of what should be possible for all our cities. Located within easy walking distance of Portland's central business district, only a block or so from the civic auditorium, and replacing substandard structures which previously had stood there, this residential-commercial development makes a sirenic stand in luring tax-paying residents back from the suburbs. The quality of its planning, architecture, and landscaping—not a little reminiscent of Le Corbusier's famous La Ville Radieuse of 1923—attains such urban civility that the three apartment blocks are almost always full, and a similar undertaking is planned to the south. Skidmore, Owings & Merrill's Portland office had been retained in 1960 to develop a comprehensive plan for the 83.5 acres/34 hectares of the overall site which had been acquired by the city's Urban Renewal Agency, a project which the city's voters had approved in 1958. Superblocks and a "green grid" of parks evolved from their studies, with a mixture of functions to generate day

and some night activity. In 1965 the land was sold, as prescribed, to the privately held Portland Center Development Company as the highest bidder; they in turn and with city approval retained SOM as architects for the first stage (29 acres/12 hectares) of the plan. The layout called for three concrete apartment towers of twenty-two to twenty-four floors each (comprising 516 units altogether), plus twenty-four two-story garden apartments, a restaurant, a broker's office, a shopping center with offices above, and several (too small) garages. The apartments, all with balconies and generally eight per floor, come in both one- and two-bedroom models.

Shopping center open daily; apartments private

The seven-story **Boise Cascade Building** (1968) and the low **Blue Cross Building** (1969), both also by SOM, lie at the north edge nearest the city center, while the imaginative **Lovejoy Park and Fountain** (1966) by Lawrence Halprin & Associates (now CHNMB Associates) fill the southwest corner of Southwest 4th Avenue at Southwest Hall Street. The fountain suggests hints of power from nearby Bonneville Dam, spray from Oregon's many mountain waterfalls, and deviltry from Rome's Trevi Fountain, combining a spirited dash of waters and angled changes of paving levels with a fey, free-geometric wooden shelter. (This latter was designed by Charles Moore and William Turnbull, who were also consultants on the fountain.) In addition to providing a lively corner, Lovejoy Park helps relax the slight rigidity of the architecture behind it. CHNMB Associates were also responsible for the landscape design of the whole Portland Center Project, including its elegant pedestrian malls, most of which had once been a street. David Thompson was assistant landscape architect. David A. Pugh was the SOM partner-in-charge. This is one of the finest urban-renewal developments that one will see.

---

15   Auditorium Forecourt Fountain (1970)
Southwest 2nd and 3rd Avenues, between Clay and Market Streets
Portland, Oregon

LAWRENCE HALPRIN & ASSOCIATES, DESIGNERS

The firm's Lovejoy Fountain seen in the nearby Portland Center Project (q.v.) was merely a warm-up for this masterpiece created four years later in front of the city's auditorium. As at Lovejoy, this is no

isolated jet that merely tinkles, splashes, and sprays for our auditory and visual pleasure, but a block-square summoning of waters which creates spontaneous involvement and gladness, a fountain for participators as well as observers, a fountain which is total theater with lines erased between audience and actors. Imagination concerning the multiform potentialities of water are brightly evident in its terraces and platforms, its cascades and still pools, its flat decks and its secret caverns, and while exhilaration leaps from its cataracts, peace can be found in its secluded corners. It is, in short, a work of genius, the finest display of urban waters that one will see anywhere: alive with grateful young in varying degrees of dampness, it serves, too, the old.

The fountain rises (via recirculated water) from the grassed and placid upper reaches of its sloping site, an area favored by both the quiescent and the very young with parents. It then gathers momentum to build up a bemused and taunted torrent searching for outlets as it dashes almost angrily between its 80-foot/24-meter-wide series of concrete embrasures and spillways, until with joy and freedom it leaps over the cunningly irregular waterfall's edges (18–20 feet/5.5–6 meters high) to surcease in the deep and blissful pools at its base. At this lower level a series of largely square concrete platforms, with slightly different heights and overlaps—to establish territoriality and bases for grouping and exploration—transfer the vertical drop of the waters to the horizontality of the urban milieu. A backup of small trees and planting gives a frame. Designed for and built of reinforced concrete, the fountain when dry acts as urban sculpture, its canted and striated walls producing a strength by themselves—and resembling somewhat the Giant's Causeway in Ireland's County Antrim. The waters start to flow at 11 A.M., pushed by a 200-horsepower vertical-flow pump, and the sight of 13,000 gallons (49,000 liters) per minute searching their destinies over the wide waterfall make it one of the attractions of Portland. It is illuminated at night—largely for the crowd in the auditorium it faces—and only on a rare winter day does the temperature force it to close down. It is probably the finest urban glory since Specchi and De Sanctis' stairs at the Piazza di Spagna (1721–25) in Rome. Satoru Nishita was partner-in-charge; Byron McCulley project director; and Angela Danadjieva Tzvetin project designer; Beamer/Wilkinson Associates were mechanical and electrical engineers. Lawrence Halprin & Associates are now known as CHNMB Associates.

Active 11 A.M.–10 P.M.

---

16   Portland Community College (Phases I and II, 1967–69)
**12000 Southwest 49th Avenue, S of IS 5 and US 99W via Capitol
    Highway exit
Portland, Oregon**

WOLFF-ZIMMER-GUNSUL-FRASCA-RITTER, ARCHITECTS

A perceptive, perhaps even brilliant, philosophy of open-door community college education can be seen here in the 125-acre/51-hectare Mount Sylvania campus on the rolling hills southwest of Portland. Distilled into a few words, the educational concept and its architectural realization seek to make the learning process so inviting, so unstructured, and the sympathetic staff so available, that the sometimes reluctant, even suspicious and alienated two-year student—often of harried background—finds here a welcoming company of peers, each working at his or her pace, each a team member with an opportunity. To achieve flexibility and to let the student literally "shop" for his course

or courses, the entire project was designed like a gigantic two-story shopping center, with an organizational mall down the middle and the various departments, or learning centers, in four major buildings opening from this. To carry the marketing analogy further, most of the classrooms are glass-faced so that a prospective student can stand outside and "browse," vicariously sampling the wares within while determining course of action. Moreover, there are few inner halls, the individual buildings instead being surrounded by a broad circulation corridor "system"—open-air "boardwalks," with frequent plazas which become animated spaces between classes. These promenades contribute a healthy student interrelation, plus creating a stimulating, double-deck architectural interlock, all the time framing a variety of distant views over the countryside. The corridors also facilitate the "window shopping" mentioned above for most of the classrooms open onto them. A student can go from his/her car (or bicycle) direct to a single classroom or shop and back without entering any "establishment."

There are five "career" divisions and, while the majority of these are more vocational and technical than academic, the college commendably minimizes the "denigration of blue-collar and semi-skilled work." The major divisions are: mathematics-science-engineering; life science-health; transportation-metals (largely shopwork); social science-business; and community and continuing education. Phase III will add the arts and radio-television. The architecture itself combines compactness with calculated views outward, constructed with a strongly emphasized (and effective) use of prestressed concrete channel slabs for roof on a poured-in-place concrete structural frame. The exterior walls are of wood panel and glass, the inner of brick. The concrete stairs joining the two levels, and the "outside" toilet and locker facilities (located between the buildings) are overly heavy, but the basic impression and the progression of spaces are very capably handled. Total enrollment in the college approaches 25,000 (there is an older, downtown campus), with some 4,000 students at the new college on most schooldays.

Open during school hours

---

17 Neighborhood Bus Passenger Shelters (1974)
located throughout city
Portland, Oregon

SKIDMORE, OWINGS & MERRILL, ARCHITECTS

The city of Portland probably has the most efficient surface transportation in the U.S.A., with a remarkable number of buses serving the central business district throughout the day. As a result of convenient and well-kept schedules—radio-controlled by supervisors at strategic spots—the buses are a welcome and much used urban asset. To make public transportation even more attractive the city commissioned Skidmore, Owings & Merrill's Portland office to design a simple prototype neighborhood bus shelter which would offer reasonable weather protection—and seats—in an oft-drizzly (in winter) climate. The result was so encouraging that 720 (500 full size, 220 slightly smaller) of these steel, wood, and polycarbonate shelters are now scattered at appropriate spots around the city. (If only Skidmore, Owings & Merrill could have designed the buses as well.) Funded under an 80 per cent grant from the Urban Mass Transportation Administration plus a three-county employer's tax on payrolls (less than $\frac{4}{10}$ of 1 per cent— and with certain firms exempted), the shelters cost less than two thousand dollars each. The polycarbonate clear sides and smoky roof (against sun) are of GE's Lexan MR-4000, stronger than acrylic plastic and mar-resistant, and in addition to enlivening the dreary days of the October-to-May rainy season by admitting a maximum of light,

they are almost invisible as street furniture. Their bottoms are open so that litter will blow out. A two-thirds-length bench (of hemlock slats) was dimensioned to accommodate both the seated and the standing. Overall the shelters measure 8.5 feet/2.6 meters long, 4.5 feet/1.4 meters deep, and 7 feet/2.1 meters high. It is instructive to compare the Portland shelters with those sprouting on the sidewalks of New York and designed by Holden, Yang, Raemsch & Corser (1975). The latter have a fiscal advantage in that they cost the city nothing, their two advertising panels (at one end) paying for their construction and installation.

In 1979 Portland's **Transit Mall** was opened. This represents the most comprehensive attempt in the nation to effect efficient mass surface transit. Though not completed when the author was last on the scene, the Mall and its shelters—also by SOM's Portland office— should be meaningful.

18 Douglas County Museum (1969/1979)
take Fairgrounds exit off IS 5 SW of town
Roseburg, Oregon

BACKEN, ARRAGONI & ROSS, ARCHITECTS; WE GROUP OF ADDITION

The purpose of this clever, if fractionalized, small museum in the southwest corner of the state "is to preserve the historical heritage and depict the resources, settlements and growth of Douglas County." (The fir tree was named for David Douglas, 1798–1834, a Scottish botanist who had traveled widely in this area: Douglas County was named for Stephen A. Douglas.) The cedar museum is divided into three major elements, their design reflective of local farm vernacular: the tall administration-curatorial building, the main exhibit building, and a shed for open-air displays. The architects took advantage of the change in grade to connect the entry level of the administration building to the second floor of the exhibit unit by a trussed, glassed-in bridge, the chief displays consequently being located on this upper level. The museum can be incrementally expanded. So successful are

the results that the architects were retained to design the nearby **Douglas Hall** (1970), a simple but flexible all-purpose sports and exhibition structure particularly useful during County Fair times.

A substantial addition to the museum, designed by WE Group of Eugene, was completed in 1979. Its exterior is completely consistent with the original structure.

Open daily 8:30–5 except legal holidays

---

19   Ladd & Bush Branch, U. S. National Bank (1869/1967)
302 State Street at Commercial
Salem, Oregon

JOHN NESTOR, ARCHITECT

This almost unbelievable building possesses facades with some of the most superb cast-iron work in the country. The bank was established as an independent downstate bank with architectural influence from the Ladd & Tilton Bank (1868) in Portland—probably through commonalty of partial ownership by Mr. Ladd. The Salem design, built the following year, was based directly on the Portland prototype utilizing cast-iron molds almost indistinguishable from the first, as the original molds were shipped to Salem where they were probably cast by the Drake Iron Works, the Willamette Iron Foundry having produced the earlier ones. In 1954 the Portland building was replaced by a new and larger structure, but its cast-iron front was carefully preserved. When the Salem bank needed expansion in 1967, having by then been acquired by the United States National Bank, the cast-iron sections of the 1868 building were purchased, moved some 40 miles/64 kilometers south, and added to the Salem core; almost nothing of the old was altered except its length, depth, and cornice. (The facades now measure 102 x 165 feet/31 x 50 meters. Note that the bay width of the addition is a tiny bit narrower.) During the renovation and expansion the structural frame was changed to reinforced concrete instead of brick, over which the cast iron was meticulously replaced. The garlanded, emblazoned, and "rusticated" main pilasters, the rich keystones and flanking voussoirs, and the positively stated solid balustrade on top—all wrapped in recollections of Venetian glory and painted to resemble stone—are superb testaments to the skill and development of cast-iron workmanship in the U.S.A. even under "frontier"

conditions. The interior has of necessity been altered, but the beautifully designed and maintained exterior (diminished by the sign over the front door) ranks among the masterpieces of its kind. Skidmore, Owings & Merrill were the architects for the expanded building.

Open during business hours

20   Bush House (1877–78)
600 Mission Street Southeast at High Street in Bush's Pasture Park
Salem, Oregon

WILBUR F. BOOTHBY, DESIGNER-BUILDER

Of subdued Italianate derivation, the Bush House provides a good regional example of the style. The exterior is on the quiet side, but the interior, including the original wallpapers and many of the original furnishings, is more determined. The barn—the Bush Barn Art Center—the grounds, and the gardens are all worth a look. The Conservatory, or Greenhouse, built c. 1882, has recently been restored: it is thought to be the oldest of its type on the West Coast. The house was built for Asahel Bush of Massachusetts, the co-founder of the Ladd & Bush Bank. Since 1953 the house and grounds have been the property of the city of Salem and are administered for the city by the Salem Art Association.

Open June–Aug., Tues.–Sat. noon–5, Sun. 2–5; Sept.–May,
Tues.–Sun. 2–5, except holidays: admission

21 Surgeon's Quarters (1857)
15th and Garrison Streets
The Dalles, Oregon

LOUIS SCHOLL, DESIGNER

This small house, looking like an illustration for one of Walter Scott's novels, is the only remnant of Fort Dalles (abandoned in 1867), and is one of the exemplary "Gothic" cottages in the Northwest. Although it has been well maintained, it should be pointed out that additions have been made, and virtually none of the furnishings are original, those now in the building being of the period and donated by descendants of pioneer families. The house today serves as a museum with numerous historic photographs. An influence from A. J. Downing's *The Architecture of Country Houses* is mentioned in the National Register of Historic Places in the design of the house.

Open May–Sept., Tues.–Fri. 10:30–5, Sat.–Sun. 10–5; Oct.–Apr., Wed.–Fri. noon–4, Sat.–Sun. 10–4, except holidays and two weeks in Jan.

South Dakota

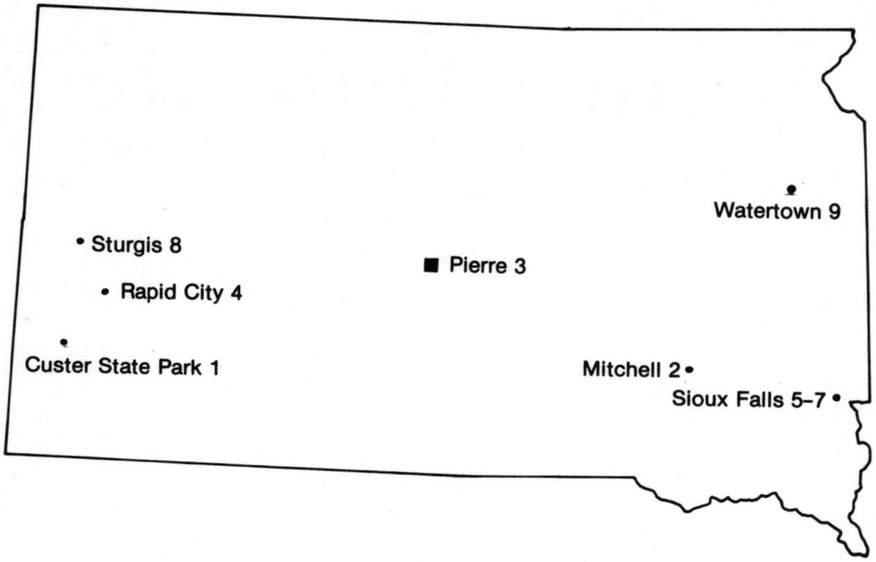

• Sturgis 8

• Rapid City 4

• Custer State Park 1

■ Pierre 3

• Watertown 9

Mitchell 2 •

Sioux Falls 5–7 •

SOUTH DAKOTA

The buildings in boldface type are of general interest. The others are for the specialist.

Custer State Park

1 The Gordon Stockade (1875; reconstructed 1968)
Mount Rushmore National Memorial (1927–41)

Mitchell

2 The Corn Palace (1892/1965)

Pierre

3 Oahe Mission School and Church (1877)
Oahe Dam (1962)—U. S. Army Corps of Engineers

Rapid City

4 St. John's School of Nursing (1968–69)—Robert B. Gay

Sioux Falls

5 **Old Courthouse Museum** (1889–90/1980)—Wallace L. Dow

6 **St. Mary's Church** (1958–59)—The Spitznagel Partners

7 McKennan Health Center (1973–76)—The Spitznagel Partners and Caudill, Rowlett & Scott

Sturgis

8 **Meade County Court House** (1965)—Gay & Gass

Watertown

9 **Holy Name Church** (1967–68)—The Spitznagel Partners

1   The Gordon Stockade (1875; reconstructed 1968)
c. 3.3 miles/5.3 kilometers E of Custer on US Alt 16
Custer State Park, South Dakota

A reconstruction of an 80-foot/24-meter-square stockade and cabins originally erected—in midwinter and in defiance of military law—by twenty-six prospectors (plus one wife and child) who sought a jump on the discovery of gold in the Black Hills. What we see today was rebuilt on the ruined fireplace of the old "fort"; it constitutes a reasonable copy and shows the extreme primitiveness of shelter in this area at that time. Distinct fringe benefits of a visit can be found in the park nearby—unfenced herds of bison and antelope, plus the more than mile-high/1,620-meter setting.

Open daily, daylight hours

The famous 60-foot/18-meter-tall heads of Washington, Jefferson, Theodore Roosevelt, and Lincoln "carved" (mostly dynamited—1927–41) into the mountains by Gutzon Borglum and his son, Lincoln, rise a score or so miles to the north at **Mount Rushmore.**

2   The Corn Palace (1892/1965)
604 North Main Street
Mitchell, South Dakota

This paean to corn affirms that agriculture is South Dakota's leading industry. (Some 92 per cent of the state's land is occupied by
farms.) Originally built in 1892, the Corn Palace was rebuilt on
this site in 1921, and in 1965 was completely remodeled. The "Palace"
serves primarily as a civic auditorium the facade of which is redeco-
rated each fall by a South Dakota artist. Only natural-colored corn,
wheat, and Sudan grass are used—some 350–400 bushels/12,300–
14,100 liters of corn and 2 tons/1.8 metric tons of grains and grasses.
It is probably the world's largest "living" mural. The Corn Palace was
extensively remodeled in 1979 following a fire.

Open June–Labor Day, daily 8 A.M.–*10* P.M., *rest of year*
Mon.–Fri. 9–5, except holidays

3 Oahe Mission School and Church (1877)
just off SD 514, c. 7.5 miles/12 kilometers N of Pierre, South Dakota

Architectural distinction is absent from this 20 x 40-foot/6 x 12-meter combined school and church, but as one of the oldest buildings in South Dakota—and as a memento of at least some white concern for the Indians—it is a useful structure, and one which served its purpose for over forty years. With dressed lumber shipped up the Missouri River, the building was put together by a missionary of the Congregational Church aided by local Indians. It proclaims simplicity throughout: even the concept of combining school with church bespeaks local conditions. When the adjacent Oahe Dam was built, the chapel, which would have been inundated, was moved to its present site overlooking lake and powerhouse.

Open Memorial Day–Labor Day, daily 8–6

The **Oahe Dam,** designed and operated by the U. S. Army Corps of Engineers, is of the rolled-earth type. Measuring 9,300 feet/2,835 meters long and 245 feet/75 meters high, it was commenced in 1944, with first power production in 1962. The lobby with exhibits is open daily, 8–4:30, except holidays. There are guided tours from Memorial Day to Labor Day (admission).

**4   St. John's School of Nursing (1968–69)
11th Street at South
Rapid City, South Dakota**

ROBERT B. GAY, ARCHITECT

These buildings join two dissimilar functions: a dormitory for 120 student nurses and facilities for instruction and recreation. These latter include, in addition to classrooms, a small medical-type auditorium with steeply raked seats, a library, and recreational rooms. The expression of the eight-story dormitory versus the lower public spaces is smoothly effected. Exposed reinforced concrete for the structural frame, red brick for the walls, and copper for trim and cornice comprise the basic materials. In spite of a low budget, materials have been well used, while the building itself has been efficiently planned.

Lounges open daily 9–5

5   Old Courthouse Museum (1889–90/1980)
Main Avenue at 6th
Sioux Falls, South Dakota

WALLACE L. DOW, ARCHITECT

This turreted municipal pile was built to house the Minnehaha County
Court House. For some years in danger of destruction when the new
Court House was completed (1962), the pride of Main Avenue has
been rehabilitated by the Siouxland Heritage Museums (1979–80),
with excellent displays on the development of prairie life and culture.
(South Dakota—the former Land of the Sioux—entered the Union in
1889 just before this structure was commenced.) The *Minnehaha
County History* declares that "At the April [1889] session, it was
moved and carried that the contract for the furnishing plans and
specifications for the courthouse be awarded to W. L. Dow," so it must
be assumed that Mr. Dow designed it, though his name does not appear on the building itself. The little-known Dow came from New England and was probably personally familiar with Richardson's work;
reputedly he designed over a hundred buildings in South Dakota during both territorial and statehood days. The building was constructed
of quartzite—locally known as Sioux Falls jasper—a rock of such

hardness that it is rarely used today for building even with sophisticated power tools. Its architecture combines stalwartness with punch, showing in its design a touch of the ubiquitous 1890s influence of H. H. Richardson (see Index) but expressed with a determination all its own. Its buildup of scale and the use of roundheaded windows on the top floors to calm this fenestrational flight upward are capably handled. The interior is largely of oak, with the usual central stairhall forming the dominant space. Thomas Brown Muths was architect in charge of historic preservation aspects; Fritzel, Kroeger, Griffin & Berg were the local architects in charge of museum transformation.

Open Mon.–Fri. 8–5, Sat.–Sun. 2–5, except major holidays

---

6 St. Mary's Church (1958–59)
5th Avenue at 29th Street
Sioux Falls, South Dakota

THE SPITZNAGEL PARTNERS, ARCHITECTS

A simple but highly satisfactory interior distinguishes St. Mary's from a plethora of fumbling churches of its period. Moreover, its art is am-

bitious and often first-rate. The rectangular nave, with low side-expansion area—together seating eight hundred—is roofed by gracefully bowed laminated beams with wood purlins forming the ceiling. The slightly angled sanctuary wall is "separated" from the nave by full-height windows hidden behind slight projections, thus receiving a wash of daylight from each side. This whole wall is of mosaic, and is dominated by a black metal cross which projects from and stretches across the sanctuary end. Note, also, the mosaic of Mary and Child, the small white cross, and the plaque of St. Mary. A cantilevered sounding board projects over the pulpit. William E. Bentzinger was project designer for TSP; Emil Frei Inc. designed the stained glass and the sanctuary wall; Robert Harmon did the Mary and Child; Robert Rambusch the Stations of the Cross; Robert Aldern the door design and pulpit canopy; and Jackson Woolley the enamels. Whereas the exterior is quietly competent, the nave is very fine.

Open daily 9–5

---

7 **McKennan Health Center** (1973–76)
7th Avenue at 22nd Street
Sioux Falls, South Dakota

THE SPITZNAGEL PARTNERS AND CAUDILL, ROWLETT & SCOTT, ARCHITECTS

Accommodating 240 beds, this new facility makes a smooth-working addition to a 1911 complex. Because of its residential location, the hospital was kept to three stories in height, and attention paid to materials and colors made it a reasonable neighbor. Services, including administration and operating rooms, are contained in a long, rectangular unit at left which abuts the old building. The ground floor of the new wing is slightly elevated and inset and made bright with awnings (in front of the cafe—open to public). There is also a garden alongside the entry road—which passes in front and bisects the project. To the right are two conjoined patient "towers," here elevated a full story to provide under-cover parking. The towers contain nursing stations and all services in semioctagonal cores, with the patient rooms grouped in modules around them. Four team-nursing units of fifteen beds each— and some architectural complexity—make up a module for a total of 120 per floor and 240 total on the two nursing levels. Single rooms were used throughout, providing not only privacy but also greater flexibility in assigning rooms (sex, disease, etc.) and maximum utilization. Construction is of lightly tanned concrete and reddish-brown brick.

Public areas open daily 9–5

---

8   Meade County Court House (1965)
5th Street at Sherman
Sturgis, South Dakota

GAY & GASS, ARCHITECTS

A courthouse for a small city (less than five thousand) which rises well above the expected. The outgrown civic building which previously stood on one corner of the site compromised the plan of the new by squeezing its dimensions, but there is no compromise with the latter's architectural expression, which is based on precast, fine aggregate wall panels of wheaten color, set in a white precast concrete framing topped by a copper roof. The plan is divided so that routine county business is transacted on one side of the central hall, while the courtroom and related functions occupy the other. This passage is unusually pleasant (except for plastic flowers), with glass-lined entrances on opposite sides (the rear one from the parking lot), highlighted by a skylight in the center. Circulation and functions are immediately graspable. The courtroom opens directly onto the hall and is also lit by a skylight; though reasonable overall, it tends to the heavy side in de-

tail. Because of the aforementioned site restrictions—the new had to be built while the old held forth—a number of offices are windowless on the below-grade lower floor, a placement which is, from a long-range standpoint, unfortunate, but considering the highly restricted space available and the even more restricted budget, fine results have been achieved.

Incidentally, the mining and ghost-town aficionado might want to explore the mountains west of Sturgis, where Deadwood, Lead, and abandoned sites offer impressive relics (some still working) of the gold rushes of a century ago. South Dakota, incidentally, is still the nation's largest producer of gold.

Open during office hours

---

9 Holy Name Church (1967–68)
10th Avenue at Sky Line Drive
Watertown, South Dakota

THE SPITZNAGEL PARTNERS, ARCHITECTS

Brick—good, red, earth-colored brick—envelops this Roman Catholic church outside and in. The low parish house to right is wrapped in brick, the angled entry court, which acts as an intermedium on enter-

ing and leaving the church, is of brick (and will later be accented by a bell tower), and the interior walls of the church fold an unbroken mantel of brick about the congregation. A unity results, with an angled plan—post-Vatican II—which creates excellent "one-room" intimacy between priest and people. A tiny (two-pew) chapel stands at left, its altar (in front of a slightly disturbing wraparound partition) visible from the main nave, while the high altar can be seen from the chapel. The chapel can also be entered directly from the outside. The church sanctuary, marked only by one step and by dark flooring, has a free-standing altar of great simplicity, and is carved, like the bishop's throne, the lectern, and the pulpit, of granite, all of which were de-signed with restraint. There is not even a communion rail to interrupt the atmosphere of closeness of congregation to sanctuary. A roof mon-itor directly above the chancel brings suffused daylight into the church, its walls being windowless. Downlights in the ceiling provide artificial illumination. Windowlessness might be a debatable approach for a church which is located in a newly opened suburb with a site offering panoramic views all around, but granted the postulate, one will not quarrel with the answer. The floor of the nave, which angles gently down to the sanctuary, is of white terrazzo, while the ceiling, which an-gles up, is of white plaster, setting a good color scheme with the red brick walls and grayish stained wood pews (which accommodate seven hundred). The choir is not isolated but placed with the congregation at right front. A warm church with an outstanding chancel. Wallace Steel was project architect for TSP; Frank Kacmarcik was liturgical consultant.

Open daily 8–7

Texas

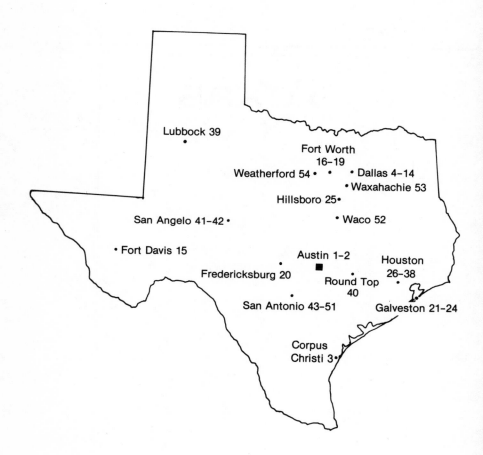

Lubbock 39 •

Fort Worth
16–19
Weatherford 54 • • • Dallas 4–14
• Waxahachie 53
Hillsboro 25 •

San Angelo 41–42 • • Waco 52

• Fort Davis 15

Austin 1–2 ■ Houston
26–38
Fredericksburg 20 • • Round Top •
40
San Antonio 43–51 •
Galveston 21–24

Corpus
Christi 3 •

TEXAS

The buildings in boldface type are of general interest. The others are for the specialist.

Austin	1	**Neill-Cochran House** (1853) **and Governor's Mansion** (1853–55)— Abner Cook
	2	State Capitol (1882–88)—Elijah E. Myers Old Land Office Building (1856–57)— Conrad C. Stremme
Corpus Christi	3	**Art Museum of South Texas** (1970–72)— Johnson/Burgee
Dallas	4	**Old City Park** (largely mid–late 19th century)
	5	Temple Emanu-El (1955–56)—Howard R. Meyer and Max M. Sandfield
	6	**Kalita Humphreys Theater** (1958–59)— Frank Lloyd Wright
	7	**One Main Place** (1967–68)—Skidmore, Owings & Merrill
	8	**John F. Kennedy Memorial** (1970)— Philip Johnson John Neely Bryan Cabin (c. 1843) Dallas County Courthouse (1891–92)— Orlopp and Kusener
	9	Mountain View College (1970–71)— Harrell + Hamilton/Chan & Rader
	10	**Dallas/Fort Worth Airport** (1968–73)— Hellmuth, Obata & Kassabaum
	11	Stemmons Towers (1962–67)—Harold A. Berry Brookhollow Plaza (1970–)—Paul Ruldolph and Harwood K. Smith & Partners
	12	**Thanks-Giving Square** (1977)—Johnson/ Burgee
	13	**The Dallas City Hall** (1975–78)—I. M. Pei; Harper & Kemp

51 **Tower of the Americas** (1967–68)—Ford, Powell & Carson

Waco

52 Suspension Bridge (1866–70)— Thomas M. Griffith

Earle-Napier-Kennard House (1867) and East Terrace (c. 1872/1966)

Waxahachie

53 Ellis County Court House (1894–97)— J. Riely Gordon

Weatherford

54 Parker County Court House (1884–86)— W. C. Dodson & W. W. Dudley

1   Neill-Cochran House (1853), **2310 San Gabriel Street**
Governor's Mansion (1853–55), **10–11th, Colorado and Lavaca**
Austin, Texas

ABNER COOK, ARCHITECT

Two distinguished Greek Revival houses designed by the same master-builder/architect and constructed within a few years of each other. Most dwellings of this style are characterized by white columns and white walls (whether of masonry or wood), but the Neill-Cochran is refreshingly "local" in that behind its stately two-story row of six Doric columns stands a wall of 18-inch/46-centimeter-thick buff-colored limestone. Opening onto the porch, which extends to protect the entire front, are four floor-to-ceiling windows which give both good scale and ventilation. Since 1958 the house has belonged to the National Society of the Colonial Dames of America in the State of Texas, which has carefully restored both house and garden to their century-old appearance (the building at one time having served as a hospital, then as an institute for the blind). The entrance hall with its circular stair is perhaps the most competent single room but the level is high throughout.

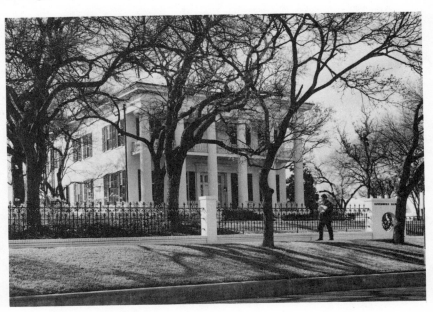

The Governor's Mansion, *bottom photo, preceding page,* follows the basic disposition of the Neill-Cochran House, but with Ionic columns, a full-width, second-story porch, and a bit more finesse in detail. It is an elegant example of the Greek Revival and, having been maintained in prime condition throughout its life, the mansion, as well as its lovingly tended gardens, is very well worth a visit.

The Neill-Cochran House is open Wed.–Sun. 2–5, except major holidays: donation
The Governor's Mansion is open Mon.–Sat. 10–12, Sun. 2–4, except major holidays

---

2   State Capitol (1882–88)
N end of Congress Street
Austin, Texas

ELIJAH E. MYERS, ARCHITECT

Straddling its hill like a pink granite behemoth, this is—of course—the largest of state capitols, being 566.5 feet/173 meters in length. Moreover its galvanized iron cornice and dome, buttressed with steel, covered with copper, and topped by a zinc Goddess of Liberty (1888), is 22.3 feet/6.8 meters higher than its prototype in Washington. Exterior finesse, however, lagged. The towering dome, for instance, merely perches on the great bulk below, it does not evolve from it. The interior, on the other hand, has surprising rewards, from the hinges on the front doors, to the spirited door framings, to the boggling space (260 feet/79 meters high) under the dome. Many of the lobbies, corridors, and stairs are also impressive. Both Senate and House chambers, however, are uninspired. Mr. Myers, who won the competition for its design, also won the competitions for the Michigan and Colorado capitols. Incidentally, the contractor for the Austin job was paid not with money but with 3,025,000 acres/1,224,187 hectares of land in the Texas panhandle. Napoleon LeBrun was an initial consultant to Elijah Myers.

Open 24 hours a day

At the southeast corner, at 108 East 11th Street, stands the sturdy, partly machicolated, **Old Land Office Building** (1856–57), Conrad C. Stremme, architect. (Open Mon.–Fri., 9–12, 1–5, except major holidays.) It is now a museum maintained by the Daughters of The Republic of Texas and Daughters of the Confederacy. There are fifty varieties of local trees on the grounds.

---

3   Art Museum of South Texas (1970–72)
1902 North Shoreline Drive
Corpus Christi, Texas

JOHNSON/BURGEE, ARCHITECTS

Seemingly sliced out of reinforced concrete (concrete chosen so as to be hurricane-proof), this smartly angled and curved, dazzlingly white, almost Greek-island block suggests on the outside few of the spatial pleasures that await within. The architects perched the museum on an embankment directly at the water's edge with an approach via a main road: thus development of three-dimensional form—plus strong identity—was of particular importance.

As soon as one enters the lofty Great Hall (all white like the exterior), the space tricks begin, the most immediate being a large, square window—"a picture"—on the far wall opposite the entry framing Corpus Christi Bay as it pulls one forward. A 60-foot/18-meter passerelle, with an access stair purposefully near the front door, cuts across the left side of the Hall with visual snatches of galleries on both floors behind. Beyond this a small, squarish gallery opens (with walled outdoor sculpture garden on top entered via second level).

In the center of the Hall, which is used for the display of large works, a freestanding elevator housing punctuates the space. To right near entry is the 231-seat auditorium with museum library, small gallery, and services beyond. In plan these elements form a loose composition to define the central hall-exhibition arena almost like a village square. After exploring the main floor, walk, don't ride, to the upper galleries, a spatial excursion that will reward no matter what works of art are on display. (The privately built but willed-to-the-city museum has a small permanent collection and an active program of loans and circulating shows.) Carefully calculated natural light, alive and changing, floods the major exhibit areas via skylights, supplemented by artificial sources when needed. Offices, shipping, storage, and classrooms—art education is a major emphasis—occupy the basement level.

Open Tues.–Sat. 10–5, Sun. 1–5, except holidays

4   Old City Park (largely mid–late 19th century)
1717 Gano Street
Dallas, Texas

Concerned citizens of Dallas and the Dallas County Heritage Society
have assembled and restored almost two dozen structures which bear
witness to much of the evolution of the city. (See also Sam Houston
Park in Houston.) Occupying land on which the Cherokees formerly
camped—the site had a natural spring—and which later (1876) became the first city park, this microcosm via its buildings gives good insight into life in early Dallas. (The city was founded as a trading post
in 1841.) The principal buildings are the Miller Cabin of 1847 (immediately left of entrance), the close-by Greek Revival Millermore House
(1855–62), an excellent jigsaw bandstand from the 1880s, a railroad
depot (c. 1886), and two side-by-side stores built in 1904. The Greek

Revival house was dismantled in 1966 and reconstructed in the park in the 1970s. All structures are original and were moved to City Park beginning in 1966. They are maintained by the Dallas County Heritage Society and the Park Department of the City of Dallas which holds title to the property.

Open Tues.–Fri. 10–4, Sat.–Sun. 1:30–4:30, except major holidays: admission

5   Temple Emanu-El (1955–56)
Hillcrest Road at Northwest Highway
Dallas, Texas

HOWARD R. MEYER AND MAX M. SANDFIELD, ARCHITECTS; W. W. WURSTER, CONSULTANT

A large religious group on the north edge of Dallas, distinguished by its handsome worship hall. Cylindrical in form (82 feet/25 meters in diameter, 70 feet/21 meters high), the walls of the interior are lined with acoustic ribs of stained wood except at the sanctuary which is of pinkish brick with mortar joints flecked with multicolored bits of glass and gold leaf. An excellent ark curtain by Anni Albers gives the proper note to the sanctuary (though the pulpit is not inspired), while the play of random-height bronze light cylinders throughout the nave, by Gyorgy Kepes, adds a fine touch. (The eye-level band of windows in daylight is, it must be added, unusual in color and from many seats bad in glare.) For High Holy Days the one-thousand-seat worship room can double its capacity by opening into the adjacent auditorium. A youth wing, designed by Howard R. Meyer, was added in 1978.

Frequently open; telephone: (214) 368-3613

---

6   Kalita Humphreys Theater (1958–59)
The Dallas Theater Center
3636 Turtle Creek Boulevard, SW off Blackburn Avenue
Dallas, Texas

FRANK LLOYD WRIGHT, ARCHITECT

At Dallas, Wright had his first chance to design a professional theater. Mr. Wright, a consummate actor himself, had long been interested in the stage as an extension of cultural expression and intergroup relations. Taliesin has its performance area, and one of the finest units at Taliesin West, Scottsdale, Arizona (q.v.), is a theater, but this at Dallas is his only one which was designed to be open to the public. Its site is a park setting, but a steeply sloping one which Mr. Wright used to maximum advantage, shoe-horning the building into the hillside so that level changes within would reflect the grade, while on the exterior he was able to create a drive-around, walk-around entity, not one with a single formal facade. The visual indifference which would normally result from a theater's many necessarily blank walls has been tempered by a play of curves versus straights and overhangs versus sheer, producing thus a satisfactory exterior.

On entering, the theatergoer is taken on an angled path before being delivered to the auditorium entrance. This widened corridor also serves

as lobby (with critically tight circulation to lower lobby and rest rooms). The auditorium itself, radiating around an apron stage and initially accommodating 416 with only 11 to 12 rows of seats, suggests a family gathering more than a theater, with admirable intimacy between audience and actors, free from any "peep-show proscenium character" (as FLW put it). Three rows of seats were recently added to the balcony to make a total capacity of 516. The stage is based on a revolving central section (32 feet/9.7 meters in diameter) within a 40-foot/12-meter cylindrical stage house, partly cantilevered over the stage itself. This doubles as a cyclorama, with side stages on both right and left. Three 4-inch/10-centimeter steps are all that separate actors from audience. If needed, a curtain bisects the revolving section. Mr. Wright originally planned to have the scene changes lugged from the basement by hand via the ramps on either side, but, in addition to the labor problem, the curves are too tight to accommodate large flats, so an elevator was installed. Other set changes can be dropped from the fly gallery. The balcony can also be used for supplemental lights. There are faults, as suggested, at the Dallas Theater Center—and some actors do not favor it—but it advanced the art of drama in its relation of actors to audience, the unreal to the real. George C. Izenour was theater consultant.

Open during performances; also daily tours, telephone for hours:
(214) 526-8210

7 One Main Place (1967–68)
Main Street at Griffin
Dallas, Texas

SKIDMORE, OWINGS & MERRILL, ARCHITECTS; HARWOOD K. SMITH & PARTNERS, ASSOCIATES

A grandiloquence characterizes this downtown skyscraper by the New York office of SOM, although its commanding presence will, perhaps, suffer in future years when the now unencumbered thirty-four-story building becomes hemmed in. This is only the first of several planned buildings on the 10-acre/4-hectare site. However, as recompense, its sunken plaza in front will then take on added significance as a central city breathing spot à la Rockefeller Center in New York. The building expresses both its concrete skeletal frame (note its slightly tapered

profile reflecting the lessening of loads as the building rises), here revetted in sand-blasted panels, and it states, too, divisible cells for flexibility in office partitioning. The window framings are square, but the glass itself is rectangular with a 26-inch/66-centimeter spandrel inset 48 inches/1.2 meters from the front edge of the structure. Thus shadow play and sun-shielding join forces with the checkerboard facades, a grid rescued from boredom by its proportions and by the extra-height windows on the ground and plaza floors. Even so there is a dryness when the skyscraper is viewed from a distance, but this impression vanishes with propinquity, especially when the sunken plaza enters the scene. This plaza forms one of the few civilized spots in Dallas' almost treeless, unrelentingly commercial downtown: it is a welcome refuge even at night when the lights glow and the fountains fount. Several levels of shops occupy the substreet (i.e. plaza) level, with an eight-hundred-car garage underneath, and the traditional Texas club on top. Paul Weidlinger was structural engineer.

Open during business hours

---

8   John F. Kennedy Memorial (1970)
Main, Market, Elm, and Record Streets
Dallas, Texas

PHILIP JOHNSON, ARCHITECT

Understated to the point of starkness, curiously unsettling in its embrace, its cantilevers at entry suggesting the tenuous forces of nature—and the balance of life—the John F. Kennedy Memorial suggests in contemporary terms the elusive, inexorable turns of fate. Construction is of seventy-two simple precast concrete slabs, eight of them longer than the others to form legs which elevate its palisade lightly above the ground. Post-tensioning binds these slabs together (note the circular metal cover plates), the design forming an enclosure of two U-shapes —"like a pair of magnets about to clamp together" says the architect.

It measures 50 feet/15 meters square and 30 feet/9 meters high. One of the weaknesses of our ethos is that we almost never produce a distinguished memorial to an individual (compare the Arch in St. Louis), but this dolmen to the late President—who was gunned down a few hundred yards from this spot—succeeds partially in evoking the disturbing concept of life, death, and even aspiration. Moreover, it

must be seen if only to jolt our conscience and shatter our coddled complacency.

Just west of the Memorial stands the 16-foot/4.9-meter-square cedar **Log Cabin** erected (probably in 1843) by John Neely Bryan—"the original speculator of North Texas" (*Dallasights,* AIA, 1978). In spite of its minute size it once served both as post office and temporary courthouse (1848–50). In 1935 it was moved to its present site and restored. Directly behind rises the **Dallas County Courthouse** (1891–92), a fine Romanesque number which until 1919 sprouted a 205-foot/62-meter-high central tower. Orlopp and Kusener were the architects. In 1966 the entire building was remodeled into up-to-date offices by architect Moffatt D. Adams.

9 **Mountain View College** (1970–71)
**Illinois Avenue at Duncanville Road (S of Dallas–Fort Worth
    Turnpike, E of Loop Road 12)**
Dallas, Texas

HARRELL + HAMILTON/CHAN & RADER, ARCHITECTS

A large, well-organized community college on the rolling hills of the westernmost edge of Dallas. The low-slung complex rests on either side of a small arroyo, here kept in constant flow by an artificial lake. The

architects skillfully utilized the sharp changes in levels, putting the instructional units on one side of the stream bank and those elements which might be used by the community (auditorium and gymnasium) on the other, and connecting them by airy bridges at two points. In addition there are separate entrances for students (west) and public (east). One of the features of the exterior is the several open-air terraces and sweeping steps, particularly those adjacent to the student center: ideal spots for personal interaction.

In the layout of the classrooms and shops a particular effort was made to develop visual relationships to encourage student awareness of what is going on outside his or her chosen field. Imaginative colors and furnishings characterize the interiors, an effort which attains high marks in the student lounge. Formalism is apparent on the entry sides of the college, but the inviting terraces between the two buildings, the visual interaction of the instructional areas, and the bright colors are very capable.

Public areas open during school hours and for performances

10 Dallas/Fort Worth Airport (1968–73)
**via TEX 114 or 183, 21 miles/34 kilometers from downtown
  Dallas**
**via TEX 121 or 183, 25 miles/40 kilometers from downtown Fort
  Worth**
Dallas–Fort Worth, Texas

HELLMUTH, OBATA & KASSABAUM; BRODSKY, HOPF & ADLER,
ASSOCIATED ARCHITECTS

D/FW is not innovative as in Dulles (Virginia q.v.) with its mobile lounges—considered here but rejected as not being large enough for jumbo jets (plus being subject to drivers' strikes); nor is it as convenient to use as Tampa International (q.v.) with its rooftop parking—initially proposed here but bypassed, some think unfortunately, for lateral garages. The Dallas/Fort Worth Regional Airport is, however, an altogether staggering achievement. It is close in basic layout to its contemporary, the smaller Kansas City International (q.v.). Like the latter, D/FW uses a series of gigantic arced-in-plan buildings, here horseshoe-shaped, off of whose outer faces up to eighteen planes per terminal, including jumbos, can berth. These extended half-circles, 2,625 feet/800 meters in inner diameter, are deployed—in a symmetrical Beaux Arts plan—on either side of a 4-mile/6.4-kilometer north-south, multilaned, vehicular spine. This automobile and bus axis can be entered from either end where (at each) it taps onto existing highways. Incredibly, no rapid transit facilities or express automotive lane to and from Dallas and Fort Worth exist: this curious short-sightedness was left to "local authorities." Four terminals have thus far been constructed with a linear potential of fourteen. Most of the open inner area described by each arc of buildings is given over to three zones of outdoor parking (beyond the attached covered garages), framed by a concentration of planting toward the center.

Passenger flow is, of course, one of the key elements in airport design, and it has been meticulously studied here. Pleasures begin when one drives one's car to the airport and swings off the central roadway to the appropriate terminal and airline. One's luggage is checked at curbside—and is whisked immediately to the flight loading platform—and one parks the car in the covered garage directly opposite (if there is room), on its deck below if it is filled, or in the open-air (and cheaper) grade-level lot just beyond, which holds up to

twelve hundred automobiles. Long-term, open-air "remote" parking is accommodated at either end of the spine, along with annoyingly far-out rental-car facilities. Having taken care of the car, one then ascends by escalator to the lobby security check and departure lounge, a distance of about 75 feet/23 meters from curbside or an average of 250 feet/76 meters from parking facilities: a simple, smooth process. The deplaning passengers move directly from plane and across the lobby to the baggage claim area and public transportation, all on one easy floor. (One's automobile might also be on this level on top of the three-decked garage.) Departure and arrival lounges are generally separate, the latter, of course, being smaller. Restaurants, rest rooms, shops, etc. are conveniently spaced in between.

If one is transferring to another airline—the greatest weakness of the airport—to long-term parking, rental cars, or the on-site, six-hundred-room hotel, one takes the Airtrans (25 cents), the automated trains which run directly below each terminal, thus obviating walking. This 13-mile/21-kilometer-long rail facility is, of course, a key to the entire airport design, and though it may take some time (up to twenty-four minutes, compare Tampa) to reach one's objective, its forty-passenger cars move along with reasonable speed and comfort. It also requires some sophistication to use without mixup on its several lines. The cross section of a building shows the central placement of Airtrans and reveals the excellent organization of a terminal's flow-lines and activities, including an under-cover service road on the outer periphery directly adjacent to baggage handling and operations.

Architecturally the buildings and details at D/FW are obviously capable from the design point of view. They are in effect straightforward, semi-industrial structures, well massed and scaled. There is, however, a tendency toward linear anonymity without a rallying accent to enliven these long-stretched masses. Close up the expression of their beige-colored concrete framework is superb, particularly the placement of beam on bracketed column. This explicit statement of structure, both outside and in, was aided and speeded by off-site prefabrication and by post-tensioning. Though the terminals form a semicircle, they are made up of straight-line components with wedge elements (often services) creating an organized planning module every 90 feet/27 meters. The development of interiors was left to the individual airlines with varying results, but in all of them one can enjoy that almost-forgotten pastime of being able to watch the planes land and take off, for each station overlooks the field. At times the surfeit of "desert" colors intrudes, but it is at least peaceful. The Braniff facility (Harper & George, interior designers) ranks among the more intimate and cheerful. All glass is bronze-colored.

The extraordinary Dallas/Fort Worth Regional Airport, which covers 17,520 acres/7,090 hectares, might well be "the bigger than Manhattan, the Year 2001 Air Terminal": it definitely has lessons— mostly positive—for all subsequent international air facilities. As the *AIA Journal* wrote (March 1978): "It must be understood the DFW's purposes were as much political as they were rational, and as much symbolic as they were functional. If it is an operational inconvenience, it is also a cultural landmark of the first order."

Among the more than score of major consultants were: Tippetts-Abbett-McCarthy-Stratton, airport planner, engineer, general consultant; Thomas M. Sullivan, Executive Director; Gyo Obata of HOK, principal in charge of design; Richard Adler of BHA, principal in charge of administration; Preston M. Geren, Jr. and Harrell + Hamilton, associate architects; LeMessurier Associates, Terry-Rosenlund & Company, structural engineers; Richard B. Myrick & Associates, landscape architects.

Always open

---

11   Stemmons Towers (1962–67)
2710 Stemmons Freeway
Dallas, Texas

HAROLD A. BERRY, ARCHITECT

Four civilized, individual office towers laid out with sensitivity to the street, to each other, and to their landscaped site. Twelve stories in height, they are shielded on all sides by a 5-foot/1.5-meter overhang of floor slabs, to provide sun protection. The ground floor of each is largely open—they house only services and vertical circulation—so that an airy lightness and mutual relationship is evident throughout the pedestrian level. Pains were taken with the landscaping to minimize visually the ranks of parked cars and to provide at least a bit of shade for them. Construction is of white concrete with gray-tinted glass. More than reasonable at a distance, the buildings are superior close up, a fresh note for semisuburban office grouping. Harwell H. Harris was chief of design.

Open during business hours

Brookhollow Plaza (1970–) stands just down Stemmons Freeway at Mockingbird Lane (open during office hours). Designed by Paul Rudolph and Harwood K. Smith & Partners, this sixteen-story building is the first of four planned, ranging from nine to twenty-two floors. Its intriguing structure is of precast concrete, "in essence a big log cabin" says Rudolph. The two sides are framed by coupled finlike "columns" 6 feet/1.8 meters wide by 1 foot/.3 meter thick, a few being as long as 43 feet/13 meters. These are post-tensioned together and project from the building face to produce the four bays seen on the exterior. Two additional "columns" 7 feet/2.1 meters wide by 1 foot/.3 meter thick support each end. The interior is column-free. Copper-colored reflective glass sets off the concrete panels. Sepp Firnkas was the consulting engineer.

12 Thanks-Giving Square (1977)
Pacific Street at Ervay
Dallas, Texas

JOHNSON/BURGEE, ARCHITECTS

Philip Johnson has designed two monuments in Dallas and there is a
hint of the Renaissance in one—the Kennedy Memorial (q.v.)—and
the Baroque in the other, Thanks-Giving Square, a half mile/.8 kilometer to the north. The latter was built as "the first center of world
Thanksgiving [and] celebrates mankind's gratitude to God." The triangular Square is entered under an open belfry which forms the major
gateway. (There are three other entries.) One then winds through a
small but surprisingly tempting and rewarding garden accented by

waters. Channels of water run along some paths; a sparkling pool awaits at the top. The garden's climax is the chapel at far end wrapped in a form taken directly from the minaret of the Great Mosque of al-Mutawakkil in Samarra, Iraq (847–52). Its cylindrical, spiraling geometry produces a day-long interaction with the sun, and gives a visual focus to a difficult street intersection. A small bridge leads to the non-denominational chapel whose nautilus interior reflects the outside. Upward swirling bands in the ceiling, highlighted by decreasing circles of stained-glass panels, establish a quietly colorful and reposeful place of contemplation. The juncture of ramped base and chapel might not be totally dextrous, but the sculptural form and its brilliant sun-consciousness, the pleasures of its garden in mid-city clutch, and the "retreat" offered by the chapel make a compelling whole. The Square was built by and is supported by the Thanks-Giving Square Foundation.

Open Mon.–Fri. 10–5, Sat.–Sun. and holidays 1–5

---

13   The Dallas City Hall (1975–78)
off Young Street between Akard and Ervay
Dallas, Texas

I. M. PEI & PARTNERS; HARPER & KEMP, ASSOCIATED ARCHITECTS

Productive urbanism and startling geometry are the chief characteristics of the new Dallas City Hall. The urban contribution—in a city where downtown graciousness is almost unknown—resides in the 425-foot/130-meter-wide plaza which stretches northward from the building toward the nearby ramparts of the central business district. This welcome disjunction is planted with local trees, highlighted by a circular pool 180 feet/55 meters in diameter, and "completed" by Henry Moore's *The Dallas Piece,* a superb work in three parts. Steps on the two edges of the northwest corner mediate the modest grade changes while three ovoid flagpoles recall (massively) the three rounded "towers" projecting from the building's facade. A garage lies under the entire plaza and accommodates 1,325 automobiles.

The building itself combines an outward-angled front (56° to the plaza) with three round-ended vertical utility-circulation cores asymmetrically disposed, defining bay divisions. The result is a seven-story facade 560 feet/171 meters long of no small monumentality. (The City Hall bears some similarity in facade angle, pier, and orientation to

Saarinen's Dulles Airport [Virginia], q.v.) The meeting of the ground floor with the plaza is "closed"—there is no liaison—except at the glazed entry. The two ends are basically triangular, which, with their horizontal cutbacks, produces a complexity of form that for some observers weakens the geometric probity of the overall. The windows on the long sunny side are inset for solar protection.

A three-story-high lobby, with entrances on both sides, forms a bright introduction to the interior. Moving stairs then take one up a single level to the dramatic Great Court, the inner focus of City Hall. This 100-foot/30-meter-high core is cheerfully top-lit by quarter-round vaulted clerestories, and each floor is surrounded by balconies lined by growing plants. (Compare this top lighting and step-backed use of balconies with Frank Lloyd Wright's Marin County Civic Center [California], q.v.) The two lower floors of this space are occupied by those municipal functions most used by the public, while the upper are more specialized.

In understanding the structure of City Hall, it is useful to realize that the first and second floors of the building establish its "basic" width, which is 122 feet/37 meters. The northerly (i.e. plaza) side of the Court level rises vertically within but each upper floor projects beyond the one below to produce the angled front. The southern "half" of the Great Court, however, steps back c. 9 feet/2.7 meters on each successive floor, thus admitting a maximum of light to the core and developing a non-rigid space. Each internal step-back equals the projection forward reflected in the angled front of the building, thus the *combined* widths of the front and back sections of each floor—the two being divided by the Court—equal that of the second (and first) level(s), even though they vary individually as the floors rise.

The space and ambience of the Great Court make an adventure of what could be a prosaic or even unpleasant task (taxes, etc.) for the citizen. It is one of our few exciting public interiors. The 250-seat, theaterlike Council Chamber, with entry on the sixth floor, holds meetings open to the public each Wednesday.

Open during office hours

---

14   Hyatt Regency and Reunion Tower (1976–78)
300 Reunion Boulevard at Stemmons Freeway
Dallas, Texas

WELTON BECKET ASSOCIATES, ARCHITECTS AND ENGINEERS

The world's oldest glass is thought to be Egyptian from around 2000 B.C., and though glass was industrialized early in the nineteenth century it only floresced as a building skin in the 1960s and 1970s. Glass then became available with insulating factors, with a variety of tints, and with reflective and mirror attributes, providing sheets of a material with tantalizing possibilities. Architects have not been slow to seize— at times overseize—these new means of sheathing a building, but it is doubtful if any new structure can equal the glass exuberance of this hotel. Mercurial by day, this compound of shapes clad in silvered reflective glass can evaporate against the sky; at sunset when the low sun emblazons its fantasia of forms, it approaches the spectacular; while at twilight the hotel glows with mystery. This act, it should be added, is fully visible from the nearby interstate highway. There are those with reservations about so much glass at Latitude 33, but *sui generis* this is one of the nation's dazzling exteriors. The interior focuses on an almost square atrium 200 feet/61 meters high which lacks the brio of the exterior. In addition to extensive public accommodations including a ballroom, there are 956 well-designed guest rooms. It should be added that the hotel's structure is very innovative in using steel plate shear walls for wind resistance.

Alongside the hotel rises the 564-foot/172-meter-high Reunion Tower, a geodesic sphere 118 feet/36 meters high, held aloft by three concrete piers. This contains a revolving cocktail lounge, restaurant, and observation deck with a geometric net of some 260 long-life exterior lights enwebbing it.

Hotel always open; Tower open 9 A.M.–midnight: admission

The area surrounding the hotel is under development both by the city and private enterprise. The nearby Union Terminal railroad station (1916—Jarvis Hunt, architect) has been rehabilitated and is directly connected to the hotel and to a series of shops, and in 1980 the city opened a Special Events Center—**Reunion Arena**—in an adjacent large park. (These have not yet been seen by the author.) Designed by Harwood K. Smith & Partners, with Paul Gugliotta consulting engineer, the Arena is a 420-foot/128-meter-square building covered by a 4-acre/1.6-hectare steel space-frame roof. Seating 17,200, it will accommodate rodeos, concerts, and a variety of other events.

15 Fort Davis National Historic Site (1854–61)
TEX 17, c. 32 miles/51 kilometers S of US 290 at Toyahvale
Fort Davis, Texas

At the mouth of a canyon, 4,900 feet/1,493 meters high in the stark Davis Mountains in westernmost Texas, Fort Davis was established to protect the San Antonio–El Paso mail and stagecoach road from depredations by Mescalero Apaches and Comanches. The Great War Trail of the Comanches lay not far to the east. Following the discovery of gold in California, Davis became a key military outpost, a position it held until 1880, when the Apaches were finally defeated. In 1891 the fort was abandoned. Its ruins and 447 acres/181 hectares were made part of the National Park System in 1961, restoration being undertaken to save what was savable and to restore groups of important buildings. Some are of stone, but many are of adobe, a few being of

adobe scored to resemble stone. For the fort buff, this stronghold represents one of the Southwest's vital outposts; for the faunaphile, Fort Davis stabled the country's first military experiment with camels (sixteen from the Levant), a successful venture which only the Civil War interrupted. The war also affected the existence of the fort itself, which was temporarily deserted, then largely wrecked by the Apaches. The fifty-plus buildings of the fort stand today as a capable (if much restored) meeting of difficult conditions set in a desolate panorama.

Open June–Aug., daily 8–6, Sept.–May, daily 8–5: admission

16 Log Cabin Village (1840s–70s)
in Forest Park, just W of
University Drive, S of Colonial Parkway
Fort Worth, Texas

A small, documentary group of frontier cabins with that architectural directness which characterizes primitive building. Brought together by the Texas Pioneer Heritage Committee and the Tarrant County Historical Society, these half-dozen original cabins have been meticulously restored. The Isaac Parker cabin (1848)—"a showplace on the frontier"—is so authentically furnished inside and out as to suggest that its inhabitants had momentarily dropped everything and gone to repel an Indian attack—as they probably often had in the past. Note its dog-run or possum-trot, an architectural Venturi carburetor for channeling the breeze and for providing a covered open-air work space. The cabins date from 1848 (the Parker house) to 1870 (the tiny Isaac Seela cabin). Although their corner mortising would not pass the critical eye of a sixteenth-century Swede from Dalarna—there is a whole science to this joinery—the logs are smartly trimmed and straight.

Open Mon.–Fri. 8–5, Sat. 9–5, Sun. 1–5, except Dec. 25:
admission

---

17   Amon Carter Museum (1961/1978)
W on Lancaster Ave to 3501 Camp Bowie Boulevard
Fort Worth, Texas

PHILIP JOHNSON, ARCHITECT

This pristine showcase for art was originally designed to display the late Mr. Carter's unequaled collection of sculpture and paintings by Frederick Remington and Charles M. Russell. It now operates on a broader scale of American art, with particular focus on the "westering" of the continent. Situated near the top of a long, gentle slope, and placed at right angles to the road (Lancaster Avenue), the museum extends its stepped terraces to possess the countryside. The terrace dimensions (approximately 140 x 300 feet/43 x 91 meters) are defined by a low wall of the same shellstone as the building, with a hint of space in its rail raised carefully above the solid balustrade. Designed by the architect, these levels and their landscaping tie the museum to the city—a city which Amon Carter partly shaped—with such terrestrial ambition that they demand possibly more of a building to back it up.

A classic formalism marks the five-arched facade, and when entering one finds a double-height but narrow exhibition space. (The main gal-

lery measures 24 feet/7.3 meters high by 24 feet/7.3 meters wide and 120 feet/36 meters long.) However, one is injected into the milieu of art as soon as one steps through the front door, and this involvement is stimulating. Opening off the major hall on the ground floor are four intimate teak-walled galleries with additional exhibition space filling the balcony. The architect's noted sensitivity to detailing is quietly stated throughout: the five tapered shellstone arches (each with 3-inch/76-millimeter steel inner column) rippling across the front are themselves works of art—in design and in their hand-carving. The lighting, worked out with Richard Kelly as consultant, allows a glarefree bath of radiance to pour over the exhibition spaces, the five black-painted eggcrate fixtures in the main gallery being the source of both natural and artificial illumination.

In October 1978 an annex to the museum was dedicated, designed by Philip Johnson and John Burgee. With 36,000 square feet/3,344 square meters, the new wing doubles the size of the original museum and includes a 105-seat theater, vastly expanded library, services, and enlarged bookstore. One of its highlights is a split-level garden area to right of the theater. Like the main building, the new is also faced with Texas shellstone.

Open Tues.–Sat. 10–5, Sun. 1–5:30, except Dec. 24–25

18   Kimbell Art Museum (1969–72)
Will Rogers Road West between West Lancaster Avenue and
**   Camp Bowie Boulevard**
(Visitor parking and entrance also off Arch Adams Road)
Fort Worth, Texas

LOUIS I. KAHN, ARCHITECT

The Kimbell's drive-in entrance is anonymous and its plan highly symmetrical (and precisely north-south oriented), but the museum's potential formality evaporates on the interior in a radiation of waves of space to create one of the country's greatest museum interiors. It is, to quote the architect, "a friendly home," a home of welcoming scale where the evanescent, non-rigid moods of natural light (with artificial backup when necessary) bathe the works of art with subtle nuances and variations throughout the day. It should be mentioned immediately that although the Texas sun furnishes by far the greater part of the illumination, no direct rays strike the paintings on the walls: they are all indirect. This is achieved by running continuous—and for a few viewers prominent—Plexiglas skylights (2.5 feet/.76 meter wide) down the center of fourteen of the sixteen lead-covered cycloidal vaults which form the building's distinctive roof. Finely pierced metal screens, suspended directly underneath the skylights, reflect and spread the light over the soffit of the vaults thence onto the works of art. "Structure is the giver of light" wrote the late Lou Kahn, and light and life are fused throughout the museum.

The overall building is 318 feet/97 meters in length—and resembles a Tunisian ghorfa with its semibarrel vaulted profile. Each of its marvelous post-tensioned vaults, the two forward of which form entry porches, measures 104 feet/32 meters long, 23 feet/7 meters wide, and 4 inches/10 centimeters thick. Note that at their ends the vaults are separated from the vertical walls by thin lunettes of light to emphasize the independence of structure from non-structure. Note, too, the subtle difference of the two curves of the lunettes. The vaults, which rest on supports only at their ends, are separated laterally by 7-foot/2.1-meter-wide concrete channels which contain air-conditioning outlets and electrical conduits.

An openness and flexibility grow under the amicable and domestic spaces of these inspired roof ripples, one which encourages gallery identity yet induces a questing spirit to probe the artistic riches hinted at behind the partitions. Exhibition space is flexible because there are

few supporting columns, while all partitions are readily movable. Two courts, the larger used for outdoor sculpture, extend the display possibilities and give accents to the interior. A 180-seat auditorium and a snack bar lie adjacent to the north court. All services and the parking entry for visitors are in the lower level. Note the pool and terraces in front. Workmanship throughout is notable, particularly in the exposed concrete vaulting, while detailing, whether in concrete, stainless steel, oak, or travertine, is impeccable. The museum was made possible by the will and collection of the late Kay Kimbell, who left his entire and considerable fortune to the Kimbell Art Foundation. The project architect was Marshall D. Meyers; Preston M. Geren, Jr., of Fort Worth was associate architect. Dr. August E. Komendant was the structural consultant, Richard Kelly and Edson Price the lighting consultants, and George Patton landscape architect. Poetry in space.

Open Tues. 10–9, Wed.–Sat. 10–5, Sun. 1–5, except holidays

NOTE: A block west up Lancaster stands the Amon Carter Museum (q.v.), while across the street is the Fort Worth Art Center, all three collaborating to give the city an enviable art museum center, with the Museum of Science and History conveniently nearby.

---

19   The Water Garden (1974)
12th, Commerce, Lancaster, and Houston Streets
Fort Worth, Texas

JOHNSON/BURGEE, ARCHITECTS

Rising immediately across 12th Street from the Tarrant County Convention Center—descending is a more appropriate word—this four-block, "sunken" oasis brings an artful retreat to the midtown hurly-burly about it. A series of irregular geometric steps and stepped gardens and pools cascade like a topographical model to create a three-dimensional stimulus to the city. This profusion of stepped-down levels offers a variety of options—some active, some quiescent, some planted, some sittable, some wet, some dry. One area cannily focuses—almost like a theater—on the "active" pool while containing its spray from baptizing the innocent. Nearby, yet with its own identity, is an "aerating" pool whose forty jets deliver a cloud of dewiness, while beyond a "quiet" pool, some 16 feet/4.9 meters below street level, thoughtfully

banishes for its users all contact with the city around it. A central plaza and a parterre area (off Lancaster) complete this solution to a tough problem. This is a brilliantly refreshing addition to the dry, dry city about it. The Water Garden was a gift of the Amon G. Carter Foundation.

Always open

---

20 19th-Century German Buildings
Fredericksburg, Texas

Sprinkled among the characterless structures of the twentieth century, and obscured by signs and utility wires, there remain in this still-Germanic town a few mementos of over a century ago when the village was founded (1846) under the aegis of The Society for the Protection of German Immigrants in Texas. It was named for Prince Frederick of Prussia, the highest-ranking member of the Society and a man well liked. These scattered relics reflect their Continental inheritance molded in central Texas yellow limestone. Among the buildings open to the public are:

1) A 1936 reproduction of the octagonal **Vereins-Kirche** of 1847 (the original of which was torn down in 1897), a building of character, with timber framing and stone walls stuccoed. Located on Pioneer Plaza between Adams and Crockett streets, it now houses the Gillespie County Historical Society Archives and Local History Collection. (Open afternoons, except holidays.)

2) **The Pioneer Museum,** 309 West Main Street, a story-and-a-half typical house of the period (1849, addition 1875) in which five generations of the Heinrich (later Henry) Kammlah family successively lived and, in the well-known Continental tradition, kept shop. It is now a small museum of the area. Note its sturdy stone walls and chimney, the outdoor oven, and typical porch across the front. (Open May–Sept., Mon.–Fri. 10–5, Sat., all year, 10–5, Sun., all year, 1–5, except major holidays: admission.)

3) **Old St. Mary's Catholic Church** (Marienkirche—1863), at corner of North Orange and San Antonio streets. A neatly shaved German "Gothic" example, it displays a fine stone tower. (Open for Sunday services.)

None of the above are of architectural importance in the history of art sense, but they all give an unusual insight, in this case a very focused one, into Texas regional architecture with its Germanic input. The locally famous "Sunday Houses"—two "boxes" of bedrooms piled one on the other—which the outlying farmers and ranchers built around 1900 for weekend-in-town marketing and churchgoing—are now zealously preserved. The Fredericksburg Historic District is listed in the National Register of Historic Places.

---

21 Ashton Villa (1858–59)
2328 Broadway
Galveston, Texas

A rich, brick, Italianate mansion, its material reflecting the fact that its New York-born owner-builder once was not only apprenticed to a brick mason but eventually owned his own brickyard in Galveston. (He also eventually owned a good deal more.) The exterior with its

double porch of delicate cast iron and its enormous brackets under the wide eaves is the most interesting part of the house. Note the triple-hung windows on the first and second floors (for maximum ventilation), and the gently rounded windows above. The interior, though not as lush as it was a century ago, is still handsome and has been well restored and refurnished. The villa was sold to the El Mina Shrine in 1927 with consequent changes including the extension of the former dining room to make a ballroom. Following the horrendous hurricane of 1900, all of Galveston Island was land-filled to make it 3–10 feet/.9–3 meters higher. Ashton Villa then lost 3 feet/.9 meter of its cast-iron fencing and its entire basement. In 1971 the property was purchased by the city and leased to the Galveston Historical Foundation, which now administers it. Ashton Villa is listed in the National Register of Historic Places.

Open Mon.–Fri. 10–4, Sat.–Sun. 12–5, except major holidays: closed Tues., Sept.–May: admission

22 U. S. Court House and Federal Building (1858–61)
20th Street at Avenue E
Galveston, Texas

This former Customs House established a surprisingly elegant Greek
Revival beachhead in Galveston, one which well over a hundred years
of hurricanes and man-made batterings have not diminished. The north
and south facades are distinguished by inset porches on both floors,
the whole suggestive of Inigo Jones's Queen's House (1616–35) near
London: the two-story portico on the west, on the other hand, projects
prominently. Almost all of the exterior details are of cast iron (reputedly from New York), including the window frames and the columns,
Ionic on the ground floor, Corinthian above. Cast iron was also used
for the interior stairs. Both shenanigans and mystery seem connected
with the erection of the building. Willard B. Robinson in his excellent
book *Texas Public Buildings of the Nineteenth Century,* with photographs by Todd Webb (published for the Amon Carter Museum by the
University of Texas Press, 1974), brings out that though the redoubtable Ammi B. Young, then Supervising Architect of the Treasury

Department (see Index), initially designed what was for his output a dull, three-story structure, work stopped in 1859 (delays, changes, shenanigans?). The Customs House was then reduced by one story and finished by C. B. Cluskey and Edwin Moore with, it should be added, more finesse than Mr. Young's earlier design. (The National Register of Historic Places [1976] cites Ammi Young as the architect.) During the Battle of Galveston (1863) it was used as Confederate headquarters. Handsomely restored in 1967, it forms one of the highlights of the Gulf Coast. Inside, the ground floor has been divided into the necessary offices and is of small interest, but the second floor beautifully houses the old courtroom and ancillary chambers.

Open during office hours

---

23   The Strand Restoration (mid-19th century/1970s)
The Strand Historic District
Galveston, Texas

Strand Street, a block from the Galveston waterfront with its picturesque shrimping fleet, and itself once the commercial heart of the city ("the Wall Street of the Southwest"), contains blocks of buildings of interest, many of cast iron, that are now undergoing extensive rehabilitation. Spurred by the Galveston Historical Foundation (founded in 1871 and Texas' oldest), aided by early efforts by the Junior League of Galveston and the Galveston County Cultural Arts Council, this heartening restoration program is transforming a recently almost-derelict section into a highly viable and attractive part of town. Now listed on the National Register of Historic Places, The Strand District comprises the area between Water (Avenue A) and Mechanic streets and from 20th to 25th streets. A century and more ago cotton flowed outward through this area and immigrants and industrial goods flowed in. The termination of the railroads in Houston rather than Galveston, the Houston Ship Channel (finished in 1914), and the September 8, 1900, hurricane combined to reverse trade trends and took away so much traffic that the city languished. However, Galveston is still the state's leading cotton port—it can berth thirty-eight ships—plus an assortment of other goods.

The urban hub of this erstwhile commerce and wealth—now adjacent to the contemporary business district—is the section being impressively uplifted. The Historical Foundation and Arts Council wisely

commissioned two broad, comprehensive studies before beginning
building-by-building attack. The first (1969), by Ford, Powell & Carson, focused on converting loft buildings into residences, while the second (1975), by Venturi & Rauch with Denise Scott Brown in charge,
encompasses a master plan for the entire length of The Strand. Its aim
—abetted by its Revolving Fund of 1973 and a Redevelopment Fund
of 1978, both granted by The Moody Foundation—is not a stage set
but bustling commercial activity with an active concern for the arts.
Among the finer structures (open during business hours but best seen
from the street) are: the Mensing Brothers Building Row, 2120–28
Strand (1882), architect unknown; First National Bank of Galveston,
2127 Strand (1866 and 1878), J. M. Brown, probable architect;
Greenleve, Block & Company Building, 2314 Strand (1882), Nicholas
J. Clayton, architect—marvelous cast-iron ground floor but decorniced
above; the sturdy Hutchings, Sealy & Company Building, 2326 Strand
(1895), Nicholas J. Clayton, architect; H. M. Trueheart & Company
Building, 212 22nd Street (1881), Nicholas J. Clayton, architect; and
the Galveston News Building, 2108–16 Mechanic Street (1884), Nicholas J. Clayton, architect, very lush.

Ongoing rehabilitating is taking place: to get up-to-date information and handy folders, contact the Galveston Historical Foundation, Hendley Building, 2014–16 Strand.

Many feel that much of the impetus for the city's vigorous activity in
restoring its fine old buildings and putting them to use stems from
Howard Barnstone's book *The Galveston That Was,* with evocative
photographs by Ezra Stoller and Henri Cartier-Bresson (Macmillan,
New York, and Museum of Fine Arts, Houston, 1966).

24 The Bishop's Palace/Gresham House (1887–93)
1402 Broadway
Galveston, Texas

NICHOLAS J. CLAYTON, ARCHITECT

Galveston, somewhat like Charleston and Mobile, has a number of historic and/or architectural gems. With few exceptions, they are—as in those other two delightful cities—not open to the public (but are visible to the stroller). With a background of Spanish discovery (1528),

Mexican seizure (1816), piratical usurpation (Lafitte from 1817–21), devastating fire (1885), and horrendous hurricane (1900), Galveston has experienced cosmopolitan vicissitudes. But since it was the largest port in the state until it was overtaken in 1914 by ambitious, canal-building Houston (whose port tonnage is now third largest in the United States), for a long time there was commerce, hence money, in Galveston, and from this came a sometimes flamboyant series of houses and commercial buildings, almost all dating from the last half of the past century. Clearly the most staggering is the mansion which Walter Gresham commissioned from his architect-neighbor Nicholas Clayton. Gresham's will was law to Clayton: it was simply to build the most elaborate house in the state, perhaps any state. Blocks from the breezes of the Gulf of Mexico, the building is strangely sited on a cramped lot, where the little-known Mr. Clayton went about his pleasurable task with enthusiasm. The exterior unfolds a catalog of almost every conceivable architectural motif: turrets with ogee "Gothic" arches, turrets with "Romanesque" round arches; chimneys (some fake) hinting of the Nile, chimneys clearly from the Rhine; stone griffins guarding the front door, bronze dragons protecting the roof; and when the ocher granite, white limestone, and red sandstone become ponderous, admirably delicate wrought-iron railings and brackets sweeten the load. With such a voluptuous introduction one enters the house—the latter "palace" trope is more descriptive—with anticipation: one is not betrayed. Though the rooms are surprisingly small, there is splendor in each, with detailing that has few rivals in late Victoriana. The stairhall is possibly the most ornate chamber, not a square inch of its oak left unseized upon, but the other main-floor rooms—each in a different wood and each projecting a supercostly mantel—are not to be outdone for conspicuous consumption. Continually occupied, the mansion has been kept in proper order. In 1923 it was sold to the Roman Catholic Diocese of Galveston, and, unfortunately, much of the original furniture was removed, though not to the impairment of the celestial stage set. The local Newman Club now occupies the lowest level.

Tours May 31–Labor Day, Mon.–Sat. 10–5, Sun. 1–5; winter tours daily 1–5: admission

The Sacred Heart Church (1903–4) stands directly across 14th Street. Brother Jiminez, S.J., achitect. (Open daily 6–6.) The first church on the site was totally destroyed by the Great Tidal Wave of September 8, 1900. Its Moresque-Indian replacement reflects that though the Moors were expelled from Spain in 1492, their 781-year

tenure of much of that sunny land had a lingering cultural impact which the Spanish occasionally carried to the New World. (The Spanish explorer Cabeza de Vaca was probably shipwrecked on Galveston Island in 1528.) On the exterior of the church, note the cusped arches in the tower and, within, the highly decorated columns of the nave. The dome, damaged by the 1915 storm, was enlarged on rebuilding.

25 Hill County Court House (1889–91)
Court House Square (off US 77/81)
Hillsboro, Texas

W. C. DODSON, ARCHITECT

A four-square, three-storied corpus of tawny limestone topped by a dazzlingly white, triple-tiered metal tower comprises this courthouse which indeed must have awed the dirt-road, wagon-transport cotton county which built it for $83,000. It makes a faith-in-law pile today. Each corner gets visual reinforcement from a squared projection with smartly handled Mansard roof (note corner detail of brackets and roof

returns), while the center of each facade bristles with a four-decker portico that might well have come out of *The Last Days of Pompeii*. The columns, the brackets, the sharply angled roof—with angled echoes on corners—all together make a stalwart mass though it has been claimed that locally it "stirs controversy." Not enough disaccord, fortunately, to keep the city fathers from renovating the entire structure (1970). The interiors, however, are of little architectural interest.

Open during office hours

26 Sam Houston Park Heritage Buildings (mid–late 19th century)
1100 Bagby Street at Lamar
Houston, Texas

The Harris County Heritage Society has given downtown Houston a
nostalgic series of buildings which re-create an architectural perspective
of the early days of this section of the country. The group and its
greenery add also a welcome respite to the concretion of skyscrapers so
near it. Anchored by the Kellum-Noble House—the only unit which
stands on its original site—three other houses, a church, a fine plantation cabin (1824) with cedar frame, and a reconstructed row of shops
have been brought together (with slightly unfocused disposition) and
rehabilitated. All of the buildings came from Harris County, and
though several were in parlous shape and the shops—Houston's
earliest—totally rebuilt from early documents, all have now been put
into mint condition. No original furniture was left in the dwellings, but
appropriate period pieces have been used. Note in the Kellum-Noble
House the functional porch which shields all four sides and both floors
from the sun and weather, undoubtedly an influence from adjacent
Louisiana. Built in 1847, it is thought to be the oldest brick dwelling

in the city. At one time serving as a private school, it was restored in 1954 as the first unit in the park. The Nichols-Rice-Cherry House (c. 1850) posseses an elaborate entrance, while an unexpected richness of wood detail within belies the chaste Greek Revival exterior. It shows a bit of upstate New York influence of the day, since its builder, Ebenezer B. Nichols, was a native of Cooperstown. St. John's Church was built by German Lutheran farmers in 1891: it is simple on the outside, but the interior is spacious and pleasant. Altogether a fine lot to which, it is hoped, subsequent additions will be made.

Tours Mon.–Fri. 10–4, Sat. 11–3, Sun. 2–5, except major holidays, Dec. 15–Jan. 1: admission

27 Old Cotton Exchange (1884–85/1907)
202 Travis Street at Franklin
Houston, Texas

EUGENE T. HEINER, ARCHITECT

Combining the Italianate with touches of Renaissance Revival, this red and white memento of the last century does much to decorate the north edge of downtown Houston. Its racy combination and array of windows begins with a double roundheaded central motif, continues with segmental and pedimented framing for the three main floors and falters with the plain sash on the fourth floor (which, however, was not added until 1907). Two prominent stringcourses tie the whole together, with a strongly bracketed cornice topping all. Note on the lower piers the alternation of brick with vermiculated blocking of stone. The trading room with its elaborate detailing has been fully restored. Though in sound structural condition, the building long stood empty until its restoration in 1973 by architect Graham B. Luhn. It is a National Registered Landmark—and fully rented.

Open during business hours

---

28 Tenneco Building (1962–63)
1010 Milam Street between Lamar and McKinney
Houston, Texas

SKIDMORE, OWINGS & MERRILL, ARCHITECTS

There is no necessity to hesitate: the thirty-three-story Tenneco ranks among a handful of great postwar skyscrapers in the United States. Although it lacks the regal approach of the Seagram Building in New York (q.v.) and the impeccability of its entrance, it exceeds that mentor of the high-rise world with the sterling quality of total urban three-dimensionality—which Seagram lacks on the back—for one can walk around the square Tenneco and find it richly identical on all four faces. (It measures 195.3 feet/59.5 meters on a side.) Much of the building's fascination stems from its subtly screened facades, for the walls are set back from the building frame to provide space for peripheral sun control. The extension of the floor slabs 5 feet/1.5 meters beyond the windows gives substantial horizontal sun and weather protection, which is augmented in each bay by a clever auxiliary louver, curved on the outer face, angled on the inner, and hollow within, with smart midpoint auxiliary suspension. As with other exoskeletal buildings, the slab projection also permits speedy window-washing (one sash per building side being openable for the window washer). Floor projection and louvers keep all but very low sun from the glass-walled offices; thus blinds and curtains are rarely needed within, while from the outside the dark, anodized aluminum space-game of the sun-measures sets up an ever-changing relationship.

The ground floor is inset on four sides, creating a sheltered 50-foot/15-meter-high "galleria" around the building, while a two-story bank is imaginatively slung from underneath the third floor, further freeing the sidewalk, and adding more spatial drama. The pink granite plaza around the building (on the ascetic side), was created by setting the building back 25 feet/7.6 meters from property lines (and thus enabling an unbroken tower). The setback also provides two truck ramps (down one, up the other) for service, with five drive-in banking kiosks on the northwesterly side, whose tellers reach them by underground circular stairs. The unusual elevator lobby employs a pinwheel arrangement of four arms of passenger lifts, plus escalators to the banking level. The office floors—the majority of which are occupied by Tenneco—are completely column-free, with a 55-foot/17-meter span of built-up girders between the square central service core and the aluminum-sheathed concrete-protected columns of the steel structural frame. One could live without the signs freighting the top (unfortunately added later: Tenneco just could not resist those seven empty bays), but its quietly stated sophistication and its answer to the stinging problem of local climate rank it with the very great. It was designed by the San Francisco office of Skidmore, Owings & Merrill.

Two other distinguished SOM skyscrapers stand nearby: **First City**

National Bank (1961) at 1021 Main Street, by the New York Office—with some sun control achieved by insetting the windows from the marble-clad frame, and the fifty-story **One Shell Plaza** (1971) by the Chicago office, one of the tallest reinforced-concrete buildings in the country.

Open during business hours

---

29 Jesse H. Jones Hall (1965–66)
615 Louisiana Street between Texas and Capitol
Houston, Texas

CAUDILL, ROWLETT, SCOTT, ARCHITECTS

Well wrapped in travertine (here from Italy), and surrounded by a stately but logical peristyle of piers which clearly support an independent roof, the Jesse H. Jones Hall for the Performing Arts sets a seignorial scene. The exterior, though formal, is not dour, while within, it is ingeniously planned. The great sheltering roof is upheld by eight slender

piers per side with the concert hall proper expressed as a freely shaped cocoon beneath, the entry to this cocoon standing clear and inviting. Moreover the peristyle surrounding the hall is illuminated at night and, as the marble facing is carried right into the inviting lobby, one finds oneself welcomed, magnetized inside before knowing it. This transfer of spaces, from out to in and back again, works easily, while the overhang of the roof on all sides facilitates arrival and departure by car in dirty weather. (There is also direct under-cover entrance via the public garage beneath the square in front.)

Inasmuch as the city block, which slopes down toward the front—and which the hall completely fills—measures 250 feet/76 meters on a side, and as a three-thousand-seat theater was desired, the architects were put to it to reconcile requests with realities. They achieved this by placing the auditorium, stage, and lobbies, and the free-form curved walls which enclose them, on a diagonal under the square roof, thus gaining maximum depth. This further permitted a wide entry in one corner, with a diminishing lobby wrapped around the sides and back of the auditorium. This extra width at the front door—facilitated by the narrow stage end adjacent—has been used to make a graciously wide, tall foyer, which steps up in three terraces to the rear of the auditorium, an ambitious Lippold wire sculpture arching over all: "the audience is part of the show." Lateral doors on stepped platforms give access to the hall proper, each door serving three rows of seats which radiate in the Continental, aisleless fashion, their bright red covering creating a cheery note. The inner walls of the auditorium are divided by piers wrapped with teak, creating an undulating effect that serves both acoustics and scale. The ceiling is made of 870 independent, bronze-colored, hexagonal panels which not only provide acoustic reflection but also screen the house downlights. Rows of these panels can be raised and lowered (as much as 27.5 feet/8.4 meters) to change seating capacity and acoustic-reverberation demands for various types of music from an orchestra to a single voice, or to a play. The system works beautifully. In addition to the main floor seating 1,781, boxes accommodate 286, a mezzanine (with distracting front edge) 326, and a balcony 608, for a total of 3,001.

Jesse Jones Hall was designed primarily for the Houston Symphony; however, it is also used for opera, ballet, and theatrical events. For concert performances the acoustic hexagons which cover the auditorium can be extended over the stage, and side "wings" pivoted into place, making "one room" of stage and auditorium. For other events this stage extension of ceiling and sides can be neatly folded and stored against the rear wall, enabling the overhead fly loft to be used. George C. Izenour, the theatrical consultant and engineer, developed the imaginative "theater mechanics" for electronically controlled acoustic flexibility; Bolt, Beranek & Newman were acoustic consultants; Charles E. Lawrence was the design partner of CRS. Jones Hall has been termed "the most sophisticated building of its kind anywhere in the world" (*Architectural Record,* February 1967).

Open during performances; some day tours; inquire

---

30   Alley Theatre (1967–68)
615 Texas Avenue, between Smith and Louisiana
Houston, Texas

ULRICH FRANZEN & ASSOCIATES, ARCHITECTS

Sheltering two separate theaters, the larger seating 798, the smaller 296, with an internal driveway separating the two while providing covered access, Alley Theatre sets high standards. It also brings a puzzlingly fortified exterior to the scene—"It is at once Southwestern and medieval, a fortress and a temple of art" says the official brochure.

(Its nine "turrets" house stairs and elevators.) The main theater provides seventeen rows of well-raked seats radiating in the Epidaurian manner 100° about its semithrust stage. No member of the audience is more than 75 feet/23 meters from the center of action, and as there is no proscenium or curtain, a fine relationship is established between actors and audience. Lateral extensions, or calipers, project from stage to envelop the auditorium. The side walls are matte black and thus disappear when the house lights are dimmed. The ceiling follows the curves of the seats in seven boldly stated bands: these are vertical on the rear, but variously angled facing the stage—their angle depending on acoustic-reflective index—and covered with natural wood strips. Though strong to the eye, they are gentle to the ear: acoustics are excellent. The stage itself is highly flexible, with numerous and effective multilevel actors' entries. A large lift for scenery is augmented by lateral "preset areas."

The smaller theater—recalling the original—is square in plan, with six ranks of seats framing its four-sided central stage, and is reached from the lobby by an almost secret passage. Its 296 seats enjoy a cockpit intimacy. Miss Nina Vance, who founded Alley Theatre—in a dance studio at the end of an alley—in 1947, worked closely with the architect on its design. MacKie & Kamrath were associate architects; George C. Izenour, lighting and theater consultant; Bolt, Beranek & Newman, acoustic consultants.

Performances Oct.–June; tours Tues.–Fri. 12:45; summer activities, July–Sept., except holidays

---

31 Superior Oil Research Laboratory (1967)
W from city on Westheimer Road, adjacent to Andrau Airport Houston, Texas

TODD TACKETT LACY, ARCHITECTS

Long and lean, this geophysical research laboratory stands as a model for a small exurban establishment. The program demanded highly flexible, column-free spaces that could be quickly altered to a variety of sizes. Adaptability was achieved—with elegance—under a broadly sheltering roof supported by exterior columns. The roof's depth contains the extensive utilities required for research activities. Rectangular in plan, the building frames an open central court, whose well-landscaped intimacy (by Garrett Eckbo) provides a fine foil to the

emptiness of the horizon. Felicity was sought in building, court, and furnishings both to keep happy the scientific staff who work on a dull plain 15 miles/24 kilometers from the city, and to create a receptive atmosphere for clients and visitors.

Reception area open during business hours

---

32 **Bates College of Law** (1966–67)
University of Houston
Gulf Freeway (IS 45) at Calhoun
Houston, Texas

FREEMAN & VAN NESS, ARCHITECTS

The first stages of a multibuilding law school for the enormously expanded university; they are keenly thought out and designed with a quiet sense of style. The library, the fulcrum of any law school, is

placed underground on its tight site, and topped by a plaza to create a nucleus for the five teaching units which are (or will be) plugged into it. These new units, the most recent by Pitts, Phelps & White, are limited to five hundred students each, representing, it is held, the optimum size for law instruction. A few details (such as entry of Administration Building) are questionable, but the overall scheme is admirable. John Freeman, Jr., was chief of design.

Open during school hours

---

33   Houston Intercontinental Airport (1966–69)
N on US 59 (Eastex Freeway), W on North Belt Road, N on
  Kennedy Boulevard
Houston, Texas

GOLEMON & ROLFE AND PIERCE, GOODWIN, ALEXANDER, ARCHITECTS

Houston Intercontinental Airport (HIA) documents the obvious precept—and was one of the first to do so—that an airport is nothing but a linkage stage of a transportation system, and not an end in itself. The

architects of most airports have been content to create a terminal, sometimes efficiently but generally indifferently, surrounded by acres of automobiles. Such a layout of necessity demands that the passenger, burdened with luggage, take a tedious hike to the check-in counter after he has locked his unattended car in left field under a broiling sun. Even if he checks his luggage at curbside, he still has his car to dispense with. The architects of the two-unit (eventually four-unit) Houston Airport (about 25 miles/40 kilometers north of downtown) brilliantly coupled automobile and plane, putting a garage on top of the terminal itself—773 cars per unit, and expandable with another floor. (A similar concept was pioneered by John B. Parkin Associates in 1961 for the Toronto International Airport.) One drives one's car up a ramp past the ticket lobby entrance either to a supervised under-cover garage, or to an open roof-top parking deck, or, if one elects (or if the terminal spaces are full) to a ground-level, 3,000-car open lot (in which lot, unfortunately, there is not one single tree for shade or to break up its mournful acreage). From roof parking the passenger takes an elevator down to the terminal departure floor and walks only a few feet/meters to his ticket counter. However, he then has to traverse the

300-foot/91-meter "concourse" to his satellite flight station, an over-all walking maximum of 600 feet/183 meters. (A basic improvement on this system can be seen in the Tampa, Florida, airport, q.v., which boasts the same concept of multidecked garage atop terminal, but cleverly—marvelously—uses automatic, horizontal, above-ground shuttles to whisk one to and from departure lounges: walking is at an absolute minimum.)

At Houston the two existing "unit terminals" (A and B) are con-nected by a closed-loop underground "train," allowing linear expan-sion—one of the system's advantages. The battery-operated trains are also used by passengers from the ground parking lots and to provide access to the terminal-area hotel. Another good feature occurs when one arrives or leaves a terminal: if by taxi or limousine one uses one side of the terminal, by rental car a second, and by private car a third, with baggage service taking up the fourth side. However, this logistic brilliance is not altogether matched by architectural elegance. Exter-nally the two terminals stand as strong masses but there is some weightiness in the elevated concourse "tubes" from terminal to flight station and in the largely enclosed automobile ramps. The terminals themselves are approximately 370 feet/113 meters square, with two public floors plus mezzanine, covered garage, and one parking deck. They send out from their diagonals the long solid walkways mentioned, each of the four ending in a circular "satellite" which accommodates five planes, with one holding station for sixty-five passengers per plane —an insufficient number if several jumbo jets, with three to four hun-dred souls each, arrive or leave at the same time. Moreover only one plane door (the front) can be employed. This situation is due to the fact that no wide-bodied planes had been designed when the terminal-construction contracts were awarded. It has been corrected in the design for the Third Terminal (June 1981). Passengers use the second floor of the satellites; baggage handling and operations occupy the ground level. The terminal interiors are of tans which produce quiet dignity. However, the lengthy tubes leading to the boarding areas are windowless, hence on the non-cheerful side. The airport's relation to the city—like that of any airport—should have commenced with a rapid transit or at least an exclusive traffic lane for buses and limou-sines. However, HIA does tap onto two freeways to downtown or the north. Engineers of the Southwest, engineers, a joint venture of Lock-wood, Andrews & Newman, Inc., Bovay Engineers, Inc., and Turner, Collie & Braden.

34 The Rothko Chapel (1970–71)
Yupon Street between Branard and Sul Ross
Houston, Texas

HOWARD BARNSTONE AND EUGENE AUBRY, ARCHITECTS

The late Mark Rothko and Barnett Newman were two of the great American artists of our time, and both have found sympathetic architectural setting in this non-denominational chapel and center for meditation. Newman's superb 26-foot/8-meter-high, weathering-steel *Broken Obelisk,* a memorial to Dr. Martin Luther King, Jr., points its shattered finger—the chapel's "steeple"—poignantly heavenward in the small reflecting pool. One then approaches the chapel, whose modified octagonal shape of salmonish brick is relieved only by the

black metal fascia over the front entrance. A darkened narthex leads via two separate doors into the inner octagon where three enormous Rothko "triptychs" and five single canvases, varying in size from 9–11 feet/2.7–3.3 meters wide and 11–15 feet/3.3–4.6 meters tall, virtually fill every wall. A sizable, centrally placed octagonal skylight, recalling —at Rothko's request—studio light, floods the chapel-gallery with natural illumination. The room itself with its grayish concrete walls, speckled gray asphalt paving-block floor, and elemental benches sets a stern stage for the art. For many observers "peace" and "transcendence" are evoked from these fourteen paintings—one gets from them more than one brings. For others these enormous purple, blackish, almost solid-color canvases—the colors "of blood and wine" —tend to weaken each other collectively. There is "mystery" but little "relief" because the pictures are so much alike. But see this chapel: it is puzzlingly provocative.

Open noon–8 P.M. *daily*

---

35   Greenway Plaza (1970–73)
off Southwest Freeway: take Buffalo Speedway exit N, c. 4 miles/6.4 kilometers SW of downtown Houston, Texas

LLOYD JONES BREWER & ASSOCIATES, ARCHITECTS

Houston, alone among major American cities, has no zoning restrictions. As a result, a plethora of freely dispersed office and office-living-shopping complexes has arisen in previous residential areas. Among the better of these is the eastern portion of Greenway Plaza, the first of four phases of an ambitious development which will not be completed until the mid-1980s. Such multi-use of land is of both urban and social significance. The 127 acres/51 hectares for the entire Greenway satellite were boldly acquired by offering far above market prices for the 305 houses and the several apartment blocks which once covered the site. (The subsequent conversion of the area to high-rise was made possible because, as mentioned, there was no zoning restriction.) Though primarily directed to providing office space, Greenway Plaza contains (or will contain) a 400-room hotel (already built), a 208-unit residential condominium (1981), a City (i.e. racket) Club, possibly another hotel, plus an extensive retail area known as The Underground. Excellent circulation, garaging, and visitor parking are found throughout. The four major buildings of Phase 1 (the eastern portion of Greenway Plaza) have a composed disposition and sense of openness. Sensitive landscaping, several large pools, and an accent of sculpture set an attractive scene. The high-rise Conoco, Kellogg, and Travelers Buildings are unified by the same light-colored, precast concrete, but vary in both window module and height. The dark hotel is not as satisfactory. The design of the recent expansion westward across Edloe Street does not measure as high as the early buildings.

Always open

36 **Contemporary Arts Museum** (1973)
Montrose Boulevard at Bisonnet Avenue
Houston, Texas

GUNNAR BIRKERTS & ASSOCIATES, ARCHITECTS

The Contemporary Arts Museum forms in plan an almost equilegged parallelogram, angled to set up a vibrant urban space with the Museum of Fine Arts diagonally across the street and the park (to be developed) in front. The building consists basically of a stainless-steel 45°/135° palisade around an open loft interior. Lest this description sound overly industrial, it forms for many an intriguing structure. A low ramp takes one to the calculatedly casual corner entry—a mere gap between wall ends: an anti-entry—and one arrives in a solid-walled, columnless, major exhibition space. Artificial lighting is used throughout. As the museum is almost exclusively devoted to changing exhibitions, partitioning is arranged on an *ad hoc* basis. The lower floor is devoted to smaller exhibitions, offices, and sales desk. A continuous line of angled windows acts as a clerestory for the basement on

most of two opposite sides. Although arbitrary in its geometry—it has been called a "corrugated metal shack"—it has been highly successful in attracting attendance.

Open Tues.–Sat. 10–5, Sun. 1–5, except major holidays

The museum was chartered in 1948, before the **Museum of Fine Arts** had a contemporary collection: it now complements the latter, which, of course, should be seen, particularly the two additions (1958/1974) designed by Mies van der Rohe. (Open Tues.–Sat. 9:30–5, Sun. 12–6, except major holidays.) Expanding the Classic Revival original museum (1924—William Ward Watkins, architect), the second—and still "classic"—Mies expansion was carried through by his office after his death in 1969. Called the Brown Pavilion, after its donors, it swings a curved facade around its formidable one-room exhibition space (83 x 300 feet/25 x 91 meters by 22 feet/6.7 meters high).

---

37 Best Products Showroom (1976)
W of Almeda Mall, off IS 45/US 75, c. 13 miles/21
    kilometers S of
Houston, Texas

SITE INC., ARCHITECT

Though this near-Gulf area is prone to hurricanes, disaster did not strike this southeast Houston catalog shop, as might seem to be the case. Jericho, possibly, was its subliminal inspiration, but neither Joshua nor Aeolus could have arranged such a gloriously imaginative "ruin" (or "unfinished building" as the architects prefer). In the bitingly competitive shopping world, attracting attention is an essential first step. However, the architects (in a personal letter) take pains to deny "that the project was conceived and sponsored as some sort of commercial advertising endeavor. This is simply not true on any level . . . The building is, in effect, a *found object* and the 'subject matter' of an art statement . . . The construction of the building has been an act of [art] patronage, pure and simple . . . Architecture is our subject matter and not necessarily our objective. In this way we hope to avoid the traditional frames of reference and formalist criteria in a search for other possibilities for public meaning." They had earlier written in an

article that "The typical response to the building has been to interpret
it as some sort of metaphor for apocalypse or destruction. The inten-
tions, however, are more concerned with 'missing parts,' with the gap
between the known and the void, with equivocation versus expectation
as sources for a new urban iconography. The impact of the building as
a public image is based upon these ambiguities" (*Skyline,* October
1978). Representing the firm's provocative philosophy of "De-
architecture" is the following: "Serving practical needs is important;
but more important is the fact that SITE's projects have, by drawing on
sources outside of the formalist/functionalist modern legacy, opened
up the question as to whether these traditions are necessarily the only
legitimate concerns of architecture" (*Architectural Review,* March
1978).

Houston's Best Products showroom is not thus to be dismissed as an
architectural billboard: because of it many architectural directions
have been questioned—and business has flourished. Maples-Jones were
associate architects.

Open during shopping hours

38   Pennzoil Plaza (1974–76)
Louisiana, Capitol, Milan, and Rusk Streets
Houston, Texas

JOHNSON/BURGEE, ARCHITECTS

In the increasingly exploratory world of skyscraper design, these twin
thirty-six-story towers establish a new and vibratory profile on downtown Houston. In plan they form two opposing trapezoids, their "opposing" ends angled at 45°. The point of each trapezoid aligns with the
rectangular base of the other to define a square block. In space, these
wedge-shaped towers set up an exquisite tension at the point of their
near meeting. This geometric interplay is accented by the 45°-angled

roof atop each, providing constantly changing silhouettes as one moves
around the city. (The angled roof was a suggestion of J. Hugh Liedtke,
the Chairman of the Board of the Pennzoil Company. He wanted the
towers "to soar, to reach, and a flat-top doesn't reach"—*P/A* 8:77.)
Abstract mathematics continue close up where the slanting roofs,
which connect the bases of the towers to form covered entries, meet
the sidewalks (not altogether smoothly). Their angled triangular
forms, again at 45°, are totally unexpected at this level, and of course
generate an interaction with the street-level viewer that changes in motion. Wind-tunnel testing was conducted with models to be certain that
turbulence would not be created by the towers' shapes, in particular by
the 10-foot/3-meter slot between them. The Pennzoil towers are
sheathed in dark glass for both windows and spandrels (the latter
backed by concrete block)—a questionable decision for a latitude parallel with south Cairo—but this native somberness is heartened by its

sharp geometry. On the interior the eight-story high, glass-roofed entries are flooded with light, trees, and people, providing a cheerful introduction. Note the white-painted space-frame of its roof: its contrast
with the dark walls is excellent. On the first basement level there is a
shopping mall and below this three levels of garage with space for five
hundred automobiles. An underground pedestrian way connects Pennzoil Plaza with a network of weatherproof communications—Houston's Downtown Tunnel System. This extends nine blocks from the
Plaza and will eventually interlace most of the central business (and
hotel) district. The building was awarded the R. S. Reynolds Memorial
Award for distinguished use of aluminum in 1978. S. I. Morris of
Houston was associate architect; Ellisor Engineers were structural consultants.

Open during business hours

---

39 Texas Tech University (1969–70)
Lubbock, Texas

Texas Tech has undergone great expansion in the last few years in the bustling city of Lubbock. Founded in 1923, it now has over 23,000 students. Among its appropriate concerns is its International Center for Arid and Semi-Arid Land Studies. Two buildings of interest are the School of Law (1969), 19th Street (US 62) at Hartford Avenue, by Harrell + Hamilton (public areas open during school year), and the Architecture Building (1970), 19th Street at Flint Avenue, by Ford, Powell & Carson (museum open during school year). The Law School is trim on the exterior, possesses friendly scale, and excellent interiors. The Architecture Building, though mannered in its facades, is a spatial delight within, especially its exhibition areas.

---

40   Winedale Historical Center (1834–1850s)
University of Texas at Austin
**17 miles/27 kilometers NE of La Grange on TEX 237 to Round
    Top, 4.5 miles/7.2 kilometers E on TEX 1457, NE on TEX
    2714, 4.1 miles/6.6 kilometers E of village**
Round Top, Texas

The restoration of the Lewis-Wagner House and the collection of ancillary buildings from nearby sites give insight into the rural work in

the last century of this section of Texas (between Austin and Houston). The earliest part of the local cedar house was a one-room cabin, built around 1834; then in the 1850s this was substantially enlarged by a new owner who added a twin section to the north, a second floor to each, and tied them together with the two-story porch seen today. It was at this time that the kitchen was built behind. A German touch—there were many mid-nineteenth-century German immigrants to central Texas—can be seen in the wall paintings and stenciling, done about 1854 by Rudolf Melchior. The buildings and the 160-acre/65-hectare farmstead were purchased in 1963 by Miss Ima Hogg and made part of the University of Texas (1967) as a study center of ethnic groups which settled the central part of the state. In addition to the Lewis-Wagner farm house, there are two Greek Revival dwellings which were moved to the site in 1967–68: the McGregor-Grimm House (1861) and the Lauderdale House (1858). Restoration is also proceeding at nearby Round Top (population 124).

Open Sat. 10–5, Sun. 12–5, by appointment weekdays: admission

---

41   Fort Concho (1868–81)
714 Burgess Street at Avenue D
San Angelo, Texas

The fort buff will want to see these seventeen buildings (of an original thirty-nine). Eight are in various stages of restoration; two have been reconstructed; seven await restoration; and several others are to be reconstructed on their original sites. Most are made of local limestone, with beams of pecan—the state tree—and wood shingles. The fort was an important base during the Indian Wars and at times housed several distinguished black cavalry regiments, nicknamed the Buffalo Soldiers. Founded as Camp Hatch in 1867, it became Fort Concho the following year. Abandoned in 1886, the fort experienced ups and downs in private hands until the Administration Building became a museum in 1930 and a restoration campaign was begun. Five buildings are devoted to exhibits that feature military and civilian history of the fort period. There is a small exhibit of Plains Indian artifacts. Fort Concho is a registered National Historic Landmark.

Open Mon.–Sat. 9–5, Sun. 1–5, except Jan. 1, Dec. 24–25: admission

42   Central High School (1957–58)
West Harris Avenue at Cottonwood
San Angelo, Texas

CAUDILL, ROWLETT, SCOTT, ARCHITECTS

As one of the pioneering schools when it was finished, the eleven buildings composing San Angelo Central High exerted a profound influence on U.S. pedagogical thinking and design. It also—rightly— helped launch its architects to national prominence. School building today has drawn away from multi-unit "campus plans," tending toward a compacted, flexible plant (see CRS's high school in Anniston, Alabama), but San Angelo remains one of the finest of the dispersed-unit, well-landscaped, one-story high schools to be seen. Frank D. Lawyer was chief of design; Max D. Lovett was associate architect.

Open during school hours

---

43 San José Mission (1740s/1768–82)
c. 5 miles/8 kilometers S of city off US 281 (Roosevelt Avenue)
at Mission Road
San Antonio, Texas

The Mission of San José y San Miguel de Aguayo—the last name belonging to the then-governor of Texas and the patron of the church —was the most important, as well as being the best fortified in New Spain. It has been referred to as the Queen of Missions. Earlier than the California missions, and sometimes more elaborate, more sophisticated than the primitive adobe churches of New Mexico, the five Spanish- and Mexican-influenced stone missions in and south of San Antonio form a vital chapter in Spanish architecture in the United States. Of these San José is by far the most impressive. The Mission (which had been founded in 1720 but moved twice) forms a large compound, approximately 500 x 550 feet/152 x 168 meters. Its eighty-four apartments for Christianized Indians (Payayas) line three walls of the enclosure, a granary (formerly the first church) stands in the northwest corner, with prefecture and quarters for the few soldiers making the fourth wall, the present church being inset at the northeast. The buildings along the walls, which were, of course, windowless on the outside, are of relatively little architectural interest except for the vaulted and buttressed granary, but the church, at least its facade, is one of the glories of the Spanish contribution to building in this country. The main entrance sparkles with its Spanish Baroque or Churrigueresque richness of ornament played off against the simple stuccoed walls of its semi-Moorish facade. (It is interesting in this counterpoint of ornamental accent leaping from a plain surface to re-

call Louis Sullivan's similar excursions in banks, especially that at Grinnell, Iowa [q.v.].) The church's external elaboration did not, however, stop at a superbly rich entry and portal window, for most of the building was—originally—covered with stucco decorated with geometric patterns. A small sample of this can still be seen near the lower right-hand corner of the tower. This strong use of color, like that which once brightened Athens' Parthenon, is now but a monochrome of former glories. The highly accomplished carvings of the front of the church and of the so-called "rose window" on the south wall were the work of Pedro Huizar, a Mexican, born in Aguascalientes in 1740, according to most sources. Many feel that this is "the finest Spanish Colonial facade in the United States" (Hugh Morrison in his *Early American Architecture,* Oxford University Press, 1952), though others might opt for San Xavier del Bac (Arizona q.v.). The church now standing—an earlier one was torn down to make way for this—was not started, according to most authorities, until 1768 and not finished until 1782. Built of thick walls of local tufa and roofed with four groin vaults and one dome (over what would be the transept), the church forms a simple and today unprepossessing rectangular interior, but one unquestionably covered with frescoes when built. A three-bay baptistry lies along one side, while behind the sanctuary stretch the intriguing ruins of the monks' vaulted cells and the cloister.

All, however, did not go well with San José—or with its sister missions. Upon partial secularization in 1794, then full secularization (1824) by the now independent Mexicans—in revolt against Church political power—desuetude set in, with only the chapel and some land remaining in Church hands. Part of the north wall collapsed in 1868, followed by most of the roof six years later. Meanwhile the magnificent portal sculpture was used for target practice and, more recently, chopped at by souvenir hunters. The original cedar front door was stolen but later reconstructed from old photographs. Then in the 1930s sentiment for the Mission's reconstruction became effective and through the combined efforts of the San Antonio Conservation Society, the Roman Catholic Church, Bexar County, and the Works Progress Administration—all working under the architectural direction of Harvey P. Smith—the complete compound was rebuilt and the church restored (except for the decorated stucco on the exterior and the frescoes within). In 1941 it was made a National Historic Site, full restoration being completed in 1949. This is one of our great examples of Spanish architecture.

Open Apr.–Sept., daily 9–8, Oct.–Mar., daily 9–6: admission

44   Spanish Governor's Palace (c. 1722–49)
105 Military Plaza, facing City Hall
San Antonio, Texas

The milieu of the Governor's Palace could stand improvement and the building's facade is hardy palatial (except for the dextrously paneled front doors), but the interior is very atmospheric. Within its massive stone walls (c. 3 feet/.9 meter thick), all of its ten rooms—the three in the center without windows—have been restored, and though they might bear problematic relation to those of 250 years ago, they do constitute a reasonable facsimile of the original. The garden behind also merits exploration. When the last governor left in 1821 (upon Mexico's independence), the "palace" gradually degenerated into a slum. In 1929 the city, spurred by conservation groups, purchased it and, aided by documentation plus an 1804 will, began complete restoration under the direction of Harvey P. Smith. The palace was opened to the public in 1931—two hundred years after the establishment of the *presidio* of San Antonio (itself founded in 1718).

Open Mon.–Sat. 9–5, Sun. 10–5, except Dec. 24–25: admission

---

45   Mission Concepción (1731–55)
807 Mission Road, near intersection IS 10 with US 281
San Antonio, Texas

Mission Nuestra Señora de la Purísima Concepción de Acuña, alas, no longer ranks among the architecturally elite of that legacy of missions which the Spanish founded from Tejas (i.e. "friends") to California in the seventeenth and eighteenth centuries. It is, however, well worthy of a visit. Its once-large compound housing 247 Indians is gone and the facade of the church (1740–55), though intact, has faded to monochrome. Moreover the front has always been marked by a lack of cohesion and harried by its geometrically determined pediment. Its cruciform interior is today simple to the point of plainness, even the contemporary main altar lacking verve (the transept altars are originals). This was not always so, as examination of the baptistry and belfry will suggest, even though their surface (but not structure) has largely disintegrated. The vestiges of former frescoes remaining inside recall that at one time both interior and facade were alive with geometric color—as at nearby San José. In 1824, following complete secularization (it had been partially secularized in 1793), the church was abandoned for thirty-one years, during which period it suffered defacement and partial destruction of the living quarters (possibly during the nearby Battle of Concepción in 1835), but the church itself

fortunately remained structurally intact, and claims to be "The oldest unrestored Church structure in the U.S." The reason for its strength resides in the 45-inch/1.1-meter-thick wall construction of dressed stone on both faces with small stone and some adobe between. Also the north and east walls were made windowless against possible attack. Shortly after World War II, the U. S. Government even marked part of the Mission (the kitchen) an official fallout shelter! The church was rededicated in 1887 and has been in active service since, its nave having been plastered and painted white. It measures 89 feet/27 meters long by 22.5 feet/6.8 meters wide.

Open daily 10–6: admission

46 The Secondary Missions (early–mid-18th century)
San Antonio, Texas

Those with missions in mind will want to see—in addition, of course, to San José and Concepción (q.v.)—Mission San Antonio de Valero, otherwise known as the Alamo, where the city was founded on Alamo Plaza, only the chapel (c. 1744) of which survives. Renovated in

1849, it now serves as a sentimental museum. (Open Mon.–Sat. 9–5:30, Sun. 10–5:30, except Dec. 24–25.) Also, San Juan Capistrano (1762) SE of the city on US 181, west on Mission Road, being restored (open daily 10–6, except Dec. 25: admission); and Mission San Francisco de la Espada (eighteenth century) beyond San Juan on Espada Road, much ruined but with rebuilt chapel still in use. (Open daily 10–6, except Dec. 25: admission.)

47 José Antonio Navarro State Historical Site (c. 1850)
228 South Laredo Street
San Antonio, Texas

The Navarro Historic Complex, located in downtown San Antonio, gives us an excellent example of Texas regional architecture of more than a century ago. The site contains a house, detached kitchen, and a two-story office or *despacho,* all of which have been carefully restored. In their design and construction they reflect a mixture of Spanish, German, French, and pioneer elements. Built of whitewashed adobe, caliche, and limestone blocks, the three were compactly laid out to create two pleasant patios, complete with grape arbor and trees. Period furnishings, interpretive displays, and guided tours provide insight into the life, times, and culture of this prominent Texas-Mexican patriot, a central figure in the formation of Texas. (He was one of only two

native-born Texans to sign the state's Declaration of Independence in 1836.) The property was acquired by the San Antonio Conservation Society in 1962, with restoration soon following. In 1975 the Society donated the site to the state of Texas, and since that time it has been operated by the Texas Parks and Wildlife Department. The complex is listed in the National Register of Historic Places.

Open Tues.–Sat. 10–4, except major holidays: admission

---

48 Edward Steves House (1876)
509 King William Street
San Antonio, Texas

ALFRED GILES, ARCHITECT

An amalgam of Victorian motifs embraces the Steves House under its Mansard roof and, as the interior and extensive furnishings are largely intact, we find a representative picture of the dwelling of a well-to-do "German" family of a century ago. Note especially the kitchen—and also the pegged picket fence in front. The property is owned by the

San Antonio Conservation Society and the dwelling is the residence of the Director of the Society.

Open daily 1–5, except Jan. 1 and Dec. 25: admission

King William Street is now listed in the National Register of Historic Places as a Historic District, bounded by the San Antonio River, Durango, Alamo, and Guenther streets. Although none of the houses except the Steves and #107—the Society's headquarters—are open to the public, a stroll will unfurl a parade of houses mostly dating from the last half of the nineteenth century, and largely built by German merchants. The Society issues a useful walking guide.

---

49   Paseo del Rio: The River Walk
San Antonio River—midtown
San Antonio, Texas

As vital as any artery of the human body, the River Walk infuses animation—and almost bucolic relief—to the asphalt midriff of San Antonio. Winding and pulsating in a horseshoe shape through the downtown area, lined with diverting shops, cafes, and restaurants, with promenades on either side and a *bateau mouche* ferrying the sightseers (with police boats making their appointed rounds), this tiny meander (about 3 miles/4.8 kilometers long) is the delight of the city. The Paseo extends non-authoritarian contact with flowing waters almost totally unencumbered by fences, barriers, or even guide rails: it is a brilliant example of responsible man and responsive nature. At night proper illumination cheers the way. Water taxis, paddle boats and sight-seeing (and dinner) barges are available: fiestas are often scheduled. A few of the pedestrian bridges are bulky, and one can quarrel with other details, but the concept is glorious, the landscaping and plant variety in general excellent—at times superb—and the overall a crown for St. Anthony of Padua for whom the city was named.

This small stream, lying some 20–25 feet/6–7.6 meters below street level—where the world above, fortunately, disappears—was sentenced to become a paved-over culvert in the 1920s (following a severe flooding). Debate ensued and a stay of execution was effected by aroused citizens. Run-off dams for flood control were erected, and during the

Depression much of the groundwork of what can be seen today was commenced under the Works Progress Administration (1937–41 —Robert H. Hugman, architect). Following World War II and the flight to the suburbs, a puzzling neglect set in. But in the 1960s, when the Paseo's potential as a tourist attraction—plus its very great value as a local amenity—was realized, a River Development Feasibility Study was completed and a River Walk Advisory Commission created (1962). Cyrus Wagner and O'Neil Ford of the American Institute of Architects' local chapter, and David Strauss, of the Chamber of Commerce, were key figures in the activity that followed. The city's 1968 HemisFair hastened the work. There are now plans to extend the development of all the river's length within the city limits (c. 10 miles/16 kilometers). Much of the river bed, incidentally, is "paved" with concrete and—like Venice's canals—is drained and cleaned at proper intervals.

The most imaginative architectural accent along the Paseo is the River Square Project (1970) off Commerce Street, Cyrus Wagner, architect, and the marvelous hundred-year-old Stockman Building (1868/1971) remodeled by Ford, Powell & Carson—all, it should be added, without commercialism. The Paseo is one of the country's great urban experiences: it might even be what downtown is all about. Don't miss it.

---

50   Ruth Taylor Theater (1965–66)
Trinity University
Stadium Drive
San Antonio, Texas

FORD, POWELL & CARSON; BARTLETT COCKE & ASSOCIATES, ARCHITECTS

The drama department of Trinity has attained national recognition, and one of the key factors has been the series of interconnected theaters and related buildings which the above-mentioned architects have designed over the years. Though all have been built with restricted, sometimes minimal funds, and though they span three decades and more of growth, all are characterized by efficiency, comeliness, and homogeneity. The Ruth Taylor Theater takes advantage of its hillside site to produce a several-level design. The main stage—Theater One— almost envelops the forward part of the auditorium level. This front

section has 140 seats that are cleverly designed to swivel so that the audience can turn comfortably to follow any action on the three stages. 186 fixed seats back these up with a balcony holding 86 more. Theater One is supplemented by a 108-seat Attic Two and a jolly Cafe Theater. All are interconnected with the Art Building (1961), making a quietly stated but rewarding university group. Funds for the theater were donated by the Ruth and Vernon Taylor Foundation.

Adjacent to and closing the three-sided court, stands the quarter-round **Laurie Auditorium** and **Communications Center** (1971), also by Ford, Powell & Carson and Bartlett Cocke & Associates. This is tied to the theater and arts complex—and all to the rolling terrain—to produce a low-key, economic, but beautifully scaled series of facilities grouped around a very hospitable brick *cortile*. Although it has been built on a minimum budget, there is no "barn" atmosphere but a fine setting for the muses and a family feeling for the audiences, inside and out. The auditorium's long, rounded rear wall (copper-finished stainless steel) is carefully handled to keep its large mass from dominating the other structures. Within, its fan-shape plan holds 3,100 seats—to accommodate the entire student body and the faculty—while its stage is flexible enough to present opera or concerts. Acoustics are excellent. Note the easy relation of auditorium to lobby. A 300-car garage is tucked underneath, utilizing the drop in grade to eliminate ramps.

Open during performances

51   Tower of the Americas (1967–68)
       HemisFair Grounds, South Alamo Street
       San Antonio, Texas

**FORD, POWELL & CARSON, ARCHITECTS; FEIGENSPAN &
PINNELL, STRUCTURAL ENGINEERS**

A stirring of lofty towers has developed throughout Europe, Japan,
and North America in the last few years, but it is doubtful if any has
been as stylishly designed or as imaginatively engineered as this which
was built for the San Antonio HemisFair of 1968. The architects

sought the simplest of silhouettes for their profile, and they used a pared shaft with a subtly molded restaurant topping, for maximum effect both by day and by night. The chief problem in a tower 652 feet/199 meters high (roof of Top House; 750 feet/229 meters to top of mast), with well over five hundred people moving around at the tip of this vertical cantilever, lies in constructional stability. Not only is wind a very demanding meteorological factor, but ice is not unknown, while the sun pushes first one side with expansion then the other to set up a bending movement. To meet best these wind and temperature forces, a twelve-sided "finned" shaft of interlocked triangles, 45 feet/14 meters in "diameter," was evolved, a design (tested in wind tunnels) which maximizes stability and minimizes sun load on any one side. It is also a design which sets up excellent scale, and, entertainingly, led to the use of three external elevators which chase up and down the tower's sides with enthusiasm. Fifty-five piers were sunk into the shale (63 feet/19 meters down) to form the foundation base. On this rests a concrete "cap" 92 feet/28 meters in diameter and 8 feet/2.4 meters thick (and made in a single pour). Above the angled buttresses of the base, the concrete for the tower was poured by slip-forming, while the steel-framed Top House was assembled on the ground and inched up the completed shaft by hydraulic jacks. (The Top House weighs 1,800,000 pounds/816,466 kilograms.) The core of the tower contains three high-speed elevators and two emergency stairwells (952 steps). At the top a revolving restaurant (a circuit an hour) occupies the first level, a stationary restaurant the second, with total seating of 452, and an observation deck on top. Great day and night. Boone Powell was the project architect.

Open daily 8 A.M.*—midnight: admission*

---

52   **Suspension Bridge** (1866–70)
     University Park Drive at Taylor Avenue
     Waco, Texas

THOMAS M. GRIFFITH, SUPERVISING ENGINEER

Wacoans claim that their 475-foot/145-meter bridge over the Brazos River was, when built, "the longest single span suspension bridge in the world," opening a good ten years before the much longer Brooklyn Bridge in New York City (q.v.). However, it should be brought out

that the 10th Street Bridge in Wheeling, West Virginia (q.v.), was over twice as long; it was opened in 1849, destroyed in 1854, and rebuilt in 1856. The cables for the Texas span were supplied by the Roebling Company and hauled by oxen from Galveston. Built privately, the Waco bridge was sold to the county in 1889 and thence operated as a free public thoroughfare. The bridge was repaired in 1885 and 1914. Now closed (1971) to vehicular traffic, it is still open to pedestrians. The four stalwart piers, faintly gothicized, are of brick stuccoed, the 2,700,000 bricks used having been made locally. The city was named for a tribe of Indians (long displaced) called Huecos by the Spanish; their once sacred spring lies near the bridge on the west bank.

There are several typical nineteenth-century houses in Waco open to the public (at least on Saturday and Sunday, 2–5 P.M.: admission). Two of the best are the Greek Revival **Earle-Napier-Kinnard House** (1867), 814 South 4th Street, with a two-story Ionic porch, and the restored (1966) Italianate **East Terrace** (c. 1872), 100 Mill Street.

53 **Ellis County Court House** (1894–97)
Main Street (US 287)
Waxahachie, Texas

J. RIELY GORDON, ARCHITECT

Towered and turreted, this is "one of the most interesting and literate of all the Richardsonian court houses" (*Court House,* edited by Richard Pare, Horizon, 1978). We find here a bastion of granite (gray for base, pink above), sandstone, and terra-cotta that will interest the specialist. The interiors are unprepossessing. Mr. Gordon (1863–1937), incidentally, supposedly designed sixty-nine courthouses in his long career, and was even commissioned to do the Texas Pavilion at the New York World's Fair of 1939–40.

Open during office hours

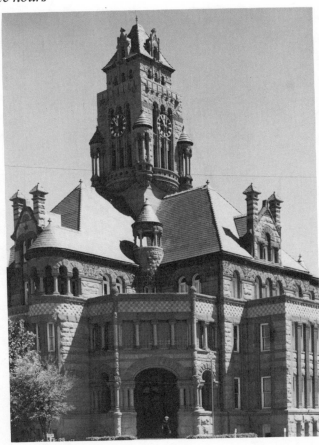

54 Parker County Court House (1884–86)
intersection of US 80/180 and TEX 51
Weatherford, Texas

W. C. DODSON & W. W. DUDLEY, ARCHITECTS

This prairie stalwart is a tamer edition of its confrere by Dodson at Hillsboro (q.v.), but its cream-colored granite aspirations are still exuberant. Its four sides are identical, each with gabled entry, the whole topped by substantial clock tower.

The rich legacy of Texas courthouses adds a vivid chapter to southwest architecture.

Open during office hours

Utah

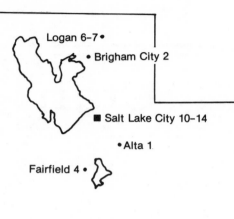

Logan 6–7 •

• Brigham City 2

■ Salt Lake City 10–14

• Alta 1

Fairfield 4 •

• Manti 8

• Fillmore 5

• Cove Fort 3

Santa Clara 15
•
• St. George 9

UTAH

The buildings in boldface type are of general interest. The others are for the specialist.

Alta	1 **Snowbird Village** (1972–)—Brixen & Christopher
Brigham City	2 Brigham City Tabernacle (c. 1876–81)
Cove Fort	3 Cove Fort (1867)
Fairfield	4 **Stagecoach Inn** (c. 1858)
Fillmore	5 Territorial Statehouse (1851–55)—Truman O. Angell
Logan	6 **Logan Tabernacle** (1865–1915) Mormon Temple (1877–84)—Truman O. Angell, Jr.
	7 Fine Arts Center (1967–68)—Burtch W. Beall, Jr.
Manti	8 **Manti Temple** (1877–88)—William H. Folsom
St. George	9 Brigham Young Winter Home (1869/ 1873–74)—Miles Romney and son
Salt Lake City	10 Beehive House (1853–55)—Truman O. Angell
	11 **Salt Lake Tabernacle** (1863–68) **and Temple Square**—Brigham Young; William H. Folsom and Truman O. Angell; Henry Grow
	12 ZCMI Department Store (1876/1976)—William H. Folsom and Obed Taylor
	13 **City and County Building** (1891–94)—Proudfoot, Bird & Monheim
	14 **Special Events Center** (1967–69)—Young & Fowler
Santa Clara	15 **Jacob Hamblin House** (1862–63)

Snowbird Village (1972–   )
**UT 210, Little Cottonwood Canyon, just S of
Alta, Utah**

BRIXEN & CHRISTOPHER, ARCHITECTS

The first phase of the Snowbird development, a 160-unit condominium
with support facilities, augurs well. Eventually there will be a sizable
Alpine village, every square millimeter of which has been carefully
analyzed and planned so that its buildings will fit into the landscape

with the minimum of intrusion. Before construction began, a ten-year overall master plan was projected to ensure logical and coherent development, one which will offer all-year recreational and convention facilities, eventually reaching a population of several thousand. An aerial tram and ski lifts, with up to 3,100 feet/945 meters of vertical rise, take one to some of the finest skiing in the country. (Located some 32 miles/51 kilometers southeast of Salt Lake City, Snowbird has a base altitude of 8,100 feet/2,469 meters.) The architects carefully avoided *Heimatstil* in their buildings, calling instead on a direct expression of reinforced concrete frame—partially for Zone 3 earthquake requirements—with walls of natural cedar, local stone, and glass.

They even went so far as to roof the lodge with sod and grass in the Scandinavian fashion, but here not for insulation but to minimize the building when viewed from above. Rectitude with élan are the result: one of the most keenly thought-out mountain recreational developments that one will see.

---

2   Brigham City Tabernacle (c. 1876–81)
Main Street between 2nd and 3rd South Streets
Brigham City, Utah

A striking tabernacle which has natural limestone and sandstone walls buttressed by sixteen red-painted brick piers. These are topped by white-painted pinnacles, the whole dominated by a white tower against a dark gray roof and accented by greenish milk-glass windows. The Box Elder Stake Tabernacle of The Church of Jesus Christ of Latter-day Saints—to use its original (and full) name—ranks as one of the most zestful members of Utahan religious monuments. A fire in 1896 destroyed parts of it, but the tabernacle was rebuilt, with some alterations of pinnacles and tower, over the next two years. A pre-fire painting, discovered in 1978, shows that the brick buttresses were an integral part of the original design.

Open late May–early Sept., daily 9–9

---

3 **Cove Fort** (1867)
**on UT 4 and 161, c. 1 mile/1.6 kilometers E of IS 15 (23
    miles/37 kilometers N of Beaver)**
Cove Fort, Utah

An unprepossessing square on the outside, the fort's interior presents an active scene. Made of local black volcanic rock and rubble, the fort measures 100 feet/30 meters square and 18 feet/5.5 meters high, its walls tapering from 4 feet/1.2 meters thick at bottom to half that at top. Its gates, the main one (on the east side) some 14 feet/4.3 meters square so as to admit a loaded wagon, were made hollow and filled with sand against flaming arrows. The prominent "crenellations" seen on the exterior are the chimneys which rise from the six rooms on both north and south sides—with firing ports between. The twelve rooms have all been restored (the north side had collapsed and was rebuilt in 1917) and furnished of the period. Cove Fort was built by the Mormons following the unrests generated by the Black Hawk War (1832) and local Ute uprisings (1865–68). The fort also served as an inn, a use to which it was again put when Indian attacks subsided. In 1903 the fort, which had by then been abandoned, was leased by the Church to the Kesler family, which purchased it outright in 1911, the Kesler heirs restoring it.

Open Apr.–Oct., daily 8–7: admission

---

4   **Stagecoach Inn** (c. 1858)
    off UT 73 at North and West Streets
    Fairfield, Utah

The Mormons were looked upon with suspicion by the federal government in the 1850s, their Church in Washington's eyes claiming precedence over civil government. To underscore federal authority, the sizable Camp Floyd (it mustered one of the largest troop concentrations in the country) was built during the so-called Utah War of 1857–58. One John Carson had earlier settled in Fairfield, erecting a walled compound in which he lived with his family. However, with the arrival of thousands of troops, Mr. Carson demolished his "fort" and put up the inn seen today—where, it might be added, the commanding general of Camp Floyd was wont to stay. It is a simple, L-shaped building of two stories, strictly compass-oriented in the approved Mormon fashion, and constructed of plastered adobe and wood. A porch and gallery grace the south side, with a one-story kitchen on the north. Given to the state (1958)—after serving almost a hundred years as a hostel—the building, which had become dilapidated, has been restored (1962 —Burtch W. Beall, Jr., architect in charge), properly furnished, and

opened to the public (1964). It is now maintained by Utah's Division of Parks and Recreation. Camp Floyd itself—which lasted only three years—was decommissioned at the outset of the Civil War, but its impact, even in its brief career, was great in that it helped open up Utah to gentiles, as non-Mormons were called.

Open mid-Mar.–mid-Nov., daily 9–5

5 Territorial Statehouse (1851–55)
50 West Capitol Avenue—behind County Court House
Fillmore, Utah

TRUMAN O. ANGELL, ARCHITECT

The simple building we see today, by the same architect who did much work in Temple Square in Salt Lake City, was to be only the first of four wings projecting in Greek-cross plan with their meeting topped by

a Moorish dome. However, as Salt Lake City became the head of the Provisional State of Deseret in 1851—deseret, in the Book of Mormon, is a honeybee—only one arm was finished. Note its Greek Revival touches. The building was restored in 1927 and opened to the public in 1930 as the state's first "park." It now functions as a regional museum.

Open summer, daily 8–7, rest of year 8–5: admission

---

6   Logan Tabernacle (1865–1915)
Main Street at Center
Logan, Utah

Quoins, that Renaissance gift of exaggerated corner edging and framing, have been called on with dedication in this tabernacle. (The word "quoin" is, of course, an Anglicization of the French *coin* for corner.) Of white-painted limestone here they give strong decorative accents to the natural quartzite walls. A sturdy wood cupola tops the stone tower. The entry was pushed forward during the remodeling of 1915. The unusual interior, which seats two thousand, is dominated by a wall-to-wall organ.

*Open June–Labor Day, Mon., Fri., Sat. 10–5, Tues., Wed., Thurs.
10–9, except holidays*

The castellated **Mormon Temple** (1877–84) on the hill to the northeast, 1st North and 2nd East streets, though not open to the general public, should also be seen for its grounds (open all year—guided
tours available) and its commanding position. Truman O. Angell, Jr.,
was its architect. It is very similar to the Temple at Manti (q.v.),
begun the same year.

---

7   **Fine Arts Center** (1967–68)
Utah State University
off 700 North Street at 1100 East
Logan, Utah

BURTCH W. BEALL, JR., ARCHITECT

Of striated natural concrete and red brick, this arts complex strongly anchors the eastern edge of an otherwise undistinguished campus. Its multiple functions of concert hall, theater, art and ballet instruction, music practice, and staff offices are well handled and expressed in its massing. The second phase of the project, the Visual Art Department, has not been built and, therefore, the chief approach on the north side is not as positive as it otherwise would be. The main focus of the capable interior lies in the theater and concert hall facilities. The concept of surrounding the performing areas with classroom facilities is strongly reflected in the massing of the building.

Art Gallery open Mon.–Fri. 8–5, except major holidays; theater/concert hall open for performances

---

8 Manti Temple (1877–88)
on US 89, N edge of town
Manti, Utah

WILLIAM H. FOLSOM, ARCHITECT

As with other temples (but not tabernacles) of the Faith, non-Mormons cannot enter the Manti Temple, but they are welcome to its grounds and to the adjacent Visitors' Center (on the north side). (As was explained to the author, a Mormon temple is not strictly a "house of worship." Temples are used for the performance of certain ordinances in favor of both the living and the dead. Congregations do not meet for worship purposes in the usual sense of the word.)

Surveying the Sanpete Valley, Manti Temple's exterior—like its three contemporaries in Utah—combines a variety of architectural influences with hints of the Gothic Revival, topped by a mixture of mid-nineteenth-century motifs in the Second Empire manner. When the Mormons first moved into this section of central Utah in 1849, they entered a land which had been a backwater of Mexico, and even though the Mexican War had ended a year earlier—with the Southwest and California ceded to the United States—the area long remained primitive. Thus the building of the Manti Temple represented an especially difficult achievement. The oolitic limestone of which the temple is built was quarried from the hill on which its stands. The exterior (95 x 171 feet/29 x 52 meters) with its elevated position (properly east-facing) and beautifully kept grounds, is the most impressive of the temples of The Church of Jesus Christ of Latter-day Saints.

Temple closed to public; grounds and Visitors' Center open daily 8–9:30 in summer, 9–9 in winter

---

9 Brigham Young Winter Home (1869/1873–74)
100 West Street at 200 North
St. George, Utah

MILES ROMNEY AND SON, ARCHITECTS

The extreme southwest area of Utah enjoys a considerably milder climate than the Salt Lake City region largely because of its lower altitude (2,760 versus 4,266 feet/841 versus 1,300 meters), plus edging the Great Basin Desert. To it the early Mormons came to raise cotton —they still call it Dixie—and to avoid winter's blasts. Brigham Young in his old age (he died in 1877 at seventy-six) frequented the town— in part to supervise the building of its temple (1871–77)—staying in an existing adobe house, built in 1869, to which additions were made (by architect Romney and his son). Though not of pretension, the

house gives a good picture of domestic building of the region. Note the modest brackets, reflecting the Italianate fad then popular. In 1975 the property was acquired by The Church of Jesus Christ of Latter-day Saints, refurbished (1976–77), and opened to the public.

Open daily 9–sunset, except some major holidays

10 **Beehive House** (1853–55)
State Street at South Temple
Salt Lake City, Utah

TRUMAN O. ANGELL, ARCHITECT

Brigham Young's official house and office combines a touch of Southern Colonial in its two-story veranda with New England in the roof treatment (captain's walk and square cupola topped by beehive) and the Victorian in its brackets. Though not stylistically pure, it offered amiable domesticity for one of Mr. Young's many wives (estimates vary from sixteen to twenty) and a few of his fifty-seven children. The interior has been painstakingly restored (1960) and refurnished to

present an excellent reflection of its time. The adobe front section was expanded to the rear by additions made in 1888. Other members of Young's large family lived in an adjacent residence, the Lion House (not open for tours), which attaches at the left. This is also used as a reception center for banquets, parties, and public meetings. In early days the houses were surrounded by a substantial wall. After Brigham Young's death, the Beehive House was used as a residence by one of his sons, and later by two presidents of the Church. Its name, incidentally, comes from the beehive on the cupola, the beehive being a favorite Mormon symbol of cooperation and industry. The Lion House is named for the statue over the entrance—Brigham Young was sometimes known as "the Lion of the Lord."

Open Mon.–Sat. 9:30–4:30, except major holidays

11 Salt Lake Tabernacle (1863–68) and Temple Square
Temple Square
Salt Lake City, Utah

**CONCEPT BY BRIGHAM YOUNG; TABERNACLE DESIGN BY
WILLIAM H. FOLSOM AND TRUMAN O. ANGELL, ARCHITECTS;
HENRY GROW, ENGINEER**

A 10-acre/4-hectare walled compound in the heart of Salt Lake City
—whose street numbering pattern originates here—Temple Square is
unquestionably the most remarkable religious enclave in the United
States. The buildings of greatest architectural interest are the Temple
(which is open only to Mormons in good standing), the famous Tabernacle, and the neo-Gothic Assembly Hall. The latter two are visitable.

The Tabernacle, with straight sides and semicircular ends, has been dear to radio audiences since 1929 for its superb 375-member (volunteer) choir and its organ recitals. (Recitals are given Mon.–Sat. at noon, Sun. at 4, throughout the year; from mid-June to mid-Sept. also nightly at seven-thirty except Thurs. and Sun. Choir rehearsal Thur. 7:30 P.M. Public welcome.) The Tabernacle's turtle-back form—subject of much folklore—was erected, like the nearby Temple, under the most primitive (i.e. oxcart) conditions. The result is somewhat scaleless, both on the exterior, with its uninterrupted aluminum roof (originally of wood shingles), and on the inside, with its smooth inverted bowl ceiling. However, the auditorium's inner space stuns. (The form must have been stupendous under construction when its arches and bracing were fully revealed.) Overall the building measures 250 feet/76 meters long and 150 feet/46 meters wide, with a periphery of forty-four masonry piers (ashlar sandstone) upholding its daring carapace. Note the classic capitals on the piers. Accoring to Mr. Paul L. Anderson, Manager, Historic Buildings and Sites Section of the Church, "The roof structure is made up of elliptically arched lattice trusses which act as rigid curved beams. There is no lateral thrust, so no tie rods are needed." (Mr. Anderson has been of inestimable help in checking Mormon data in this book.) The nine trusses are spaced 12 feet/3.6 meters apart and span 132-foot/40-meter clear inner width. Trusses in half-arch form rise from the semicircular ends, their "fanned" juncture with the straight arches ingeniously butted (to judge from the drawings). The plaster ceiling shell hangs from the trusses. The 10-foot/3-meter-deep, bridge-like arches—Henry Grow had designed lattice-truss bridges in Pennsylvania, New Jersey, and elsewhere in Utah before tackling the Tabernacle's roof—are fastened together with wooden dowels and reinforced with rawhide if the wood split. Little metal was employed until some handmade bolts were added later. (Iron was scarce in Utah before the coming of the railroad.) The wide U-shaped balcony, put in by Angell in 1869–70, not only increased the seating capacity to approximately 8,000, it made the acoustics—for choirs—superb. (Some authorities feel that the horsehair in the plaster helps control echoes.) The slight blandness of the plastered interior is offset by an ebullient organ of 10,814 pipes (twice rebuilt and enlarged, the last time in 1948–49). Architecturally impressive, the Tabernacle from the constructional point of view ranks among the wood engineering masterpieces of the last century. William H. Folsom, the father of one of Brigham Young's wives, drew the original floor plan of the Tabernacle, but the arched roof was Brigham Young's idea, engineered by Henry Grow. Truman Angell, in addition to the gallery, was responsible for the exterior cornice and the interior woodwork.

The Temple, standing in adjacent splendor, was begun in 1853 but not finished for forty years. Its basic design, like that of the Tabernacle, is largely attributable to Brigham Young—a carpenter and cabinetmaker by trade—with the help of Truman O. Angell as architect. Joseph Don Carlos Young, Brigham's son, took over in 1887 upon Angell's death. The Temple measures 186.5 x 118.5 feet/ 56.8 x 36 meters, with the east center tower (always the tallest) being 210 feet/64 meters high. Many feel that the Temple is "the most impressive religious edifice in the West."

It might be useful to digress here for a moment on Mormon temples and their religious and architectural derivation, for although they are not open to the public (after their dedication), they form an impressive element on the Utah landscape and their exteriors and grounds can be seen by all. Beginning in 1820 Joseph Smith, then a lad of fourteen in western New York State, had, the Faith holds, a series of visions: six years later he was led by an angel's instructions to a hill in Palmyra, New York, and there he found a neatly packed series of thin gold plates incised with inscriptions. Their characters resembled, it is said, those used by the ancient Egyptians. Joseph Smith miraculously translated these plates—which the angel retrieved in 1829—calling them the Book of Mormon, and thenceforth establishing The Church of Jesus Christ of Latter-day Saints. This Egyptian-Hebrew background, evident in the language of the Book of Mormon (which supplements the Old and New Testaments), is slightly suggested in the architecture of Mormon temples. It would seem—at least to some observers—that an influence from the Near East was sought when the Salt Lake Temple was designed. Its towered ends and crenellations, for instance, recall, if vaguely, the Palace, of Sargon at Khorsabad (722–705 B.C.). In addition there are certainly Gothic Revival influences in the buttresses, and, according to some, Masonic touches. Note, incidentally, the profusion of symbolic representations of the earth, sun, moon, and stars on the temple's exterior walls.

The separate Assembly Hall, 1877–80, is an example of Victorian neo-Gothic with seemingly dozens of spires piercing the heavens. Obed Taylor was the architect. It is employed for public worship and as a conference center, being also used by the community. Altogether, Temple Square is one of the world's most unusual architectural complexes, a compact, fascinating religious compound.

Temple Square grounds open June 15–Sept. 15, daily 6 A.M.– 10:30 P.M., rest of year, 8 A.M.–9:30 P.M.; one-hour guided tours every thirty minutes

12   **ZCMI Department Store** (1876/1976)
      15 South Main Street
      Salt Lake City, Utah

WILLIAM H. FOLSOM AND OBED TAYLOR, ARCHITECTS

Zion's Co-operative Mercantile Institution (ZCMI), the country's first
department store (Wanamaker's emporium opened the same year),
reflects excellent nineteenth-century cast-iron work. The three-story
central bay was finished in 1876 with Corinthian columns, roundheaded, double-hung windows, and bold pediment. The south unit or
bay was added in 1880 and the bay to the north in 1902. This last bay
was made of formed metal and wood—not cast iron. In 1975–76 the
double-hung windows and glass were removed and the facade kept as
an open screen fronting a modern building in one of the country's largest downtown shopping centers. Gruen Associates were the architects.

Open during business hours

13 City and County Building (1891–94)
4th South and State Streets
Salt Lake City, Utah

PROUDFOOT, BIRD & MONHEIM, ARCHITECTS

This neo-Romanesque bulwark of officialdom presides over a flowered and treed setting with determined, almost fortified solidity (which withstood a 1934 earthquake). Its sandstone bulk is spruced by an en-

ergetic change of scale at the entry which progresses from tripartite
arches (note the polished granite columns)—in the H. H. Richardson
manner—to a four-part, tall and airy loggia. Three squared towers
soar above, with conically capped half-turrets on either side. Behind,
and turreted itself, rises the five-story central tower which pulls all
forces together. Sturdy on the outside, it also provides a strong silhouette for the city. The interiors are disappointing because they have
been changed and modernized so often. (Many, however, are now
being restored.) The north half of the building serves as City Hall, the
south as County Courthouse. In addition the building served as territorial capitol (1894–96), then as the first capitol of the state from 1896
to 1916 when the present capitol was completed. (Utah finally attained statehood in 1896 when the Mormons renounced polygamy.)
Architecturally—and considering the eclecticism of the era—it is by
far the best of the end-of-the-century buildings in the state and one of
the finest in the West. Burtch W. Beall, Jr., is in charge of a careful
long-range restoration program.

Open during office hours

---

14   Special Events Center (1967–69)
University of Utah
South Campus Drive, off 5th South Street
Salt Lake City, Utah

YOUNG & FOWLER, ARCHITECTS; H. C. HUGHES, STRUCTURAL
ENGINEER

A circular multipurpose sports and special events facility carefully
eased into the hillside to take maximum advantage of change of
grades. Though it accommodates fifteen thousand spectators, its bulk,
being half in and half above the ground, does not intrude on the scale
of the campus. The exterior, somewhat overly fractured, is of natural
concrete and glass with brick used at entrances, the whole topped by a
shallow dome. The interior carries more conviction than the outside,
largely because the underside of the dome produces a smartly stated
structure of dark wood ribs and well-detailed artificial light panels.
The dome represents considerable technological achievement, forming
the world's largest clear-span wood roof at 344 feet/105 meters in
diameter. It is built of laminated timber sections, 12.5 x 27.6

inches/31.7 x 70 centimeters maxiumum size, set in a low-rise
triangulated web. The main members average 30 feet/9.1 meters in
length with smaller purlins filling each triangle. Resting on forty-eight
reinforced concrete columns, its lateral thrust contained by a steel tension ring, the dome was preassembled in sections on the ground, which
sections were then lofted into place beginning at the perimeter. The
tension ring (of five horizontal steel plates each 1 x 12 inches/2.5 x 30
centimeters in cross section) is anchored to the reinforced concrete
ring which encloses it, the concrete then stepping down to form the
arena's seats. The seats, incidentally, are bright red, adding to inner
festivities. A huge steel-framed "cloud" (it weighs 180 tons/163 metric tons) hangs from the center of the dome, and provides lighting, television facilities, scoreboard, and an access elevator direct to the center of the court. The same architects also designed the natatorium
directly behind the center. Robert A. Fowler was partner-in-charge.

Open during events

15   Jacob Hamblin House (1862–63)
off US 91, W edge of
Santa Clara (St. George), Utah

This rugged, outback, semifortified house was built well over a century ago by one of the legendary leaders of this southwest corner of Utah. A famous friend of Indians—he was an exemplary missionary to the Hopi and Navajo—Hamblin did much to settle the area. His two-story house was built of red sandstone taken from the hills which rise behind. Note the casual disposition of the windows and doors. How the Ohio-born Hamblin, several wives (he was an official of the Mormon Church), and two dozen children fitted into this modest dwelling is a mystery: togetherness incarnate. Given to the state of Utah by his heirs (1959), the house—which had long lain empty—has been carefully restored and its interior furnished with handmade furniture in the manner of its time. The house forms a valuable Southwest example of frontier building. It is now administered by the Mormon Church.

Open daily 9–5, except major holidays

Washington

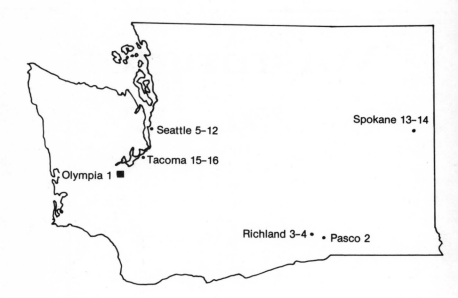

Olympia 1 ◼

• Seattle 5–12

•Tacoma 15–16

Spokane 13–14
•

Richland 3–4 • • Pasco 2

WASHINGTON

The buildings in boldface type are of general interest. The others are for the specialist.

Olympia

1 **The Evergreen State College** (1968–72)— Durham Anderson Freed Company and others

Pasco

2 **Art-Drama-Music Complex** (1970–71)— Brooks Hensley Creager

Richland

3 Battelle Memorial Institute's Pacific Northwest Laboratories (1967–68)—Naramore, Bain, Brady & Johanson

4 Central United Protestant Church (1963–65)— Durham Anderson Freed Company

Seattle

5 **Pioneer Square Historic District** (1890s/1970s) Pike Place Market Historic District (1907)

6 L. C. Smith Building (1914)—Gaggin & Gaggin

7 **Seattle-First National Bank** (1968–69)— Naramore, Bain, Brady & Johanson

8 **North Seattle Community College** (1968–70)— Edward and John Mahlum

9 **Juanita High School** (1970–72)—Kirk, Wallace & McKinley

10 Seattle Central Community College (1973–76)— Kirk, Wallace & McKinley

11 **Freeway Park** (1974–76)—Lawrence Halprin & Associates

12 **Seattle Aquarium** (1977)—Fred Bassetti & Company

Spokane

13 Spokane County Court House (1894–95)— Willis A. Ritchie

14 **Riverpark Center Opera House** (1972–74)— Walker, McGough, Foltz & Lyerla

Tacoma

15 **Christ Episcopal Church** (1968–69)—Paul Thiry

16 **Weyerhaeuser Headquarters** (1969–71)— Skidmore, Owings & Merrill

1 **The Evergreen State College** (1968–72)
**Cooper Point Peninsula, W on Harrison Avenue and Mud Bay
    Road, N on Overhulse Road, c. 5 miles/8 kilometers NW of
Olympia, Washington**

**DURHAM ANDERSON FREED COMPANY, PLANNERS; ARCHITECTS
AS NOTED**

The Evergreen State College—the adjective is aptly applied—is seemingly carved out of its bosky site. A knife neatly cleared minimal
swaths through 990 acres/401 hectares of trees, then man, Silvanus
beside him, designed a setting for students where visual rewards and
physical retreats are always at hand. Intimacy of students with nature
and students with professor is part of the school's informal philosophy.

(It is the first four-year college, incidentally, to be built in the state of Washington since 1899.) The campus plan is deeply respectful of its site, banishing the automobile from the entire central core, the service roads branching from an outer ring. The buildings which loosely enclose the excellent central mall consist of (1) the airy Library (Durham, Anderson, Freed) facing on and properly overseeing the space with its 122-foot/37-meter-high bell tower; (2) the Activities Building (Kirk, Wallace & McKinley) at right, with somewhat agitated facades but a fine interior; (3) the cylindrical Group Instruction Building (Harris, Reed & Litzenberger) at left, with (4) the Laboratory Building (Naramore, Bain, Brady & Johanson) adjacent. The residence halls for 425 students (The Bumgardner Partnership) lie through the woods at the northeast corner. When opened in 1972 the college had an enrollment of 1,200, a figure which is expected to rise to as many as 12,000 by the mid-1980s. Though it rains much in this western edge of the state, it is more of an "Oregon mist" than a downpour, hence there was no need for covered walks. Well planned and designed throughout.

Campus always open

---

2   Art-Drama-Music Complex (1970–71)
Columbia Basin Community College
2600 North Chase Street, immediately N of US 12
Pasco, Washington

BROOKS HENSLEY CREAGER, ARCHITECTS

An architectural arcanum whose startlingly plain, box-form walls brilliantly serve two masters: enclosure and as heroic screens for after-dusk films and slides. Works of art, announcements, and casual delights are projected from machines in the eight turrets built into the berms surrounding the building. As a two-year community college with a substantial evening attendance, it would be difficult to imagine a more tempting come-on. The three-level complex combines art studios, drama (with multiform theater), music studios, speech classrooms, and administration.

The narrow slotted entrances of the simple square exterior, which measures 135 feet/41 meters on a side, unexpectedly open onto a tantalizing inner labyrinth of "streets" and small courts. These separate

and demarcate the four divisions, each discipline taking the form most suited to its functions. These inner spaces—suggestive of Middle East urban patterns—are cool and shaded in the desert-like climate of this part of Washington. Their heavy concrete walls twitch with the changing geometry of sunshine and shadow, while overhead several bridges add spatial accents to this cultural casbah. At night invisible-source theater spotlights maintain the drama and cast people-shadows. Although it might seem that this compact composition might be more suited to an urban campus than one with almost endless plains surrounding it, the reverse is true: it offers an inner focus and life in a flat, featureless landscape. One of the most imaginative buildings in the United States.

Open during school hours

---

3 **Battelle Memorial Institute's Pacific Northwest Laboratories**
   (1967–68)
   George Washington Way at Battelle Boulevard, c. 5 miles/8
   kilometers NW of
   Richland, Washington

NARAMORE, BAIN, BRADY & JOHANSON, ARCHITECTS

Battelle Northwest engages in a broad and exotic spectrum of scientific investigations; beginning in the mid-1940s the company has pioneered in the environmental effects of atomic energy. To facilitate such research these laboratories were built near the Hanford Atomic Energy plant. (The laboratories are operated by the Battelle Memorial Institute for the United States Department of Energy.) The "use of science for the benefit of mankind" lies behind all inquiry, whether in arid land ecology, clinical dentistry in miniature swine, or ceramic oxide nuclear fuels, almost ad infinitum. Most of the work at Battelle is done by individuals or small teams, thus when this new "campus" was built, the architects provided private facilities but stressed public gathering spots, generally out of doors and situated around the "lake" and bank of fountains which greet one on entering, waters on which most buildings face. Open garden courts in the center of each unit offer more protected gathering areas. The layout will eventually encompass fifteen divisions. Architecturally there is formalism but this is much helped by the landscaping. The buildings are constructed of precast concrete

panels with an exposed aggregate surface which picks up the color and texture of the adjacent desert landscape. The same module was used throughout, which makes for unity, flexibility, and economy. Although the research facilities are closed to the public, visitors are welcome to the grounds. Co-designers were William Bain, Jr., partner-in-charge; Michael Ossewaarde as managing architect; and James Jonassen as technical architect.

Grounds and reception area open during business hours

---

4   Central United Protestant Church (1963–65)
1124 Stevens Drive (N of hospital)
Richland, Washington

DURHAM ANDERSON FREED COMPANY, ARCHITECTS

Off-white brick, natural wood ceiling and pews, plus a simplicity of inner shape combine to produce a restful, worshipful interior, one reminiscent of the new churches in Switzerland. Natural light floods across the sanctuary wall from a recessed, full-height window, giving

emphasis to the chancel, the suspended cross, and the cantilevered, freestanding altar. The wall at right carries a series of splayed windows (of somewhat heavy embrasure) with richly colored, thick stained glass by the Willet Studio; note that the window spacing increases from the chancel to the rear, lending a subtle perspective to the nave. Artificial illumination comes from a series of downlights flush with the ceiling. The choir and organ are recessed at left where they can directly encourage congregational singing. Nave capacity is four hundred. The sharp, angled planes of the exterior are in places compromised by previously existing church buildings, but manage to hold their own with aplomb. A four-hundred-seat fellowship hall adjoins.

To visit apply at church office, Mon.–Sat. 9–5, except holidays

5 Pioneer Square Historic District (1890s/1970s)
Yesler Way at 1st Avenue South and vicinity
Seattle, Washington

Seattle, like an increasing number of cities, is awakening to the architectural heritage of its early years. Though the depths and merits here are not startling—the city was founded in 1852 and a fire in 1889 de-

stroyed much—the redevelopment of the 8-acre/3.2-hectare Pioneer Square Historic District will reward the stroller. This section is a former skid road area just off Elliott Bay where the city first flourished. (Skid roads—hence rows—evolved in the timberlands of the northwest. Consisting of short logs spaced about 5 feet/1.5 meters apart, they facilitated hauling of timber to mill or river.)

Among the District's most distinctive single features is the Pergola (1909), at Yesler and 1st Avenue, restored (1972) by the Park Department. This glass and cast-iron pavilion, now used as a bus shelter, originally was a streetcar transfer point and stood over the underground municipal rest rooms. Money for its restoration was given to the city by United Parcel Service, which was founded in Seattle in 1907. Obviously influenced by Hector Guimard's famous Art Nouveau entrances to the Paris Métro, the shelter finds an antipodal touch in the Tlingit Totem Pole on the same little (triangular) square. It is a replica of the 140-year-old original brought to Seattle in 1899 and which stood on this site until 1939. Directly facing stands the Pioneer Building (1889) of doughty Richardson influence, restored (1973) by the Theta Company and architect Ralph D. Anderson, who has done much sensitive work in the area, including changing (1973) the Grand Central Hotel (1890) to the Grand Central Arcade with numerous shops, offices, and restaurants.

It is also pertinent to point out that one can explore portions of the buildings underneath Pioneer Square, for following the fire the street level was raised a full floor, and Underground Tours (daily, except major holidays, apply at 610 1st Avenue: admission) enable one to inspect these relics of long ago. One should also stroll along Occidental Avenue—closed to the automobile—and neighboring streets, where much rehabilitation of old commercial structures has taken place. The Pergola, Totem Pole, and Pioneer Building are National Historic Sites.

Daily tours: inquire at 610 1st Avenue

Rehabilitation is also progressing (1978–79) on the **Pike Place Market Historic District** (1907), 1431 1st Avenue (open Mon.–Sat. 9–6, except holidays). This is a multilevel, picturesque collection of shops and restaurants, plus a colorful assortment of farmers (who can sell only what they grow), fish merchants, butchers, etc. Once threatened by a proposed new development, the Market's future has been assured and protected through designation as a Historic District.

6 L. C. Smith Building (1914)
Yesler Way at 2nd Avenue
Seattle, Washington

GAGGIN & GAGGIN, ARCHITECTS

A too-little-known, thirty-five-story skyscraper, for many years the tallest north of San Francisco and west of the Mississippi. It conforms with gusto to its irregular site, it expresses zoning regulation with finesse, its windows admit a maximum of light and air, and its historical trappings—it was finished in 1914—are barely visible. Good show, L. C. Smith.

Open during business hours

7   Seattle-First National Bank (1968–69)
    **4th Avenue between Madison and Spring Streets (secondary entry
       on 3rd Avenue)
    Seattle, Washington**

NARAMORE, BAIN, BRADY & JOHANSON, ARCHITECTS

Dominating the Seattle skyline with assertiveness, the fifty-story nearly
square shaft of Seattle-First proclaims that downtown is here to stay
and that this is the place to be. A more bold—or more handsome—
affirmation of faith would be hard to find. In front, it boasts a Henry
Moore *Vertebrae* of strangely disturbing interaction which is one of
the country's noted pieces of urban sculpture. The tower, which measures 144 x 126 feet/44 x 38 meters, was set back on its site to create
an entry-level plaza (on 4th Avenue), this piazza easing the very
difficult, two-way grade dropoffs. The gradients are so sharp that the
main entrance is on the fifth floor—3rd Avenue is 47 feet/14 meters
lower—and there is a drive-in bank on the fourth floor! The Moore
sculpture and a low wall in front, plus trees on the sides, lend framing
to the main entry. The entry space is "expanded" by the fact that the
walls of the lobby at plaza level are set back from the four gigantic

corner columns and are of clear glass: only the inner elevator core is solid. The resulting openness, particularly under such topographical conditions, is startling. The main banking room stands semidetached at north (on Spring Street), and though dropped a floor from the plaza level because of the gradient, is tied to it by escalators.

Seattle-First is extremely tidy structurally, with four enormous, aluminum-clad, steel columns at the corners—which taper from an 8-foot/2.4-meter-wide built-up, double-plate column at base to a 14-inch/36-centimeter-wide flange at top—and a square central elevator utility core: no inner columns are used in the tower floors. Fireproofing and insulation are placed between outer skin and inner column, and the plenum or space between is air-conditioned to equalize temperature differentiation. The walls were designed as Vierendeel trusses, with load transfer beams at the sixth floor. Spandrels are steel, again aluminum-faced, with four double-height utility floors for air conditioning, etc., one each at top and "bottom" and at the nineteenth and thirty-fourth levels.

The interiors of the public banking floors—by the architects—and the tower banking offices were smartly carried out and are enriched with a distinguished collection of contemporary art. The bank itself occupies eighteen floors, the rest being rental space. A six-hundred-car garage takes up much of the lowest section; a heliport at 609 feet/186 meters tops all. Detailing throughout is meticulous. Perry B. Johanson was partner-in-charge; Robert J. Pope, project architect; Donald A. Winkelmann, project designer; Skilling, Helle, Christiansen, Robertson, structural engineers; Pietro Belluschi, consultant.

Open during business hours

---

8 North Seattle Community College (1968–70)
**Exit 172 from IS 5 (follow signs), W on North 85th Street, N on
     Meridian Avenue**
Seattle, Washington

EDWARD AND JOHN MAHLUM, ARCHITECTS

Combining clarity of disposition of elements with spatial pleasures between them, this north campus of Seattle Community College achieves a high level of both unity and detail. A small city in itself, with six thousand students at work throughout the day and part of the night,

the plan of the college is based on a stretched-out instructional spine with special rooms offset as needed. Access is by means of continuous sheltered balconies, the long lines of which give a horizontal emphasis and a human scale. Construction is of concrete throughout. The main entrance is formal but the scale otherwise is inviting. Terraces, planting, gardens, and fountains quicken the spaces between all units, as does the stimulating interaction on several levels of the covered walks. First-rate.

Open during school hours

---

9   Juanita High School (1970–72)
N on IS 405, take Exit 20B (NE 124th Street), W on 124th to
**   100th Avenue NE, N to 132nd Street, E to school**
Seattle (Kirkland), Washington

KIRK, WALLACE & McKINLEY, ARCHITECTS

Planned "for the next fifty years," this innovative high school for 1,600 pupils is full of provocative notions. The basic concept, one carefully worked out with educators two years before construction began, de-

manded an academic complex with a completely open central area. This takes the form of a Greek cross with arms 275 feet/84 meters long and a ceiling height of 14.8 feet/4.5 meters with skylights helping with illumination. A module of columns 55 feet/17 meters on center almost invisibly punctuates this great space, their bay size permitting maximum flexibility. This open area of 63,690 square feet/5,917 square meters is subdivided by movable furniture and partitions 4–5 feet/1.2–1.5 meters in height, all of which can readily be changed. The floor is completely carpeted and the ceiling acoustically designed. Across the ends of the four arms of the cross plan are rectangles containing a large assembly hall and those instructional functions requiring sight, sound, or odor (i.e. kitchen) isolation. The result is a flexible central space flanked by specialized facilities. Covered walks lead from the academic complex to the physical education building, stressing Juvenal's *mens sana in corpore sano*. In addition to its own 56,000 square feet/5,202 square meters, there is a handsome quota of outdoor athletic facilities on the 40-acre/16-hectare site.

Open during school hours: apply at office

---

10 Seattle Central Community College (1973–76)
Broadway at East Pine Street
Seattle, Washington

KIRK, WALLACE & McKINLEY, ARCHITECTS

"Unregimented" fenestration and three-dimensional facade development, both functionally generated, have been used to advantage in this block-long community college just northeast of the central business

district. Though its main facade closely edges an undistinguished avenue, the four-story building succeeds in maintaining the quiet scale of
the street (where only three floors, basically, show, the fourth being
carefully set back). Moreover, as one walks or drives by, relationships
between flush solid (brick) and deeply recessed transparent (glass)
make the passage a pleasure. In plan the college is divided into two
sections by a full-length inner "pedestrian street," which welcomes the
community, with library and administration on the Broadway side and
a deep complex of professors' offices and classrooms on the other. At
midpoint a festive two-story, skylighted inner "forum" with adjacent
cafeteria creates a natural core and meeting place, plus injecting a vertical spatial escape. The college, which enrolls 5,500 day students and
1,300 evening ones, offers three main curricula: Occupational-
technical, College Parallel, and Community Service Functions. It was
planned as a "look-in," "walk-in" campus, closely reflecting "the scale,
character, and needs of the community." Construction is of concrete
with brick facing.

Open Mon.–Thurs. 7 A.M.–*10* P.M., *Fri. 7–6, except holidays*

11 Freeway Park (1974–76)
Seneca Street between 6th and 8th
Seattle, Washington

LAWRENCE HALPRIN & ASSOCIATES, LANDSCAPE ARCHITECTS

Freeway is an urban park created out of thin air by bridging the gulch containing Interstate 5. Instead of an ugly gash of a roaring, noisome highway carrying over 130,000 cars a business day, one finds trees, flowers, waters, and even a secret canyon where one can lose oneself by tumbling waterfalls and forget the immanent city. (The park also forms the roof of two garages.) No expensive land, public or private, was expropriated, no demolition involved.

The design of the 5-acre/2-hectare "lid-park" takes full advantage of the sharp change in grade (33 feet/10 meters) to establish a series of strolling, resting, and exploring spots, all different, all with their rewards. The most important elements are oriented for maximum sunshine. The prime focus is a wildly stepped waterfall which spews 28,000 gallons/127,291 liters per minute of recirculated water to create a

visual center and—literally—wash out the freeway noise. Near the
lower reaches of these rushing waters there is a window so that one
can observe the madcap vehicular world beneath. The variety of planting from evergreens to geraniums was chosen for seasonal changes, and
to withstand a certain amount of carbon monoxide. Its flowers are supported by donations, primarily from neighboring banks and the Friends
of Freeway Park. The park forms a key element in tying a residential
and retirement section to the business core. Angela Danadjieva was
project designer for Lawrence Halprin & Associates; Edward MacLeod
& Associates worked with the Halprin firm; Naramore, Bain, Brady
and Johanson were the architects concerned with bridge design and the
municipal parking garage under the East Plaza.

Always open

---

12   Seattle Aquarium (1977)
Pier 59 on Waterfront Park
Seattle, Washington

FRED BASSETTI & COMPANY, ARCHITECTS

Architect Bassetti and engineers-biologists Kramer, Chin & Mayo have transformed and expanded a disused pier into an intriguing aquarium. The rectangular, lofty old building forms its entrance and contains introductory exhibits and a bookshop. To this is attached the new wing of poured concrete and natural wood. This contains a meander of both open and enclosed exhibits displaying marine life from oysters to frolicking seals, from snails to ladder-climbing salmon—all from the Puget Sound region. The unexpected architectural spaces and levels, the contrast of sheltered and open, and the quality of the exhibits all get very high marks. It is, as the folder states, "filled with surprises"—and a great deal of information. The clever graphics were by Gideon Kramer and Associates.

Open May–Sept., daily 10–9, Oct.–Apr., daily 10–5: admission

---

13   Spokane County Court House (1894–95)
1116 Broadway between Jefferson and Madison Streets
Spokane, Washington

WILLIS A. RITCHIE, ARCHITECT

It doesn't matter which château gave the inspiration—the end turrets of de Bury and Chambord come to mind—the fact remains that this is a surprisingly competent, albeit anachronistic example of America's château-seeking for a courthouse. As the official folder describes the building's origin: "Back in the 1890s the County Commissioners were faced with the necessity of constructing a new courthouse and offered a prize for the most original plan. Architect W. A. Ritchie, then 29 years old and said to have had no formal training and a background consisting of a correspondence course conducted by the superintendent of architecture of the United States Treasury Department, submitted the winning design and you are witness of the results." An addition dates from 1953. Threatened with destruction, it has fortunately been spared, refurbished, and is the rightful pride of the city. Exterior detailing is excellent: the interiors are not of architectural moment. The Court House is listed in the National Register of Historic Places.

Open during office hours

---

14 Riverpark Center Opera House (1972–74)
Spokane Falls Boulevard at Washington Street
Spokane, Washington

WALKER, McGOUGH, FOLTZ & LYERLA, ARCHITECTS AND ENGINEERS

A smart-looking opera house-theater combined with exhibition hall on the north edge of downtown (the former railroad area). It overlooks the Spokane River and the island site of the city's 1974 Expo, of which this is the permanent building. The overall profile is expressive with auditorium angling upward to stagehouse at west, and separated by a well-scaled glass hallway from the flat-roofed one-level exhibition hall at east. Both units are wrapped by smooth concrete panels (superbly poured) with dark glass for contrast. Beyond the far end of the entry hall there are steps down to the river, where outdoor concerts (on floats) are given in summer, the steps serving as seats. The lobby area of the theater-concert hall is capacious with several levels and views, and in summer enjoys the use of the river terrace for intermissions. (More works of art, especially tapestries, would spruce up the public areas.) The auditorium relies on elegant simplicity with concrete walls topped by a ceiling of slightly convex curves of wood which sweep over the red plush rows of Continental seating. Acoustics are report-

edly very good. There are 1,803 seats in the orchestra, 476 in the terrace, 345 in the balcony, and 76 in the pit for a total of 2,700. The
148-foot/45-meter-wide stage is basic proscenium and can accommodate a variety of uses from opera to lectures. Backstage facilities are
first-rate.

The one-level exhibition hall has under-cover docking facilities for
the largest trucks. Altogether a very fine "restrained" example, handsomely direct in appearance, very functional in use.

Open for events

---

15   Christ Episcopal Church (1968–69)
310 North K Street
Tacoma, Washington

PAUL THIRY, ARCHITECT

The exterior of Christ Church combines a series of semi-independent,
concrete wall planes, both squared and angled, whose intersections,
perforations, and projections interlock and suggest cubistic three-
dimensionality. It constitutes a building which must be walked around:
one cannot remain static in front of such tension. A 45-foot/14-

meter-high concrete cross, with tapered stem, pivots the space play.
Exaggeration is there but it extends a dynamic invitation to enter. The
interior, roughly a square in plan with stepped entry at one diagonal
and rounded chancel opposite, is by contrast a room of peace. Its main
source of daylight floods from a setback, hence unseen, stained-glass
window onto the sanctuary wall, supplemented by "dormers" (also unseen) in the change of roof levels above the chancel. A series of minute colored windows on two sides and a low band of clear glass opening onto a small outside pool lessen any suspicion of confinement. A
large suspended corona (effective) supplies much of the artificial illumination, augmented by wall brackets. The nave seats 450 with
overflow space at the rear. The choir occupies a niche of its own, also
at back. The building replaces the former wooden church which stood
on the site, relics of which (such as baptismal font) have been incorporated in the new. A well-scaled arcade connects the church to the
old parish house.

To visit apply at church office, Mon.–Fri. 9–5, except holidays

16 **Weyerhaeuser Headquarters** (1969–71)
from Tacoma (c. 8 miles/13 kilometers) N on IS 5, exit 142 B, E
   on WA 18, first road N
from Seattle (c. 22 miles/35 kilometers) S on IS 5, exit South
   320th Street, S on WA 99, R on South 348th Street (WA 18)
near Tacoma, Washington

SKIDMORE, OWINGS & MERRILL, ARCHITECTS

Built in stepped layers as it fills a small valley, and clutched by trees at
each end, this extraordinary headquarters building by the San Francisco office of SOM constitutes one of the great corporate structures. Its
fascinatingly stretched-out low mass—oriented east and west—with its
elongation intensified by open-air extensions to parking areas, hugs the
ground. It worships the earth with its horizontality, stepping outward
longitudinally to mesh with the valley's contours as the building's floors
increase, then retiring modestly at the top (fifth floor) over its brood
of offices. It also steps back in lateral (i.e. cross) section as it rises, so
that the widest (and shortest) floor is that on the ground, the four
above each being narrower, with the top scarce more than one third
the breadth of the bottom. In short, the building waxes in length and
wanes in breadth as its floors (except the top one) increase. It resembles a low-slung, "reversed," stepped pyramid enamored of its valley
and forest setting. (To increase the horizontal emphasis, observe
that the vertical columns on each floor alternate in line.)

   The narrowing of the cross section as the height rises is taken up on
the exterior by wide, uninterrupted, full-length "planting boxes," slightly
triangular in section. (The longest measure almost 1,300 feet/396 meters.) With flowers and plants—over two dozen varieties—thus outside
each row of windows or corridors, and a sizable, 10-acre/4-hectare
artificial lake lying northward, contact with the outside world from
inside offices is never lacking. (The lake was made by damming an
existing stream by the building itself and carrying the southbound
overflow underground.) Even the parking lots, carefully right-angled
on opposite sides of opposite ends of the building, and holding 1,300
cars, are terraced and landscaped. A substantial menhir, sensitively installed by Gordon Newell (and chemically treated to encourage lichen
and moss), dominates the main (west) entrance with appropriate symbolism, fulfilling the encompassing Mother Earth syndrome.

The inset fifth floor, which is covered by a low gambreled, copper-clad roof, is devoted to top management, plus small executive dining area (most executives prefer to eat in the cafeteria), and an enclosed briefing room. The fourth floor, which also serves as entry level, contains a receptionist at each end, with lounge, 350-seat cafeteria, and kitchen in center. The three lower floors are filled with various research and specialized group facilities. An unusual feature of the interior—and the genesis of the design of the building—is that all office floors, except for small special rooms, are completely open and partitionless, with individual divisions being made by 5-foot/1.5-meter-high movable standard components (of red and white oak and mohair). This "office landscape," or *Bürolandschaft* as the Germans who "invented" it use the term, permits maximum flexibility and a sense of openness and greatly facilitates personal communication, yet in most cases maintains a sufficient degree of privacy. The decision to use it here, one reached after lengthy space-planning studies by Sydney Rodgers Associates, made possible the very wide lower floors: rows of partitioned offices would have been intolerable. The building thus materialized from its initial philosophy of office disposition. It was probably the first 100 per cent open landscape commitment for a major building in the United States.

The interiors were impeccably designed by the architects. The north and south walls of all floors are glazed from end to end, their glass being end-butted, hence mullionless for outward-bound freedom: "a landscape in a landscape" as *Interiors* (March 1972) put it. Sasaki, Walker Associates were the landscape architects, and it is important to note that they were on the scene with the architects from the very beginning—before a specific building was even thought of—helping with site selection and development, then tying building to site—and vice versa, the "terraces" of planting boxes playing no small part in this. Altogether superb.

Road viewing only unless on official business

Wyoming

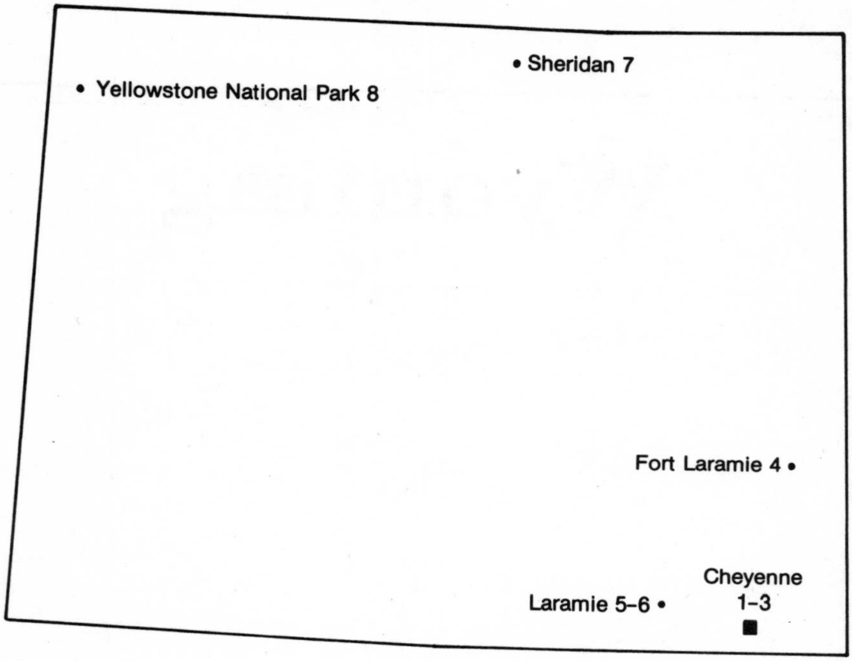

• Sheridan 7

• Yellowstone National Park 8

Fort Laramie 4 •

Cheyenne
Laramie 5–6 •   1–3
■

WYOMING

The buildings in boldface type are of general interest. The others are
for the specialist.

Cheyenne

1 Union Pacific Railroad Station
(1886–87)—Van Brunt & Howe

2 **State Capitol** (1886–88)—
D. W. Gibbs

3 First United Methodist Church
and Education Building
(1890/1967)—J. P. Julien/
Muchow Associates

Fort Laramie

4 **Fort Laramie** (1849–75)

Laramie

5 **Ames Monument** (1881–82)—
H. H. Richardson

6 Old Main (1886–87)—
Frederick A. Hale

Sheridan

7 Sheridan Inn (1892–93)—
Thomas R. Kimball

Yellowstone National Park

8 **Old Faithful Inn** (1903–4)—
Robert C. Reamer

1 Union Pacific Railroad Station (1886–87)
Capitol Avenue at W 15th
Cheyenne, Wyoming

VAN BRUNT & HOWE, ARCHITECTS

Henry Van Brunt (1832–1903), whose first base was Boston, then Kansas City, built a number of stations across the West for the Union Pacific, being not only a distinguished architect but good friend of the railroad's president. Among the better buildings of that vanishing communication breed is this, the once-busy passenger station of Cheyenne. The well-paced asymmetry of its tower (marred by the UP shield) and the parade of arches across the ground level—both influences from Richardson—make the station a respectable contributor of its day. Additions were made as late as 1937. The interior is intact but disappointing.

Open daily 9–6

2   State Capitol (1886–88)
Capitol Avenue at 24th
Cheyenne, Wyoming

D. W. GIBBS, ARCHITECT

The Cheyenne Capitol—at the other end of the street from the railroad station, and majestically parlaying the Classic versus a modified
Romanesque—falls into the dome pattern popularized by Washington,
but does so with less bombast than most. Wyoming's architecture is
"generally characterized by utilitarianism," as the *Wyoming State
Guide* (Oxford University Press, 1941) put it, but this capitol
represents a distinct jump beyond. Designed—via a small invitation competition—when the area was still a territory (it became a
state in 1890), it represented considerable technical ability and opti-
mistic confidence in the area's future. The east wing was added in
1888–90, the west 1915–17. The interiors while good are not out-

standing. In 1979 the gold leaf was replaced on the dome and the rotunda restored to its original elegance. There is a fine view from the top (June–Aug.).

Open Mon.–Fri. 8–5, except holidays

---

3 First United Methodist Church and Education Building
   (1890/1967)
18th Street between Central Avenue and Warren Avenue
Cheyenne, Wyoming

J. P. JULIEN/MUCHOW ASSOCIATES, ARCHITECTS

A fine, old downtown church, typical of its period, which was given a substantial infusion of faith by the building of an adjacent Fellowship Hall, classrooms, and office addition. This handsome new unit by

Muchow Associates is sensitively related to the old church, with good spaces between, mutual regard, and careful landscaping. The addition provides several large meeting halls which are used not only by the congregation but also by the community, a secular concern which fortunately more and more churches are showing. The interior of the church provides comfortable relation between chancel and congregation. The church is listed in the National Register of Historic Places.

Open Mon.–Fri. 8–4, Sun. service

---

4 **Fort Laramie** (1849–75)
off US 26, 2.7 miles/4.3 kilometers SW of
Fort Laramie, Wyoming

The significance of Fort Laramie lies less in its buildings than in its role as chronicler of the opening of the West: it was the nation's chief military outpost west of the Mississippi from 1849 to 1890. The fort's palisaded beginnings, measuring about 150 feet/46 meters square, and initially called Fort William, were actually commenced by private fur traders in 1834, mostly those specialized beaver-pelt seekers whose income was dependent on the ephemeral fashion of men's beaver hats. In 1841 the log stockade was replaced by an adobe-walled compound. (When it later came under army control all enclosures were removed.) Francis Parkman, en route to Oregon—like thousands of others after him—visited Fort Laramie and commented enthusiastically about the fort, but not about the American Fur Company, which he described as being "exceedingly disliked in this country." Brigham Young and his wagon train, fleeing persecution in Illinois, tarried there briefly in 1847 en route to Utah, to be followed by multitudes of later Mormons. And when the gold rush to California began in 1849, the U. S. Government purchased Fort Laramie and rebuilt it as the prime link of a chain of forts across the West—the *indigènes* becoming sometimes more than restless at the take-over of their hunting lands. After "pacification" of the Indians, the fort was decommissioned (1890), many of the buildings were sold for their lumber, and its 35,000 acres/14,164 hectares were made available to homesteaders. The state in 1937, realizing the historic importance of the by then semiruined fort, purchased it, and in 1938 it became part of the National Park System, with reconstruction commencing. The visitor today will see an uneven but broad collection of buildings, ranging from "visible foundations" to accurately restored and furnished military quarters. The oldest, and architecturally the

most interesting, of these is the white clapboarded (over adobe) Officers' Quarters, otherwise known as Old Bedlam, part of which dates from 1849 with additions around 1855. Probably designed in the East, there are a few Greek Revival touches in its porches. Other structures, the last dating from 1884, have been and are in the process of restitution.

In leaving the fort, note the sparse, well-engineered, three-span suspension bridge over the Laramie River, built in 1875 and in use until 1960; it was fortunately left standing alongside the new one.

Open mid-June–Labor Day, daily 7–7, rest of year, daily 8–4:30, except Jan. 1, Dec. 25

---

5 Ames Monument (1881–82)
**off IS 80 at Veedauwoo exit, SW c. 2 miles/3.2 kilometers on
   Blair Road (c. 18 miles/29 kilometers SE of Laramie, c. 31
   miles/50 kilometers W of Cheyenne) near
Laramie, Wyoming**

H. H. RICHARDSON, ARCHITECT

This lonely pyramid on a desolate summit (8,640 feet/2,633 meters high) surveys the land which the Ames brothers opened to settlement when they pushed through the nearby Union Pacific Railroad

(1865–69)—the first to span the continent. It is Richardson's only work west of the Mississippi, the commission stemming from his buildings for the Ames family in North Easton, Massachusetts (q.v.). Its angled mass of random ashlar, 60 feet/18 meters high, and 60 feet/18 meters square at the base, suggests the influence of the Bent Pyramid at Dahshur of Egypt's IV Dynasty (2680–2565 B.C.), while in its powerful silhouette—visible from the railroad (which is now relocated)—it vividly recalls the great mountains around it. Near its top, on opposite sides, are plaques to Oakes and Oliver Ames designed by Augustus Saint-Gaudens. Henry-Russell Hitchcock, in a phrase of early enthusiasm, wrote that "This is perhaps the finest memorial in America" (*The Architecture of H. H. Richardson and His Times,* Museum of Modern Art, 1936; MIT paperback, 1966).

---

6 Old Main (1886–87)
University of Wyoming
9th Street at Ivinson Avenue
Laramie, Wyoming

FREDERICK A. HALE, ARCHITECT

A virile, textbook-be-damned pride marks this, the first building of the University of Wyoming. (At 7,165 feet/2,184 meters above sea level this is the highest campus in the U.S.A.) Although an architectural pi-

oneer, Old Main still has more character than most of the later build-ings around it. A previously existing tower was removed as a safety measure, and the window sashes are now of metal, but otherwise the building is as saucy as ever, being remodeled as Administration Build-ing in 1938–39 and the 1950s. The interiors are of little interest.

Open during business hours all year

7　**Sheridan Inn** (1892–93)
Broadway at 5th Street
Sheridan, Wyoming

THOMAS R. KIMBALL, ARCHITECT

Buffalo Bill was one of the first managers of this famous inn and, for-tunately, it has changed little since he sat on its 145-foot/44-meter-long porch and selected cowboys for his Wild West Show. It was built

by the Sheridan Land Company and the Burlington & Missouri Railroad (now the Chicago, Burlington & Quincy), whose tracks lie just across the street. Its design was supposedly inspired by an inn which the architect had seen in Scotland. In addition to the encompassing porch, the roof is of note as it sprouts a startling collection of shed and gable dormers—at last count sixty-nine. The setting is lent nostalgia by the nearby 4-8-4 steam locomotive (of 1940) given to the city by local citizens and the CB&Q. The inn had been closed and was in danger of being destroyed in 1965 when members of the Sheridan County Chapter of the Wyoming State Historical Society and Mrs. Neltje Kings joined forces, Mrs. Kings purchasing the inn in 1967. The ground floor has been completely restored (1969), and though no longer in use as a hotel, the dining room, parlor, and the Buffalo Bill Bar (made of oak and mahogany in England) are very active. A gift shop, art gallery, and convention facilities have been added. The inn is listed in the National Register of Historic Places.

Open Mon.–Sat. for lunch and dinner

8   Old Faithful Inn (1903–4)
opposite Old Faithful Geyser
Yellowstone National Park, Wyoming

ROBERT C. REAMER, ARCHITECT

The Swedes introduced the log cabin into the American Colonies in
1638, but it is doubtful if any of them could have envisioned a log
(and frame) structure as mammoth as Old Faithful Inn. With 356
bedrooms, 196 baths, and public areas pyramiding to an eight-story
overall height in the center, it would be imposing of almost any material. There is an authentic rustic quality to the inn's log, boulder, and
lava block construction which typifies a high-mountain, Western resort
hotel at the turn of the century. It has, indeed, potent architectural validity today. (If only we could find workmen as dedicated as those who
erected this in extremes of cold, snow, and difficult logistics of material.) The interiors of the public rooms form an almost unique period
piece: to quote the 1908 Haynes *Guide,* "Windows of diamond-shaped
panes and dainty French curtains are exquisitely beautiful against the
setting of rough logs. Elbows of natural branches from the neighboring
forests form braces for the numerous gables and frame the many balconies and stairways surrounding the office while timbers braced this
way and that support the high roof" (reprinted in *Wyoming History
News,* May 1975). Mr. Reamer, a Seattle architect, added the east

wing in 1913 and the west wing in 1928. Listed in the National Register of Historic Places, the inn forms a wonderfully sympathetic introduction to the nation's first (1872) and largest National Park.

Open May–Sept.

Glossary

abacus   The topmost, blocklike element of a capital, that
                        on which the architrave (i.e. beam) rests

acropolis   Literally a city on a hill, the most famous
                        example being in Athens

acroterion   A small pedestal at ends and/or on top of a
                        pediment to hold a statue (Greek or Roman
                        temples); the word often includes the figure(s);
                        also commonly an eave ornament

Adam/Adamesque   Influenced by the Scot Robert Adam (1728–92)
                        and his brother James (1732–94), the most
                        important British architects of their time

adobe   Sun-dried brick generally mixed with straw binder

aggregate   Gravel or crushed stone mixed with cement and
                        water to form concrete

agora   An open square or marketplace in ancient Greece
                        generally surrounded by a peristyle

allée   An avenue of trees

anthemion   Foliated leaf pattern in clusters in Greek and
                        Roman friezes

architrave   The bottom part of an entablature—that which
                        rests on the columns

archivolt   The outside molding of an arch; also the
                        ornamental molding on the face of an arch

Art Deco   The "jazzed," zigzag design approach popular in
                        the late 1920s and the 1930s. Its name stems
                        from L'Exposition Internationale des Arts
                        Décoratifs et Industriels Modernes of 1925 in
                        Paris; also known as Moderne

ashlar masonry   Stone cut in rectangles: it can be smooth or
                        rough-faced, aligned or random

atrium   An open inner courtyard in a Roman house
                        generally surrounded by a colonnade

baldachino   The canopy supported over an altar. Also called a
                        ciborium

balloon frame   Framing of precut light wood studs, generally
                        2 x 4's, often two stories long and spaced less than
                        2 feet/.6 meter apart

baluster   The upright supports of a railing

balustrade   The railing around the head of stairs or atop
                        some buildings

band course   See stringcourse

barge board   A decorative, often scroll-cut board at gable ends

batten	A narrow board nailed to cover the joint of two vertical boards
bay	A vertical wall module (as between structural columns in a skyscraper)
belt course	See stringcourse
bema	A raised platform from which religious services are conducted, generally applied to synagogues
berm	A man-made low earth 'boundary'
betonglass	Thick faceted glass (1 inch/2.5 centimeters generally)
blind arcade	An "arcade" indicated by pilasters applied to a wall surface
blind arch	A relieving arch built into a wall to distribute overhead weight
bolection mold	The prominent roll mold which covers the juncture of door panel and frame
box girder	A rectangular, hollow girder usually of steel
brackets	Angled supports, often elaborate, to uphold an overhang
brise-soleil	Exterior louvers, fixed or movable, to control sun load on a building
cartouche	A shield or coat of arms used as a decorative panel on a wall
cavetto cornice	An outward-curved, usually quarter-round, cornice used in Egyptian Revival
CBD	The Central Business District of a city
cella	The inner room(s) of a Classical temple, primarily the sanctuary
chamfer	A beveled edge at the meeting of two planes
chancel	The (east) end of the church, the part reserved for the clergy and choir
Chicago window	A large fixed central pane of plate glass flanked by sash windows
ciborium	See baldachino
clapboard	A covering board thin on inner (upper) edge, thicker at butt; the boards are overlapped horizontally for weather protection. Sometimes called weatherboards
clerestory	The topmost windows of a church nave, those above the aisle roof, thus any high band of windows

console	An elaborate bracket, often scroll-shaped
coquina	A soft limestone of marine origin found in Florida; it hardens on exposure to air
corbel	A (series of) cantilevered short projection(s) supporting an overhang
Corinthian Order	The richest of the Greek and Roman orders, the capital representing stylized acanthus leaves; at ten diameters its column is the most slender of all
cornice	Technically the top and most projected element of an entablature; in contemporary buildings it refers to the entire projecting eave
cortile	A small courtyard
crockets	Ornamental decorations, usually vegetation-derived, on Gothic members
cupola	A domed accent on a roof with either round or polygonal base
curtain wall	An enclosing wall or wall panel independently attached to the frame of a building
dendrochronology	Dating of a wooden building by counting annual tree rings in a beam cross section or core. The method was developed by Professor A. E. Douglass of the University of Arizona
dentils	A continuous line of small blocks in a Classical molding just under the fascia
dependencies	Smaller buildings symmetrically placed on either side of a major one: flankers
distyle in antis	Two Classical columns set between end walls
dogtrot	A breezeway separating two sections of a (log) house, early popular in Southern vernacular
Doric Order	The oldest and simplest of the Classical orders. The Greek Doric column is fluted and has no base
drum	The (circular) base and support of a dome
Eastlake Style	The Eastlake Style, named for the English architect C. L. Eastlake, was popular toward the end of the nineteenth century. It helped popularize the Stick Style
ell	An addition to a house making an L-shape
English bond	A brick pattern with alternating rows of headers (brick ends) and stretchers (brick sides)
entablature	The horizontal element which tops Classical columns. The lowest part—that resting on the

	columns—is the architrave, the middle (and often decorated) the frieze, and the top the cornice
entasis	The slight swelling profile curve of a Greek or Roman column as it diminishes upward (an optical correction)
exedra	A semicircular (or rectangular) niche, often half-vaulted and with seats
extrados	The outside face or edge of an arch
facade	The face of a building, usually the main elevation
fanlight	A window over an entry, either semicircular or semielliptical
fascia	The flat band(s) of an entablature; also the flat top edge of a building
Federal Style	The planar, tightly restrained yet elegant style which budded in the U.S.A. following the Revolution. Found largely in the Northeast, it lasted until the 1830s
fenestration	The disposition of the windows of a building
flankers	Flanking wings or dependencies usually symmetrically disposed about the main building
Flemish bond	Alternate brick headers and stretchers in the same row
Four Corners area	The juncture of Utah, Colorado, New Mexico, and Arizona
frieze	The mid-member of the three-part entablature (architrave, frieze, cornice), often with decorative panels
furring	Inner blocking of an exterior wall to create air space with inside wall
gable	The (triangular) upper wall established by the roof planes
galleria	Typically a glass-roofed urban passageway
gambrel roof	A roof with two slopes on each side, the lower sharply pitched. It stems from the French Mansard roof
Georgian architecture	In the U.S.A. the period of increasing architectural richness beginning under the reign of George I (1714–27) to the Revolution. Symmetry and Classically derived details are characteristic
ghorfas	A series of long, mud-brick paraboloid

	"warehouses" (like horizontally piled cigarettes) found in south Tunisia
girder	A major horizontal supporting beam
girt	A heavy beam at the ends (and often flanking the chimney) of a Colonial house to receive upper floor joists and sometimes the summer beam
Greek cross	A (church) plan with all four arms of equal length
Greek Revival	A style based on Greek architectural prototypes or details, popular in the first half of the nineteenth century
hall	The name given to the living room of a seventeenth-century New England house
hammer beam	A short cantilevered beam or bracket supporting a timber roof arch
hatchment	An escutcheon with armorial insignia
headers	Bricks laid with their ends facing out
hexastyle	Having six columns at one end
hip roof	A roof with four sloping planes, at times meeting in a flat roof-deck
hogans	The traditional semirounded, earth-covered log dwellings of the Navajo
Howe truss	A (bridge) truss made up of a series of X-frames; similar to Long truss but with vertical wrought-iron or steel tie rods
hyphen	A connecting link between the main house in Georgian architecture and the flanking dependencies
impost	The springing point or block of an arch
in antis	The end of a (Classical) building with columns between the side walls
International Style	The first organized architectural movement against Academism; it dates largely from the 1920s and '30s
intrados	The under surface or soffit of an arch
Ionic Order	One of the major Classical orders; its capitals are immediately identified by their volutes or scrolls
IS	Abbreviation of Interstate Highway
jalousies	Slatted exterior blinds, often adjustable to control light and air
jerkin-head	The small triangular nipping off of the gable end of a roof

joist	The parallel secondary beams upholding a floor
lantern	A small geometric structure atop a roof, most frequently glazed and usually for appearance only
lights	The panes of glass of a window
lintel	A beam over an opening, or over two or more vertical members (post-and-lintel)
Long truss	A bridge truss composed of continuous boxed X-panels
lunette	Small round or half-round window generally in a gable
Mansard roof	Like the gambrel roof (q.v.), a roof with two sloping planes per side, the lower much more sharply pitched. Named for François Mansart (1598–1666)
mastaba	A flat-roofed, slope-sided tomb from Egypt's Old Kingdom
metope	The panel between the triglyphs of a Doric frieze, either plain or sculptured
Moderne	See Art Deco
modillions	Small scroll brackets, larger and wider than dentils
mortise	A cut-out hole in a beam or member which receives a tenon
mullion	The vertical division between windows (and windows and doors)
muntin	The pane divider within a window frame
oculus	A circular opening in the crown of a dome
oriel window	A bay window projecting on brackets or corbels
P/A	The abbreviation of *Progressive Architecture* magazine
Palladian	Architecture influenced by the Italian architect Andrea Palladio (1508–80). Characterized by majestic symmetry often with flanking dependencies. Palladian windows have a broad arched central section with lower flat-headed side portions
passerelle	A footbridge
pavilion	A projecting center section—for prominence—of a (usually) symmetrical building
pediment	The triangular space of the gable end of a building; also at small scale used over doors and

	windows—triangular, segmental (curved), and "broken" pediments
pendentive	A triangular spheroid section used to effect the transition from a square or polygonal base to a dome above
pent roof	A small "attached" roof used over first-floor windows
peripteral	Having columns completely surrounding a temple (or building)
peristyle	A colonnade surrounding a building on the outside or a court inside
piano nobile	The main floor of a mansion, generally elevated a full floor above grade
pilaster	In effect a column reduced to a thin rectangle to establish wall divisions; an engaged pier
pilotis	Columns which uphold the upper floor(s) of a building leaving ground level largely open
plate	The top horizontal member of a wood-framed wall: the rafters spring from the plate
platted	Surveyed and laid out, as of a town
plinth	The square block under a column; also the base for a statue
portal(es)	The covered porch or veranda fronting a Spanish building
portico	A columned shelter at entry; a porch
post-and-lintel	Construction by vertical uprights supporting horizontal beams
prestressed concrete	Reinforced concrete whose end-threaded steel bars or cables are prestretched to develop extra strength
purlin	Secondary horizontal beams supporting roof rafters
quadriga	A representation of a four-horse Roman chariot used as decorative feature
Queen Anne Style	A late-nineteenth-century, almost frantic mélange of styles, often with prominent triangular gable
quoins	Prominently beveled stones (or wood in imitation of stone) used to give emphasis to corners: from French *coins* or corners
rafters	The (generally) angled framing members which directly support the roof
raised basement	A "basement" partly or totally above grade

random ashlar	Miscellaneously sized, non-aligning, rectangular stones
reredos	An ornamental screen placed on the wall behind an altar
retable (retablo)	The niches and shelves behind a Spanish altar (in Gothic architecture often an encased shrine)
return	The carrying of a molding partly around a corner, often on gabled ends
reveal	The depth of inset from the wall face of a window or door
ridgepole	The topmost horizontal roof member receiving upper ends of rafters
rinceau	A low-relief vine-like running ornament
riser	The vertical measure between stair treads
roundel	A small circular opening or window
rustication	Exaggeration of joints and/or surface of stone or wood imitating stone
saltbox	The name for a New England cottage with rear addition and asymmetrically extended roof
segmental arch	A partial arch over a window
shaft	The part of a column between base and capital
shakes	Hand-split shingles, generally large and thick
sheathing	Boards or panels enclosing a structural frame
shed roof	A one-slope roof
Shingle Style	A late-nineteenth-century domestic style using (unpainted) shingles on walls as well as for roof; a term made popular by Professor Vincent Scully
sill	A wood (or metal) member atop and fastened to foundation walls to which the upright framing is attached
single-loaded	Rooms on one side only of a corridor
soffit	The underside of an arch or overhead beam
spandrel	In high-rise construction the enclosing panels between window head below and windowsill above; the solid bands between rows of windows
spire	The tapered section of a steeple
steeple	A church tower and its spire
stepped gable	A gable whose slope or rake is stepped rather than straight (or curved). Also called crow-foot and Dutch gable

stereotomy	The art of stone cutting and placing
Stick Style	A middle-late-nineteenth-century style of complex projections, roof, and wood outrigging
stile	The vertical framing member of a door or window
stretchers	The long sides of bricks laid facing out
stringcourse	A generally flat band of minute projection horizontally stretching across a brick facade. Also called a belt course or band course
studs	The (secondary) upright members of a wood-framed wall, often 2 x 4's
stylobate	The base, usually stepped, for a columned building or colonnade
summer beam	A heavy intermediate beam, mainly used in seventeenth-century New England, which carries floor joists and is itself supported by chimney and end girts
tache	Literally a spot, used here as a wall accent
temenos	A sacred confine
tenon	A projection on a wooden beam designed to fit the mortise in another beam to effect juncture. The two are fastened with a dowel
tholos	A round building, especially Greek
tie beam	A horizontal beam connecting the ends of rafters to make a truss
Town truss	A lattice panel truss with alternate closely spaced diagonals
trabeated	Post-and-lintel construction
tread	The step of a stair
triglyphs	The rectangular blocks in a Doric frieze with two vertical channels and half channels on edges
truss	A combination, generally triangulated, of wood, concrete, or metal members to span a space and provide structure for supporting the roof
Tuscan Order	A Roman adaptation of the Greek Doric without fluting but with base; the frieze is plain
tympanum	The framed (triangular) inner area of a pediment; also framed semicircular panel above door
vermiculated	Grooved stone imitations of worm tracks
vigas	The projecting roof beams in Indian pueblo and Spanish Colonial architecture

volutes	Spiral ornament as on an Ionic capital
voussoirs	The wedge-shaped stones or bricks which make up an arch
wainscot	The paneled protective wall lining of a domestic interior, usually not to ceiling
weatherboard	Lapped horizontal wood siding using boards often of parallel faces—as opposed to radial-cut clapboards which they resemble

Index

Kidder Smith is an architect and Fellow of the American Institute of Architects who has devoted most of his professional life trying to make architecture a more significant part of our culture. Supported by a number of major foundation grants, he has produced a series of distinguished articles, books, and exhibitions on the architecture of twenty-four countries. He has also lectured on four continents, often under the auspices of the Department of State. Mr. Smith received the ENIT Gold Medal from the Italian Government for his *Italy Builds*, and he and the late Philip L. Goodwin were decorated by the Brazilian Government for their *Brazil Builds* book and exhibition for the Museum of Modern Art. His *New Architecture of Europe* and *New Churches of Europe* were published in the U.S.A., England, Italy, and Germany; his *Pictorial History of Architecture in America* was one of the major books at the Moscow International Book Fair of 1979. He has also contributed to the Encyclopaedia Britannica. The twelve-year undertaking which produced these volumes on *The Architecture of the United States* represents his most ambitious effort.

Mr. Smith was born in Birmingham, Alabama (1913), and received his A.B. and M.F.A. from Princeton University. He and his wife, Dorothea, live in New York City, with one son teaching in California and the other in Switzerland.